How can the intelligence of monkeys and apes, and the huge brain expansion that marked human evolution, be explained? In 1988, *Machiavellian Intelligence* was the first book to assemble the early evidence suggesting a new answer: that the evolution of intellect was primarily driven by selection for manipulative, social expertise within groups where the most challenging problem faced by individuals was dealing with their companions. Since then a wealth of new information and ideas has accumulated. This new book will bring readers up to date with the most important developments, extending the scope of the original ideas and evaluating them empirically from different perspectives. It is essential reading for researchers and students in many different branches of evolution and behavioural sciences, primatology and philosophy.

Machiavellian Intelligence II: Extensions and Evaluations

Machiavellian Intelligence II
Extensions and Evaluations

EDITED BY

ANDREW WHITEN AND RICHARD W. BYRNE
University of St. Andrews

PUBLISHED BY THE PRESS SYNDICATE OF THE UNIVERSITY OF CAMBRIDGE

The Pitt Building, Trumpington Street, Cambridge CB2 1RP, United Kingdom

CAMBRIDGE UNIVERSITY PRESS

The Edinburgh Building, Cambridge CB2 2RU, United Kingdom

40 West 20th Street, New York, NY 10011-4211, USA

10 Stamford Road, Oakleigh, Melbourne 3166, Australia

First published 1997

Typeset in Lectura 9.25/13.5

A catalogue record for this book is available from the British Library

Library of Congress Cataloguing in Publication data

Machiavellian intelligence II: extensions and evaluations/edited by A. Whiten and R. W. Byrne.

    p.   cm.

Includes bibliographical references and index.

ISBN 0 521 55087 4 (hc). – ISBN 0 521 55949 9 (pbk.)

1. Primates – Behavior. 2. Animal intelligence. 3. Intellect. 4. Machiavellianism (Psychology). 5. Social behavior in animals. 6. Primates – Evolution. 7. Human evolution. I. Whiten, Andrew. II. Byrne, Richard W.QL737.P9M274   1997

599.8'1513–dc21   96-48233CIP

ISBN 0 521 55087 4 hardback

ISBN 0 521 55949 9 paperback

Transferred to digital printing 2002

Contents

Preface   xi

1   Machiavellian intelligence
    RICHARD W. BYRNE & ANDREW WHITEN   1

2   Friendships, alliances, reciprocity and repair
    MARINA CORDS   24

3   Why Machiavellian intelligence may not be Machiavellian
    SHIRLEY C. STRUM, DEBORAH FORSTER & EDWIN HUTCHINS   50

4   Social intelligence and success: Don't be too clever in order
    to be smart
    ALAIN SCHMITT & KARL GRAMMER   86

5   Minding the behaviour of deception
    MARC D. HAUSER   112

6   The Machiavellian mindreader
    ANDREW WHITEN   144

7   Exploiting the expertise of others
    ANNE E. RUSSON   174

8   Primates' knowledge of their natural habitat: As indicated
    in foraging
    CHARLES R. MENZEL   207

9   Evolution of the social brain
    ROBERT A. BARTON & ROBIN I. M. DUNBAR   240

10 The modulatory of social intelligence
    GERD GIGERENZER   264

11 The Technical Intelligence hypothesis: An additional evolution-
    ary stimulus to intelligence?
    RICHARD W. BYRNE   289

12 Protean primates: The evolution of adaptive unpredictability
    in competition and courtship
    GEOFFREY F. MILLER   312

13 Egalitarian behaviour and the evolution of political intelligence
    CHRISTOPHER BOEHM   341

14 Social intelligence and language: Another Rubicon
    ESTHER N. GOODY   365

    Index   397

Contributors

ROBERT BARTON
Department of Anthropology
University of Durham
43 Old Elvet
Durham DH1 3HN
England

CHRISTOPHER BOEHM
Department of Anthropology
University of Southern California
Los Angeles
CA 90089-0032
USA

RICHARD BYRNE
School of Psychology
University of St Andrews
St Andrews,
Fife KY16 9JU
Scotland

MARINA CORDS
Department of Anthropology
Columbia University
New York
NY 10027
USA

ROBIN DUNBAR
Department of Psychology
University of Liverpool
P.O. Box 147
Liverpool L69 3BX
England

DEBORAH FORSTER
Department of Cognitive Science
University of California, San Diego
La Jolla
CA 92093-0515
USA

GERD GIGERENZER
Centre for Adaptive Behavior and
Cognition
Max Planck Institute for Psychological
Research
Leopoldstrasse 24
80802 München
Germany

ESTHER GOODY
Department of Anthropology
University of Cambridge
Free School Lane
Cambridge CB2 3RF
England

KARL GRAMMER
Ludwig–Boltzmann–Institut fur
Stadtethologie
Institut fur Humanbiologie
Althanstrasse 14
A1090 Wien
Austria

MARC HAUSER
Departments of Anthropology and
Psychology
Harvard University
Cambridge
MA 01238
USA

EDWIN HUTCHINS
Department of Cognitive Science
University of California, San Diego
La Jolla
CA 92093-0515
USA

CHARLIE MENZEL
Ethologie und Wildforschung
Zoologisches Institüt
Universität Zürich-Irchel
Winterthurerstrasse 190
CH 8057 Zürich
Switzerland

GEOFFREY MILLER
Max Planck Institute for Psychological
Research
Leopoldstrasse 24
80802 Munich
Germany

ANNE RUSSON
Department of Psychology
York University
2275 Bayview Avenue
Toronto, Ontario M4N 3M6
Canada

ALAIN SCHMITT
Ludwig–Boltzmann–Institut fur
Stadtethologie
Institut fur Humanbiologie
Althanstrasse 14
A1090 Wien
Austria

SHIRLEY STRUM
Department of Anthropology
University of California, San Diego
La Jolla
CA 92093
USA

ANDREW WHITEN
School of Psychology
University of St Andrews
St Andrews
Fife KY16 9JU
Scotland

Present addresses

CHARLIE MENZEL
Language Research Center
Georgia State University
3401 Pathersville Road
Decatur GA 30034
USA

GEOFFREY MILLER
ESRC Research Centre for Economic
Learning and Social Evolution (ELSE)
University College London
Gower Street
London WC1E 6BT
England

SHIRLEY STRUM
Box 62844
Nairobi
Kenya

Preface

Machiavellian Intelligence II is not just a second edition of *Machiavellian Intelligence*. All but one of the authors are new. The one author in common is writing on a different topic, as are the editors themselves. Moreover, the titles and contents of the chapters are not simple updates of those in the original volume. Instead, this book complements our earlier one in rather particular ways. This means that although we provide an introductory chapter to bring readers new to the area up to speed, the significance of the papers in this new book will be much better appreciated if the contents of its predecessor volume have been assimilated. We trust that serious new students of Machiavellian intelligence will take the time to do this and – although we would say this woundn't we? – we strongly believe that there is no substitute for this route to a rounded grasp of the subject.

Machiavellian Intelligence brought together the scattered origins of the idea that primate intellect had its roots in the problems posed by complex social life, and additional chapters explored the reasons for its plausibility. Since, then, 'Machiavellian intelligence' has become a commonplace phrase in the literature, even to the point of acceptance where it sometimes appears with a small 'm'! We felt the time was ripe to assess progress.

Machiavellian Intelligence II is designed to move things forward in two main ways, as suggested by our subtitle. One falls mainly under the heading of *extensions* of the earlier body of empirical work and accompanying theory. Since the first volume was published in 1988, a profusion of papers has been published in the 'heartland' of the idea of Machiavellian intelligence, the social manoeuvrings of non-human primates. Indeed, whole books and edited volumes on aspects of primate social complexity have appeared, as we anticipated in our 1988 preface, and papers on the topic swell journal pages such that a comprehensive account of them is no longer feasible in our pages. Two chapters do, however, review the highlights of the principal advances made in these areas and offer their evaluations.

Another feature of this volume compared to the first is a greater emphasis on studies of our own species, which we have come to realise is a perspective from which many interested readers approach the topic. One chapter here explores extension of the idea of Machiavellian intelligence to the social strategies observed in groups of young human children.

Other chapters extend our knowledge of important specific topics including deception, mindreading and the exploitation of others' expertise. These were subjects on which research was often only embryonic by 1988, but in which there has been a significant rise in empirical and theoretical activity, generating fascinating and often surprising results.

Next come four chapters that are more concerned with *evaluation* of the principal hypotheses at stake (although they provide their own extensions too). The evaluations concern the Machiavellian intelligence hypothesis of a social origin of intellect, which has now been tested in formal ways not even contemplated in our original volume. Between them these chapters describe the principal competing hypotheses, which in one form or another concern cognitive adaptations for dealing with complexities of primates' particular styles of foraging. The evaluations are very varied in scope, in part because they concern interesting and quite fundamentally different forms of both the social and foraging hypotheses.

The final three chapters explore further 'extensions' to the intellectual terrain of Machiavellian intelligence that go well beyond the scope of the evaluation chapters that precede them. The first of the chapters offers an explanation for the rapid encephalisation that occurred in hominid evolution, which extends the idea of social intellect beyond its previous bounds to the context of sexual selection. Another considers the puzzle of human egalitarian behaviour: does this set our species apart from selection pressures for Machiavellian intelligence? The last chapter addresses the implications of a social origin of intellect for social anthropology, and in particular the extensions of the idea that follow from the addition of spoken language to the species' toolkit for social manipulation.

Amongst its authors, this book has come to be known affectionately as 'Mach II'. With due modesty, we cannot but hope that the supersonic allusion becomes increasingly apt for the excitement of the intellectual journey we here aim to share with our readers.

Andrew Whiten
Richard Byrne
St Andrews, Scotland: June 1996

1 Machiavellian intelligence

RICHARD W. BYRNE AND ANDREW WHITEN

After a very slow germination in the more than 20 years leading up to 1988, the 'Machiavellian intelligence hypothesis' has subsequently been evoked as an explanatory theory in a wide range of contexts: neurophysiology (Brothers, 1990), social anthropology (Goody, 1995), medicine (Crow, 1993) and even news broadcasting (Venables, 1993), in addition to its impact on psychology and studies of primate evolution. All of a sudden, the idea that intelligence began in social manipulation, deceit and cunning co-operation seems to explain everything we had always puzzled about. This popularity may, of course, simply reflect its correctness. However, the vagueness of the theory may also have helped, allowing it to be 'all things to all men'. The book that brought in the name did not even contain a single, clear definition of the Machiavellian intelligence hypothesis (Byrne & Whiten, 1988a)! This was not simply carelessness, but a reflection of the reality. In many ways, 'Machiavellian intelligence' is better seen, not as a precise theory, but as a *banner* for a cluster of hypotheses that have been under active investigation since before we coined the label.

All these hypotheses share one thing: the implication that *possession of the cognitive capability we call 'intelligence' is linked with social living and the problems of complexity it can pose*. In the mid-1980s, we thought we could discern a rise in the number of studies that acknowledged the potential explanatory power of the hypothesis. However, these were often rather disparate strands: the time, we felt, was ripe for an attempt to orchestrate them into what we hoped would be the beginnings of a more coherent and focused appraisal. In '*Machiavellian Intelligence: Social Expertise and the Evolution of Intellect in Monkeys, Apes and Humans*', the volume we edited in 1988, we therefore did two things (Byrne & Whiten, 1988a). We reprinted those theoretical and empirical contributions that seemed to us to have been seminal, and then in addition we invited 18 scientists to make specific new contributions. A measure of the need for integration of the topic in those days was that none of the empirical papers we considered important at that time made much direct reference to the theoretical ones. However, since publication of that volume, the links between the themes it developed have become well recognised and the subject of an exciting flurry of research activity. In this chapter, we aim to orientate the reader – particularly the reader new to Machiavellian intelligence – with an overview of the research strands that seemed most important in 1988, and the subsequent developments that have guided us in preparing 'Machiavellian Intelligence II'.

Origins of the theory

The origins of the general idea are diverse, and extend back many years before 1988. Perhaps most famously, Nicholas Humphrey (1976) argued that primates appear to have 'surplus' intelligence for their everyday wants of feeding and ranging. So, since evolution is unlikely to select for surplus capacity, we scientists must have been missing something. Humphrey identified that 'something' as the *social complexity* inherent in many primate groups, and suggested that the social environment might have been a significant selective pressure for primate intelligence. Group living, he suggested, must be beneficial overall to each member or it would not occur, yet only individual (and kin) benefits drive evolution. For each individual primate, this sets up an environment favouring the use of *social manipulation* to achieve individual benefits at the expense of other group members, but without causing such disruption that the individual's membership of the group is put in jeopardy. Particularly useful to this end would be manipulations in which the losers are unaware of their loss, as in some kinds of *deception*, or in which there are compensatory gains, as in some kinds of *co-operation*. Intelligence is thereby favoured as a trait, and since this selective pressure applies to all group members, an evolutionary arms-race is set up, leading to spiralling increases in intelligence. (Rather than getting bogged down in the philosophical quagmire of defining 'intelligence', let us – like Humphrey – simply treat it as whatever mechanisms enable an individual to take into account these complexities of social or other life and devise appropriate responses.) Humphrey suggested that the resulting intelligence in social primates would probably be of a sort particularly suited to social problems and not well-tested by the gadgetry of psychologists' laboratories, so explaining the many failures to find differences in intelligence between animals (see Warren, 1973; Macphail, 1982). This implies that there might in principle be a 'non-social intelligence', which perhaps we might seek in other groups of animals than primates, or indeed in computer science laboratories.

Ten years earlier, Alison Jolly (1966) had had a similar insight. The lemurs she studied in Madagascar *lacked* the intelligence evident to her in monkeys, yet they lived in similar-sized groups. Jolly realized that this was inconsistent with the idea — popular at the time — that monkey-level intelligence is necessary for long-term group living, and she suggested instead that *group living, arising without great need of intelligence, would subsequently tend to select for intelligence.* She did not suggest, as Humphrey later did, that primate intelligence is especially tuned to social problems.

Even earlier, in 1953, Michael Chance and Allan Mead had linked primate social complexity to *neocortical enlargement*, although they did not explicitly mention intelligence. Specifically, they pointed to the extended receptivity of female primates and the conflict situations that this sets up for males, arguing that taking into account the movements of both the female and a competing male during manoeuvring poses a peculiarly difficult problem for a male (Chance & Mead, 1953). In the early 1950s, sexual conflict was still seen as the basis of primate society (Zuckerman, 1932), but by 1988 this exclusive emphasis on male–male conflict as demanding intelligence found little support. Nevertheless, Chance and Mead's theoretical speculations foreshadowed those of Jolly and Humphrey many years later, and interestingly (in the light of future controversies; see Chapter 9) Chance and Mead assumed that the absolute size of the neocortex was linked to dealing with complex problem solving.

This brief recap brings out several of the questions underlying the early variants of the Machiavellian hypothesis:-

- *Sources of complexity.* If intelligence is hypothesised to be an adaptation for dealing with complexity, can we validly compare complexity in social living and complexity in exploitation of the physical environment; and if so, which one is in fact the greater, for a species?

- *Domain specificity.* Is primate intelligence particularly tuned to social problems, making primates less able to deal with logically comparable problems in non-social domains? If so, are some species tuned to other sorts of problem domain; in particular, is human intelligence socially 'biased'?

- *Mechanisms of social competition.* Where intelligence is shown in the social domain, does it manifest mainly as 'nasty' deceit and exploitation, or is 'nice' co-operation also enhanced? (The more general issue here is whether the terms 'nice' and 'nasty' have any useful meaning in an evolutionary context, since to evolve a behavioural trait needs simply to be adaptive for the individuals that possess it. More sensibly, we might ask: does mutualistic co-operation require more or less intelligence than competitive manipulation?)

- *Brain evolution.* Is greater intelligence reflected in changes in size or structure of the brain, and if so, how are these best measured?

The extent of primate social complexity

Psychologists and primatologists have long asserted and aimed to demonstrate that primates are socially complex animals; indeed, that is many people's reason for studying them. What, specifically, does this social complexity amount to?

A structured society is suggested by the existence of stable dominance hierarchies, extensive matrilines, and regular patterns of long-term group membership and intergroup transfer; and these features have been known in primates for many years. In some monkey species, the influence of kin support is so profound that it appears that dominance rank is 'inherited', not earned by demonstrations of power and skill (Kawamura, 1958; Sade, 1967; see Chapais, 1992). Further, the influence of third parties on the outcomes of contests is pervasive (see references in Harcourt & de Waal, 1992). Kummer (1967) was a pioneer in documenting the female hamadryas baboon's use of a powerful male to enable her to make threats with impunity; and Harcourt (1988, 1992) marshalled studies showing that primates use alliances far more than non-primates, and unlike them, choose potential allies on the basis of their competitive value. In Old World monkeys and apes, evidence began to appear that individuals use grooming to build up relationships that can be drawn upon for later support (e.g. Seyfarth, 1977; Seyfarth & Cheney, 1984), and that temporarily impaired relationships could be patched up with deliberate and distinctive acts of reconciliation (de Waal & van Roosmalen, 1979; de Waal and Luttrell, 1988). In some species, notably chimpanzees, the manoeuvring to gain alliances and influence powerful individuals appeared to be so subtle that the terms 'political' and 'Machiavellian' came to be used to describe it (de Waal, 1982; Nishida, 1983). These issues of alliance formation and repair, coalitions and political behaviour have since been extensively explored in Harcourt & de Waal (1992: see also Chapters 2 and 3).

It is tempting to describe these aspects of complexity as if only we, the primatologists, were aware of them. However, a programme of work by Dorothy Cheney and Robert Seyfarth, in which field playback experiments were used to ask what vervet monkeys know about their calls, has shown that this would be misleading (Cheney & Seyfarth, 1990). Vervets' reactions have demonstrated that they are aware of the relative ranks of third parties (not simply the rank with respect to themselves), the group membership of individuals belonging to other troops, and some aspects of kinship among matrilines. The last point has been directly addressed in experiments by Dasser (1988). Macaque monkeys were rewarded for picking the right picture of a monkey face, given a cue of the face of another monkey that was systematically related to the rewarded picture; the particular relationship was, in different experiments, 'mother–daughter' or 'sibling'. Monkeys were able to learn this task, showing that they appreciate the closeness of connection among these pairs of individuals. Cheney & Seyfarth (1990) have explored the social knowledge of vervet monkeys in great depth, but the extent to which other primates are similar to these small Old World species is a topic in its infancy.

Another way in which an intelligent primate can exploit the social group it lives in is in its use of *other* individuals' knowledge or skill. Emil Menzel showed as long ago as 1974 the extraordinary ability of chimpanzees to pick up small cues from the behaviour of others, so learning the location and nature of objects they had not seen themselves (Menzel, 1974). Social learning is invaluable for many birds and mammals (Zentall & Galef, 1988): living socially provides many opportunities for safely learning what predators to avoid, what foods to eat and where to find them, for example. But if primates can in addition imitate the adaptive behaviour patterns of others, their potential for profiting from social living is greatly enhanced. Hauser (1988) carefully documented a case of the rapid spread of a specific feeding technique among vervet monkeys that appeared to rely on imitative learning, and that helped the animals to exploit a special food during a drought crisis. However, the extent of cultural learning through imitation has become a subject of surprising controversy (Whiten, 1989). Visalberghi & Fragaszy (1990), for example, showed in a series of careful experimental tests that the efficiency of capuchin monkeys' learning of tool use rested on individual discovery rather than imitation. The role and nature of observational learning in primates has thus become the subject of renewed research activity (see Chapter 7).

The issue of whether *any* species of animal can imitate, and if so in what fashion, remains controversial; but several lines of evidence point to some sort of imitative ability in great apes. For example, wild mountain gorillas rapidly acquire complex techniques for preparing plant foods, and the overall structure of the procedures are remarkably standardised, despite great individual variations in the details of finger movements and lateral biases (Byrne & Byrne, 1991, 1993); the inherent improbability of such complex sequences being determined by individual learning has been used to argue that gorillas imitate at 'program-level' (Byrne, 1994; Byrne & Russon, 1998). Such foraging skills are the most likely functional context for imitation in the wild, but identification of imitation as a learning process can be easier under relatively novel, or non-natural conditions: for example, at a forest camp during the process of 'rehabilitation' from captivity to the wild, orangutans copy many distinctive human procedures (Russon & Galdikas, 1993; see Chapter 7). Alternatively, the novel actions may be provided experimentally. The capacity of apes to imitate has been so much *assumed*, that proper experimental tests have only recently been conducted, with unexpected and interesting results; some data suggest that home-rearing by humans imparts an ability to imitate in ways that wild apes cannot, as if the home-reared ape's mind is 'programmed' by distinctively human mother–infant patterns of interaction (Tomasello *et al.*, 1987, 1993; and see Chapter 6).

Alongside the new debates about mechanisms in social learning that this has engendered, researchers have continued to document *cultural* differences in wild apes, most strikingly amongst chimpanzees, which underscore the capacity of these animals to benefit from local opportunities to learn from others (Nishida, 1987; Wrangham *et al.*, 1994). Questions about imitation and other acquisition mechanisms aside, primates can profit from other individuals' skills in more direct ways. Stammbach (1988) trained one individual in the skill needed to operate a food-dispenser, and other group members rapidly adjusted to the possibilities of scrounging, learning to refrain from displacing the skilled individual, whose social status increased (see Chapter 7).

Our own introduction to primate complexity was in discovering that deception was being practised among the baboons whose behavioural ecology we were investigating (Byrne & Whiten, 1985). At the time, deception of a tactical nature, practised on fellow group members, was only known from chimpanzees. Our subsequent surveys (Whiten & Byrne, 1988b; Byrne & Whiten, 1990, 1992), pooling data contributed by a large number of experienced primatologists, showed that deception was used by all families of monkeys and apes, but not definitely by strepsirhine primates (but see Chapter 5). In most cases, the deception served to manipulate the *attention* of conspecifics: distracting them from their current actions, preventing them noticing things, deflecting their attention onto other stimuli (Whiten & Byrne, 1988a). Perhaps the greatest sophistication in primate deception is shown by the great ape individuals who were reared in human-like ways for 'ape-language' studies (see Savage-Rumbaugh & McDonald, 1988).

Some instances of primate tactical deception may be deliberately planned, but in the great majority of cases it is plausible that the deceptive tactic is learnt, reflecting the very rapid learning capacity of monkeys and apes (Byrne & Whiten, 1992; Byrne, 1995). Monkeys and apes are relatively large-brained compared with strepsirhine primates or any other mammals (Passingham, 1982; Martin, 1990), suggesting that there could be a link between the extent to which subtle social manipulation is expressed, and brain enlargement allowing rapid learning. This was tested by Byrne (1993), who showed that the amount of tactical deception reported, in excess of that expected from the overall number of field studies done on a species, was significantly related to the species' neocortical expansion (see Chapter 9).

The depth of primate understanding

In parallel with this body of work demonstrating the complexity of interactions among social groups of primates, evidence has also grown that individuals of some species have a deeper, more 'human-like' understanding of each other. Central to these claims is the topic of *theory of mind*. The term was introduced by Premack & Woodruff (1978) to explain the actions of a chimpanzee, but has since become a major topic for other disciplines including human developmental psychology and philosophy (e.g. Astington *et al.*, 1988; Whiten, 1991; Lewis & Mitchell, 1994; Carruthers & Smith, 1996).

If an individual is able to respond differentially, according to the beliefs and desires of another individual (rather than according only to the other's overt behaviour), then it possesses a theory of mind. In Premack and Woodruff's experiments, a chimpanzee was shown a film clip, depicting a human attempting to solve a problem, and failing; for instance, a man trying to get a bunch of bananas above his reach. The chimpanzee was then offered, without training, a choice of photographs, one of which showed the solution to the filmed man's problem (here, stepping onto a chair, rather than, say, pushing a stick through an opening, or eating a banana). The chimpanzee performed above chance, leading the authors to argue that its behaviour was based on understanding the goals of the human in the film clip, not merely a physical sequence of events: a 'theory' of mind.

A second experimental paradigm, used to support this conclusion, concerns the relation between *seeing* something (an observable) and *knowing* what happened (a state of belief). Premack (1988) allowed a chimpanzee to see that one of two trainers was able to see which container was being baited — but not to see which container it was. The chimpanzee then chose between the trainers by pulling a string, and the one chosen then indicated a bait container (in the case of the trainer who had not witnessed the baiting, this was always the wrong one). Three of the four chimpanzees tested in this experiment chose the 'knowledgeable' trainer significantly above chance. Povinelli and his co-workers (Povinelli *et al.*, 1990, 1991) have conducted an extensive series of experiments on this basic idea, and compared the performance of chimpanzees with rhesus macaques. Whether the 'ignorance' of one trainer was created by absence from the room during baiting, by an occluding screen, or by a paper bag pulled over the head, most chimpanzees were able to successfully follow the indications of the 'knowledgeable' person, whereas the monkeys remained at chance.

Premack (1988) argued that such experiments are the only way we possess of discovering whether animals recognise states of mind, and that they provide *unequivocal* evidence, whereas purely observational data can never resolve the basic ambiguity of whether performance is based on understanding or learning by conditioning. He singled out ourselves, along with Goodall, as relying on mere, unreliable anecdotes. This attack on observational data was taken up by Kummer *et al.* (1990), Kennedy (1992) and Heyes (1993a). The consensus of these researchers is that unlike observational data, the result of a good experiment is unequivocal. There is no dispute about the value of appropriate experimentation (e.g. see Byrne & Whiten, 1988b, p. 267; de Waal, 1991). However, in the untidy, real world, experiments also require interpretation. Indeed, by 1988, Premack had concluded that the results of his 1978 experiment on theory of mind were equivocal and that 'there is, on the whole, only suggestive evidence for theory of mind in the chimpanzee' (Premack, 1988, p. 179). Heyes (1993a) pointed out that Povinelli's refined version of Premack's knowledge/ignorance experiment is also ambiguous in its interpretation, because only the subject's reaction to the *first* trial in which the trainer's gaze was occluded gives clear evidence that a chimpanzee *understands* the consequences of visual occlusion for knowledge, rather than rapidly learns a new reward schedule. Povinelli (1994) re-analysed his data, and found that on these crucial first trials performance was at chance levels even for the chimpanzees: the 'killjoy' alternative that the animal learns to associate a particular physical arrangement with reward, without understanding mental states, remains distinctly possible. We remain convinced that experiments – no less than observations – require very careful interpretation, and that a single instance of either is unlikely to be a compelling test of a theoretical position.

Fortunately, there is now an extensive body of evidence, from observation and experiment, suggesting differences between apes and monkeys in the ability to take the mental perspective of others. For instance, Povinelli's team (Povinelli *et al.*, 1992a, *b*) have devised a two-player co-operative task, and tested both rhesus monkeys and chimpanzees. One player can see which handle will provide both with food rewards, but not operate the handle; the other cannot see which to pull, but can reach the handles. Both species learn either role in the task. However, when an individual that has learnt one role is placed in the other, the results are quite different: for the monkeys, the whole task has to be learnt again, while the chimpanzee is able to assume the other role without training. This result shows understanding of the physical cause-and-effect logic of the co-operative task, but whether this requires an understanding of mental states of the other individual is less definite (see Byrne, 1995). Further experiments and observations that relate to this issue are discussed in Chapter 6.

Convergent findings come from our own analyses of deception in primates. We attempted to tackle the question of intentionality by adopting the approach of constructing the *most plausible history* that might have conditioned each observed tactic (Byrne & Whiten, 1990, 1991; Byrne, 1997). In most cases, we found this *could* be done without having to imagine anything very improbable in the individual primate's history: we treated such cases as probably reflecting a tactic learned without any insight into the mental processes of the deceived victim. However, in a significant number of cases, the scenario we were forced to imagine was so remotely unlikely ever to occur in the lives of the animals, that an explanation based on theory of mind appeared *more* plausible (Byrne & Whiten, 1991). These cases concerned both species of chimpanzee, gorillas and orangutans, but not monkeys.

Intriguingly, a similar monkey/ape rubicon occurs in several other capacities: imitation of actions, pretence in play, mirror self-recognition, and so on. The coincidence of the same pattern – monkeys fail, apes succeed – has perhaps led some authors to relate this to the distribution of theory of mind ability (e.g. Gallup, 1982; Whiten & Byrne, 1991); yet these phenomena are much less obviously dependent upon theory of mind – as we have already discussed in the case of imitation. Similarly, the relevance to Machiavellian intelligence, of recognising that a reflection in a mirror is that of oneself, needs to be established by more than correlation. There is now abundant evidence that some chimpanzees, orangutans and gorillas can show by their behaviour that they can recognise a reflection in a mirror as an image of themselves; whereas monkeys cannot (Gallup, 1970; Suarez & Gallup, 1981; Patterson & Cohn, 1994). Gallup's classic test of this, to mark with odourless paint a part of the anatomy not visible without a mirror, has been criticised for poor controls and possible artefacts due to the use of anaesthetic (Heyes, 1993b). However, a version of this test recently applied to two gorillas did *not* use anaesthetic, yet met with success (Patterson & Cohn, 1994); and much film exists showing the reaction of apes catching sight of their marked faces that leaves no doubt in the minds of viewers that the result is genuine. Its meaning is less clear. Early claims that mirror self-recognition indicates self-consciousness and a sense of mortality seem far-fetched; some would go so far as to argue that no more than cross-modal matching is involved (e.g. Mitchell, 1993; Heyes, 1993b).

On current evidence, then, great apes appear to have a greater depth of social understanding than monkeys or strepsirhine primates (see Chapter 6). This would interact, of course, with the 'complexity' of their societies: if great apes have, but monkeys lack, a theory of mind, then apes' social lives would be *inherently* more complex, even where superficially their behaviour may seem the same. Just as Chance & Mead (1953) argued that a monkey, taking the probable actions of a third party into account, is facing a more challenging world than an animal that only interacts dyadically, if an ape in the same circumstance is taking into account the probable thoughts as well as actions of its partners in interaction, then the social problems it is tackling are greater still.

Domain specificity

Humphrey (1976), alone of the original proposers of the Machiavellian intelligence hypothesis, suggested that primate intelligence is biased towards social problem-solving by its evolutionary origins. This idea has been taken up by Cheney & Seyfarth (1988, 1990), who studied the reactions of vervet monkeys to aspects of natural history by experiment and observation. These monkeys, known to take account of subtleties such as rank, kinship and group membership of other vervets, and capable of using alarm calls (of other vervets and of superb starlings) to identify the particular type of predator hazard that is nearby, seem relatively unsophisticated when it comes to general natural history. Confronted with experimentally faked tracks of python, or signs of leopard (the distinctive hanging carcass of an antelope in a tree), they show no reaction. This is unlikely to be because vervets discriminate these fakes as such: when the observers once noticed the group walk across a natural track of a python, the monkeys *also* failed to react – until they encountered the snake, and ran back screaming! (Note this use of Cheney and Seyfarth's carefully recorded 'anecdotal' evidence in validating their experimental data.)

Negative data is always hard to deal with, but – if real – the surprising incompetence of monkeys may be less likely to apply to chimpanzees. When engaged in raids into the range of neighbour communities, they routinely examine signs of chimpanzees on the trail and sniff at old chimpanzee nests, convincing observers they are fairly skilled trackers (Goodall, 1986). Perhaps instead of implying that 'primate intelligence is socially biased', we have here another case of monkey/ape difference in understanding. That is, perhaps skills we recognise as 'intelligent' developed *first* in the early ancestors of all modern monkeys and apes, but at that time only applied to the social arena; more recently, the ancestors of modern great apes developed an enhanced intelligence that gives insight in both technical and social domains (Byrne, 1995). If this were the case, there might be no reason to expect a legacy of *socially*-biased intelligence in humans (see Chapter 11).

Nevertheless, there has been increasing interest in recent years in a legacy of characteristically social cognitive adaptations in our species (e.g. Barkow *et al.*, 1992; Baron-Cohen *et al.*, 1993; Erdal & Whiten, 1994; Goody, 1995). Smith (1988) showed that children demonstrate concepts of rank and transitivity in dealing with other children, well before these skills can be detected using non-social tests. Cosmides (1989) argues more radically still, that human intelligence consists entirely of discrete 'modules' of ancient (and often social) origin, producing strong biases in current abilities (see Chapters 10, 12, 13 and 14).

Theoretical issues

Several issues of interpretation or disagreement, within the broad compass of the Machiavellian intelligence hypothesis, have already emerged in the course of this summary. Other disagreements exist, some going to the heart of the issue, others more tangential.

In what sense is 'Machiavellian' to be understood?

In an effort to make links with references to Machiavelli by evolutionary biologists like ourselves, Wilson *et al.* (1996) have recently reviewed the literature on what is called 'Machiavellianism' in social psychology. In this psychological literature, which now exceeds 300 references, Machiavellianism is seen as a kind of personality trait, with its own tests on which individuals may score as 'high-Machs' or 'low-Machs'. Machiavellianism is defined by Wilson *et al.* as 'a strategy of social conduct that involves manipulating others for personal gain, often against the other's self-interest', in line with its common colloquial usage.

Wilson *et al.* (1996) suggest that our own use of the term implies something broader than this, such that all forms of social intelligence in primates (and perhaps other taxa) are included. This is true: we include not only actions consistent with Machiavellianism in the colloquial sense of relatively short-term personal gain, such as deception, but also acts such as helping and co-operation that are conventionally seen as alternative strategies. Our reason for this was spelled out in the Preface of *Machiavellian Intelligence*. A central tenet of recent evolutionary theory is that animals' behavioural strategies are geared to maximising 'personal' gain in the ultimate currency of reproductive success (inclusive fitness). From a biological perspective, we felt we were using the term 'Machiavellian' in an entirely apt way, to describe relatively complex social strategies fulfilling (ultimate) personal gain. In addition, Machiavelli himself actually gave advice more consistent with this broad interpretation than with what we might call 'narrow Machiavellianism'. Not for the first time, we had best quote directly:

> For a prince . . . it is not necessary to have all the [virtuous] qualities, but it is very necessary to appear to have them . . . [It] is useful, for example, to appear merciful, trustworthy, humane, blameless, religious – *and to be so* – yet to be in such measure prepared in mind that if you need to be not so, you can and do change to the contrary.
>
> (Machiavelli, 1514/1961, our italics).

However, it is clearly important to recognise the different emphases of usage of 'Machiavellian' in these literatures, each justified by the contrasts that are of interest. In the human social psychology literature, the principal interest lies in contrasting immediate self-interest with alternative attitudes that are unselfish, altruistic, and so on. From the evolutionary, comparative perspective, 'Machiavellian' intelligence is an expression used instead for contrast with the simpler social repertoires widespread in the animal kingdom (as well as with non-social uses of intelligence). It is the complex, indirect nature of the strategies we wish to highlight, and this usage seems to have become commonplace in our discipline. Accordingly, it may sometimes be helpful to distinguish 'narrow Machiavellianism' when referring more specifically to the high-Mach/low-Mach dimension of variation.

What is the scope of the theory: Animals, primates, humans?

Up to now, we have only mentioned non-human primates; however, the subtitle of our 1988 book also mentioned humans, and the considerable subsequent interest in Machiavellian intelligence often seems to be motivated by the hope that it might also explain recent, hominid-line intellectual changes.

Researchers are currently divided in the scope they accord social pressures in the evolutionary line that has led from the earliest primates to humans. There are at least three principal branch points in primate evolution at which there is some evidence of intellectual change in one descendant line. To sharpen the focus of the Machiavellian intelligence hypothesis, we need to identify the selective pressure causing increased intelligence in each of : (a) the haplorhine (monkey and ape) line, which is characterised by larger brains, relatively greater investment in neocortex, greater social sophistication and greater social complexity than the strepsirhine line; (b) the great ape line, which is characterised by an apparently different level of understanding, absolutely larger brains, but no greater proportional investment in neocortex than the monkey line; and (c) the later *Homo* line, which is characterised by massive brain enlargement, and extensive stone tool use. Some consider social pressures as of proven relevance only to the first, haplorhine/strepsirhine transition, and most unlikely to be related to the second, monkey/ape one (e.g. Byrne, 1995); others attribute all intellectual advances among primates to social pressure (e.g. Dunbar, 1992; Aiello & Dunbar, 1993).

Further, according to the Machiavellian hypothesis, an evolutionary selective pressure towards greater social intelligence must surely apply to *any* species meeting the basic criteria, of living in large, semi-permanent social groups of long-lived individuals. Signs of this should be visible, for instance, in carnivores, elephants, cetaceans, some bats, and some herbivores (see, for example, Connor *et al.*, 1992; Harcourt, 1992; Zabel *et al.*, 1992; see also Chapter 9).

What is claimed by the theory: Social origin, social bias, social module?

Intellectual advancement in response to social challenge may not result in a particularly social 'kind' of intelligence: a domain-general ability might be incremented, with consequent side-effects on any task benefiting from the increase. Alternatively, the social origin of intelligence may leave a legacy in the cognitive machinery itself, detectable now in various ways (e.g. references in Goody, 1995). If the intelligence is merely *biased* towards social tasks, then we would expect greater efficiency in social versions of a logically identical problem than in non-social ones. There is some evidence that this is the case even for humans (Smith, 1988; Cosmides, 1989). However, a stronger claim would be that it has resulted in specific development of a social *module* or modules, independent from other modules used for non-social tasks (Cheney & Seyfarth, 1990; Baron-Cohen, 1994; Leslie, 1994; and see Chapter 10).

What alternative is there?

The 1988 volume brought together a diversity of evidence that was *consistent* with the Machiavellian intelligence hypothesis, and in the eyes of many made it the more plausible. However, piling up results that are consistent with a hypothesis has long been realised as inadequate in testing scientific theories. Since there is evidently no single diagnostic of the truth in this case, we are led to adopt a Bayesian approach, comparing the relative likelihoods of the various possible theories in the light of the impact of the evidence on all of them. To discuss what constitutes evidence-in-favour, it is necessary to consider the alternative possible accounts.

Milton (1981, 1988) has made a spirited defence of one popular alternative model, the hypothesis that environmental complexity, in the form of *cognitive mapping skill*, was the challenge that led to primate intelligence. The patchy and sparse, but potentially predictable, distribution of fruits in tropical forests, with many species fruiting on non-annual cycles, constitutes a formidable problem for memory (see also Chapter 8). This hypothesis is encouraged by the facts that:

- Monkeys and apes, unlike Strepsirhines, tend to rely on ripe fruit in their diet;
- The relative brain size of primates is correlated with their home range area, and is a crude index of this memory problem (Clutton-Brock & Harvey, 1980);
- Folivores, which need only small home ranges compared with frugivores, have relatively small brains.

The latter two effects may however reflect evolutionary changes to body size instead of brain size (Shea, 1983; Deacon, 1990). Species, such as folivores, which require larger guts (and hence larger body frames in which to accommodate the guts), will inevitably appear 'smaller-brained' if brain size is scaled against body size. More folivorous primates require access to smaller areas to guarantee their year-round supply of food; thus the 'smaller brained', more folivorous species will be just those with smaller home ranges. Byrne (1994) has argued that scaling brain against

body size is quite inappropriate anyway: if brain tissue is used computationally, then its absolute size will determine its power, unaffected by
body size variation. Brain size relative to body size is a good index of the
extent of metabolic and other energy invested in brain tissue, and thus
of the strength of selection for large brains or small bodies in the species'
recent evolution; however, it is not a proper measure of what, computationally, that brain is capable of. One's desktop computer will not work
more efficiently in a smaller room!

Certainly, when primates' absolute brain sizes (or their neocortex sizes,
relative to the rest of the brain) are used instead, the result is a clear
relationship to social group size, but no correlation with range area
(Sawaguchi & Kudo, 1990; Dunbar, 1992; see also Chapter 9).

The other broad alternative class of theory posits that *technical skill* in
dealing with environmental problems selected for increased intelligence.
In its traditional cast, this 'man the tool maker' hypothesis implicates
bipedalism in freeing the hands; given the existing manipulative skill and
relatively large brains of ape-like early hominids, this led to an increase
in tool-making, which in turn selected for increased brain capacity and
manipulative ability (Oakley, 1949). The lack of any simple relation
between hominid brain size and the fossil record of tool development (e.g.
Wynn, 1988) has questioned this view, but it has to be admitted that
hominid brain volumes and hominid tools are imperfectly known, and
likely to remain so. A related theory points to the special challenge of
extractive foraging in primate diet acquisition: the need to detect and
extract food items from a substrate that conceals them from view
(Parker & Gibson, 1977, 1979). In its strict form, this theory applies only
to the common chimpanzee and humans (see Chapter 11), and is therefore hard to test; but Dunbar (1995) has tested the more general assertion
that extractive foraging promotes intelligence, using brain size to index
intelligence, and found no relationship.

On a broader interpretation, various ways in which great apes show
an ability exceeding that of monkeys might be seen as evidence in favour
of selection for *technical skill* (Byrne, 1995). Whereas monkey abilities
seem tied to the social world, in a number of ways great apes seem to
understand 'how things work'. Great apes make tools to a pattern, albeit
not stone ones, and sometimes in advance of the situation in which the
tool will be used (McGrew, 1992); even their selection of 'found' tools,
in the absence of tool manufacture, implies possession of a prior specification of what a good tool should be – a mental representation of a physical

object. Monkey tool-using and tool-making, when analysed carefully, show clear signs of trial-and-error acquisition, and no signs of possession of mental representation of the tool (see Chapter 11 for details). Great apes may also require computational, representational skill in other ways than tool use – for instance in some forms of plant-feeding, where an understanding of the hierarchical structure of behaviour is suggested by the data (Byrne & Byrne, 1993; and see Chapter 11), or in careful, planned arboreal clambering, where success seems to require treating the body as an engineering problem (Povinelli & Cant, 1992). Further, some great ape achievements that have been labelled 'social' are open to re-interpretation as 'technical' successes. For instance, in mirror self-recognition, it is often argued that success depends on understanding 'the self', a social insight, but alternatively we might view as a purely technical matter the ability to work out that the body of tactile and propriocep-tive experience was the same as the body reflected in the mirror (e.g. see Heyes, 1993a). Imitation of motor actions is often claimed to imply theory of mind ability (see Chapter 6), but alternatively the skill may be to comprehend the organisational structure of actions, a technical achieve-ment (see Chapter 11).

We appear confronted, at present, with 'either/or' choices, between Machiavellian manipulation, cognitive mapping, extractive foraging, and technical skill, as pressures for intelligence. However, given the multi-faced nature of intelligence, and the long evolutionary history leading to modern humans, it is perhaps unlikely that the answer will be so simple. Most likely, more than one of these spheres may have had some role in shaping intelligence at different periods of primate and human evolution; and quite other spheres of challenge may have been important for the evolution of intelligence in other groups of animal. More tricky to tease out, it may be that interactions between various selective pressures, were crucial in selecting for intelligence, rather than any one in isolation. It is even possible that disparate pressures, social and non-social, have resulted in a legacy of separate 'intelligences' within one brain *at the same time* (e.g. Rozin, 1976; Gardner, 1983; Cosmides, 1989).

References

Aiello, L. C. & Dunbar, R. I. M. (1993). Neocortex size, group size and the evolution of language. *Current Anthropology*, 34, 184–93.

Astington, J. W., Harris, P. & Olson, D. R. (1988). *Developing Theories of Mind.* Cambridge: Cambridge University Press.

Barkow, J. H., Cosmides, L. & Tooby, J. (ed.). (1992). *The Adapted Mind: Evolutionary Psychology and the Generation of Culture.* Oxford: Oxford University Press.

Baron-Cohen, S. (1994). How to build a body that can read minds: Cognitive mechanisms in mindreading. *Cahiers de Psychologie,* 13, 513–52.

Baron-Cohen, S., Tager-Flusberg, H. & Cohen, J. D. (ed.). (1993). *Understanding Other Minds: Perspectives from Autism.* Oxford: Oxford University Press.

Brothers, L. (1990). The social brain: A project for integrating primate behavior and neurophysiology in a new domain. *Concepts in Neuroscience,* 1, 27–51.

Byrne, R. W. (1993). Do larger brains mean greater intelligence? *Behavioural and Brain Sciences,* 16, 696–7.

Byrne, R. W. (1994). The evolution of intelligence. In *Behaviour and Evolution,* ed. P. J. B. Slater & T. R. Halliday, pp. 223–65. Cambridge: Cambridge University Press.

Byrne, R. W. (1995). *The Thinking Ape: Evolutionary Origins of Intelligence.* Oxford: Oxford University Press.

Byrne, R. W. (1997). What's the use of anecdotes? Attempts to distinguish psychological mechanisms in primate tactical deception. In *Anthropomorphism, Anecdotes, and Animals: The Emperor's New Clothes?,* ed. R. W. Mitchell, N. S. Thompson & L. Miles, pp. 134–50. New York: SUNY Press Biology and Philosophy.

Byrne, R. W. & Byrne, J. M. E. (1991). Hand preferences in the skilled gathering tasks of mountain gorillas (*Gorilla g. beringei*). *Cortex,* 27, 521–46.

Byrne, R. W. & Byrne, J. M. E. (1993). Complex leaf-gathering skills of mountain gorillas (*Gorilla g. beringei*): Variability and standarization. *American Journal of Primatology,* 31, 241–61.

Byrne, R. W. & Russon, A. E. (1998). Learning by imitation: A hierarchical approach. *Behavioral and Brain Sciences.* (In press.)

Byrne, R. W. & Whiten, A. (eds) (1985). Tactical deception of familiar individuals in baboons (*Papio ursinus*). *Animal Behaviour,* 33, 669–73.

Byrne, R. W. & Whiten, A. (1988a). *Machiavellian Intelligence: Social Expertise and the Evolution of Intellect in Monkeys, Apes and Humans.* Oxford: Clarendon Press.

Byrne, R. W. & Whiten, A. (1988b). Towards the next generation in data quality: A new survey of primate tactical deception. *Behavioral and Brain Sciences,* 11, 267–73.

Byrne, R. W. & Whiten, A. (1990). Tactical deception in primates: The 1990 data-base. *Primate Report,* 27, 1–101.

Byrne, R. W. & Whiten, A. (1991). Computation and mindreading in primate tactical deception. In *Natural Theories of Mind: Evolution, Development and Simulation of Everyday Mindreading,* ed. A. Whiten, pp. 127–41. Oxford: Basil Blackwell.

Byrne, R. W. & Whiten, A. W. (1992). Cognitive evolution in primates: Evidence from tactical deception. *Man,* 27, 609–27.

Carruthers, P. & Smith, P. K. (eds) (1996). *Theories of Theories of Mind.* Cambridge: Cambridge University Press.

Chance, M. R. A. & Mead, A. P. (1953). Social behaviour and primate evolution. *Symposia of the Society of Experimental Biology Evolution*, 7, 395–439.

Chapais, B. (1992). The role of alliances in social inheritance of rank among female primates. In *Coalitions and Alliances in Humans and Other Animals*, ed. A. H. Harcourt & F. B. M. de Waal, pp. 29–59. Oxford: Oxford University Press.

Cheney, D. L. & Seyfarth, R. M. (1988). Social and non-social knowledge in vervet monkeys. In *Machiavellian Intelligence: Social Expertise and the Evolution of Intellect in Monkeys, Apes and Humans*, ed. R. W. Byrne & A. Whiten, pp. 255–70. Oxford: Clarendon Press.

Cheney, D. L. & Seyfarth, R. M. (1990). *How Monkeys See the World: Inside the Mind of Another Species*. Chicago: University of Chicago Press.

Clutton-Brock, T. H. & Harvey, P. H. (1980). Primates, brains and ecology. *Journal of Zoology, London*, 190, 309–23.

Connor, R. C., Smolker, R. A. & Richards, A. F. (1992). Dolphin alliances and coalitions. In *Coalitions and Alliances in Humans and Other Animals*, ed. A. H. Harcourt & F. B. M. de Waal, pp. 415–43. Oxford: Oxford University Press.

Cosmides, L. (1989). The logic of social exchange: Has natural selection shaped how humans reason? Studies with the Wason selection task. *Cognition*, 31, 187–276.

Crow, T. J. (1993). Secual selection, Machiavellian intelligence, and the origins of psychosis. *Lancet*, 342, 594–8.

Dasser, V. (1988). Mapping social concepts in monkeys. In *Machiavellian Intelligence: Social Expertise and the Evolution of Intellect in Monkeys, Apes and Humans*, ed. R. W. Byrne & A. Whiten, pp. 85–93. Oxford: Clarendon Press.

de Waal, F. B. M. (1982). *Chimpanzee Politics: Power and Sex Among Apes*. London: Jonathan Cape.

de Waal, F. B. M. (1991). Complementary methods and convergent evidence in the study of primate social cognition. *Behaviour*, 118, 297–320.

de Waal, F. B. M. & Luttrell, L. M. (1988). Mechanisms of social reciprocity in three primate species: symmetrical relationship characteristics or cognition? *Ethology and Sociobiology*, 9, 101–18.

de Waal, F. B. M. & van Roosmalen, A. (1979). Reconciliation and consolation among chimpanzees. *Behavioral Ecology and Sociobiology*, 5, 55–6.

Deacon, T. W. (1990). Fallacies of progression in theories of brain-size evolution. *International Journal of Primatology*, 11, 193–236.

Dunbar, R. I. M. (1992). Neocortex size as a constraint on group size in primates. *Journal of Human Evolution*, 20, 469–93.

Dunbar, R. I. M. (1995). Neocortex size and group size in primates: A test of the hypothesis. *Journal of Human Evolution*, 28, 287–96.

Erdal, D. & Whiten, A. (1994). On human egalitarianism: An evolutionary product of machiavellian status escalation? *Current Anthropology*, 35, 175–83.

Gallup, G. G., Jr (1970). Chimpanzees: Self-recognition. *Science*, 167, 86–7.

Gallup, G. G., Jr (1982). Self-awareness and the emergence of mind in primates. *American Journal of Primatology*, 2, 237–48.

Gardner, H. (1983). *Frames of Mind: The Theory of Multiple Intelligences*. New York: Basic Books.

Goodall, J. (1986). *The Chimpanzees of Gombe: Patterns of Behavior*. Cambridge, MA: The Belknap Press.

Goody, E. N. (1995). *Social Intelligence and Interaction. Expressions and Implications of the Social Bias in Human Intelligence.* Cambridge: Cambridge University Press.

Harcourt, A. (1988). Alliances in contests and social intelligence. In *Machiavellian Intelligence: Social Expertise and the Evolution of Intellect in Monkeys, Apes and Humans*, ed. R. W. Byrne & A. Whiten, pp. 132–52. Oxford: Clarendon Press.

Harcourt, A. (1992). Coalitions and alliances: Are primates more complex than non-primates? In *Coalitions and Alliances in Humans and Other Animals*, ed. A. H. Harcourt & F. B. M. de Waal, pp. 445–71. Oxford: Oxford University Press.

Harcourt, A. H. & de Waal, F. B. M. (eds) (1992). *Coalitions and Alliances in Humans and Other Animals.* Oxford: Oxford University Press.

Hauser, M. D. (1988). Invention and social transmission: New data from wild vervet monkeys. In *Machiavellian Intelligence: Social Expertise and the Evolution of Intellect in Monkeys, Apes and Humans*, ed. R. W. Byrne & A. Whiten, pp. 327–43. Oxford: Clarendon Press.

Heyes, C. M. (1993a). Anecdotes, training, trapping and triangulating: Do animals attribute mental states? *Animal Behaviour*, 46, 177–88.

Heyes, C. M. (1993b). Imitation, culture and cognition. *Animal Behaviour*, 46, 999–1010.

Humphrey, N. K. (1976). The social function of intellect. In *Growing Points in Ethology*, ed. P. P. G. Bateson & R. A. Hinde, pp. 303–17. Cambridge: Cambridge University Press.

Jolly, A. (1966). Lemur social behaviour and primate intelligence. *Science*, 153, 501–6.

Kawamura, S. (1958). Matriarchal social ranks in the Minoo-B troop: A study of the rank system of Japanese monkeys. *Primates*, 1, 148–56.

Kennedy, J. S. (1992). *The New Anthropomorphism.* Cambridge: Cambridge University Press.

Kummer, H. (1967). Tripartite relations in hamadryas baboons. In *Social Communication among Primates*, ed. S. A. Altmann, pp. 63–71. Chicago: University of Chicago Press.

Kummer, H., Dasser, V. & Hoyningen-Huene, P. (1990). Exploring primate social cognition: Some critical remarks. *Behaviour*, 112, 84–98.

Leslie, A. M. (1994). ToMM, ToBy and Agency: Core architecture and domain specificity. In *Mapping the Mind: Domain Specificity in Cognition and Culture*, ed. L. Hirschfeld & S. Gelman, pp. 119–48. Cambridge: Cambridge University Press.

Lewis, C. & Mitchell, P. (1994). *Children's Early Understanding of Mind: Origins and Development.* Hove: Lawrence Erlbaum Associates.

Machiavelli, N. (1513/1961) *The Prince.* Harmondsworth: Penguin Books. (Translated from the Italian by G. Bull).

Macphail, E. (1982). *Brain and Intelligence in Vertebrates.* Oxford: Clarendon Press.

Martin, R. D. (1990). *Primate Origins and Evolution.* London: Chapman Hall.

McGrew, W. C. (1992). *Chimpanzee Material Culture: Implications for Human Evolution.* Cambridge: Cambridge University Press.

Menzel, E. W. (1974). A group of chimpanzees in a 1-acre field: Leadership and communication. In *Behaviour of Nonhuman Primates*, ed. A. M. Schrier & F. Stollnitz, vol. 5, pp. 83–153. New York: Academic Press.

Milton, K. (1981). Distribution patterns of tropical plant foods as a stimulus to primate mental development. *American Anthropologist*, 83, 534–548.

Milton, K. (1988). Foraging behaviour and the evolution of intellect in monkeys, apes and humans. In *Machiavellian Intelligence: Social Expertise and the Evolution of Intellect in Monkeys, Apes and Humans*, ed. R. W. Byrne & A. Whiten, pp. 285–305. Oxford: Clarendon Press.

Mitchell, R. W. (1993). Mental models of mirror self-recognition: Two theories. *New Ideas in Psychology*, 11, 295–325.

Nishida, T. (1983). Alpha status and agonistic alliance in wild chimpanzees (*Pan troglodytes schweinfurthii*). *Primates*, 24, 318–36.

Nishida, T. (1987). Local traditions and cultural transmission. In *Primate Societies*, ed. B. B. Smuts, D. L. Cheney, R. M. Seyfarth, R. W. Wrangham & T. T. Struhsaker, pp. 462–74. Chicago and London: University of Chicago Press.

Oakley, K. P. (1949). *Man the Tool Maker*. London: Trustees of the British Museum.

Parker, S. T. & Gibson, K. R. (1977). Object manipulation, tool use, and sensorimotor intelligence as feeding adaptations in early hominids. *Journal of Human Evolution*, 6, 623–41.

Parker, S. T. & Gibson, K. R. (1979). A developmental model for the evolution of language and intelligence in early hominids. *Behavioural and Brain Sciences*, 2, 367–408.

Passingham, R. E. (1982). *The Human Primate*. Oxford: W. H. Freeman.

Patterson, F. G. B. & Cohn, R. H. (1994). Self-recognition and self-awareness in lowland gorillas. In *Self-awareness in Animals and Humans: Developmental Perspectives*, ed. S. T. Parker, R. W. Mitchell & M. L. Boccia, pp. 273–90. Cambridge: Cambridge University Press.

Povinelli, D. J. (1994). Comparative studies of mental state attribution: a reply to Heyes. *Animal Behaviour*, 48, 239–41.

Povinelli, D. J. & Cant, J. G. H. (1992). Arboreal clambering and the evolution of self-conception. *Quarterly Journal of Biology*, 70, 393–421.

Povinelli, D. J., Nelson, K. E. & Boysen, S. T. (1990). Inferences about guessing and knowing by chimpanzees (*Pan troglodytes*). *Journal of Comparative Psychology*, 104, 203–10.

Povinelli, D. J., Parks, K. A. & Novak, M. A. (1991). Do rhesus monkeys (*Macaca mulatta*) attribute knowledge and ignorance to others? *Journal of Comparative Psychology*, 105, 318–25.

Povinelli, D. J., Nelson, K. E. & Boysen, S. T. (1992a). Comprehension of role reversal in chimpanzees: Evidence of empathy? *Animal Behaviour*, 43, 633–40.

Povinelli, D. J., Parks, K. A. & Novak, M. A. (1992b). Role reversal by rhesus monkeys; but no evidence of empathy. *Animal Behaviour*, 44, 269–81.

Premack, D. (1988). 'Does the chimpanzee have a theory of mind?' revisited. In *Machiavellian Intelligence: Social Expertise and the Evolution of Intellect in Monkeys, Apes and Humans*, ed. R. W. Byrne & A. Whiten, pp. 160–79. Oxford: Clarendon Press.

Premack, D. & Woodruff, G. (1978). Does the chimpanzee have a theory of mind? *Behavioural and Brain Sciences*, 4, 515–26.

Rozin, P. (1976). The evolution of intelligence and access to the cognitive unconscious. In *Progress in Psychobiology and Physiological Psychology*, ed. J. M. Sprague & A. N. Epstein, pp. 245–77. New York: Academic Press.

Russon, A. E. & Galdikas, B. M. F. (1993). Imitation in ex-captive orangutans (*Pongo pygmaeus*). *Journal of Comparative Psychology*, 107, 147–61.

Sade, D. S. (1967). Determinants of dominance in a group of free-ranging rhesus monkeys. In *Social Communication Among Primates*, ed. S. Altmann, pp. 99–114. Chicago: Chicago University Press.

Savage-Rumbaugh, S. & McDonald, K. (1988). Deception and social manipulation in symbol-using apes. In *Machiavellian Intelligence: Social Expertise and the Evoution of Intellect in Monkeys, Apes and Humans*, ed. R. W. Byrne & A. Whiten, pp. 224–237. Oxford: Clarendon Press.

Sawaguchi, T. & Kudo, H. (1990). Neocortical development and social structure in primates. *Primates*, 31, 283–9.

Seyfarth, R. M. (1977). A model of social grooming among adult female monkeys. *Journal of Theoretical Biology*, 65, 671–98.

Seyfarth, R. & Cheney, D. (1984). Grooming alliances and reciprocal altruism in vervet monkeys. *Nature*, 308, 541–2.

Shea, B. T. (1983). Phyletic size change and brain/body allometry: A consideration based on the African pongids and other primates. *International Journal of Primatology*, 4, 33–61.

Smith, P. K. (1988). The cognitive demands of children's social interactions with peers. In *Machiavellian Intelligence: Social Expertise and the Evolution of Intellect in Monkeys, Apes and Humans*, ed. R. W. Byrne & A. Whiten, pp. 94–110. Oxford: Clarendon Press.

Stammbach, E. (1988). An experimental study of social knowledge: Adaptation to the special manipulative skills of of single individuals in a *Macaca fascicularis* group. In *Machiavellian Intelligence: Social Expertise and the Evolution of Intellect in Monkeys, Apes and Humans*, ed. R. W. Byrne & A. Whiten, pp. 309–326. Oxford: Clarendon Press.

Suarez, S. & Gallup, G. G. (1981). Self recognition in chimpanzees and orangutans, but not gorillas. *Journal of Human Evolution*, 10, 175–88.

Tomasello, M., Davis-Dasilva, M., Camak, L. & Bard, K. (1987). Observational learning of tool-use by young chimpanzees. *Human Evolution*, 2, 175–83.

Tomasello, M., Savage-Rumbaugh, E. S. & Kruger, A. C. (1993). Imitative learning of actions on objects by children, chimpanzees, and enculturated chimpanzees. *Child Development*, 64, 1688–705.

Venables, J. (1993). *What is News?* Kings Ripton, Huntingdonshire: ELM Publications.

Visalberghi, E. & Fragaszy, D. M. (1990). Do monkeys ape? In *'Language' and Intelligence in Monkeys and Apes: Comparative Developmental Perspectives*, ed. S. T. Parker & K. R. Gibson, pp. 247–73. Cambridge: Cambridge University Press.

Warren, J. M. (1973). Learning in vertebrates. In *Comparative Psychology: A Modern Survey*, ed. D. A. Dewsbury & D. A. Rethlingshafer, pp. 471–509. New York: McGraw Hill.

Whiten, A. (1989). Transmission mechanisms in primate cultural evolution. *Trends in Ecology and Evolution*, 4, 61–2.

Whiten, A. (ed.) (1991). *Natural Theories of Mind: Evolution, Development and Simulation of Everyday Mindreading.* Oxford: Basil Blackwell.

Whiten, A. & Byrne, R. W. (1988a). The manipulation of attention in primate tactical deception. In *Machiavellian Intelligence: Social Expertise and the Evolution of Intellect in Monkeys, Apes and Humans,* ed. R. W. Byrne & A. Whiten, pp. 211–23. Oxford: Clarendon Press.

Whiten, A. & Byrne, R. W. (1988b). Tactical deception in primates. *Behavioural and Brain Sciences,* 11, 233–73.

Whiten, A. & Byrne, R. W. (1991). The emergence of metarepresentation in human ontogeny and primate phylogeny. In *Natural Theories of Mind: Evolution, Development and Simulation of Everyday Mindreading,* ed. A. Whiten, pp. 267–81. Oxford: Basil Blackwell.

Wilson, D. S., Near, D. & Miller, R. R. (1996). Machiavellianism: A synthesis of the evolutionary and psychological literatures. *Psychological Bulletin,* 119, 285–99.

Wrangham, R. W., McGrew, W. C., de Waal, F. B. M. & Heltne, P. G. (eds). (1994). *Chimpanzee Cultures.* Cambridge, MA: Harvard University Press.

Wynn, T. (1988). Tools and the evolution of human intelligence. In *Machiavellian Intelligence: Social Expertise and the Evolution of Intellect in Monkeys, Apes and Humans,* ed. R. W. Byrne & A. Whiten, pp. 271–84. Oxford: Clarendon Press.

Zabel, C. J., Glickman, S., Frank, L. G., Woodmansee, K. B. & Keppel, G. (1992). Coalition formation in a colony of prepubertal spotted hyaenas. In *Coalitions and Alliances in Humans and Other Primates,* ed. A. H. Harcourt & F. B. M. de Waal, pp. 113–135. Oxford: Oxford University Press.

Zentall, T. R. & Galef, B. G. (eds). (1988). *Social Learning: Psychological and Biological Perspectives.* Hillsdale, NJ: Lawrence Erlbaum Associates.

Zuckerman, S. (1932). *The Social Life of Monkeys and Apes.* London: Kegan, Paul, Trench & Trubner.

2 Friendships, alliances, reciprocity and repair

MARINA CORDS

Sociality is not limited to primates. Other animals, such as corals and colonial hydrozoans, are far more impressively social in the extent to which individuals co-operate, even forsaking their autonomies, as part of a colonial 'superorganism' (Wilson, 1975). To consider the hypothesis that primate intelligence evolved in response to the demands of social life therefore requires us to do more than identify common aspects of sociality in this order: we should identify ways in which primate social systems differ from those of other animals.

All primates are social, but not all are gregarious. Gregarious primates live in groups that typically persist beyond the lifetimes of their individual members. These groups are largely 'closed', in that entrance of strangers is resisted. The most distinctive features of primate societies, however, are that their members (a) recognise and interact with one another as individuals (b) over the course of relatively long lifetimes in such a way that (c) earlier interactions influence later ones. Thus every individual is part of a network of individualised social *relationships*, and each relationship has a unique and potentially long history. Because the occurrence and outcomes of interactions between individuals at one time may influence the occurrence and outcome of their subsequent interactions, the pair's history of interaction becomes one relevant factor in predicting the future course of the relationship by observers and by the animals themselves.

Members of non-human primate groups have social relationships with each of their group-mates, although these relationships vary in form. At one level, social relationships function to maintain group integrity, and thus to solve the ecological problems to which group-living is a characteristic primate adaptation. At another level, however, social relationships may be formed to deal with some of the problems *caused* by group-living: the need for co-ordination of individuals' activities and priorities, increased intra-group competition, or the proximity of potentially dangerous conspecifics may require co-operative action between familiar individuals.

The degree to which these distinctive features of primate societies are limited to primates is debatable: as a set, they clearly differentiate primates from social invertebrates. But individual recognition also occurs in other social mammals and birds, and some of these species (such as elephants) also live for long periods in stable social units. Unfortunately social behaviour of non-primates has generally been studied less than that of primates (Harcourt, 1988), which automatically biases our perception of potentially unique primate characteristics. It is especially sobering when primatologists turn to other taxa and find similarly complex social organization (e.g. Rowell & Rowell 1993, studying sheep). The possibility remains that the difference between other long-lived social animals and primates lies not in general features of their individualised social organisation, but rather in the details of how social relationships are developed, maintained and used. This chapter provides an overview of such behavioural mechanisms.

Before proceeding further, it is worth considering more closely what the words 'social relationship' mean. Hinde (1979) used this term to refer in a descriptive way to the content, patterning and quality of interactions between two individuals. Even individuals who neither benefit from nor desire interaction with each other have relationships: what matters is the particular sequence of interactions that characterises the dyad because of the specific ways in which each individual responds and responded previously to the other. From such a description, emergent features of the relationship (such as reciprocity) may be abstracted and aspects of underlying affective systems may be inferred. Kummer (1978) emphasised a more functional perspective by describing relationships as investments that benefit the individuals engaged in them. In this context, interactions are viewed as ways of shaping the relationship to maximise the value of the social partner, as well as expressions of the relationship's benefit. Even if a social partner's value is negative, so that s/he does not increase Ego's chances of survival or reproduction, individuals should be selected to influence their partners' qualities, behavioural tendencies and availability, so as to cut their losses. Hinde's and Kummer's formulations are both valuable and they are not mutually exclusive. Kummer's perspective is especially useful in interpreting the behavioural mechanisms involved in the development, maintenance and adaptive expression of social relationships.

Friendship

In primates that live in larger groups, it is particularly obvious that individuals do not interact similarly with all group-mates, even when these belong to the same age, sex or kinship class. Especially affiliative relationships often occur among relatives, but are not limited to relatives (Silk, 1994; van Hooff & van Schaik, 1994). In savanna baboons, for example, certain adult males and anoestrous females form special friendships in which the partners spend extraordinary amounts of time in close proximity, and groom more frequently than with other partners. Females, as well as males, play a role in maintaining proximity, which is not true among non-friends (Smuts, 1985). Similar distinctions have been made among dyads in other species (e.g. Goodall, 1986; Dunbar, 1988; Watts, 1994), with more 'friendly' dyads characterised by more frequent and sometimes more extreme affiliative interactions. Not all particularly friendly dyads comprise individuals with obvious common reproductive interests, such as mothers and offspring or potential mates.

Assessing friendship

When used to describe social relationships of non-human primates, the terms 'friendship' or 'bond' usually imply affiliation in the form of extraordinary proximity or grooming or both. These behaviour types were used to indicate affiliation in early naturalistic studies of primates (e.g. Carpenter, 1964; Lindburg, 1973), and have remained popular ever since. The main practical reason for their use is that grooming and being in proximity are relatively frequent and long-lasting behavioural states, and sufficient accurate data can therefore be easily gathered. The meaning of interactions involving either of these behaviour types has never been studied, however, and the validity of adding up grooming bouts or time spent in proximity to get a summary measure of dyadic 'affiliative tendency' is questionable. What exactly are we measuring? A single act of grooming, for example, could represent (a) either partner's *testing* or *confirming* its partner's readiness or availability to interact, (b) the dispensing of a direct *benefit* of an established relationship (such as skin cleaning), (c) the groomer's attempt to *develop* a more friendly relationship with the recipient (see next section), or (d) an attempt to *repair* an established relationship that has been damaged by previous aggression (see below; Kummer, 1978; Goosen, 1981). Thus the relationships of two dyads that groom equally often could actually be very different. The fact that grooming is asymmetrical, involving a groomer and a recipient, further complicates comparisons of dyads. A period of grooming may have different meaning if the active role is assumed mostly by one individual rather than being more equitably assumed by both.

As an indicator of friendship, spatial proximity might seem even harder to interpret than grooming because it is less obviously affiliative. There is evidence, however, that feeding competition and agonistic interference are associated with proximity maintenance (Pereira, 1988; Janson, 1990; Barton, 1993), and such associated costs support its interpretation as social investment. In any case, some primates, especially some New World monkeys, groom rarely if ever (e.g. squirrel monkeys, Baldwin & Baldwin, 1981; Boinski, 1994: night monkeys, Wright, 1981: muriquis, Strier, 1992), and spatial association is the most obvious alternative indicator of affiliative social relationships.

Validation of grooming and proximity measures as indicators of social bond strength comes from correlations between them and other types of behaviour. Individuals that spend more time in proximity often engage in more frequent, more diverse or more reciprocal sociopositive interactions of other types, and engage less frequently in aggression (e.g. Fairbanks, 1980; Colvin & Tissier, 1985; de Waal & Luttrell, 1988; O'Brien, 1993; Watts, 1994; but see Furuichi & Ihobe, 1994). Animals that are near each other might be expected to interact frequently (Goosen, 1981), but even when the number of interactions is corrected for time spent in proximity, frequent spatial associates show affiliation at higher rates (Kurland, 1977; Berman, 1982) and agonism at lower rates (Bernstein *et al.*, 1993; Watts, 1994) than indivduals that associate less often.

Recently, increasing attention has focused on the role of vocalisations in mediating group cohesion during travel and interindividual conflicts (Boinski, 1993; Harcourt *et al.*, 1993). Analysis of call contexts suggests that quiet vocalisations regulate social life. Furthermore, many calls occur in vocal exchanges. Studies of captive guenons (Gautier & Gautier-Hion, 1982) and squirrel monkeys (Smith *et al.*, 1982) have suggested that the frequency of calling between particular animals reflects, and even communicates to others about, affinitive aspects of their relationships. In the case of squirrel monkeys, however, the interpretation of calls as having primarily an affiliative social function has been questioned on the basis of comparative field research (Boinski & Mitchell, 1992). Further study is needed: vocal exchanges, which are relatively frequent and easily scored interactions, might be more satisfactory and more general indicators of social bonds among primates than measures such as grooming and proximity.

Developing and servicing friendly relationships

Although grooming is often interpreted as an expression of affiliation, it has also been viewed as a behavioural mechanism that establishes and maintains (and hence causes) affiliative relations. As such, it might seem an ideal behaviour to use in evaluating social priorities and strategies. The notion of grooming as social investment would be supported if one could demonstrate that this behaviour is costly to the groomer. Possible costs include energetic costs, time costs (especially reduced foraging time) and potential health complications from hair in the caecum (Kurland, 1977; Silk, 1982). Although these costs of grooming are widely assumed, there is little evidence that they apply to natural populations (Maestripieri, 1993; Cords, 1995). Costs may also result from reduced vigilance, an automatic consequence of the visual attention that grooming requires of its practitioners, and lost social opportunity, since grooming involves only one partner at a time. Two studies have supported the notion of vigilance costs. In captive rhesus macaques, grooming mothers were less vigilant than usual, and their infants were more likely to be harrassed by group-mates (Maestripieri, 1993). In wild blue monkeys, grooming was associated with much lower levels of predator vigilance relative to other activities (Cords, 1995). Social opportunity costs of grooming have yet to be assessed.

There are other kinds of data suggesting that grooming can function to develop or maintain social bonds (Dunbar, 1988). The fact that frequency and duration of grooming are related to sex, age, rank, kinship and reproductive state of partners suggests that grooming has more than a merely hygienic function. More importantly, the time that individuals spend grooming is positively related to group size across catarrhine species (Dunbar, 1991), as if maintaining a larger social network requires more effort. The most convincing evidence that grooming relates to developing and maintaining social bonds comes, however, from studies of particular relationships, in which grooming frequency is inversely related to the degree to which the relationship is stably established. For example, in a series of shifting alliances among captive male chimpanzees, grooming peaked during periods of tension, and was interpreted as an attempt to reduce such tension (de Waal, 1982, pp. 131). Among geladas, younger males are more likely than older ones to groom all the females in their harem: older males concentrate on preferred females. Dunbar (1984) interpreted this age-related reduction in grooming with less preferred females as a function of how established a male's relationships with these females was: young males, newer to their one-male units, must invest more than older males in establishing relationships with all the females. Finally, in an experimental analysis, Stammbach & Kummer (1982) found that grooming among hamadryas females convened temporarily in small groups occurred most among individuals who preferred one another as social partners (where preferences were independently measured); in isolated dyads, however, the same females groomed less with preferred partners. The change in female grooming behaviour was interpreted as an effect of social competition: animals with an established relationship assert or reinforce their bond when faced with potential competitors.

The function of friendship

From an evolutionary perspective, the fact that primates form special friendships or bonds would be of little interest if these relationships did not confer on the participants some advantage related to survival and reproduction. Kummer (1978) has addressed this issue with a general framework that considers the value of social partners in terms of their qualities that might benefit a partner (such as age, experience, skills), their tendencies actually to perform behaviour that benefits their partners, and their availability as partners. Engaging in a relationship is a way of improving the value of a partner, for it allows an individual to monitor and learn to predict the partner's behaviour, and even to modify the partners qualities, tendencies or availability. But what particular tendencies are important among non-human primates?

We should distinguish between benefits of relationship formation generally, and special benefits associated with that subclass of relationships termed 'friendships'. Among gregarious primates, most group-mates have some sort of relationship with one another that is special when compared to their relations with other members of their population. Members of a given group are relatively tolerant of one another in feeding and social contexts, provide protection against predators either through alarm-calling or active defence, and may support one another in contests with other groups over feeding areas or territorial boundaries.

To explain special friendships within a group, however, one must invoke additional benefits that accrue to friends. For example, firstly, primate friends may show even greater tolerance to one another than an average pair of group members. Friends are thus permitted joint access to small food patches (de Waal, 1991), or are able jointly to interact with third parties without being harrassed, or are simply guaranteed a position in the group that is relatively safe from predators. Secondly, friends may actively support one another in aggressive encounters with third parties in their groups (Cheney et al., 1986). In various species, alliance-formation is known to be important in the acquisition and maintenance of dominance rank (Chapais, 1992), in obtaining access to females or to food, and as a form of protection against harrassment. Thirdly, friends may make food resources available to one another by direct action (Boesch-Achermann & Boesch, 1993), as a result of tolerance (de Waal, 1989a) or by indicating where food is located. Fourthly, improved access to other individuals, or social resources, may result if an individual offers tolerance and/or protection when its friend attempts to interact with a third party. Finally, primate friends sometimes prefer one another as mates (Smuts, 1985; Small, 1989).

The fact that social relationships are mutual investments complicates the picture, because the perspectives of the two partners are likely to differ. Asymmetries in the value each partner attaches to the other arise when one individual possesses useful qualities lacking in the other, or is more apt to behave in a useful way, or is simply more available as a partner (Kummer, 1978; Noë et al., 1991). These asymmetries are important, because they are at the root of the idea that some form of negotiation or book-keeping is needed if individuals exchange benefits or services in a way that is mutually advantageous. Furthermore, since the value of social partners may differ in kind, and not just degree, negotiation and book-keeping will require conversion between currencies.

Coalitions and alliances

Of all the benefits that special friends may enjoy, intervention in ongoing aggression, or coalition formation, has attracted most attention.

Coalition formation is not strictly limited to special friends, however; male chimpanzees may form coalitions with non-affiliated partners under special circumstances (de Waal, 1992), and an entire social group can be considered an alliance competing with similar groups (Wrangham, 1980; Dunbar, 1989). We shall focus, however, on coalitions and alliances operating within groups and especially among friends. Following de Waal & Harcourt (1992), we shall use the word coalition to describe the joining of forces by two or more parties during a conflict of interests with other parties. In terms of actual behaviour, coalitions involve an ongoing aggressive encounter that a third party joins, taking sides with one of the original opponents by directing aggression to the other. The term *alliance* refers to an enduring, co-operative relationship, in which repeated coalitions are formed.

Coalition formation has attracted much interest among primatologists for two reasons. Firstly, in several well-studied species (especially some Cercopithecines and chimpanzees), it is a conspicuous form of social interaction that appears to have significant fitness consequences for recipients of support. These individuals may increase their immediate access to resources, may increase their long-term competitive abilities through effects on dominance rank, or may be protected from potentially harmful conspecifics or predators (Harcourt, 1992). Secondly, engaging in coalitions can be a particularly costly form of co-operation: an animal that joins an ongoing fight risks both physical injury and erosion of its own relationship with its opponent. From an evolutionary viewpoint, such willingness to suffer costs should be more than balanced by beneficial consequences.

Why coalition formation is socially complex

The degree to which participation in coalitions is costly has been debated, however, and is probably variable. Two dimensions of the triadic system influence this variability. Firstly, an individual that intervenes in dyadic aggression can do so either on behalf of the original aggressor or on behalf of the victim. If the identities of aggressor and victim are generally correlated with their relative power, it may be less costly to join the already prevailing opponent than to try to turn the tables on that opponent by defending the victim. Secondly, the relationship between the intervening animal and the target of its aggression needs to be considered: even defending a victim may cost little if the intervening individual is more powerful than the original aggressor.

Similarly, the benefits of coalition formation are not always clearly one-sided in favour of the individual who received coalitionary support. Most studies assume that receipt of support increases the likelihood of winning an aggressive encounter, and a few have actually shown this to be the case (Harcourt, 1992; Silk, 1992a). It is much harder, however, to show conclusively that the intervening animal is *not also* gaining something from the interaction: sometimes there is an obvious concrete benefit to participation in a coalition, as when that coalition functions to secure access to a resource immediately present. But whether or not an immediate resource is at issue, offering coalitionary support may provide an animal with a chance to solidify its own dominance relationship with the target of the coalition, or its solidarity with the individual it supports, both at relatively low cost (Chapais, 1992; Noë, 1992). Several recent studies of coalition types that were originally considered altruistic have concluded that mutualistic co-operation is a better description, precisely because benefits do not accrue to only one coalition partner (Bercovitch, 1988; Noë, 1990).

The above considerations suggest that primates that form coalitions strategically, so that benefits outweigh costs (at least in the long run), must integrate a complex set of information. Harcourt (1988) has analysed in detail why such interactions are more complex than dyadic interactions. Not only must a potential supporter assess its own relationships with the original antagonists, but also their relationship with each other. It must incorporate information on the abilities, tendencies and availability of group members that are uninvolved in the ongoing dispute, and maybe even absent from its vicinity, for these individuals may become involved and could change the balance of costs and benefits. Insofar as the payoffs of participating in coalitions vary with their context, it must further integrate information on what the various players stand to gain (or lose) in any given interaction. Several rules may be used to make strategic decisions: for example, support may be given preferentially to kin or to partners who have the most to gain from the support, because this will increase net benefit; or intervention may occur preferentially against targets that are lower-ranking, because this will decrease costs. These rules may conflict with one another, and strategic decisions will also depend on resolving the conflicts. The decisions are even more difficult because they must often be made quickly, when opportunity arises. Thus, according to Harcourt (1988, p. 143) 'the decisions made are not simply dichotomous support/not support ones, but complex choices about who to support, when, under what circumstances, and with what beneficial consequence to be achieved'.

Evidence for the strategic nature of coalitions

Do non-human primates form coalitions in a strategic manner? Several descriptive reports of primates seizing appropriate opportunities to institute social change through coalition formation (de Waal, 1982; Harcourt, 1988) suggest that they do so. For example, de Waal describes how a young adult male chimpanzee, Nikkie, overturned his dominance relationship with an older male cage-mate by challenging him only in the presence of a third male, whose support was critical for Nikkie's success.

More systematic evidence of strategic coalition formation comes from a few species whose coalition formation has been extensively documented. These reports vary according to whether they measure coalition formation in absolute terms, or relative to the number of opportunities for its occurrence (i.e. per bout of dyadic aggression). Most agree, however, that (a) at least females support close kin more often than distant kin or non-kin (note than non-philopatric males have fewer opportunities to support kin, and most studies concern species in which only females are philopatric), (b) intervention occurs more often when it is less risky, e.g. when the target is surbordinate to the supporter, (c) those interventions that are especially risky are especially kin-biased, and (d) support of young animals is more likely if they face higher risks (for reviews, see Gouzoules & Gouzoules, 1986; Walters, 1987; Harcourt, 1988; Bernstein, 1991; Ehardt & Bernstein, 1992; Silk, 1992b).

Kinship and risk are not the only variables related to coalition formation. Reciprocity has also been linked to the patterning of coalitions within groups, such that individuals are more likely to support partners from whom they also more frequently receive support. One of the earliest reports of reciprocity among coalition partners concerned adult male baboons forming coalitions to wrest an œstrous female from her original consort partner (Packer, 1977). Although this report was taken as a text-book example (Goodenough et al., 1993), subsequent research and re-examination of the original data suggest that this particular system is a poor example of reciprocity (Bercovitch, 1988; Noë, 1990, 1992). More recently, however, reciprocity among supporting coalition partners has been reported in groups of chimpanzees, macaques and vervet monkeys (Hunte & Horrocks, 1987; de Waal & Luttrell, 1988; Hemelrijk, 1990a; Hemelrijk & Ek, 1991; Silk, 1992b).

A coalition involves not only supporting one of the original opponents, but also opposing the other one; thus reciprocity could also exist between the intervening animal and its opponent. In such a 'revenge system', individuals are more likely to intervene against those who intervene against them. This sort of reciprocity in coalitionary aggression has been reported for male bonnet macaques (Silk 1992b) and chimpanzees (de Waal & Luttrell, 1988), though Hemelrijk & Ek (1991) failed to replicate the results on the same chimpanzee colony.

Reciprocity in any behaviour, such as coalition formation, might seem to suggest that the reciprocators keep mental records of prior interactions that are used to determine their roles in current or future interactions. Simpler explanations of reciprocity are possible however (de Waal & Luttrell, 1988; Hemelrijk, 1990b). For example, if an animal supports those individuals with whom it spends much time, reciprocity in support will automatically result from the fact that its proximity to others necessitates their proximity to it. To rule out simpler explanations like this, potentially confounding variables (such as proximity) must be taken into account in analyses of coalition data (Hemelrijk, 1990b). Not all studies demonstrating reciprocity in coalitionary support have done so, however, and even when such adjustments are made, researchers have disagreed about the interpretation of results. For example, de Waal & Luttrell (1988) suggested that reciprocity in supportive coalitions among chimpanzees is 'calculated' (i.e. requires mental book-keeping because the exchange of behavioural acts is contingent on previous acts), as their analysis controlled for the effects of factors related to general intimacy, such as kinship, proximity and the fact that partners are of the same sex. Based on analyses that incorporated additional factors, however, Hemelrijk and colleagues (Hemelrijk & Ek, 1991; Hemelrijk et al., 1991) interpreted the same apparent reciprocity, at least among males, as a by-product of selfish strategies of individuals with similar goals.

The strategic nature of coalition formation is evident not only in the behaviour of individuals that intervene, but also in would-be recipients of support. These animals often solicit support, or at least solidarity, from particular partners in the course of their initially dyadic aggressive interaction (de Waal & Harcourt, 1992). Among captive chimpanzees and long-tailed macaques, for example, solicitation gestures are directed preferentially toward powerful, high-ranking individuals (Hemelrijk et al., 1991; de Waal, 1977), i.e. those most likely to be useful partners.

Manipulating support by cultivating friendships: A peculiarly primate tactic?

Potential coalition partners may have ways of encouraging coalitionary support other than making direct appeals during aggressive encounters (Harcourt, 1992). For example, they could coerce others into giving support by punishing them for failing to do so; evidence for this mechanism in primates is weak however (Harcourt, 1992). They could also induce support either by reciprocating specific supportive acts, or by cultivating generally friendly relations that increase the likelihood of support over the long term (Cheney *et al.*, 1986; Harcourt, 1989). Harcourt (1988, 1989, 1992) has argued that a major difference between primates and other social animals lies in the use of such tactics by primates in competition for access to the most effective (or dominant) alliance partners. Other animals, he argues, do not attempt to induce either more or higher-quality support in such ways; in fact, they do not attempt to manipulate the kind of agonistic support received at all, and do not compete for the attention of the best supporters. Insofar as tactics to induce support from the best partners require integration of all the information relevant to single coalitionary acts, as well as knowledge of contingencies between acts which may involve different currencies, the use of such tactics would seem to require even greater cognitive abilities.

Most discussions of primates using friendship to foster alliance formation concern a limited set of Old World species and focus on the role of grooming. Thus who an animal chooses to groom, and how hard it competes for grooming opportunities, are interpreted in terms of who it wants as a supportive partner, and how much it values the potential support. An influential model by Seyfarth (1977) predicted how grooming would be distributed among adult females of differing dominance rank. High-ranking females would be attractive, he argued, because they are the most effective coalition partners. Later publications emphasised additional benefits of cultivating relationships with high-ranking females, including increasing their tolerance around resources to which they control access, protection from harrassment, and increased predator defence (Seyfarth, 1983; de Waal & Luttrell, 1986). Because of competition to groom high-ranking individuals, which would be affected by the rank of the competitors, females would end up grooming most with partners of adjacent dominance rank. This predicted grooming distribution was documented in several catarrhine species, but that does not mean the model is correct

(Seyfarth, 1983; de Waal & Luttrell, 1986). In the species tested, rank distance is correlated with kinship, so grooming adjacently ranked animals might alternatively be explained by the attractiveness of relatives, or otherwise socially similar animals. Such an alternative mechanism does not imply social competition or the trading of services, just the recognition of social similarity (de Waal & Luttrell, 1986). Also, the predicted pattern of grooming relationships has not been found universally across primates (O'Brien, 1993).

However one explains the patterning of grooming within primate groups, the link to alliance formation assumes that grooming increases the likelihood of receiving support. Evidence relevant to this proposition comes from observational and experimental studies. As we shall see, none of these makes an air-tight case for a causal relationship between grooming and receiving support, though the data are consistent with such a relationship.

Observational studies summarise grooming and supporting activities over relatively long periods, providing data that may reveal positive correlations across dyads between grooming received and support given, and between grooming given and support received. They thus address the hypothesis that individuals establish longer-term social relationships with particular partners through frequent grooming, thereby increasing the chance that their partners will act as supporters. Correlations between grooming and support have been reported for vervets (Seyfarth, 1980), baboons (Seyfarth, 1976; Hemelrijk, 1990b), chimpanzees (Hemelrijk & Ek, 1991), capuchins (O'Brien, 1993) and bonnet macaques (Silk, 1992b), although other studies have failed to find such correlations (Silk, 1982; de Waal & Luttrell, 1986).

The results of correlational studies may be difficult to interpret for two rather different reasons. Firstly, as elementary statistics books warn, correlations need not reflect causal relationships. A correlation between grooming and receipt of support across dyads could result as an epiphenomenon when grooming and receiving support are both causally related to some third variable (Hemelrijk, 1990b). For example, Hemelrijk (1991) argued that the correlation between grooming received and support given reported for vervet monkeys was a by-product of correlations between grooming given and grooming received, and grooming given and support given. In other words, reciprocity in grooming, and the tendency for animals to groom frequently those whom they support frequently, could interact to produce the observable but spurious correlation between grooming received and support given. Partial correlation tests can assess the association between two variables after removing statistically the effects of a third that is correlated with both (Hemelrijk, 1990b).

While it may be true that correlations need not reflect causal relationships, it may also be true that causally related variables are not correlated most strongly. For example, although a monkey might try to induce support by grooming partners most likely to act supportively, an individual female deciding who to groom might base her choice on a feature correlated with the likelihood of support, rather than on previously received support *per se* (Seyfarth, 1991). Thus the absence of a correlation between grooming and receipt of support when other variables are partialed out may not mean that these two types of behaviour are causally unrelated, only that the causal relationship is indirect. Another reason that a causal relationship may not be revealed by correlation relates to possible differences among individuals in the costs and benefits of participating in acts of grooming or support. For example, a low-ranking female may frequently groom a high-ranking one, and yet receive help from her only rarely; the same low-ranking female may groom a mid-ranking female only moderately often, yet receive help from her frequently. The low-ranking female's behaviour can be understood by recognising that she is willing to 'pay' more for the more valuable support of the higher-ranking female; consequently, there is imperfect reciprocity between her grooming and the support she receives (see also Boyd, 1992).

Because of difficulties associated with interpreting observational evidence, experimental studies that examine the contingency of single interactions might better demonstrate a causal link between grooming and receipt of support. Seyfarth & Cheney (1984) examined the short-term influence of grooming on subsequent coalition formation in a field experiment on vervet monkeys, in which each subject's willingness to support another individual was compared when it had recently received grooming from that other individual, and when it had not. As an indicator of an individual A's willingness to support individual B, Seyfarth & Cheney measured A's response to a playback of B's threat call, controlling for baseline response levels. The call played back is normally given when threatening or chasing an opponent, and vocalisers are often joined by others; the call thus seems to solicit support from nearby individuals (Cheney & Seyfarth, 1990). The response measured was attention to the source of the played-back call, namely looking toward a hidden speaker, and its intensity was measured by its duration. Unrelated vervets did show a stronger response to the playback if they had recently been groomed by the caller, but prior grooming did not affect the response of relatives. These results are consistent with the notion of a causal link between grooming and receiving subsequent support, at least among non-relatives. However, the results fall short of demonstrating such a link unless one assumes (a) that attending to the call does indicate readiness to form a coalition, and (b) that different durations of attention accurately reflect different likelihoods of supporting.

In a recent experimental study, Hemelrijk (1994) directly measured the likelihood of supporting as a function of the receipt of prior grooming. Trios of female macaques were temporarily removed from a larger group, and each trio was held together for a short period in which the two higher-ranking females either (a) engaged in unidirectional grooming spontaneously or were induced to groom (through the application of syrup and seeds to the hair of one of them), or (b) did not groom. Then, one of these females was provoked to attack the lowest-ranking female, and the behaviour of the grooming partner was monitored. Females supported others more often after being groomed by them than when no grooming had occurred. The likelihood of support was not increased when the would-be supporter had taken the active role (as groomer, rather than recipient) in the preceding grooming bout. These results suggest quite strongly that grooming is related to the receipt of support.

These two experiments leave two issues unresolved, however. Firstly, both were concerned with support that benefits the aggressor, so the question remains open whether grooming can be used to induce victim support, which may be more costly to the supporter (see above). Secondly, neither experiment addresses the question of whether varying amounts of grooming lead to varying amounts of support.

Managing aggression

Reconciliation: Repairing social relationships

If some social partners are valuable in an adaptive sense, individuals should not only cultivate relationships selectively but should also maintain them once they are established. Maintenance might require occasional demonstrations that partners are still available and willing to interact. It also includes protecting the relationship from disruption by aggressive conflict. Aggression can be avoided altogether by settling disputes before they escalate according to conventions such as dominance (Jones, 1983) or prior ownership (Kummer & Cords, 1991). Some primates increase the rate of affiliative behaviour before predictable periods of conflict (namely feeding times), although it is not known if such increases reduce the amount or intensity of subsequent aggression (de Waal, 1987; Mayagoitia et al., 1993). Should aggression erupt, its effects can be buffered in several ways. Firstly, relatively mild forms of aggression may predominate: for example, only 20% of aggressive interactions in captive rhesus macaques involved contact, and less than 7% involved biting (Bernstein & Ehardt, 1985). Secondly, aggressive interactions can be shortened by third party interference (e.g. Bernstein & Gordon, 1974; Pereira, 1988; Petit & Thierry, 1994) or by reducing the opponent's aggressive motivation with appeasement gestures (de Waal, 1989a). Finally, relationships that have been disturbed by conflict can be repaired once the aggression has ceased. Such repair has been termed 'reconciliation' (de Waal & van Roosmalen, 1979).

Reconciliation has been recognised in many primates, including prosimians, monkeys and apes, by the friendly reunions that former opponents have after aggressive conflicts (for reviews, see Kappeler & van Schaik, 1992; de Waal, 1993). These reunions typically occur within minutes of the preceding conflict, and, in some species, involve behavioural elements specific to the post-conflict context. The facts that aggression seems to increase the likelihood of such friendly interactions, and that they occur selectively between former opponents, suggest a causal connection between the conflict and the reunion, and are consistent with the idea that reunions function as social repair mechanisms. This interpretation has been corroborated by experimental and observational studies of macaques. By manipulating the behaviour of pairs of macaques before they were confronted with a food source, Cords (1992) showed that characteristic tolerance levels around this food decreased if dyad members had previously interacted aggressively, but that post-conflict reunions could restore tolerance levels to baseline. Reunions decreased both the dominant's tendency to exclude its partner aggressively, and the subordinate's hesitancy to feed near the dominant opponent. Insofar as tolerance around resources is one benefit of relationships with valuable partners, this experiment directly demonstrated the adaptive significance of post-conflict reunions. Aureli & van Schaik's (1991) observations suggested further that reunions reduce tension levels in the victims of previous fights, and that tension levels are related to the likelihood of receiving further aggression from group-mates. Rates of receiving aggression after an initial aggressive conflict were elevated over baseline if there was no friendly reunion, but remained at baseline levels if a friendly reunion had occurred.

Primates reconcile selectively with particular social partners. Within a group, there are typically dyads that reconcile nearly all their conflicts, while others reconcile rarely. Attempts have been made to relate this variation in conciliatory tendency to characteristics of the dyad, such as friendship and kinship (Kappeler & van Schaik, 1992; Castles et al., 1996). Across studies, results have been somewhat inconsistent, however, partly because of methodological complications (Veenema et al., 1994), and partly because neither factor seems sufficiently explanatory. Kinship and friendship were investigated because both are likely to be related to relationship value; thus the underlying expectation was that primates should reconcile more often with valuable social partners. An experiment that tested this hypothesis directly supported the prediction: when macaque partners depended on each other to get food in a co-operative task, they reconciled three times more often than when co-operation was not required of them (Cords & Thurnheer, 1993). Because the study dyads were used as their own controls, this experiment showed not only that reconciliation was directed strategically to valuable partners, but also that the likelihood of its occurrence could be adjusted when the value of partners changed. It is likely, however, that a social partner's value is not the only relevant variable: access to the partner, determined perhaps by general levels of compatibility, as well as the security of the social relationship, may also influence the tendency to reconcile (Cords & Aureli, 1993; Watts, 1995a).

Animals that reconcile must switch rapidly from an agonistic to an affiliative motivation. The cognitive prerequisites for reconciliation, however, may be rather simple: former opponents must be capable of individual recognition and have reasonably good memories (de Waal & Yoshihara, 1983). Such abilities are not limited to primates, so it is not surprising that friendly post-conflict reunions have been reported in other social mammals as well (e.g. mouflon, hyenas: Cords & Thurnheer, 1993). Studies of non-primates have not focused on reconciliation, however, so it is impossible to judge whether the nature or function of their reunions differ relative to primates. The strategic nature of reconciliation documented in some primates seems more clearly to presuppose a Machiavellian intelligence. Again, however, there are no comparable data from non-primates, so we cannot yet determine whether primates are distinctive in this respect.

Third party conflict resolution

The resolution of aggressive conflicts by the opponents themselves is only one option. Among monkeys and apes, third parties who were not part of the aggression are sometimes involved in its sequelae in ways that suggest their roles as pacifiers, mediators and consolers.

Third parties may resolve conflicts in their group directly by attacking one or both of the original opponents, or by engaging one of them in friendly interaction. In either case, the original conflict is simply stopped. Among Tonkean macaques, for example, high-ranking males intervene in ongoing fights by making friendly overtures to the original aggressor. Petit & Thierry (1994) interpreted these peaceful interventions as protecting the victim, while preserving the intervening animal's relationship with the aggressor. Interventions were more likely to benefit closer kin.

In several monkey species, aggressive conflict increases the chance that an individual will interact affiliatively with its former opponent's kin (York & Rowell, 1988; Cheney & Seyfarth, 1989; Judge, 1991; but see Aureli et al., 1993). Judge's study of pigtail macaques suggested that it was particularly the aggressor that was likely to interact with kin of the victim: victims did not increase their interaction rate with the aggressor's kin (see also Aureli & van Schaik, 1991). While the effects of these post-conflict interactions with the opponent's kin have not been documented, it has been suggested that they prevent aggression from 'spreading' to relatives of the original opponents, or protect the original victim if its relatives reconcile with the aggressor on its behalf (Aureli & van Schaik, 1991; Judge, 1991). Alternatively, such interactions might fall into the same class as interactions between aggressors and their own kin, which may occur at elevated frequencies after conflicts because of a general social arousal directed toward nearby and available partners. Further research is needed to exclude simpler explanations of this sort.

The idea that third parties may mediate reconciliations between opponents comes mainly from observations of power struggles among captive male chimpanzees (de Waal, 1982). After inter-male aggression, a female would sometimes groom one of the males, and then appear to lead him over to his former opponent, eventually leaving the two males to groom one another (de Waal & van Roosmalen, 1979). While such direct attempts at apparent mediation have not been observed in macaques, de Waal (1989b, p. 238) reports a case in which a mother rhesus monkey was grooming her juvenile son's former aggressor, but yielded her position to her son when she noticed him approaching, thus facilitating a friendly reunion between the former opponents. De Waal & Aureli (1996) have argued that these observations indicate that primates recognise social relationships between others, including the course of conflict and reconciliation in those relationships; they propose, however, that chimpanzees have a deeper understanding of the process of reconciliation than macaques, in accord with the way chimpanzee bystanders can become more fully involved in mediation.

Consolation refers to friendly post-conflict interactions that occur between the victim of aggression and third parties that function to reduce the victim's state of fear or arousal through reassuring friendly contact. The notion of consolation again stems mainly from observations of conflicts in chimpanzees (de Waal & van Roosmalen, 1979; de Waal & Aureli, 1996; but see Watts, 1995b on gorillas), in which victims may receive friendly contact, especially embraces and gentle touches, from third parties. Because conflict elevates the occurrence of such contacts, victims show a greater increase in affiliative contacts than aggressors, and rates of contact with victims are higher if the aggression was more intense, it seems that these third party interactions are consolatory (de Waal & Aureli, 1996). Although descriptive accounts of apparently consoling interactions with victims exist for macaques (Lindburg, 1973), quantitative analyses have failed to document an increase in friendly contacts with third parties after aggression relative to baseline levels, even when the analysis was limited to the victim's close kin, who should be most likely to console (de Waal & Aureli, 1996). These results stand in contrast to demonstrations that macaque aggressors do increase their rate of contact to their own kin (Judge, 1991). de Waal & Aureli (1996) suggested that the occurrence of apparently consoling behaviour between chimpanzees and its absence in macaques may be understood partly in terms of the looser, more egalitarian nature of chimpanzee societies, which makes consolations both less risky and more effective. They also consider it possible, however, that consolation in chimpanzees is based on empathy, and hence dependent on the attribution to others of mental states that differ from one's own.

Before leaving the topic of third party conflict resolution, we should note how much we *do not* know about it. Firstly, the function of these third party interactions has been substantiated mainly through circumstantial evidence and intuition; future research must rule out simpler alternative hypotheses. Secondly, most data come from macaques and chimpanzees; the degree to which similar social phenomena occur across the order is unknown. Furthermore, only a few macaque species have been investigated, so that even reported differences between macaques and chimpanzees must be considered to be preliminary. Finally, comparative data from non-primates are, again, utterly lacking.

Conclusion

A hallmark of research on the social behaviour of primates has been its focus on individuals and their social relationships over relatively long lifetimes. Regardless of the particular social system involved, primates form different kinds of relationships with different members of their population and even of their own social unit. Not all such relationships involve animals with immediate joint reproductive interests. Primates are not unique in these respects, however. Where their social behaviour may be distinctive is in the way these social relationships are cultivated, protected and used. Some of the evidence relating to these processes has been presented in this chapter. The complexity involved in strategically managing a dynamic social world certainly appears considerable, but the data still leave room, in many cases, for skeptical interpretation.

In two important respects, our knowledge of primate social life is limited. Firstly, most data come from a very limited number of species, especially semi-terrestrial Old World monkeys and chimpanzees (Strier, 1990). From what is known about these species, it is understandable that social complexity would be linked to the ways in which social bonds are used, and even formed, to influence competitive outcomes through asymmetries in power (de Waal & Harcourt, 1992). Similar Machiavellianism may not characterise other primate taxa however: reduced agonism and salience of dominance, reduced kinship among non-philopatric females, a lack of conspicuous communicative signals for mediating complex interactions, and even anatomical constraints (Rowell, 1988; Strier, 1990; Pereira, 1995) may limit either the usefulness or the effectiveness of co-operating to compete. Negative evidence always accumulates more slowly than positive evidence; for less well studied primates (which include most species), it is therefore hard to say whether evidence of Machiavellian strategies is negative, or if we simply cannot yet judge.

Secondly, as cautioned several times already, data from non-primate species are also lacking, which makes it impossible to put the primate data, such as they are, into a wider perspective. In a sense, this chapter is an invitation to further research on other animals that also live in individualised societies, research that might be partially guided by an appreciation of how primates behave.

References

Aureli, F. & van Schaik, C. P. (1991). Post-conflict behaviour in long-tailed macaques (*Macaca fascicularis*): I. The social events. *Ethology*, **89**, 89–100.

Aureli, F., Veenema, H. C., van Panthaleon van Eck, C. J. & van Hooff, J. A. R. A. M. (1993). Reconciliation, consolation, and redirection in Japanese macaques (*Macaca fuscata*). *Behaviour*, **124**, 1–21.

Baldwin, J. D. & Baldwin, J. I. (1981). The squirrel monkey. In *Ecology and Behavior of Neotropical Primates*, ed. A. F. Coimbra-Filho & R. A. Mittermeier, pp. 277–330. Rio de Janeiro: Academia Brasileira de Ciencias.

Barton, R. A. (1993). Sociospatial mechanisms of feeding competition in female olive baboons, *Papio anubis*. *Animal Behaviour*, **46**, 791–802.

Bercovitch, F. B. (1988). Coalitions, cooperation, and reproductive tactics among adult male baboons. *Animal Behaviour*, **36**, 1198–209.

Berman, C. (1982). The ontogeny of social relationships with group companions among free-ranging infant rhesus monkeys, I. Social networks and differentiation. *Animal Behaviour*, **30**, 149–62.

Bernstein, I. S. (1991). The correlation between kinship and behaviour in non-human primates. In *Kin Recognition*, ed. P. G. Hepper, pp. 6–29. Cambridge: Cambridge University Press.

Bernstein, I. S. & Ehardt, C. L. (1985). Intragroup agonistic behavior in rhesus monkeys (*Macaca mulatta*). *International Journal of Primatology*, **6**, 209–26.

Bernstein, I. S. & Gordon, T. P. (1974). The function of aggression in primate societies. *American Scientist*, **62**, 304–11.

Bernstein, I. S., Judge, P. G. & Ruehlmann, T. E. (1993). Kinship, association and social relationships in rhesus monkeys (*Macaca mulatta*). *American Journal Primatology*, **31**, 41–53.

Boesch-Achermann, H. & Boesch, C. (1993). Tool use in wild chimpanzees: New light from dark forests. *Current Directions in Psychological Science*, **2**, 18–21.

Boinski, S. (1993). Vocal coordination of troop movement among white-faced capuchin monkeys, *Cebus capucinus*. *American Journal of Primatology*, **30**, 85–100.

Boinski, S. (1994). Affiliation patterns among male Costa Rican squirrel monkeys. *Behaviour*, **130**, 191–209.

Boinski, S. & Mitchell, C. L. (1992). Ecological and social factors affecting the vocal behavior of adult female squirrel monkeys. *Ethology*, **92**, 316–30.

Boyd, R. (1992). The evolution of reciprocity when conditions vary. In *Coalitions and Alliances in Humans and Other Animals*, ed. A. H. Harcourt & F. B. M. de Waal, pp. 473–89. Oxford: Oxford University Press.

Carpenter, C. R. (1964). *Naturalistic Behavior of Non-human Primates*. University Park, PA: The Pennsylvania State University Press.

Castles, D. L., Aureli, F. & de Waal, F. B. M. (1996). Variation in conciliatory tendency and relationship quality across groups of pigtail macaques. *Animal Behaviour*, 52, 389–403.

Chapais, B. (1992). The role of alliances in social inheritance of rank among female primates. In *Coalitions and Alliances in Humans and Other Animals*, ed. A. H. Harcourt & F. B. M. de Waal, pp. 29–60. Oxford: Oxford University Press.

Cheney, D. L. & Seyfarth, R. M. (1989). Redirected aggression and reconciliation among vervet monkeys, *Cercopithecus aethiops*. *Behaviour*, 110, 258–75.

Cheney, D. L. & Seyfarth, R. M. (1990). *How Monkeys See the World: Inside the Mind of Another Species*. Chicago: University of Chicago Press.

Cheney, D. L., Seyfarth, R. M. & Smuts, B. B. (1986). Social relationships and social cognition in nonhuman primates. *Science* 234, 1361–6.

Colvin, J. & Tissier, G. (1985). Affiliation and reciprocity in sibling and peer relaltionships among free-ranging immature male rhesus monkeys. *Animal Behaviour*, 33, 959–77.

Cords, M. (1992). Post-conflict reunions and reconciliation in long-tailed macaques. *Animal Behaviour*, 44, 57–61.

Cords, M. (1995). Predator vigilance costs of allogrooming in wild blue monkeys. *Behaviour*, 132, 559–69.

Cords, M. & Aureli, F. (1993). Patterns of reconciliation among juvenile long-tailed macaques. In *Juvenile Primates: Life History, Development and Behavior*, ed. M. E. Pereira & L. A. Fairbanks, pp. 271–284. New York: Oxford University Press.

Cords, M. & Thurnheer, S. (1993). Reconciling with valuable partners by long-tailed macaques. *Ethology*, 93, 315–25.

de Waal, F. B. M. (1977). The organization of agonistic relations within two captive groups of Java-monkeys (*Macaca fascicularis*). *Zeitschrift für Tierpsychologie* 44, 225–82.

de Waal, F. B. M. (1982). *Chimpanzee Politics: Power and Sex Among Apes*. New York: Harper and Row.

de Waal, F. B. M. (1987). Tension regulation and nonreproductive functions of sex in captive bonobos (*Pan paniscus*). *National Geographic Research*, 3, 318–35.

de Waal, F. B. M. (1989a). Foodsharing and reciprocal obligations among chimpanzees. *Journal of Human Evolution*, 18, 433–59.

de Waal, F. B. M. (1989b). *Peacemaking Among Primates*. Cambridge: Cambridge University Press.

de Waal, F. B. M. (1991). Rank distance as a central feature of rhesus monkey social organization: A sociometric analysis. *Animal Behaviour*, 41, 383–95.

de Waal, F. B. M. (1992). Coalitions as part of reciprocal relations in the Arnhem chimpanzee colony. In *Coalitions and Alliances in Humans and Other Animals*, ed. A. H. Harcourt & F. B. M. de Waal, pp. 233–257. Oxford: Oxford University Press.

de Waal, F. B. M. (1993). Reconciliation among primates: A review of empirical evidence and unresolved issues. In *Primate Social Conflict*, ed. W. A. Mason, & S. P. Mendoza, S. P., pp. 111–44. Albany: State University of New York Press.

de Waal, F. B. M. & Aureli, F. (1996). Consolation, reconciliation, and a possible cognitive difference between macaques and chimpanzees. In *Reaching into Thought: The Mind of the Great Apes*, ed. A. E. Russon, K. A. Bard & S. T. Parker, pp. 80–110. Cambridge: Cambridge University Press.

de Waal, F. B. M. & Harcourt, A. H. (1992). Coalitions and alliances: A history of ethological research. In *Coalitions and Alliances in Humans and Other Animals*, ed. A. H. Harcourt & F. B. M. de Waal, pp. 1–19. Oxford: Oxford University Press.

de Waal, F. B. M. & Luttrell, L. M. (1986). The similarity principle underlying social bonding among female rhesus monkeys. *Folia Primatologica*, 46, 215–34.

de Waal, F. B. M. & Luttrell, L. M. (1988). Mechanisms of social reciprocity in three primate species: Symmetrical relationship characteristics or cognition? *Ethology Sociobiology*, 9, 101–18.

de Waal, F. B. M. & van Roosmalen, A. (1979). Reconciliation and consolation among chimpanzees. *Behaviour Ecology and Sociobiology*, 5, 55–66.

de Waal, F. B. M. & Yoshihara, D. (1983). Reconciliation and redirected affection in rhesus monkeys. *Behaviour*, 85, 224–41.

Dunbar, R. I. M. (1984). *Reproductive Decisions: An Economic Analysis of Gelada Baboon Social Strategies*. Princeton, NJ: Princeton University Press.

Dunbar, R. I. M. (1988). *Primate Social Systems*. London: Croom Helm.

Dunbar, R. I. M. (1989). Social systems as optimal strategy sets: The costs and benefits of sociality. In *Comparative Socioecology*, ed. V. Standen & F. A. Foley, pp. 131–49. Oxford: Blackwell Scientific Publications.

Dunbar, R. I. M. (1991). Functional significance of social grooming in primates. *Folia Primatologica*, 57, 121–31.

Ehardt, C. & Bernstein, I. S. (1992). Conflict intervention behaviour by adult male macaques: Structural and functional aspects. In *Coalitions and Alliances in Humans and Other Animals*, ed. A. H. Harcourt & F. B. M. de Waal, pp. 83–111. Oxford: Oxford University Press.

Fairbanks, L. A. (1980). Relationships among adult females in captive vervet monkeys: Testing a model of rank-related attractiveness. *Animal Behaviour*, 28, 853–9.

Furuichi, T. & Ihobe, H. (1994). Variation in male relationships in bonobos and chimpanzees. *Behaviour*, 130, 211–28.

Gautier, J. P. & Gautier-Hion, A. (1982). Vocal communication within a group of monkeys: An analysis by biotelemetry. In *Primate Communication*, ed. C. T. Snowdon, C. H. Brown & M. R. Petersen, pp. 5–29. Cambridge: Cambridge University Press.

Goodall, J. (1986). *The Chimpanzees of Gombe: Patterns of Behavior*. Cambridge, MA: The Belknap Press.

Goodenough, J., McGuire, B. & Wallace, R. A. (1993). *Perspectives on Animal Behavior*. New York: John Wiley and Sons, Inc.

Goosen, C. (1981). On the function of allogrooming in Old-World monkeys. In *Primate Behaviour and Sociobiology*, ed. A. B. Chiarelli & R. S. Corruccini, pp. 110–20. Berlin: Springer-Verlag.

Gouzoules, S. & Gouzoules, H. (1986). Kinship. In *Primate Societies*, ed. B. B. Smuts, D. L. Cheney, R. M. Seyfarth, R. W. Wrangham & T. T. Struhsaker, pp. 299–305. Chicago: University of Chicago Press.

Harcourt, A. H. (1988). Alliances in contests and social intelligence. In *Machiavellian Intelligence: Social Expertise and the Evolution of Intellect in Monkeys, Apes and Humans*, ed. R. W. Byrne & A. Whiten, pp. 132–52. Oxford: Clarendon Press.

Harcourt, A. H. (1989). Social influences on competitive ability: Alliances and their consequences. In *Comparative Socioecology*, ed. V. Standen & R. A. Foley, pp. 223–42. Oxford: Blackwell Scientific Publications.

Harcourt, A. H. (1992). Coalitions and alliances: Are primates more complex than non-primates? In *Coalitions and Alliances in Humans and Other Animals*, ed. A. H. Harcourt & F. B. M. de Waal, pp. 445–71. Oxford: Oxford University Press.

Harcourt, A. H., Stewart, K. J. & Hauser, M. (1993). Functions of wild gorilla 'close' calls. I. Repertoire, context, and interspecific comparison. *Behaviour*, 124, 89–122.

Hemelrijk, C. K. (1990a). Models of, and tests for, reciprocity, unidirectionality and other social interaction patterns at a group level. *Animal Behaviour*, 39, 1013–29.

Hemelrijk, C. K. (1990b). A matrix partial correlation test used in investigations of reciprocity and other social interaction patterns at group level. *Journal of Theoretical Biology*, 143, 405–20.

Hemelrijk, C. K. (1991). Interchange of "altruistic" acts as an epiphenomenon. *Journal of Theoretical Biology*, 153, 137–9.

Hemelrijk, C. K. (1994). Support for being groomed in long-tailed macaques. *Animal Behaviour*, 48, 479–81.

Hemelrijk, C. K. & Ek, A. (1991). Reciprocity and interchange of grooming and 'support' in captive chimpanzees. *Animal Behaviour*, 41, 923–5.

Hemelrijk, C. K., Klomberg, T. J. M., Nooitgedagt, J. H. & van Hooff, J. A. R. A. M. (1991). Side-directed behaviour and recruitment of support in captive chimpanzees. *Behaviour*, 118, 89–101.

Hinde, R. A. (1979). *Towards Understanding Relationships*. London: Academic Press.

Hunte, W. & Horrocks, J. A. (1987). Kin and non-kin interventions in the aggerssive disputes of vervet monkeys. *Behavioural Ecology and Sociobiology*, 20, 257–63.

Janson, C. H. (1990). Social correlates of individual spatial choice in foraging groups of brown capuchin monkeys, *Cebus apella*. *Animal Behaviour*, 40, 910–21.

Jones, C. B. (1983). Social organization of captive black howler monkeys (*Alouatta caraya*): 'Social competition' and the use of non-damaging behavior. *Primates*, 24, 25–39.

Judge, P. G. (1991). Dyadic and triadic reconciliation in pigtail macaques (*Macaca nemestrina*). *American Journal of Primatology*, 23, 225–37.

Kappeler, P. M. & van Schaik, C. P. (1992). Methodological and evolutionary aspects of reconciliation among primates. *Ethology*, 92, 51–69.

Kummer, H. (1978). On the value of social relationships to nonhuman primates: A heuristic scheme. *Social Science Information*, 17, 687–705.

Kummer, H. & Cords, M. (1991). Cues of ownership in Macaca fascicularis. *Animal Behaviour*, 42, 529–49.

Kurland, J. (1977). Kin selection in the Japanese monkey. *Contributions to Primatology*, 12, 1–130.

Lindburg, D. G. (1973). Grooming behavior as a regulator of social interactions in rhesus monkeys. In *Behavioral Regulators of Behavior in Primates*, ed. C. R. Carpenter, pp. 124–48. Lewisburg, PA: Bucknell University Press.

Maestripieri, D. (1993). Vigilance costs of allogrooming in macaque mothers. *American Naturalist*, 141, 744–53.

Mayagoitia, L., Santillan-Doherty, A. M., Lopez-Vergara, L. & Mondragon-Ceballos, R. (1993). Affiliation tactics prior to a period of competition in captive groups of stump-tailed macaques. *Ethology, Ecology and Evolution*, 5, 435–46.

Noë, R. (1990). A veto game played by baboons: A challenge to the use of the prisoner's dilemma as a pradigm for reciprocity and cooperation. *Animal Behaviour*, 39, 78–90.

Noë, R. (1992). Alliance formation among male baboons. In *Coalitions and Alliances in Humans and Other Animals*, ed. A. H. Harcourt & F. B. M. de Waal, pp. 285–321. Oxford: Oxford University Press.

Noë, R., van Schaik, C. P. & van Hooff, J. A. R. A. M. (1991). The market effect: An explanation for pay-off asymmetries among collaborating animals. *Ethology*, 87, 97–118.

O'Brien, T. G. (1993). Allogrooming behaviour among adult female wedge-capped capuchin monkeys. *Animal Behaviour*, 46, 499–510.

Packer, C. (1977). Reciprocal altruism in *Papio anubis*. *Nature*, 265, 441–3.

Pereira, M. E. (1988). Effects of age and sex on intra-group spacing behavior in juvenile savannah baboons, *Papio cynocephalus cynocephalus*. *Animal Behaviour*, 36, 184–204.

Pereira, M. E. (1995). Development and social dominance among group-living primates. *American Journal of Primatology*, 37, 143–75.

Petit, O. & Thierry, B. (1994). Aggressive and peaceful interventions in conflicts in Tonkean macaques. *Animal Behaviour*, 48, 1427–36.

Rowell, T. E. (1988). The social system of guenons, compared with baboons, macaques and mangabeys. In *A Primate Radiation: Evolutionary Biology of the African Guenons*, ed. F. Bourliere, J. P. Gautier, A. Gautier-Hion & J. Kingdon, pp. 439–51. Cambridge: Cambridge University Press, .

Rowell, T. E. & Rowell, C. A. (1993). The social organization of feral *Ovis aries* ram groups in the pre-rut period. *Ethology*, 95, 213–32.

Seyfarth, R. M. (1976). Social relationships among adult female baboons. *Animal Behaviour*, 24, 917–38.

Seyfarth, R. M. (1977). A model of social grooming among adult female monkeys. *Journal of Theoretical Biology*, 65, 671–98.

Seyfarth, R. M. (1980). The distribution of grooming and related behaviours among adult female vervet monkeys. *Animal Behaviour*, 28, 798–813.

Seyfarth, R. M. (1983). Grooming and social competition in primates. In *Primate Social Relationships: An Integrated Approach*, ed. R. A. Hinde, pp. 182–90. Sunderland, MA: Sinauer Associates.

Seyfarth, R. M. (1991). Reciprocal altruism and the limits of correlational analysis. *Journal of Theoretical Biology*, 153, 141–4.

Seyfarth, R. M. & Cheney, D. L. (1984). Grooming, alliances and reciprocal altruism in vervet monkeys. *Nature*, 308, 541–3.

Silk, J. B. (1982). Altruism among female *Macaca radiata*: Explanations and analysis of patterns of grooming and coalition formation. *Behaviour*, 79, 162–88.

Silk, J. B. (1992a). Patterns of intervention in agonistic contests among male bonnet macaques. In *Coalitions and Alliances in Humans and Other Animals*, ed. A. H. Harcourt & F. B. M. de Waal, pp. 215–32. Oxford: Oxford University Press.

Silk, J. B. (1992b). The patterning of intervention among male bonnet macaques: Reciprocity, revenge and loyalty. *Current Anthropology*, 33, 318–25.

Silk, J. B. (1994). Social relationships of male bonnet macaques: Male bonding in a matrilineal society. *Behaviour*, 130, 271–91.

Small, M. F. (1989). Female choice in non-human primates. *Yearbook of Physical Anthropology*, 32, 103–27.

Smith, H. J., Newman, J. D. & Symmes, D. (1982). Vocal concomitants of affiliative behavior in squirrel monkeys. In *Primate Communication*, ed. C. T. Snowdon, C. H. Brown & M. R. Petersen, pp. 30–49. Cambridge: Cambridge University Press.

Smuts, B. B. (1985). *Sex and Friendship in Baboons*. New York: Aldine.

Stammbach, E. & Kummer, H. (1982). Individual contributions to a dyadic interaction: An analysis of baboon grooming. *Animal Behaviour*, 30, 964–71.

Strier, K. B. (1990). New World primates, new frontiers: Insights from the woolly spider monkey, or muriqui (*Brachyteles arachnoides*). *International Journal of Primatology*, 11, 7–19.

Strier, K. B. (1992). *Faces in the Forest: The Endangered Muriqui Monkeys of Brazil*. New York: Oxford University Press.

van Hooff, J. A. R. A. M. & van Schaik, C. P. (1994). Male bonds: Afilliative [sic] relationships among nonhuman primate males. *Behaviour*, 130, 309–37.

Veenema, H. C., Das, M. & Aureli, F. (1994). Methodological improvements for the study of reconciliation. *Behavioural Processes*, 31, 29–38.

Walters, J. R. (1987). Kin recognition in non-human primates. In *Kin Recognition in Animals*, ed. D. J. C. Fletcher & C. D. Michener, pp. 359–93. New York: John Wiley & Sons.

Watts, D. P. (1994). Social relationships of immigrant and resident female mountain gorillas, II. Relatedness, residence and relationships between females. *American Journal of Primatology*, 32, 13–30.

Watts, D. P. (1995a). Post-conflict social events in wild mountain gorillas (Mammalia, Hominoidea). I. Social interactions between opponents. *Ethology*, 100, 139–57.

Watts, D. P. (1995b). Post-conflict social events in wild mountain gorillas, II. Redirection, side direction, and consolation. *Ethology*, 100, 158–74.

Wilson, E. O. (1975). *Sociobiology*. Cambridge, MA: The Belknap Press.

Wrangham, R. W. (1980). An ecological model of female-bonded primate groups. *Behaviour*, 75, 262–300.

Wright, P. (1981). The night monkeys, genus *Aotus*. In *Ecology and Behavior of Neotropical Primates*, ed. A. F. Coimbra-Filho & R. A. Mittermeier, pp. 211–40. Rio di Janeiro: Academia Brasileira de Ciencias.

York, A. D. & Rowell, T. E. (1988). Reconciliation following aggression in patas monkeys, *Erythrocebus patas*. *Animal Behaviour*, 36, 502–9.

3 Why Machiavellian intelligence may not be Machiavellian

SHIRLEY C. STRUM, DEBORAH FORSTER
AND EDWIN HUTCHINS

Introduction

The discovery of primate social complexity during the last 20 years stimulated a reinterpretation of the nature and evolution of primate intelligence. In this chapter we attempt to do three things. Firstly we present a short background highlighting some inherent difficulties with the current 'social complexity/cognition' model from which the Machiavellian Intelligence hypothesis derives. Next we explore the consequences of these problematic issues with data on sexual consorts in baboons. Finally we present another way to frame the social complexity/cognition link that we feel has the potential to more fully explain our consort data and to resolve some of the inherent ambiguities in the social complexity model of intelligence. In the process we are left to wonder whether Machiavellian intelligence is really 'Machiavellian'.

The model

The intellectual events that culminated in the Machiavellian Intelligence hypothesis look slightly different from the description offered by Byrne and Whiten (Chapter 1) when seen from the perspective of primate field studies (Strum & Fedigan, 1997). This vantage point may help to explain why the Chance–Jolly–Kummer–Humphrey (Chance & Mead, 1953; Jolly, 1966; Kummer, 1967; Humphrey, 1976) hypotheses about 'social intelligence' did not actually begin to constitute a 'domain' of knowledge and research for nearly 20 years. Field data and shifts in theoretical orientations were crucial. Long-term studies of chimpanzees (see Goodall, 1986 and references therein) and baboons (Altmann, 1980; Ransom, 1981; Strum, 1981; Stein, 1984), in particular, documented an array of social relationships. These were initially treated as mere 'social noise' resulting from many social animals living together (e.g. Ransom & Ransom, 1971; Ransom, 1981; Goodall 1986). The era of sociobiological theory, which began in 1975 (Wilson, 1975) reframed behaviour in terms of individual tactics and strategies that had evolutionary importance and placed social behaviour and social relationships in context. Sociobiological theory transformed the social noise of longitudinal field data into 'social strategy' (e.g. Strum, 1982, 1983a,b; Dunbar, 1984; Stein, 1984) making the creation and maintenance of social relationships (whether they were kin, peer, friend, etc) central to individual reproductive success (Kummer, 1978; Strum 1982; Smuts, 1985).

This shift in ideas about the value of social relationships occurred independently of considerations of the evolution of intelligence, in part because the reigning sociobiological view assigned tactics and strategies to the genes and not to individual minds (Dawkins, 1976; Crist, 1994). The sociobiological assumption was easy to accept given the behaviourist tradition inherited *via* classical ethology (Marler & Hamilton, 1966), which insisted that mind was not crucial to the production of behaviour (Strum & Fedigan, in press) and rejected individual agency (Crist, 1994).

If social relationships reflect evolutionary strategies then individuals must be manipulating others for selfish gain. This assumption had at least two consequences. Firstly, a group composed of such actors becomes suddenly and increasingly complex. Secondly, it was the inclusion of social manipulation as part of competition between individuals that later made the term 'Machiavellian' seem an appropriate way to characterise both individual abilities and the social world. But the cognitive soup didn't really begin to boil until studies presented detailed and careful documentation of individual tactics and strategies (e.g. Bachmann & Kummer, 1980; de Waal, 1982; Strum, 1983a,b; Goodall, 1986). These data suggested the need for a cognitivist rather than a behaviourist framework and a consideration of mind in addition to genes.

The field data interacted with results from laboratory studies. Researchers tested individual abilities on a range of primate species in a variety of contexts (see examples in Parker & Gibson, 1990). The ape-language experiments about the production and comprehension of symbol reference systems similar to human language were especially influential. Premack & Woodruff (1978) even asked whether chimpanzees had a 'theory of mind'.

The stage was set for a 'cognitive revolution' in primate behaviour as this combination of field and laboratory results made precise claims about the social world and about intelligence. Social complexity came to be seen as the motor for the evolution of higher cognition (although not without earlier and continuing counter claims about ecological complexity and cognition (Parker & Gibson, 1977; Milton, 1981; Byrne, 1995)) and Machiavellian intelligence became a short-hand way to restate the most essential aspects of 'social intelligence'.

What is Machiavellian intelligence? There is no explicit or simple definition (see Byrne & Whiten, 1988; and Chapter 1). Machiavellian intelligence is defined by reference to three issues: the intelligence that is needed in dealing with conspecifics in the context of social interaction; the special nature of the social environment and its distinction from the 'technical' world; and the claim that it is this kind of intelligence that stimulated the evolution of non-human primate and human cognitive skills. In all versions of the Machiavellian intelligence hypothesis, social life is seen as highly problematic because of special characteristics of social interactions that require, for example, constant monitoring, accurate prediction, appropriately timed behaviour, all taking place in a context of social complexity. Byrne and Whiten claim that Machiavellian intelligence is a special kind of social intelligence that allows the actor to change tactics creatively as the social game evolves (Byrne & Whiten, 1988). They suggest that Machiavellian intelligence may involve 'declarative knowledge', social problem-solving, innovation, flexibility, social expertise, memory, conditional social rules, 'mindreading', imitative learning and self-reflection. Current research has proceeded along these lines, exploring such issues as 'theory of mind' (Cheney & Seyfarth, 1990; Whiten, 1991). But the Machiavellian intelligence hypothesis in its various guises rests on a number of assumptions about the link between social complexity and cognition that have not been scrutinised. What exactly is social complexity and how is it generated? Is it simply the result of long lifetimes and overlapping generations (Humphrey 1976) or the consequence of an increase in the number of actors and the increase in the number of social conditions (Byrne & Whiten, 1988; Cheney & Seyfarth, 1990)? What makes any social situation 'complex'? How is social complexity distributed within the system? In what manner does social complexity affect the individual? How are the links between social complexity and cognition created during interactions and during evolution?

We will examine these questions using data on sexual consorts and consort turnovers in a troop of wild baboons. These data are particularly appropriate because sexual behaviour has played a central role in the history of ideas about social intelligence beginning with Chance & Mead's (1953) assumption that sexual competition between males was the primary source of the need for special intelligence. Consort tactics have provided some of the earliest and most convincing examples for the Machiavellian intelligence hypothesis.

Data on consorts in these baboons (Strum, 1975, 1981, 1982) were part of new formulations about social manipulation as part of social strategies (Western & Strum, 1983). The data took two forms. The first, on consort success, resulted in the 'residency model' of consort success (Strum, 1982). Male success was not predicted by male dominance rank but rather by length of tenure in the troop. This was because males had alternatives to aggressive strategies of competition but these non-aggressive social alternatives took time to implement since they depended on the creation and maintenance of social relationships as part of a system of reciprocity. Females co-operated with males from whom they derived benefits through friendship. For their part, males who invested in female friends subsequently gained co-operative partners and an advantage in both reproduction and defence.

The second source of insights emerged from data on the dynamics of consort turnovers. Males employed a variety of non-aggressive 'social' tactics that minimised the risk of injury and yet increased their ability to get the receptive female. For example, the 'sidelines' turnover tactic occurred when a male who had been watching from some distance, seemingly uninterested in the consort, timed his involvement to coincide with aggression between the consort male and those males who were following the consort closely (male followers). While those males were preoccupied with each other, the 'sidelines' male would rush in, claim the female and move her away. Thus it was not the winner of the conflict but the 'clever' male who was the female's new consort. Similar 'smart' ways to get receptive females implied that social manipulation depended on skill and knowledge integrated into sophisticated tactics, which because of their flexibility and variability were not so easily explained by deterministic genetic mechanisms. The patterning of consorts and the dynamics of consort turnovers appeared among the most socially complex baboon behaviour suggesting the need for a cognitivist interpretation such as Machiavellian intelligence.

Now, nearly 20 years later we would like to reconsider these ideas. Are social strategies central to successful consorts and are cognitive assessments involved? Do baboon consort interactions demonstrate a link between social complexity and cognition and provide evidence of Machiavellian tactics?

The consort data

We will use two sets of data similar to the original sets to further explore these questions. The first comprises longitudinal data on the consort success of individual males spanning the period from 1972 through 1987 from a troop of wild baboons who live in Kenya (see Strum, 1982, 1987, 1994b for details). The goal of this analysis was to discover whether there are robust patterns in *consort scores* (a male's monopoly of consorts with females during his residency) that could represent consort tactics and strategies as predicted from the earlier interpretation. Four variables were chosen because they are reasonable surrogates for the two consort strategy options: traditional aggressive strategies as seen in weight and age, and non-aggressive social strategies linked to social manipulation as seen in residency status and friendships with females (Strum, 1994b). These variables could be reliably extracted from the longitudinal records to produce a 15 year data-base. Male baboons were weighed during several research projects and males are categorised as heavy or light based on the mean weight from each set of weighings. Adult ages were estimated based on criteria developed during two decades of observing adult males. Six broad categories are used ranging from 'just matured' to 'oldest' (roughly more than 20 years of age). Friendship is defined as the strong affiliative bond between individuals (in this case a male and a female) that includes close proximity, mutual assistance, preferential grooming and orientated following (Strum, 1975, 1982). Both adult and adolescent males are part of the sample. For adolescent males the variable *age* was translated into *size class* (small, medium and large subadults) to allow the inclusion of immigrants whose actual ages were unknown and *migration status*, whether the male was natal or immigrant, replaced the variable *tenure* that was used for adults. A complete presentation and interpretation of these data can be found in Strum (1994b).

The second set of data concerns the dynamics of consort turnovers from 1989–1991 (Forster & Strum, 1994). In particular we examine a specific pattern of turnover, 'sleeping near the enemy' (SNE), and treat it as a social manipulation in order to investigate the nature of cognition.

Before we present the data, a short description of a baboon consort may be useful (see also Strum, 1987 for specific examples). Males and females form sexual consortships during a period of about 7 days around ovulation. Consorts can start much earlier and last much longer depending on the 'who, when and why' of the interactions. Copulation is not a sufficient criterion for a 'consort', although it is an important aspect. The most striking feature is the association between the consort pair. The male usually maintains the proximity (but see Strum, 1981) as the consort male and female co-ordinate their drinking, feeding and resting. In contrast to other times, the male does the majority of the grooming. The consort male may also be possessive of the female when other males are near. The female can be helpful and co-operative with the male or resist his efforts at maintaining proximity, co-ordinating activities and even copulation. Very often, the consort pair is surrounded by other interested baboons who comprise the 'consort party' (Forster & Strum, 1994). Interested males follow the consort, orientate themselves to the pair, track their movements and may harass, challenge or try to take over the female. The consort party can also contain the female's kin, competing females who try to interfere with the consort female or are possessive of the consort male, immature friends of the consort male or of a male follower, and sometimes an 'unrelated' juvenile who harasses copulations. This diverse and complex social context includes individuals intent on disrupting the consortship for a variety of reasons. It is not surprising that a particular consort configuration rarely lasts a whole day or that there are a large number of configurations with nearly unique characteristics. Each time someone leaves or joins the consort party, options and potential outcomes shift. And every change in an essential characteristic, such as the day of the female's reproductive cycle, also remakes the party and the dynamics of the consortship.

Longitudinal data on consorts as social manipulation

The data are derived from 3460 consorts involving 32 adult males and 40 adolescent males, 12 of whom became part of the adult male sample after they matured. Details of how consort scores were assigned and how age, weight, residency and friendship with females were measured can be found in Strum (1994b). Consort scores can be viewed as a measure of a male's success in getting and keeping receptive females. The statistical analysis (both multiple regression and multi-factorial analysis of variance) suggests a highly significant patterning within consort scores for both adult and adolescent males. This means that despite the almost infinite variety of consort party configurations and the large number of consort pairs, some outcomes are more likely than others. Adding the adolescent data to that on adult males yields a life-history trajectory for male tactics and strategies.

Adult Males The success of an adult male depends on his residency, whether he has friendships with females and his age but not on his weight (see Strum, 1994b for statistical analysis and discussion):

- Males who had resided with the troop for 2–5 years did better than newcomers and than males who had stayed longer.
- Males who made friends with females did better than those who did not.
- Middle aged and older males did better than young males or the oldest males.

Interactions between factors also account for a major part of the variation:

- A male's performance for his age improves when he has friendships.
- Weight interacts with both friendship and with age in a complex manner.
- There is a trade-off between weight and friendship in determining consort success.

Examining each factor individually confirms these relationships and elaborates the nature of the interaction between variables. For example the low scores of newcomers improved when they had friendships with females or if they were younger males, among males with friends certain combinations (such as old resident or young newcomer) were the most successful, and a male's weight was important only when interacting with other factors.

Adolescent Males The analysis of adolescent consort scores includes weight, size class, friendship with females and migration status. Only a male's size class and friendship with females were important main effects although other factors interacted to yield significant differences in consort scores:

- Among large subadults, heavier males did best.
- Among small subadults, lighter males did best.
- Scores of natal males with friends were higher than those of immigrants without friends.
- Light adolescents with friends did better than heavier counterparts without them.

Factor by factor analysis supports these patterns and elaborates their dynamics as in the data on adult males. For example, friendship and weight were traded off against each other for both middle-sized and large subadult males, scores for males with friends increased with size class, and the most successful immigrants were small and light or large and heavy.

Summary The long-term data argue for the existence of robust patterns in the factors that influence consort success across individuals and across male life history. These suggest the operation of at least two kinds of consort strategies: aggressive competition and social manipulation. They also demonstrate that no variable alone can explain male consort success. At a minimum, 2–4 factors contribute and they contribute in complex ways. For some categories of males, two- and three-way interactions between variables account for more variation than any one factor on its own. Furthermore, most of the complexity observed in the data is not just the co-variance of characteristics entraining each other. Clusters of variables appear to represent meaningful complexes, some of which strongly suggest trade-offs between strategic alternatives. The most obvious and important is that between weight and friendship. Light males can compensate for any aggressive disadvantage by having female friends. By implication non-aggressive social strategies are as effective, and in these data at times more effective, than aggression.

Some clusters may be part of strategic complements. The residency model implied that if social strategies took time to develop, newcomers would not yet have these social alternatives. We would predict that among newcomers who are dependent on aggressive tactics, younger males at the height of their aggressive potential should do best. In contrast, social alternatives are paramount among residents. We would predict that older resident males would have more experience and more skill in creating and maintaining friendships, and in social manipulation. The longitudinal data bear this out: young newcomers fare better than older newcomers while older residents are more successful than younger residents.

Age was initially chosen as a surrogate for aggressive strategies but this analysis shows that the situation is more complicated. Certainly both the potential for aggression and individual resource holding power (RHP: Parker, 1974) declines with age. But at the same time social expertise so central to males using non-aggressive options increases with age. This may explain why the effect of age may not be independent of the other factors.

The data on adolescent males add a developmental dimension to the adult male framework. Consort score rises during adolescence but does not achieve adult standards. Size class makes the greatest independent contribution but friendship accounts for the most variation. Yet even among adolescents, the factors that influence consort success are complex, as weight and migratory status interact with size class and friendship to explain a large part of the variation. When we examine the adolescent scores and factors chronologically the following picture emerges. Among the smallest subadults, neither aggressive competition nor social alternatives are operating. The essential feature of success is 'newness' giving immigrants an advantage over natal males, perhaps a short-lived version of the initial but temporary attractiveness of adult immigrants (Strum, 1987). But middle-sized adolescents already exhibit both types of strategies since friendship has begun to influence consort success. And although weight has no independent effect, it now enters into a trade-off with friendship. Large subadults have just finished a period of rapid growth (Strum, 1991) and are nearly adult weight. Weight is the only single factor that influences these males' scores suggesting the operation of aggressive strategies of competition. Although heavy males do best, light males with friendships do just as well and the interaction of weight and friendship accounts for more of the variation than weight does alone.

Among subadult males we also find meaningful clusters of characteristics that imply strategic trade-offs or strategic complements. Just as with adults, friendships with females can act to equalise otherwise asymmetrical males. The ontogeny of non-aggressive alternatives begins early. Since no heavy adolescent had friendships, non-aggressive alternatives may be employed initially by light males to compensate for lower aggressive potential.

Together, adult and adolescent data suggest that strategic options develop over a male's lifetime. Across this period, a male's choice of tactics depends on his acquisition of aggressive and social competence, the successful construction of non-aggressive strategies, the loss of physical prowess with age, the accumulation of skill and knowledge with age, and perhaps inbreeding avoidance after a long period of tenure (Strum, 1989, 1994b). Aggression and social manipulation may be mutually exclusive for brief periods because of ontogenetic, historical or physical constraints. During most of a male's life, however, the two are likely to co-exist. These data demonstrate how aggression and social strategies are integrated, first during the transition to adulthood and again in the stages of social progress during a male's adult tenure.

Baboon consorts and the Machiavellian hypothesis

The consort data provide evidence that both aggressive and social strategies operate in the context of consorts. These data also seem particularly appropriate to Dennett's search for 'creative intelligence', which reveals itself in 'changing behaviours' observed only over the long-term and in the mixture of novel and appropriate advances 'with a smattering of false starts, unlucky breaks and "bad ideas"' (Dennett, 1988) and to Machiavellian intelligence, which requires changing tactics as the social game evolves. –

However, drawing conclusions about cognition and Machiavellian intelligence turns out to be surprisingly difficult. As discussed below, the difficulties fall into four classes that reflect some of the central problems with the social complexity model of cognition and the Machiavellian intelligence hypothesis.

1. *What is social complexity?* We claim that consorts are part of social complexity for baboons but what *is* social complexity? In primatology, the term 'social complexity' has had an intuitive appeal without being grounded in theory or generating a theoretical framework. In fact *complexity* has been used without precise and operational definitions (Strum & Latour, 1987; but see Strum, 1994a) in contrast to the use of the concept in other disciplines (for an accessible overview see Waldrop, 1992). A variety of phenomena are glossed over as being part of, or contributing to, social complexity including 'reactive social environment' (Chance & Mead, 1953), long lifetimes and overlapping generations (Humphrey, 1976), increase in the number of actors and in the number of social conditions (Byrne & Whiten, 1988; Strum, 1994a; Byrne, 1995), group size (Dunbar, 1992), heterogeneity of actors (Western & Strum,

1983; Strum, 1994a) response time and turnover rate (Strum, 1994a), societies structured by relationships (kin, rank and friendship: Bachmann & Kummer, 1980; de Waal, 1982; Cheney & Seyfarth, 1985), any type of social manipulation such as agonistic buffering (Strum, 1983a,b) or coalitions (Harcourt & de Waal, 1992) and particularly social manoeuvres that have a long history (de Waal, 1982), or involve deception (Whiten & Byrne, 1988). Consort dynamics seem an intuitively natural context in which some of these are played out but no one has made explicit whether the 'complexity' derives from the number of conditional rules, the number of interactants, the rate of change of consort party configurations, or deception. All primates have relatively long lifetimes, overlapping generations and reactive social environments but not all primate societies seem socially 'complex'. Without better and more rigorous criteria we remain uncertain how consort behaviour fits into the category 'social complexity' or what else should be included. The difficulty of classification without definition is certainly a handicap. More important, we cannot investigate or interpret the *cognitive challenges* of social complexity without a better framework for the idea of social complexity.

2. *What is complex about social complexity?* Even when we have defined what phenomena fall into the domain of social complexity and what factors may give rise to situations of increasing complexity, we must still consider what it is that makes them complex. What is complex about consorts? It could be the presence of two strategic alternatives (aggression and social manipulation), the need to develop, integrate and sequence these options, or the challenges of implementation in specific contexts. We are left to wonder whether newcomers with only aggressive strategies live less or more complex lives and whether the creation of alternatives is an active enterprise or an unintended consequence of other social events. One can imagine that the cognitive tasks in implementing consort tactics and strategies might be very different depending on what actually constitutes the source of its complex nature.

3. *How does social complexity affect the individual?* Even if we know what social complexity is and what is 'complex' about it, we face a dilemma. How does that complexity affect the individual? A dull-witted thug surrounded by sharp-witted social manipulators is likely to have a very unhappy and complex life without having very complex thoughts about it! An infant on its mother's belly at the edge of a consort turnover does not 'experience' the consort's social complexity in the same way as an adult. What can we safely assume about the other actors: the consort

female, the consort male, the followers, the male on the sidelines, the consort female's infant, the harassing juvenile and the rest of the troop? The Machiavellian intelligence argument that links social complexity to cognition assumes that individuals are necessarily embedded in the surrounding social complexity, that they must respond to it if they are to be reproductively successful and that their response is itself selected to be increasingly complex. Yet in many species, including humans (Marchman, 1992), we know that a subject does not automatically perceive the complexity of the stimulus environment and therefore does not necessarily react to it. The perceptual apparatus can extract simple features from a complex environment to be processed in a number of ways. Specialised forms of communication such as bird song or human language have sensitive periods that give temporal restrictions to the relevant features in the learning environment (Elman, 1990; Bates & Elman, 1993; Elman *et al.*, 1996). Thus one solution for coping with a complex environment is to find ways to simplify it, the result being 'complicated' (composed of many single factors linked together over time or space) but not 'complex' (composed of many factors acting simultaneously; Strum & Latour, 1987). Looked at it from another perspective, both complexity theory (Waldrop, 1992) and computer modelling of cognitive processes using neural nets (McClelland *et al.*, 1986; Elman *et al.*, 1996) demonstrate that complexity can be a system's property, an emergent phenomenon from the interaction of simple agents and/or simple rules without the agent itself being complex. Thus the existence of social complexity does not guarantee the existence of behavioural or cognitive complexity in individual agents. For example, after we describe the complexity in sexual consorts (that we the observers can cognise), we still have to identify how the individual perceives and responds, how males discriminate options and the way perceptions and discriminations are manifest in behaviour. Only with this type of evidence can we argue forcefully for the link between social complexity and cognition and for the operation of a complex type of cognition such as Machiavellian intelligence.

4. *What links social complexity to cognition?* The evolution of Machiavellian intelligence can be represented by a simple flow diagram: social complexity enters a black box and sophisticated social cognition emerges from the other end. We are not quite certain, however, about the nature of cognition or what happens in this black box, for example how social complexity stimulates the evolution of advanced intelligence in individuals. The distinction between the nature of cognition and the

evolution of cognition is not trivial and has implications for the kind of data pursued. Evolutionary arguments require a broad cross-species perspective that relies on population level behavioural patterns within species that can be directly linked to the reproductive success of individuals. Evolutionary arguments present the scenario for the evolution of 'averaged out' intelligence rather than a discussion of the nature of cognition in actual interactions. The nature of the cognitive process, however, has much to do with the way variation in the behaviour of an individual reflects the influence of experience on performance and local, specific contextual detail. Often the two levels of explanation are conflated. When they are not, arguments for one type of explanation often take for granted the essentials of the other: that we know the nature of cognition or that we know the evolutionary mechanisms that make possible the evolution of intelligence.

The longitudinal baboon data give hints about the evolutionary context and hints about cognition (see criteria in Dennett, 1988). Yet they do not provide concrete answers about either or about the links between social complexity and cognition. The most they do is suggest the developmental trajectories necessary to any 'cognitive' story.

To summarise our argument so far, the factors that contribute to consort success are multiple; they interact in a complex fashion that is explicable at any one time or over the lifetime of a male. The variables can be linked with some confidence to 'tactics' that males employ and to the organisation of tactics into strategies that have a developmental and historical ontogeny. The trade-offs that males make between factors are strongly suggestive of 'cognitive' assessment because they seem too dynamic to be controlled by deeply embedded deterministic mechanisms. In the past, similar data were used to *demonstrate* 'social complexity'. The social complexity/cognition model then argued that the existence of social complexity meant the existence of a special type of cognition (and the evolution of this new type of cognition), a seductive circularity that tempts us even now. As Thompson (1988) suggests in a related context the 'causality is semantic not physical' (see also Heyes, 1988). In reality, both the origins of the model and later tests about the link between complexity and cognition have lacked data on cognition. The ease with which current arguments can flow from the notion of 'tactics' to the notion of 'cognitive assessment' may be the result of a subtle but dramatic shift in the use of the term 'tactic'. Sociobiology and behavioural ecology made evolutionary deterministic tactics and strategies the common currency of behavioural interpretation: any well organised behaviour with reproductive pay-offs must be the result of natural selection. Now in the new cognitivist environment it is just as easy to assume that any complex or flexible tactic/strategy must be the product of 'mind'.

We can start the search for the missing cognitive data in the dynamics of baboon consorts. If there is cognition in consort strategies, it would be most critical during consort turnovers. Next we will explore what we can learn about the nature of cognition from the details of actual interactions.

Consort dynamics – sleeping near the enemy

Consorts can be overturned by both aggression and by social manipulation (Strum, 1982, 1987) but for the moment we will concentrate on non-aggressive social strategies. There are a variety of these types of consort turnovers, for example the 'sidelines' tactic already described. 'Sleeping near the enemy' (SNE) is a label we have attached to a night-time turnover in consort partners, a common pattern in savannah baboon groups (Hausfater, 1975; Rasmussen, 1980; Bercovitch, 1985; Smuts, 1985).

The data come from one small group of baboons (the Malaika group), which is the daughter troop of the baboons in the longitudinal data. During our study, the group consisted of 36 baboons including 7 reproductively active males and 9 reproductively active females. In 1989–1991 there was an 11 month period of concentrated breeding with 292 consortships and 122 consort turnovers. On 39 occasions, observations were extended into the evening to collect data about which males ascended the sleeping site as the consort partner (Forster & Strum, 1994). Both complete and partial records showed one common pattern. In a significant majority of cases a turnover occurred near or on the sleeping rocks. The consort male approaching the sleeping site was an older male while the changeover resulted in a new partner who was younger, who had been a passive follower of the consort and who had not overtly challenged the consort before. The older male appeared to be avoiding aggressive conflict by employing a variety of tactics. He might suddenly leave the female, as if losing interest, despite his attention and possessiveness minutes before. He might abandon the consort, 'saving face' (Strum, 1987) by choosing a low risk opponent to attack. Many times the older male actively tried to control the consort female all the way *to* the rocks, even blocking her from climbing up. However, once she decided to climb, he would not follow despite showing signs of distress at her departure. The younger male would be just ahead of the consort pair. When the female began to climb the rocks, this male would follow her and become her next consort.

We have interpreted these behaviours as indicating a shift in strategies over a very short time period (Forster & Strum, 1994) for both the consort male and the passive follower male (i.e. classic Machiavellian intelligence). A key factor seems to be the actual location of the animals and the opportunities or restrictions on competitive tactics that the topography permits. Older males employ a variety of tactics in competition over œstrous females. They try very hard to avoid aggression by diverting it, seeking out coalitions with male allies, using infants and female friends as agonistic buffers and other social manipulations. These tactics require a high degree of visual contact and co-ordination with others for their success. Younger males lack experience, allies and friendships and employ fewer social strategies. They are forced to use their aggressive potential to resolve conflicts by challenging other males, although these challenges are often successfully countered by social manipulations. The cost of day-time guarding can be reduced by staying separate and even by the acts of travelling and foraging, which permit flexibility in tactics utilising both visibility and space. When either space or visibility is reduced, tension increases and so do the chances of a consort turnover. Guarding a receptive female overnight may be much more costly than during the day. It is this change that seems to make night-time different from day-time for an active consort.

Thus when older and younger males come into close proximity at the sleeping rocks, the change in both proximity and visibility increases the likelihood of aggression. At the same time, the aggressive tactics of younger males gain an advantage against the social strategies of older males. At the rocks mobility is very restricted, there is nowhere to hide and few opportunities to 'manipulate' the situation. The challenge of manoeuvring on the rocks is compounded by the quick action, constant monitoring and communication required by the social dynamics surrounding consorts. Although the actors may remain the same, the change in topography significantly changes opportunities and constraints for males.

This interpretation is reinforced by what happens the next day. An older male usually takes over the consort female in the morning, sometimes within the first hour after leaving the sleeping rocks but usually before midday. Once again, the physical and social context changes, this time to the advantage of the older male. Putting the entire picture together we might say that an older male may choose to avoid the risk of guarding a female against a younger male during the night knowing that he has a high probability of getting the female the next day.

Yet five cases of all-night guarding by an older male also suggest that the costs and benefits of gaining and maintaining access to a receptive female shift not only between day and night but also within a female's cycle. Older males do not give up their females when the female is near ovulation. These shifts in consort dynamics and decisions between day and night suggest that males may make very sophsticated assessments of small but important changes in the relative costs and benefits of competition and the use of specific tactics and strategies.

What can we conclude about the male's cognition? Unfortunately, we still do not have the type of cognitive data that we need although it is tempting, as in the past, to take the data as anecdotal evidence for mental structures such as 'who knows/believes what about whom'.

Neither the longitudinal data nor the data on turnovers seem able to address the nature of the cognitive process except through a too-ready reinterpretation of the notion of tactics and strategies (from evolutionary to cognitive) or in vague ways such as that the implied 'process' may have age-related effects, experience related effects, or social status effects. What is missing still is the (cognitive) process by which social history affects the outcome of a consort.

We conclude that it is difficult to make interpretations about Machiavellian intelligence from these data. This is in part because of important unanswered questions about social complexity (what it is, what makes it complex, how the individual is affected and whether complexity is emergent or essential) that have not been addressed in past and present efforts, including our own. By failing to precisely define or situate complexity and without a 'theory of complexity' we are handicapped in discussions about the interaction between social complexity and the nature of cognition and about social complexity and the evolution of intelligence. But equally troublesome is the lack of real data on cognition, particularly in the naturalistic evidence linking social complexity and cognition. This may have been inevitable, given the implicit ideas about cognition embedded in both the social complexity model and the Machiavellian intelligence hypothesis.

A different approach to cognition

The recent change in attitudes to animal 'mind' as best exemplified by the new field of cognitive ethology (Ristau, 1990) was primarily a deductive rather than an inductive move (Griffin, 1976) and greatly stimulated by the revolution in human cognitive sciences that took place several decades earlier (see Gardner, 1985). In the process of shifting from a behaviourist to a cognitivist stance, cognitive ethology assimilated the then current view of human cognition as mental states and internal representations lodged inside individual minds (see, for example, work on tactical deception, social imitation, theory of mind and Machiavellian intelligence among non-human primates). The 'classical' view delivered the world as a set of symbolic descriptions manipulated according to formal rules. The body and its relations to the physical and social environment were rendered irrelevant to cognition ('disembodied cognition', Bobrow, 1991; Norman, 1991). The result was models of cognitive process where models could easily do things that people find very difficult, and could not do at all things that people (and other animals) do effortlessly. Furthermore, thinking of cognitive processes as symbolic operations made it very difficult to imagine how the cognitive skills of humans could have evolved.

In the past decade a number of lines of research have converged on an alternative conception of cognition that puts emphasis on cognitive activity as part of social and physical environments. During the 1960s and 70s, a socio-historical perspective developed in the U.S.A. in response to the introduction of the early 20th-century Soviet psychology of Vygotsky (1978), Luria (1979), Leont'ev (1981) and others. The Soviet school had its motivational roots in Marxist dialectical materialism. By emphasising the study of behaviour as developmental processes of change they focused on social activity rather than the individual as the appropriate unit of analysis. As a result, they linked psychological processes to social processes by suggesting how intrapsychological processes can be appropriated from interpsychological processes that are enacted in social interaction (Scribner, 1984; Wertsch, 1985; Cole & Engestrom, 1993).

In the U.S.A., the Soviet school gave rise to a 'situated action' approach (Suchman, 1987; Lave, 1988; Clancey, 1993). Situated action interprets behaviour as organised through continual negotiation with elements of the environment rather than being read from stored representations (which may in fact be *post-hoc* justifications for action rather than blueprints for its generation). The focus on the role that structure in the environment plays in cognition is coupled with a new definition of cognition in terms of systems of co-ordination among elements both inside and outside the organism (Schmidt *et al.*, 1990). This reaffirmed the need to expand the unit of analysis for cognition beyond the individual to include both organisms and their environments (Bateson, 1972; Neisser, 1976).

The framework provides a link between cognitive events at the individual level and those that emerge in interaction. Hutchins (1995) developed a language of co-ordination as a way to describe observable constraints on cognition and as a means to describe phenomena both inside and outside of individuals using the same terms. Social interactions become dynamic systems in which individuals use a variety of 'structures' to get into co-ordination with each other (where structure refers to any regularity that is stable enough to be treated as an entity – a friendship, a sentence, a stable spatial configuration). Two systems are said to be in co-ordination when regularities in one system constrain the regularities achieved by the other system. Such abilities need not be autonomous representations of the behaviour produced. Rather they are contingent on the context in which they operate (they are situated actions). The language of co-ordination is a first step towards defining what is cognitively relevant to an activity, for example, what the animal would need to remember and what distinctions would need to be made in order to manage an observed co-ordination.

In addition, interactions among humans also have distributed cognitive properties that are not the same as the properties of the individual participants (Hutchins, 1995, chapter 5). These imply that the properties of interactions emerge from the dynamic interplay of the contributions of the participants.

Seeing social interactions in these ways builds a foundational link between the social and the cognitive in two directions. Firstly, an important class (initially possibly the most important class) of cognitive challenges faced by individual animals resides in the tasks of establishing and maintaining co-ordination with the behaviours of others. Secondly, social interactions are the locus of cognitive functions that cannot be produced by any individual alone and the structure of these interactions may form a zone of 'proximal development' (Vygotsky, 1978; Wertsch, 1985) for the ontogeny of cognitive processes in individuals. This suggests how social living can be both a cognitive challenge and a source of cognitive solutions.

These new directions have produced research results with profound implications for ideas about human cognition. For example, it is often possible to produce complex behaviour by getting into co-ordination with structure in the task world (Norman, 1988; Hutchins, 1995). The cognitive processes required to do the task this way may be much simpler than the processes that would be required to produce the same behaviour while not taking advantage of structure in the world, which means that less 'cognition' needs to occur inside the individual than we have assumed (Norman, 1988, 1993; Hutchins, 1995).

We have drawn on these ideas to create an alternative approach to exploring cognition in non-human primates (Forster *et al.*, 1995). The framework begins by using the language of co-ordination to translate traditional social interactions into systems of linkages between individuals that are specific to their contexts. This implies that the meaning of co-ordination events and situated action resides in the interaction and not in the individual. Therefore, at least to some extent, we can investigate primate cognition by examining these more easily observed socially distributed cognitive processes.

Applying the new framework to primate cognition

This new way of thinking about cognition has particular relevance to non-human primates. It is obvious that the conceptual and methodological problems of 'disembodied' cognition present even greater obstacles for studying non-human animals. For this reason alone, alternative approaches are appealing. But we suggest that a situated action and a distributed cognition perspective may constitute the new direction needed to resolve the current behaviourist/cognitivist tension in interpretations of primate behaviour (Dennett, 1981; Dunbar, 1988; Heyes, 1988; Menzel, 1988; Thompson, 1988; Crist, 1994). It is particularly appropriate to the social complexity model of primate intelligence and may address some of the model's inherent problems about how the *social* molds the *cognitive* in interaction and in evolution. Once we recognise that systems larger than the individual have cognitive properties, that these properties are emergent (they cannot be simply reduced to actions or processes inside individual elements of the system) and that interactions between individuals are part of the cognitive process, not just manifest clues to internal mental structures, a whole new arena opens up for the study of the dynamics and principles of cognitive processes. When the unit of analysis is expanded beyond the individual, we can 'see' cognition. In fact, the social organisation of the group can then be read as the cognitive architecture of the larger system (Roberts, 1964; Chandresekeran, 1980; Hutchins, 1991, 1995). Using the perspective and language of co-ordination, we begin to specify 'cognitive data', the minimal set of cognitive challenges faced in social interaction. Then, once we know more about the cognitive processes that occur 'outside' the individual we are in a better position to know what needs to be 'inside' the individual and the mechanisms for the ontogeny and phylogeny of a new type of social intelligence.

Baboon consorts as situated action and distributed cognition

Before we tackle baboon consorts as situated action and distributed cognition it is useful to review some of the main claims of the new framework :

- Social living does not present any single cognitive challenge; challenges change with the nature of social interactions.
- Both the minds of individuals and social interactions themselves are considered loci of cognitive processes.
- The cognitive processes in social interactions have elements that are distributed among structures in the environment, most relevant here are other social actors.
- Actors in interaction produce cognitive processes that some of the participants could not produce alone.
- Actors in interaction can participate in distributed cognitive processes that none of the participants could have produced alone.
- Distributed cognition or jointly produced processes provide learning targets for participants.

What happens to baboon consorts when we use our new lens? Our tools include extending the boundaries of the unit of analysis beyond the individual and looking at social interactions as situated action with distributed cognitive properties using the language of co-ordination.

We can revisit 'sleeping near the enemy' although the data were not collected for this framework. The first step is to convert the behavioural sequences into co-ordination events such as when the younger male positions himself ahead of the consort pair as they approach the rocks and when he follows the female as she climbs. Day-time and night-time co-ordination events can be compared. At the rocks, the older male can abandon the female by walking away from her, he can let the female walk away without following her or look for a distraction that would allow him to save face while giving up, he can enlist a male ally or redirect aggression to an innocent bystander. Each of these options can be reached through a number of micro-co-ordination possibilities. When the behavioural sequence is de-composed in this way, the analysis begins to specify the functional abilities of individuals such as the skills and knowledge that would be necessary to maintain the observed co-ordinations (e.g. the recognition of specific other animals or memory of interaction histories).

Next we treat 'sleeping near the enemy' as situated action. This makes the boundaries of the unit of analysis flexible but demands that we define the system. What elements are necessary and sufficient to explain the observed regularities? At the very least the elements include consort female, older consort male, young male follower, time of day (evening), location (proximity to the sleeping rocks), female sexual state and 'normal' troop activity. Other elements may make up the system on any given occasion, with their own constraints and influences on the outcome of the process. For example, the consort female may have a young infant who coordinates its sleeping activity with her, or friends who want to sleep nearby, or higher ranking females who interfere.

As a situated action, 'sleeping near the enemy' is like a *conversation* between actors about the night-time consort party configuration. These conversations of actions are distributed processes with an almost 'script-like' character that can be analysed for the factors or contingencies that produce the regularities in outcome that we observe. They can also be used to investigate constraints on conversations such as the limits to the number of steps, limits to the number of elements, limits to the order of a sequence and to its duration. As in the dynamics of any human conversation, the sequence and the outcome cannot be attributed to a single individual. Furthermore the meaning of the conversation or its elements is also not individually produced. Therefore what takes place in such *conversations* is not just distributed action but also distributed cognition. No matter what the young male had 'in mind', what actually happens, the system we call 'sleeping near the enemy', is best understood in terms of situated co-ordination events rather than as the external manifestation of some internal plan of action. Later we can ask if these properties are also cognised by individuals in the system. In the meantime, the decomposition of co-ordination events and the reassembly of these into a functional system can be our entry point into the functional abilities of individuals and their cognitive properties.

This brief reframing of 'sleeping near the enemy' helps to illustrate how a different approach can begin to address some of the problematic aspects of the social complexity model of cognition. What is the *nature of the cognitive processes* involved in social interactions such as 'sleeping near the enemy'? We can begin to specify cognitive processes in terms of the need to co-ordinate with the behaviour of others. This is facilitated by scaffolding onto existing structure in the social (relationships, history, etc) and physical environment (space, visibility, etc). The cognitive challenges of *co-ordination* are likely to involve limitations based on the number of actors, the speed with which the actors interact, the number of relationships simultaneously at play, the unpredictability of outcome, the length of the behavioural sequence, the asymmetry of response, and the turnover rate of actors or characteristics (Strum, 1994a), elements raised in previous discussions of complexity and cognition. The new framework, in particular the language of co-ordination, allows us to examine these claims, whether and how such factors impinge on cognition rather than just assume that they do. In 'sleeping near the enemy,' it is apparent that the physical constraint of space becomes the critical over-riding influence on the ability to co-ordinate with others.

The language of co-ordination creates a conceptual tool with which to probe *what links social complexity to cognition*. Certainly the nature and number of co-ordination patterns provides a useful socio-cognitive measure of complexity (e.g. number, diversity and types of co-ordination) for social interactions such as 'sleeping near the enemy'. This helps specify how features of participants and of interactions contribute to social complexity (*what is social complexity*) and indicates *what makes it complex?* Since the limits on co-ordination become the limits of the possible interaction, we should not ask whether consorts or consort turnovers are socially complex but rather how complex, for whom and in what way. The same consort can have differing degrees of social complexity for different actors (compare adolescent and adult males, male without a friend and male with a friend) while different consorts can be more or less socially complex for the same individual depending on the context (compare a male when he is a newcomer to when the same male is a resident).

How is social complexity generated? The social dynamics of 'sleeping near the enemy' imply at least two things: that the 'averaged' vision of individual strategic action is not very useful in understanding the outcome of any instance of 'sleeping near the enemy' and that the distributed properties of the system are indeed complex. Furthermore, the complexity of the system might exist without a comparable complexity in the individual. 'Sleeping near the enemy' could be a regularity in interaction, given the appropriate constraints, even if it is not part of a 'larger plan' for those involved. Thus it is important to be able to distinguish whether social complexity is emergent or also the property of the individual agents. The new approach offers testable hypotheses about the generation of social complexity. By de-composing interactions into systems of co-ordination we can investigate whether they are constructed out of simpler components, whether the complexity of an interaction depends on the properties of the participants, whether it depends on properties of the interaction that are not properties of the individual participants or whether system level characteristics such as changes in established patterns of interaction that increase complexity because they require participants to partially reorganise the co-ordination system are the most important.

The remaining question, *what evolutionary mechanisms link social complexity and changes in cognition*, is not addressed by the consort turnover data. Current discussions of the evolution of intelligence and the Machiavellian intelligence hypothesis focus on how things *change* without explaining how they *are*. The new approach, by trying to understand how things work, will have the story of 'change' built in. Beyond that, the framework makes some heuristic suggestions for understanding the phylogenetic development of intelligence. Vygotsky argued that socially enacted (interpsychological) cognitive processes can be both learning targets and can be resources appropriated for intrapsychological processes during development. That is how the challenges of social living can also provide its solutions when cognitive processes are socially distributed and the emergence of such phenomena is closely coupled with social complexity. Rather than imagine the spontaneous appearance of complex neural structures that support previously non-existent cognitive abilities, it is much easier to contemplate how and why individuals can scaffold onto social interactions ontogenetically and how socially distributed cognitive processes could provide a rich resource for phylogenetic appropriation for internal cognitive processes. In this scenario, what went inside the head was first outside the head. However, the framework also adds a cautionary note about what and how much needs to be represented by any individual. In a distributed cognitive system, what actors build in interaction often goes beyond what each could have built (or represented) individually (for humans see Hutchins, 1995 and references therein).

Conclusions

Baboons appear to live in a socially complex world and the social strategies involved in consorts may be an important part of this social complexity. The social manipulations of getting and keeping a consort female seem intuitively strong reasons to claim the operation of Machiavellian intelligence. But the data on baboon consorts do not provide a compelling argument either about social complexity or about the evolution of Machiavellian intelligence not because they are 'poor' data but, we suggest, because the current view of social complexity is not formalised enough to be predictive and the cognitive aspects of the behavioural data are not normally specified. We have proposed using another approach. The situated action, distributed cognition framework begins to unravel the relationship between social complexity and cognition both in terms of the nature of cognition and in terms of its evolution. It provides a way to measure social complexity as systems of co-ordination, suggests what is complex about social interactions, and specifies the cognitive challenges posed by this complexity. It also intimates how changes in cognitive skills might arise both during the course of development and of evolution. In all these ways it resolves some ambiguities of the model and helps to break the current circularity in the argument. But the framework contributes something more fundamental. It argues for the distributed nature of cognition, for the importance of cognitive work that is done by structure in the world (social and physical), for the centrality of co-ordination between individuals in both social interaction and in the essential challenge of cognition. If these claims are correct then they undermine the very narrow individualistic language of tactics and strategies and the disembodied view of cognition that have been the basis of our approach to primate mind in the new cognitivist era.

When Byrne and Whiten proposed the term 'Machiavellian intelligence' to refer to the individual mental abilities necessary to cope with the complexity of social living, in particular the ability to change tactics as the social game evolves, they had in mind Machiavelli's The Prince whose basic premise is 'do what works'. But the ordinary view and most common connotation of 'Machiavellian' derives from the book as a guide to the cunning and unscrupulous tactics and strategies that a ruler can employ to maintain power and authority. We suggest that Machiavellian intelligence may be a misnomer. In the first place, the negative connotation places undue emphasis on exploitation, domination and deception of others. In contrast, primate social complexity seems an intricate tapestry of competition and co-operation, of aggression and reconciliation, of non-aggressive social alternatives, and of behaviours and relationships that cannot be so easily dichotomised. Thus seeing primates through Machiavelli's eyes limits and simplifies our vision of the challenges of social life. But more importantly, primate social intelligence may not really be captured by talk of individual tactics and strategies and traditional views of cognition. Situated action, distributed cognition, the challenges and constraints of co-ordination during social interactions, the reality of being part of a system that no one actor could create alone, these may prove more useful ways of thinking about primate cognition among baboons in consort and even for Machiavelli's 'Prince'. This approach certainly seems an appropriate starting point for the story of how special forms of social intelligence could have evolved among primates living in socially complex groups. Perhaps we should look to the court of Henry the Navigator in 14th-century Portugal rather than to Machiavelli for our metaphor. Henry gathered to his court a variety of individuals to tackle the social (and cognitive) challenge of 'exploration'. Together they created a novel system, the science of navigation, which in turn opened up new social and cognitive worlds. 'Navigational intelligence' was only later appropriated by individuals and written onto cognitive artefacts. The navigation metaphor may be particularly apt as Hutchins (1995) has used case studies of modern day navigation to show how cognition is socially distributed, how representational structures move across media, and how crucial co-ordination is to both social and cognitive challenges among humans. We might even stretch the imagination a bit to suggest that a baboon's social world is like a sea upon which individuals must navigate (not just compete or co-operate or negotiate). This requires co-ordination between the individual and its social world. In the end, where one goes on this sea (and in interactions) is as dependent on the position of others at that particular moment and on existing social regularities (structure) as it is on a preconceived plan of optimal route. The navigation image and the new approach might also help in the controversy over the the relative importance of social or ecological origins of intelligence. Treating each social interaction as a situated action requires that we explain the observed regularities in clearly defined terms without making *a priori* distinctions between the social and ecological domains. This makes sense since the 'sea' of the world of baboons is composed of both. Successful navigation requires co-ordination with all elements, *simultaneously*. The interesting question then becomes not which is more important, the social or the ecological environment of any situated action, but how co-ordination is accomplished, how is the system assembled from the co-ordination events, and how do the tasks of co-ordination with the social and with the physical elements resemble or differ from each other. Ultimately we will want to know, as in 'sleeping near the enemy', how the social and physical elements interact to constrain or facilitate each other and the consequences this has for the nature and evolution of cognition.

Acknowledgements

We would like to thank David Western, Debbie Custance and Catherine Kenyatta for helpful comments.

References

Altmann, J. (1980). *Baboon Mothers and Infants.* Cambridge, MA: Harvard University Press.

Bachmann, C. & Kummer, H. (1980). Male assessment of female choice in hamadryas baboons. *Behavioral Ecology and Sociobiology,* 6, 315–21.

Bates, L. & Elman, J. (1993). Connectionism and the study of change. In *Brain Development and Cognition: A Reader,* ed. M. Johnson, pp. 623–42. Oxford: Blackwell Scientific.

Bateson, G. (1972). *Steps to an Ecology of Mind.* New York: Ballantine Books.

Bercovitch, F. B. (1985). Reproductive Tactics in Adult Female and Adult Male Baboons. PhD thesis, University of California, Los Angeles.

Bobrow, D. (1991). Dimensions of interaction. *American Association of Artificial Intelligence Magazine,* 12, 64–80.

Byrne, R. (1995). *The Thinking Ape: Evolutionary Origins of Intelligence.* Oxford: Oxford University Press.

Byrne, R. & Whiten, A. (eds) (1988). *Machiavellian Intelligence: Social Expertise and the Evolution of Intellect in Monkeys, Apes and Humans.* Oxford: Clarendon Press.

Chance, M. & Mead, A. (1953). Social behavior and primate evolution. *Symposia of the Society for Experimental Biology, Evolution,* 7, 395–439.

Chandrasekaran, B. (1980). Natural and social system metaphors for distributed problem solving: Introduction to the issue. *Institute of Electrical and Electronic Engineers Transaction on Systems, Man and Cybernetics,* 11, 1–5.

Cheney, D. & Seyfarth, R. (1985). The social and nonsocial world of nonhuman primates. In *Social Relationships and Cognitive Development,* ed. R. Hinde, A. Perret-Clermon & J. Stevenson, pp. 33–44. Oxford: Clarendon Press.

Cheney, D. & Seyfarth, R. (1990). *How Monkeys See the World: Inside the Mind of Another Species.* Chicago: University of Chicago Press.

Cole, M. & Engestrom, Y. (1993). A cultural-historical approach to distributed cognition. In *Distributed Cognitions: Psychological and Educational Considerations,* ed. G. Salomon, Cambridge: Cambridge University Press.

Clancey, W. (ed.) (1993). Situated cognition: A neuropsychological interpretation on response. *Cognitive Science,* 17, 87–116.

Crist, E. (1994). The Significance of Language in Portraying Animals: Anthropomorphism and Mechanomorphism in Behavioral Studies. PhD thesis, Boston University.

Dawkins, R. (1976). *The Selfish Gene.* New York: Oxford University Press.

de Waal, F. (1982). *Chimpanzee Politics: Power and Sex Among Apes.* London: Jonathan Cape.

Dennett, D. (1981). Three kinds of intentional psychology. In *Reductionism, Time and Reality,* ed. R. Healey, pp. 37–62. Cambridge: Cambridge University Press.

Dennett, D. (1988). Why creative intelligence is hard to find. *Behavioral and Brain Sciences,* 11, 253.

Dunbar, R. (1984). *Reproductive Decisions: An Economic Analysis of Gelada Baboon Social Strategies.* Princeton, NJ: Princeton University Press.

Dunbar, R. (1988). How to break moulds. *Behavioral and Brain Sciences,* 11, 254–5.

Dunbar, R. (1992). Neocortex size as a constrain on group size in primates. *Journal of Human Evolution,* 20, 469–93.

Elman, J. L. (1990). *Incremental Learning or The Importance of Starting Small.* Technical Report no. 901. San Diego: University of California, Center for Research in Language.

Elman, J., Bates, L., Johnson, M., Karmiloff-Smith, A., Parisi, D. & Plunkett, K. (eds) (1996) *Rethinking Innateness: Connectionism in a Developmental Framework.* Cambridge, MA: MIT Press.

Forster, D. & Strum, S. C. (1994). Sleeping near the enemy: Patterns of sexual competition in baboons. In *Current Primatology. Vol. 2: Social Development Learning and Behavior,* ed. J. Roeder, B. Thierry, J. Anderson & N., Herrenschmidt, pp. 19–24. Strasbourg: Université Louis Pasteur.

Forster, D., Hutchins, E. & Strum, S. C. (1995). Essence and boundaries: Ontogeny of distributed social skill in baboons. Paper presented at the 25th Annual Symposium of the Piaget Society, Berkeley, CA, June, 1995.

Gardner, H. (1985). *The Mind's New Science: A History of the Cognitive Revolution.* New York: Basic Books.

Goodall, J. (1986). *Chimpanzees of Gombe: Patterns of Behavior.* Cambridge, MA: The Belknap Press.

Griffin, D. R. (1976). *The Question of Animal Awareness.* Los Altos, CA: Kaufmann.

Harcourt, A. & de Waal, F. (eds) (1992). *Coalitions and Alliances in Humans and Other Animals.* Oxford: Oxford University Press.

Hausfater, G. (1975). Dominance and Reproduction in Baboons. *Contributions to Primatology*, 7, 1–150.

Heyes, C. (1988). The distant blast of Lloyd Morgan's Canon. *Behavioral and Brain Sciences*, 11, 256–7.

Humphrey, N. (1976). The social function of intellect. In *Growing Points in Ethology*, ed. P. Bateson & R. Hinde, pp. 303–17. Cambridge: Cambridge University Press.

Hutchins, E. (1991). The social organization of distributed cognition. In *Perspectives on Socially Shared Cognition*, ed. L. Resnick, J. Levine & S. Teasley, pp. 283–307. New York: APA Press.

Hutchins, E. (1995). *Cognition in the Wild*. Cambridge, MA: MIT Press.

Jolly, A. (1966). Lemur social behaviour and primate intelligence. *Science*, 153, 501–6.

Kummer, H. (1967). Tripartite relations in hamadryas baboons. In *Social Communication Among Primates*, ed. S. Altmann, pp. 63–72. Chicago: University of Chicago Press.

Kummer, H. (1978). On the value of social relations to nonhuman primates: A heuristic scheme. *Social Science Information*, 17, 687–705.

Lave, J. (1988). *Cognition in Practice*. Cambridge: Cambridge University Press.

Leont'ev, A. (1981). *Problems in the Development of Mind*. Moscow: Progress Publishers.

Luria, A. R. (1979). *The Making of Mind*. Cambridge, MA: Harvard University Press.

Marchman, V. (1992). Language learning in children and neural networks: Plasticity, capacity, and the critical period. Technical Report no. 9201. San Diego: University of California, Center for Research in Language.

Marler, P. & Hamilton, W. (1966). *Mechanisms of Animal Behavior*. New York: Wiley and Sons.

McClelland, J., Rumelhart, D. & the PDP Group (eds) (1986). *Parallel Distributed Processing: Explorations in the Microstructure of Cognition*. vol. 2: *Psychological and Biological Models*. Cambridge, MA: MIT Press.

Menzel, E. W., Jr (1988). Mindless behaviorism, bodiless cognitivism or primatology? *Behavioral and Brain Sciences*, 11, 258–9.

Milton, K. (1981). Distribution patterns of tropical plant foods as a stimulus to primate mental development. *American Anthropologist*, 83, 534–48.

Neisser, U. (1976). *Cognition and Reality: Principles and Implication of Cognitive Psychology*. San Francisco: W. H. Freeman.

Norman, D. (1988). *The Psychology of Everyday Things*. New York: Basic Books.

Norman, D. (1991). Approaches to the study of intelligence. *Artificial Intelligence*, 47, 327–46.

Norman, D. (1993). *Things That Make Us Smart: Defending Human Attributes in the Age of the Machine*. Reading, MA: Addison Welsley Publishers.

Parker, G. A. (1974). Assessment strataegy and the evolution of fighting behavior. *Journal of Theoretical Biology*, 47, 223–43.

Parker, S. T. & Gibson, K. (1977). Object manipulation, tool use, and sensorimotor intelligence as feeding adaptations in cebus monkeys and great apes. *Journal of Human Evolution*, 6, 623–41.

Parker, S. T. & Gibson, K. (eds) (1990). *'Language' and Intelligence in Monkeys and*

Apes: Comparative Developmental Perspectives. New York: Cambridge University Press.

Premack, D. & Woodruff, G. (1978). Does the chimpanzee have a theory of mind? *Behavioral and Brain Sciences*, 1, 515–26.

Ransom, T. (1981). *Beach Troop of the Gombe.* Lewisburg, PA: Buckness University Press.

Ransom, T. & Ransom, B. (1971). Adult male–infant relations among baboons (*Papio anubis*). *Folia Primatologica*, 16, 179–95.

Rasmussen, K. (1980). Consort Behaviour and Mate Selection in Yellow Baboons. PhD. thesis, University of Cambridge.

Ristau, C. (ed.) (1990). *Cognitive Ethology: The Minds of Other Animals.* Hillsdale, NJ: Lawrence Erlbaum Associates.

Roberts, J. (1964). The self-management of cultures. In *Explorations in Cultural Anthropology: Essays in Honor of George Peter Murdock*, ed. W. Goodenough, pp. 433–54. New York: McGraw Hill.

Schmidt, R., Carello, C. & Turvey, M. (1990). Phase transitions and critical fluctations in the visual coordination of rhythmic movements between people. *Journal of Experimental Psychology, Human Perception and Performance*, 16, 227–47.

Scribner, S. (1984). Studying working intelligence. In *Everyday Cognition: Its Development in Social Context*, ed. B. Rogoff & J. Lave, pp. 9–40. Cambridge MA: Harvard University Press.

Smuts, B. (1985). *Sex and Friendship in Baboons.* New York: Aldine.

Stein, D. (1984). *The Sociobiology of Infant and Adult Male Baboons.* Norwood, NJ: Ablex.

Strum, S. C. (1975). Primate predation: Interim report on the development of a tradition in a troop of olive baboons. *Science*, 187, 755–7.

Strum, S. C. (1981). Processes and products of change: baboon predatory behavior at Gilgil, Kenya. In *Omnivorous Primates*, ed. G. Teleki & R. Harding, pp. 255–302. New York: Columbia University.

Strum, S. C. (1982). Agonistic dominance in male baboons: An alternative view. *International Journal of Primatology*, 3, 175–202.

Strum, S. C. (1983a). Why males use infants. In *Primate Paternalism*, ed. D. Taub, pp. 146–87. New York: Van Nostrand Reinhold.

Strum, S. C. (1983b). Use of females by male olive baboons. *American Journal of Primatology*, 5, 93–109.

Strum, S. C. (1987). *Almost Human.* New York: Random House.

Strum, S. C. (1989). Longitudinal data on patterns of consorting among male olive baboons. *American Journal of Primatology*, 78, 310.

Strum, S. C. (1991). Weight and age in wild olive baboons. *American Journal of Primatology*, 25, 219–37.

Strum, S. C. (1994a). La société sans culture matérielle. In *Intelligence Sociale des Technique*, ed. B. Latour & P. Lemonnier. Paris: Decouverte.

Strum, S. C. (1994b). Reconciling aggression and social manipulation as means of competition, part 1: Lifehistory perspective. *International Journal of Primatology*, 15, 739–65.

Strum, S. & Fedigan, L. (1987). Theory, method and gender: What changed our views of primate society? In *The New Physical Anthropology* , ed. S. Strum & D. Lindburg. Englewood Cliffs, NJ: Prentice Hall. (In press.)

Strum, S. & Latour, B. (1987). Redefining the social link: From baboons to humans. *Social Science Information*, 26, 783–802.

Suchman L. (1987). *Plans and Situated Actions: The Problems of Human-machine Communication*. New York: Cambridge University Press.

Thompson, N. (1988). Deception and descriptive mentalism. *Behavior and Brain Sciences*, 11, 266.

Vygotsky, L. (1978). *Mind in Society: The Development of Higher Psychological Processes*. Cambridge, MA: Harvard University Press.

Waldrop, M. (1992). *Complexity: The Emerging Science at the Edge of Order and Chaos*. New York: Simon and Schuster.

Wertsch, J. (1985). *The Social Formation of Mind*. Cambridge, MA: Harvard University Press.

Western, J. & Strum, S. (1983). Sex, kinship and the evolution of social manipulation. *Ethology and Sociobiology*, 4, 19–28.

Whiten, A. (ed.) (1991). *Natural Theories of Mind: Evolution, Development and Simulation of Everyday Mindreading*. Oxford: Basil Blackwell.

Whiten, A. & Byrne, R. (1988). Tactical deception in primates. *Behavioral and Brain Sciences*, 11, 233–44.

Wilson, E. O. (1975). *Sociobiology: The New Synthesis*. Cambridge, MA: Harvard University Press.

APPENDIX

Analysis of a SNE consort turnover using the new framework

Description

Towards the end of the day, the Malaika (MLK) troop is making its way to White Rocks sleeping site. Low-ranking mature adult male Ndovu (ND) has been in consort with high ranking adult female Mavis (MV) for the last few hours (he took over in a typical 'sidelines' pattern from middle-ranking young adult male Herakles (HK) who is also in the process of establishing an alliance with ND). Top-ranking large subadult male Robert (RT) had been with MV during the night but lost her to low-ranking mature adult male Ron (RL) soon after MLK left the sleeping site for their day's journey. RT has been following and challenging the consort the whole day except for a short period right after his morning loss. (RT has no male allies and has strong friendships with the three top-ranking females in MLK: Desire (DE), Zilla (ZL) and MV). The consort party also includes bottom-ranking small subadult Sharman (SQ) as a low-key but constant follower. The switch between RL and HK as consort males occurred around midday when MV (who avoided all of RL's copulation attempts) took off into the thicket and RL, HK, RT, ND and SQ went chasing out of sight. HK emerged with MV as the new consort partner while RL and ND (who are long-term allies) avoided RT's threatening pursuit.

MV's youngest infant Griffin (GN) is just about 1 year old and still goes to nurse occasionally and sleeps on his mother's ventrum during the night. The two older siblings in MLK are juvenile Gamma (GX) and juvenile Gideon (GD) and they often 'baby-sit', play and groom with their younger brother.

The rest of the troop is slowly making its way to the sleeping rocks, climbing the face of the rock, settling down in clusters. Some of the other males that were part of the consort party at various points throughout the day are in positions from which they can see the consort pair.

- ND is possessive (example 2: see analysis for an operational definition) of MV around RT as the consort party moves closer to the sleeping site. ND initiates long grooming bouts with MV; every time she gets up to move closer to the rocks, he follows with intense lip smacking and grunting and resumes grooming her.

- RT followed more quietly as the consort party approached the rocks, synchronising his activity with that of the consort pair.

- RT shifts to sitting a bit ahead of the consort pair, moving towards the rocks a few steps, looking back at the consort pair, and then sitting down facing them. From time to time RT exchanges 'come hither' facial expressions with MV. Sometimes, these exchanges were followed by ND shifting from resting to grooming MV or to grooming her more intensely (lip smacking and grunting intermittently). He even got up and shifted his position so that now he was right in the line of sight between RT and MV.

- MV's two youngest sons groom a few metres away from the consort pair. GN keeps looking towards his mother and when the consort party moves, so does he. GX begins to climb the face of the rock, pausing to look back at his younger brother. GN follows alternating between looking at GX and orienting toward the consort party. He sits down, giving a low intensity whimper. GX grunts in his direction, climbs down to sit near him and resumes grooming.

- MV moves a few steps towards the rocks. RT goes ahead a few steps, grunting in her direction. ND quickly steps in front of her and with rapid grunts and lip smacking movements sits down between her and the rock and tries to groom her. The grooming bouts get shorter, all terminated by MV moving towards the sleeping rocks.

- Top-ranking female DE approaches, stands facing MV, and gives her a quick eyelid flash (threat – example 1). MV jumps away, disrupting the grooming bout. ND grunts and shifts closer, resumes grooming, with his back towards DE. DE walks past the consort and climbs the sleeping rocks.

- When MV begins to climb the base of the rock, ND does not follow her as before but agitatedly looks around and gives a low intensity enlisting scream in HK's direction.

- RT grunts and as MV passes by him on the rock he glances back in ND's direction and then follows her close behind.

- ND stays at the base, now joined by HK. They both alternate looking at each other and at the departing newly formed consort. ND whimpers but makes no attempt to follow or challenge RT.

- HK sits, grunts and then moves off to join female friend ZL's family.

- MV and RT settle on the top of the rock after they copulate.

- GN follows the pair visually checking RT and then gradually joins MV who embraces him on her ventrum.

- ND also climbs the sleeping rock and settles next to the family of female friend RM.

Analysis

The most striking aspect of this narrative is that the meaning of the action sequences all depends on more than a single individual. Even the most robust pattern, that of settling on White Rocks for the night, is the result of the accumulated interactions in the troop movement towards the rocks.

The framework we use allows us to situate individuals as participants in social interactions and to describe these interactions as *systems of co-ordination*. There are micro *co-ordination events* such as communication gestures, but interactions can also be read as co-ordination events between bits of social structure we call relationships (e.g. relative rank, friendship, alliance).

Co-ordination events – communication gestures

Example 1: 'Threat' In this example we can say that DE and MV co-ordinated a threat event but DE and ND did not. If ND had not turned his back to her and chose to respond as if the gesture was directed at him as well, the co-ordination event would have had a different meaning and possibly a different outcome. Note that it does not matter to this analysis if DE 'intended' to threaten ND as well as MV. If ND responded as if he was threatened, the meaning of DE's gesture (i.e. its effect on the outcome) would have been the same as if she 'really intended' to threaten him. In this sense the meaning of communication gestures cannot reside solely 'inside' individuals but rather are distributed both inside (we cannot observe and thus refrain from making any claims about 'inside' individuals at this point in the analysis) and in the dynamics between them (which we can both observe and record).

Example 2: 'Possessive' We use the label 'possessive' as a shorthand for a very specific type of co-ordination event: when animal A directs communication gestures towards animal B, interrupting co-ordination of gestures between animal B and animal C (we use 'possessive towards' rather than the more grammatically correct 'possessive near' or 'possessive around' since other troop members may also be 'around', yet A synchronises his gestures specifically with B and C and not the others). Thus, when the narrative claims that ND(A) is possessive of MV(B) towards RT(C) it means that a co-ordination event that takes place between RT and MV (e.g. RT approaches MV, RT directs a 'come hither' facial expression towards MV, MV wanders towards RT, or MV exchanges 'come hither' expressions with RT, etc), is interrupted by ND directing his own gestures toward MV (e.g. ND approaches MV quickly, ND begins grooming MV, or even ND approaches quickly and directs an eye flash toward MV, or toward RT. The gestures toward MV all involve ND orientating his back to RT, or positioning himself between MV and RT). When we record possessive events we also note gestures or actions directed by animal C right after the interruption (e.g. RT may display a submissive gesture towards ND, or avoid eye contact, turn away from MV, or make no changes). The event and its meaning (i.e. its effect on the outcome) cannot be ascribed to one of the participants without reference to the other(s).

Co-ordination events – social relationships

(Note that this analysis extends beyond the particular example and relies on the accumulated project records of interaction patterns between individuals, which vary in stability and duration).

Example 1: 'Threat' If we go back to the interaction between DE, MV and ND that we analysed in the previous section with respect to the co-ordination of communication gestures, we can now analyse the same interaction at the level of the various social relationships that are brought into alignment. DE and MV have a rank differential (DE is top-ranking and MV is third). ND has a history of interactions with both females that make each more or less 'a friend'. In this case ND has a stronger grooming partnership with MV than he has with DE. Furthermore, in the more immediate context, ND has a consortship with MV that had lasted since midday. Of potential additional consequences (which did not play out in this incident) are the relationships between RT and each of the participants, since he is within potential interaction radius, being in close proximity and constant visual monitoring. RT and ND have a rank differential (RT is top ranking and ND is sixth). RT also has strong friendships with both DE and MV but the friendship with DE has a longer history. In the more immediate context, RT and MV have a 'sleeping-together' history during the days of active consortship. SQ is also part of the consort party although not active in this interaction. He is lower ranking than the other males, newly dominant over adult females having used extensive aggressive harassment, and likely to be a brother of RT. Although RT and SQ did not participate actively in this interaction it took place within their field of view and potential field of interaction.

Example 2: 'Possessive' If we return to the possessive interaction we analysed in the previous section, we can apply a similar analysis of the co-ordination of social relationships: ND was possessive of MV toward RT. By interrupting the co-ordination event between MV and RT, ND brings into alignment his most recent relational history with MV as her consort partner and his rank differential with RT.

Situated action

There appears to be a multiple interaction between relationships and the value any relationship carries in a specific interaction. although the ND–RT rank differential is quite large, and RT has a stronger long-term friendship with MV than does ND with MV, the fact that ND has been the consort partner for the last hours constrains what can be 'said in this conversation'. The extent to which a female tries to co-ordinate with consort followers (in contrast with the extent to which these attempts are initiated by the follower male(s)), is usually correlated with her partner's interruptions (i.e. 'possessiveness' in our terminology). Together, the female's actions and the male's possessiveness and other males' reactions increase the likelihood of a change in consort configuration.

Distributed cognition

The switch in the consort configuration at the rocks cannot be explained by any single individual's actions. It involved the negotiated co-ordination between MV, RT, ND and to some extent, HK. Moreover, a blow-by-blow analysis of the social dynamics does not make sense unless the interpretation takes into account details that might be considered contextual but here are explicitly included within the boundaries of the unit of analysis. Thus, for example, MV's timing of the climb to the sleeping rock might have been affected by GN's attempt to co-ordinate physical contact with her, RT's invitations, the approaching darkness, etc. (as well as by other factors that are not recognised by or observable to us). In a similar vein RT could not 'pick up' the female so easily if ND showed more resistance. The SNE pattern gains explanatory coherence only when the constraints of physical space on manoeuverability are considered.

The negotiation near the sleeping rocks and the repeated regularity with which it was observed in this troop, suggests that individual baboons may anticipate the outcome. RT shifts position to 'leading' the consort pair to the rocks, rather than following, and shifts from challenging to waiting (synchronising his movement with that of the consort pair). But it also seems that the baboons are limited in their options by specific contexts, and that baboon decision-making is often opportunistic. If RT was planning to take over the female at the rocks, why did he spend the time and energy following the consort pair throughout the day? This implies that although a pattern is reproduced repeatedly and reliably, it may still require particular elements and an unfolding dynamic for it to mean what we, as observers, recognise as 'sleeping near the enemy'. Given the appropriate constraints, we suggest that SNE may occur just as reliably even if the individuals cannot mentally grasp it as a 'larger plan'. Thus SNE is distributed in the system but may or may not be 'inside' any of the individual heads.

4 Social intelligence and success: Don't be too clever in order to be smart

ALAIN SCHMITT AND KARL GRAMMER

Consequences of behaviour and meta-learning, and social intelligence

Don't be too clever in order to be smart

Our title alludes to *Clever* and *Smart*, comic figures created by Ibañez, which contrast in the behaviour they use to reach goals. Whereas *Clever* shows much refinement, *Smart* acts without many detours, and succeeds as often as *Clever*. This result would be surprising to common sense or to analysts of social interaction, Machiavellian intelligence and cognitive competence (Handel, 1982; Hinde, 1983; Anderson, 1985). Indeed, the analysis of the cognitive prerequisites of social interaction would normally lead to the conclusion that sophisticatedly planned and performed behaviour is *the* means to achieve social goals. Yet there is a caveat. The point we want to make is that the consequences of behaviour, not the degree of underlying cognitive complexity, determine social success. Straightforward action–reaction behaviour such as reciprocity (an eye for an eye) may be as efficacious as subtle diplomacy. For example, reciprocity may be well suited to stop overt physical aggression such as a child's temper tantrum. Watzlawick *et al.* (1967) tell illuminating stories of unsuccessful communication resulting from either endless recursive mindreading or ignorance of quite simple interaction rules (a man who needs a hammer imagines that his neighbour may be unwilling to lend one, and after a lot of thinking on the neighbour's possible motives, knocks angrily at the other's door shouting that he would never accept even a donated hammer).

Watzlawick *et al.* call on interactants to communicate on their communication rules (to meta-communicate) to resolve problems, and like Dennett (1983), think that we can manage only few embedded propositions. The growing knowledge in attribution psychology (Weiner, 1991) and the notorious failures of political planning point in the same direction.

In everyday life, the consequences of behaviour are very prominent selection forces, particularly success and failure. We learn from consequences. In situations that are rare or unique or involve danger for life, the consequences are even more important selective agents. However, learning from them is then very risky. A child normally cannot learn to traverse a road by testing the consequences of a contact with a car. In this case, belief in tradition, imitation, imprinting or even innate knowledge are more effective learning mechanisms. An example of the innateness of 'social intelligence' is the eye-contact maintaining behaviour of newborns, which, if absent, strongly frustrates care-givers and may weaken the mother–child bond (Eibl-Eibesfeldt, 1995).

From the importance of the consequences of behaviour it follows that it is not sufficient to master social interaction behaviour *per se*, e. g. how to fight, be polite or tell lies (subsequently called *procedural rules*), but it is also necessary to learn when to use which behaviour and how to combine behaviours. Establishing connections among procedural rules, and between procedural rules and particular contexts, we call social *meta-learning*. Such *meta-rules* indicate the range of social applicability of procedures. In contrast to learning how to proceed (e.g. how to lie), which can be transmitted more or less easily from teacher to pupil (make poker face, but be not too disinterested, smile but take care to include upper-face muscles), meta-learning is much more an experiential process, rules being acquired by doing. A meta-rule would say 'never lie', with the addition 'unless you are in an emergency situation or there is zero chance of detection' to enhance practicability. But what is an emergency situation? When reputation is at stake? My own or the other's? Which other is so significant that I lie to save his face? How does one assess the probability of detection? Children need about 10 years to be perfect liars (Ekman, 1989).

Learning meta-rules is more difficult and time-consuming than learning procedural rules. The three most complicating factors are the ambivalence of sociality, the frequency dependence of social behaviour, and the combinatorial explosion arising from the many possibilities of rule–situation interactions. Ambivalence and frequency dependence are particularly obvious in deceptive behaviour. Once deception is known as a possibility in social interaction, one can never again be sure that the other's overt behavior is what s/he 'really' intends to do. Also, frequent deception increases the likelihood of both detection and development of countermeasures (Byrne, 1995). Thus, deception is predicted to be rare and actually is both among non-human primates (Byrne & Whiten, 1992) and pre-schoolers (see below). This however drastically reduces the *real life* occasions to learn meta-rules on deception. 'Nice, fair and forgiving' tactics such as tit-for-tat and reciprocal altruism also depend on the frequency of tactics competing with them (Maynard Smith & Price, 1973; Axelrod, 1984).

Ontogenetically, social meta-learning follows the learning of procedural rules. This is comparable to the acquisition of language and memory use. Children first acquire examples of grammatically correct language (*like– liked; stand–stood*), then recognise the rules (if you need past tense, add -ed to the infinitive form) and go through a phase where they make 'errors' that they did not make before (*stand–standed*). Finally, they learn exceptions to the rule and rules governing exceptions. A similar pattern holds for memory use. At first sight, 5 year olds are not able to remember a seven-digit number. This is not a problem of will, since they like to participate and predict that they can do it. It is not a problem of memory capacity either, but one of knowledge about using memory. Typically, children look at the number and turn to something else. This leads to forgetting. However, when told to mentally repeat the number, something they seldom do spontaneously, they can learn even longer numbers (Anderson, 1985).

Meta-learning and social intelligence: Simulating the future

We think that the need for meta-learning of social interaction rules is a major force driving social intelligence. It is at this point that cognitive complexity, memory capacity and mental simulation are really needed. Relationships between Ego and others and among others, the consequences of action on these relationships, thousands of different situations experienced with at least dozens of individuals have to be memorised and predicted for a sufficiently long time period (Smith 1988). Costs and benefits have to be assessed, risks and chances inferred, both in the case of failure and success, both for Ego and others. The other's mind has to be read, his/her knowledge, intentions and behavioural capabilities have to be considered. Finally, the most promising tactic has to be selected from a host of available procedures (Whiten & Byrne, 1988). One has always to go beyond the information given, often under competition, time pressure and memory strains. Imagine a goal (finding a mate within a week) that can be reached after six steps and that there are three alternatives at each step. This gives at least 729 (3^6) possible ways to reach the goal. Often, this combinatorial explosion is reduced by the utilisation of 'pre-existing' time and memory saving knowledge structures (lexica of procedural rules, heuristics; Tversky & Kahnemann, 1974; Nisbett & Ross, 1980). However, there are some complications that may enforce the use of extensive mental simulation of how to proceed. Firstly, few heuristics apply to new situations, which leads to shortcomings when they are applied nevertheless (Nisbett & Ross, 1980). Secondly, 'real' intentions may have to be concealed and thus detours constructed. Thirdly, moves must not restrict the possibilities for further action (Chisholm, 1976). That is, one has to be able to stop action without losing face or to continue action with more pressure (imagine escalating fights alternating between show-off and retiring). Tactics made up of many steps allow such a policy of graduation, but complicate planning. Most probably high risk of failure or losing face induce gradual tactics (entering a clique among adolescents), intentions being revealed step by step. Low risk leads to direct moves (borrowing a book from a friend). Again, one of the most intricate problems is to decide when to use heuristics or to develop new tactics.

Mental models simulating social situations and predicting own and other behaviour (Lorenz, 1973; Harris, 1991) may be gradually improved by trial-and-error, imitation, pretence play, Pavlovian conditioning, and instrumental conditioning (learning by consequences, the most widespread learning mechanism in higher organisms). *Real life* occasions to test and learn the consequences of social interaction are limited in number. This is particularly obvious with deception, events involving danger for life and mate choice. In contrast, the number of future situations where procedural rules may have to be used is very large. Thus, informed guesses on the outcomes of future situations must be based on mental simulations, or on belief in traditional rules, but can rarely be deduced from experience. In order to reach an acceptable degree of plausibility, simulations must be numerous. The need for simulation may explain our almost unquenchable curiosity for 'stories' modelling social situations (narrative fiction such as fairy-tales, theatre, films etc.) and for life-events and biographies reported by gossip and mass-media. This curiosity turns into sensationalism with accounts of establishing and breaking relationships, criminal or political deception and violent death. Children enter into drama and fiction and participate in make-believe worlds within the second year of life (Harris & Kavanaugh, 1993).

What data are needed

To our knowledge, no data exist on the ontogeny and phylogeny of social meta-learning. For children there is some patchy empirical work on procedural rules that is in great need of an encompassing functional theory. Investigations are at hand on establishing contact with others, telling lies, excuses, pretence, reciprocity, helping, crying, comforting, conciliatory gestures (e.g. Hartshorne & May, 1928; Ginsburg, 1980; Eisenberg & Garvey, 1981; Sackin & Thelen, 1984; Marcus, 1986; Schropp, 1986; Darby & Schlenker, 1989; Putallaz & Wasserman, 1990; Leekam, 1991; Bussey, 1992; Grammer, 1992; Zahn-Waxler, et al., 1992; Harris & Kavanaugh, 1993; Mosier & Rogoff, 1994; Verba, 1994). In this list, naturalistic studies predominate, which is not actually representative of the published literature. However, only work based on naturalistic observation can tell something about the *real life* consequences of behaviour. Naturalistic data on the social consequences and on how children take account of them are essential in discovering how and when social meta-knowledge appears. They are not intrinsically difficult to collect, the major problem being that naturalistic observation is utterly time-consuming and thus not very productive in number of publications.

Theoretical work on the systematics and *real life* frequencies of social interaction behaviours is also needed. An open issue is the nature and complexity of problems confronting an individual, which in part determine the cognitive and behavioural methods used to solve them. Piaget (1967) saw technical, sensorimotor and cognitive problems as the driving forces of the ontogeny of intelligence, social conflicts being only important in moral development. For a long time, 'mechanical' selective agents were also postulated to be prominent in the phylogeny of intelligence (for a brief history of extracted-foraging and tool-maker hypotheses, see Lewin, 1993; Byrne, 1995) until Jolly (1966) and Humphrey (1976) suggested that sociality may have been of outstanding importance. This suggests a reassessment of human ontogeny: in fact, there seems to be a developmental lead of children's skill in the social over the technical domain (Smith, 1988). Charlesworth *et al.* (1976) observed that 88% of all problems 5 year olds encounter are social blocks, and concluded that the art of block removal is a major adaptive function of intelligence (Charlesworth 1978). The remaining 12% were physical and cognitive problems (an object is too heavy or complex to manipulate). Moreover, Hay & Ross (1982) have shown that even in 2 year olds, experimentally induced conflicts over objects are only *apparently* about objects. Actually, they are largely centred on the other child, e. g. on teasing. Common sense knowledge of adult life also suggests that most problems lie in the resistance of others, not things.

Thus, although some bodies of data and arguments are at hand, much quantifying observation on the problems, solutions and consequences encountered in the 'wild' has to be done. The most burning question is the assessment of co-variation between the complexity of a problem, the complexity of its cognitive appraisal and behavioural solution, and the success of this solution. Do complex problems always require complex thinking and complex solutions? How successful are complex solutions as compared to simple ones? Unfortunately, no satisfactory operationalisation of the variables involved has yet been found.

Social intelligence: Arrière-pensées, or not arrière-pensées?

Social intelligence is more than manipulating others, or skillfully causing them to behave in a way we want them to. Nobody has ever empirically determined how many *real life* social interactions are manipulative and how many are not. For example, Ekman (1992, pp. 150–60) describes 18 kinds of felt, non-deceptive smiles, and contrasts them to one 'false' or feigned type, but he does not know how often they occur. This holds also for lying. Although a lie seems to be an outstanding social event, it is unknown how many people lie how often in everyday life (Ekman, 1989, 1992).

Logically, it does not follow from the omnipresent eventuality of covert intentions that there is no behaviour without arrière-pensée [without reserve or ulterior motives]. It is only awfully difficult if not logically impossible to demonstrate that a behaviour has no arrière-pensée. This is clear with deception. Once it is raised as a serious possibility, it becomes almost immune to disconfirmation (compare the endless spiral of espionage and counter-espionage). Another case in point is altruism, which in theory may always be discovered to be in some way self-interested (Karylowski, 1982; Heal, 1991). But take a greeting smile, which may be interpreted either as a manipulation of the other's mood and will to communicate, or as an expression of friendly feelings towards the other. What about people co-operating in maintaining an interesting conversation, or in consoling empathically a crying child? Is the pursuit of a joint goal not rewarding enough to co-ordinate action? Does the parsimony principle not command that we first take into account that a greeting smile is an expression of friendly feelings, and nothing else? The use of the term *manipulation* in the above cases seems to have too much of a pejorative connotation. To sum up, in our view, social intelligence is the ability to skillfully enable or manage social interaction, with or without having something at the back of the mind.

Markl (1985, *contra* Dawkins & Krebs, 1978) has argued in the same direction, but from a very different viewpoint. Communication within (exclusive) social groups should, as a rule, be co-operative and mutually informative. In contrast, exploitative communication should be transitory and restricted to special cases, such as triadic and between-species interaction. The main reason for this is that communication in social groups is repetitive, prolonged, based mainly on role-switching between sender and receiver, and thus has co-evolved under mutual control to honesty and to the benefit of both interactants. Markl illustrates this by the recruiting behaviour of workers of the American desert ant *Novomessor*. If a worker has unsuccessfully tried to drag a piece of prey to the nest, she starts stridulating and emits a pheromone while continuing her efforts to displace the object. Others begin to help in dragging and recruiting. As soon as the prey-object is moved, signal emission stops and no more workers are attracted. Markl has never seen a finder calling for help and letting others do the carrying. Clearly, it is nevertheless possible to call the finder's behaviour 'manipulation', but this would be misleading terminology.

Although deception is theoretically predicted to be rare and empirically found to be uncommon in 'natural' social environments (Byrne & Whiten, 1992 on non-human primates; below on children), the literature on social intelligence is somewhat overloaded with deception and manipulation, the frequency of which is quantitatively unknown, as compared to other socially intelligent behaviours. Although there are logical and methodological advantages in focusing on egoistic manipulators, animals and man may nevertheless be also altruistic socialisers (see Chapter 13). In fact, we probably are both, and each behaviour may be used in an overt, non-manipulative and non-deceptive way, but also in the contrary manner. It is a matter of empirical enquiry to determine when and how often each mode is used, and what costs and benefits each has.

There are some empirical data on children that indirectly illuminate this issue. All authors who by naturalistic observation have quantified friendly *versus* non-friendly behaviour in children have found that friendly, prosocial or co-operative behaviour prevails, the ratio of prosocial to anti-social actions ranging from 1–10 with a median of 4 (Green, 1933; Radke-Yarrow *et al.*, 1976; Montagner, 1978, 1988; Strayer & Trudel, 1984; Kontar & Soussignan, 1987; Montagner *et al.*, 1988; Atzwanger, 1991; see Schropp 1986 for a counter-example: objects are more often demanded than offered). None of these authors explicitly assessed intentionality of the observed behaviours, but almost all excluded feigned friendliness, e.g. 'smiling at another child while teasing it'. Overall, these data may be interpreted as showing that friendliness prevails because it is the most successful strategy, independent of whether it is used honestly or in a deceptive manner. However, the exclusion criterion makes it more plausible that much of the friendly behaviour was indeed friendly, or at worst, aimed at socialising.

Social intelligence: Epistemological and psychological trap,
and trust as a way out of it

The preceding sections have repeatedly shown that the task of acquiring knowledge about the social environment is laden with ambivalence. In particular, the omnipresent eventuality of arrière-pensées leads to an epistemological situation where there is no way out. Interestingly, Freud has found that our mind seems to function similarly: thoughts are not only determined, but over-determined, that is, influenced by a host of motives and ideas that endlessly and circularly refer to each other. This led Freud (1937) to speak of 'endless psycho-analyses', and Popper (e.g. 1989) to find psycho-analysis to be unfalsifiable and to deny it the status of a scientific theory (this is only one of the half-dozen of non-falsifiabilities Popper found). The same holds for the interpretation of the intentionality of a behaviour: there are many conjectures, but only very rarely definite refutations. In particular Machiavellian behaviour leaves things unsettled and evades both confirmation and falsification of what 'actually' happened. We have the same state of the art at the level of theory and data:

we do not (yet?) exactly know if and which social systems evolved towards honesty or deception, and when manipulation and direct tactics are expected to occur.

Although Machiavelli, Freud and Popper deserve credit for having systematically investigated the fuzziness of (social) knowledge, the morass of epistemological uncertainties caused by social complexity and ambivalence has been with us throughout our recent evolutionary history (say since 2 million years, but possibly many more, see below). An increase in cognitive complexity is one way to reduce uncertainty, but since it is self-reinforcing, it is open to run-away selection (see Chapter 12). Deception and counter-deception spirals are such arms-races of social cognitions. We propose that trust was and is the ultimate counter-measure against this trap. Some emotions may indeed be very simple social intelligence devices, which may be very well suited for reducing cognitive uncertainty, to speed decision taking and to facilitate memorising. Falling in love is another instance of such a device, love drastically diminishing uncertainty during mate choice. Clearly there are also drawbacks: cognitive complexity coupled with trust reduces uncertainty (Boon & Holmes, 1991), but coupled with distrust, it increases uncertainty and may reduce the capacity to action. Paranoia is a case in point. Trust involves some risk-taking and risk calculations, and paradoxically is even one of the prerequisites of successful deception. To reiterate two of our main theses: (a) The cognitively simple (trust) and cognitively complex (embedded mind-reading) may have similar social consequences and thus may be similarly adaptive or non-adaptive. (b) It is not sufficient to know how to let oneself into trust and how to mindread, but one has also to learn when to trust or mistrust.

There is only little empirical research on (mis)trust (Deutsch, 1973, 1983, 1991; Fincham et al., 1990, Boon & Holmes, 1991). But interestingly, Sigmund and Anna Freud, and particularly Erikson (1950), have postulated that the acquisition of fundamental trust in others is the most important and earliest developmental step in human life. If distrust then dominates, it may disturb social relationships throughout life (Boon & Holmes 1991). Research on attachment has produced similar results, both in humans and animals (for a review, see Rajecki et al., 1978): The bond to the mother is formed at birth and strongly influences the well-being and social functioning in child- and adulthood (e.g. 'secure base for exploration' effects or conflict management abilities, Suess et al., 1992).

Phylogeny: Comparators

Ambivalence arises with incompleteness of information and the necessity to reduce uncertainty. Uncertainty appears in phylogeny when organisms must discern useful information from noise (i.e. spurious, uninformative behaviour and transmission obstacles) and when they must compare, and take a decision on how and when to act.[1] This happened early in evolutionary history. Feeding sites have to be assessed, and exploited or not. Females have to compare males with one another and males have to decide when to fight a rival. In such conflict situations, even lower animals such as spiders behave as if making risk evaluations (Krebs & Davies, 1978f, 1984, 1991). Semi-permeable or exclusive sociality, in contrast to solitary life and living in anonymous groups, raised many new occasions to compare. Almost all exclusive groups of animals are socially stratified, i.e. there is some form of hierarchy based on repeated comparing.

There are many ways to cope with ambivalence. Even random behaviour may be adaptive (see unpredictable 'protean' escape behaviour: Chapter 12). Flexibility varies greatly, from conditional strategies where individuals follow only one of some alternatives present in the population (e.g. silent sneaker males *versus* calling males in some frogs: Alcock, 1993) to tactical behaviour where each individual may switch between all alternatives available to the species (e.g. promiscuous mating or single-male centred consorting in chimpanzee females: Goodall, 1986). Man clearly has the largest behavioural flexibility. In most of the above cases, the fundamental problem is again not to know the procedural rule (e.g. fight or flight or submit when threatened), but when to use it (if the other is x-times larger, if the resource is worth n energy units, if benefits exceed costs).

Firstly, it follows from the above that the need for having some capability to compare and to choose among alternatives and thus for 'metalearning' may have been present very early in phylogeny. Secondly, once social and other comparison mechanisms were present, a run-away process may have been started, social and other complexity intensifying itself through an increasing capacity of individuals to learn and to be flexible. Play may have a special role in acquiring this flexibility since it has often

---

[1] We focus here on comparing, which is more relevant than noise in the analysis of social intelligence. Comparing may or may not be a conscious process.

been distinguished from 'serious' behaviour by its openness to new combinations of known procedures. Thirdly, great flexibility goes along with high centralisation of the nervous system, also seen within primates (Byrne, 1993; see Chapter 9). However, there seems to be no clear relationship between flexibility and ecological success. Indeed, aeromonads, cockroaches, gulls, rats and man are very successful ecologically, but have very different degrees of behavioural flexibility. Thus again, the consequences of behaviour, and not the underlying 'cognitive' complexity, ultimately determine success. *Homo sapiens sapiens* may be a noteworthy exception since s/he seems to be both the most flexible and the most successful. However at present, it is not easy to reliably quantify our ecological success.

Social success in children (with an essay into classification)

A functional and systematic approach

The following empirical findings illustrate some of the preceding theoretical points. We concentrate on proximate functional aspects by examining the contexts and consequences of behaviour (Hinde, 1975). A systematic approach to the consequences has to differentiate at least three inter-related dimensions: time (from the immediate to the reproductive phase of the next generation), costs and benefits, and the resources at stake (Alcock, 1993 gives a good introduction to the analysis of adaptive significance; see Borgerhoff Mulder, 1991 on human foraging and mating). There are enormous practical, methodical and logical difficulties in the study of adaptation. A complete analysis would require (a) longitudinally following many subjects and their relevant environments over a long time, (b) ensuring that the scrutinised behaviour is really adaptive, not a random by-product of other adaptations, and (c) measuring the critical consequences and their costs and benefits. This brief excursion into perfectionism shows that there is much to do.

Resources in children's lives: Material and socio-emotional

Material resources are those necessary to the physiological homeostasis of the organism (food, shelter, etc). Quite early, a sense for ownership develops that may encompass any accessible object or area such as food, toys or bed. Socio-emotional resources are body-contact and interaction with one, a few and many others that provide relief from distress and are objects of attachment, friendship, sociality and group affiliation. The need for autonomy and control coupled with playfulness and curiosity appear early. Moreover, children tend to demand to be the centre of attention from which they gain prestige, dominance, self-confidence and identity. From birth, material resources can almost only be acquired through inter-action with others. Once acquired, some material resources such as food and toys, and later money and its analogues, may be used to gain socio-emotional resources such as interaction, friendship or regard, which in turn may lead to a social standing that facilitates access to resources, and so on.

Since almost all resources are limited, and since their acquisition is very often blocked by others, social conflict is one of the most important dimensions of life in groups. Most conflicts occur with familiar and friendly individuals (Hartup et al. 1988). Thus social block avoidance and removal, conflict management, and interaction and relationship repair are prominent elements of children's daily lives.

Short-term resource acquisition (immediate to weeks)

Short-term social goals that kindergarteners try to reach are contact to talk (20%), access to an object (7%) or play group (7%), getting infor-mation (16%) or attention (16%), changing the behavioural flow of others (11%) and asking for help, persuading others to common play and searching for affection (21%). Others resist about equally often (average 40%) to all of these attempts, which is one resistance about every 2 minutes in a group of 15 children (Krasnor & Rubin, 1983). Overall and in the end, children are successful in about one third of all attempts, quite independent of whether they begin by verbally commanding, suggesting, describing, demanding, proposing co-operation or non-verbally using physical aggression, pointing or patting (Charlesworth et al., 1976; Charlesworth, 1978; Krasnor & Rubin, 1983). B resists A's first attempt with a simple 'no' (35%), which leads almost always to A's insistence, or with a justified 'no', which is accepted by A in about half of the cases (Eisenberg & Garvey, 1981). A for its part insists either unsuccessfully by repeating its first attempt, or by somewhat more successfully justifying its demand. Child A rarely proposes a compromise (4%), although it is a very efficient tactic (75% success). Most conflicts in young children con-sist only of a few turns and are then skipped (Shantz, 1987).

Thus, there are many occasions to remove blocks, many ways to proceed, and tactics vary in effectiveness. Subsequently, we describe more of preschool children's problems and solutions, but focus on interaction dynamics. All this indicates that there is ample room for meta-learning.

Managing conflicts by crying Infants' crying typically elicits care-giving, but might also produce anger and other negative emotions (Murray, 1979; Zahn-Waxler *et al.*, 1983). Thus, the typical benefits of crying are to be comforted and nourished, and to have contact. However, babies that cry incessantly may activate anger, neglect and even abuse.

Effectiveness of crying is also frequency dependent in peer groups. In most kindergarteners, crying is very efficient since it elicits helping and comforting in about 95% of cases (Sawin, 1970 in Radke-Yarrow *et al.*, 1983; Grammer, 1988). However, counter-measures develop against children who cry too often. They are branded as 'cry-babies' and ignored. This label may stick on them for weeks. Once their rate of crying has been low for some time, the effectiveness of their cries increases again. A similar social dynamic applies to sneakers who 'tell the teacher' to resolve conflicts, to discovered liars and to cheaters feigning conciliatory intentions. Note that crying and telling-the-teacher are tactics that are quite easy to learn, to perform and to understand for an observer, as compared with pretending conciliation and lying. Despite this, they elicit similar social dynamics when overused.

Resuming play and relieving stress: Conciliatory gestures Co-operative propositions, object offering, stroking, kissing, apologies, symbolic offers and repairing the concrete damage are typical gestures preschoolers use to make up (Sackin & Thelen 1984; A. Schmitt unpublished results, the following is based on 65 reconciliations). On average, children spontaneously repair about 30% of their conflicts. This rate increases to over 80% with increasing conflict intensity. Conciliatory gestures are very efficient since in 91% of all cases, they are accepted by the addressee and former opponents resume play. Playful togetherness and relief from conflict distress appear to be the main resources at stake.

The comparison of crying and conciliatory gestures illustrates well that tactics of very different degrees of cognitive and behavioural complexity may have similar immediate success and elicit similar counter-measures when it is discovered that they are used deceptively. Actually, the large majority of conciliatory gestures are honest, as suggested by three observations. Firstly, play is resumed for a long time. Thus, opponents seem to agree on its meaning. Secondly, the probability of reconciliation does not co-vary with friendship, power, dominance and rank in attention structure, whereas there is a strong and significant correlation with conflict intensity. Moreover, conflict instigators tend to initiate reconciliation. Thus, proximate factors are more strongly associated with conciliation than distant factors such as relationship and group structure. This seems to indicate that few arrière-pensées are involved. Thirdly and most importantly, straightforward deception is rare (2 cases, 3%). In one case, child A stretched out her hand toward B, smiled, approached and said that she had something to tell B. B approached, received two blows, screamed and took flight. The other case involved the three highest ranking boys and is a rare instance of overt tactical use of conciliatory behavior for the purpose of manipulating own and others' social standing.

> EKO (5.1 years; 2nd in attention rank), at the end of a quarrel with DAL (5.11; alpha) lasting 20 minutes. EKO to DAL: *We are friends again?* DAL: *Yes, but only if you are no longer friend with* MIC. EKO: *OK.* He runs to MIC (6.1; 3rd) who is playing alone, and screams: *We are no longer friends.* MIC lifts his eyebrows in surprise, than frowns.
> EKO runs back to DAL: *Are we friends?*
> DAL: *Yes.* They separate and each plays alone.
> Five minutes later. EKO goes to MIC, smiles: *I was kidding. We are friends, are'nt we?*
> MIC: *Yes.* MIC smiles brightly.

[Comment: As a response to EKO's conciliatory gesture, DAL tries to break up the relationship between EKO and MIC; EKO counters by pretending to do this. This deception is detectable only in retrospect, by taking into account the fact that EKO returns to MIC and repairs the break by saying that was joking. Thus, it is not clear if EKO intended to deceive at the very moment when he overtly renounced MIC's friendship.]

Entering a peer group of familiar children An impressive consistency of results exists in the literature on children's entry behaviour, (for a review, see Putallaz & Wasserman, 1990, to which the following owes much). The successful initiation of entrance into a peer group is a prerequisite for further interaction or for relationships to develop, these being among the most wanted short- and long-term resources in children's lives. However, there is a high potential of rejection (54% among well acquainted 3–4 year olds, Corsaro, 1981; even 26% in popular children, Putallaz & Gottman, 1981). Actually, the entry situation has been identified both by teachers and clinicians as posing serious problems to children, and as being a key element in long-term peer acceptance and a quick diagnostic of social competence.

The most successful tactic (>95%) to enter a familiar peer play group is to wait, circle around the area and observe, to greet and make an empathic statement on the group's activity and then to request access and engage in a behaviour similar to that underway. This tactic seems to be a demonstration of sharing the group's frame of reference. However, 3–4 year olds most often (>70%) use non-verbal tactics (physical contact, watching and circling, entering and smiling) or disruptive verbal tactics (making a claim on the area or on play objects, presenting self), that are quite ineffective (about 20%). Moreover, most of the ineffective tactics used are only one step in length, consisting of waiting and watching, or in non-verbal entry. The successful tactics however are those consisting of many steps, i.e. persistent tactics of a high escalative potential. Overall, Corsaro (1979) identified 15 entry tactics, the least successful being used the most often. The most parsimonious explanation for this seems to be that the learning process underway is trial-and-error. Its low effectiveness is easy to understand since 15 tactics, many alternatives at each step and the necessity to use indirect multi-step procedures leads to the previously mentioned combinatorial explosion. Moreover, children instruct each other very incompletely and the meta-rules have thus to be inferred by observation or by lonesome experience. Thus, at 3–4 years, social intelligence seems to be inadequate to definitely solve the entry problem, although many tactics are tried.

Sometimes, while apparently trying to enter a group, children present themselves ('I have a larger car'), derogate group members ('your drawing is awful'), force inclusion, either by citing a rule mandating it or by threatening or otherwise asserting power. This is an inefficient tactic. However, these children may not be interested in joining the group, but they may want to confirm or improve their social standing *vis-à-vis* the group or individual group members. This actually works (Hold-Cavell & Borsutzky, 1986). Thus, children may have very different motives in approaching others.

Long-term resource acquisition (months to years)

Long-term resources are objects (that are valued by themselves *and* as a means to facilitate interaction; for a brief review, see Schropp, 1986), access and affilliation to a peer group, relationships with group members (friendship, dominance) and social status (prestige, reputation, popularity). One principle pervades all analysis of social intelligence, and particularly of relationships and group structure: linear cause–effect relations do not hold, or, put positively, each of the above descriptors may be a cause as well as an effect of social organisation; for example popularity facilitates access to a play-clique. Since playing together is fundamental for childrens' friendships (Youniss, 1986), participation increases popularity, which in turn improves the chances of making friends and entering other play groups, and so on. The same self-reinforcing dynamics hold for rejection (Hymel *et al.*, 1990) and supporting others in conflict (see below). To complicate things, high status, friendship and dominance, and particularly being a member of a group of high-ranking friends results in high levels of access to and utilisation of limited material resources (Charlesworth & LaFrenière, 1983). Possession of desired objects increases prestige, etc. Consequently, it is very difficult to determine if a behaviour is a resource in itself or a means to another end. In fact, both immediate and long-term, and both material and socio-emotional resources may simultaneously be at stake. These may conflict and produce ambivalence, and thus complicate the social judgement of those involved and observing, including scientists.

Entering a peer group: Newcomers Newcomers need 1–2 months to accommodate to an existing group. In newly forming groups, about 5–10% of the children are never accepted, even after months (our informed guess; we are not aware of data). They have no friends, are disliked and spend most of their time alone. In the first week, newcomers are 'the antithesis of aggressive: arms kept down and close to trunk, face and eyes averted, movements slow, silent' (McGrew, 1972). They observe continuously and then start to engage in behaviours practiced by in-groups. Again, as in the case of entering familiar groups, this demonstration of sharing the group's frame of reference efficaciously triggers acceptance. Premature attempts to influence group members are ignored or rejected. ' . . . as the newcomer observes his peers interacting, he comes to recognize the behavioural contingencies of inclusion, approval, and acceptance. By relying on the actions of more knowledgable hosts and the observable consequences of their behaviour, new children may learn to act appropriately without having to discover what is positively or negatively sanctioned from direct experience' (Feldbaum *et al.*, 1980).

The above points to the difficulties associated with contacting familiar play-cliques and a new group. While the former is essential in determining social standing within a group, the latter may have been among the most challenging and life-threatening of social situations encountered throughout the history of our species. Indeed, xenophobia and ethnocentrism are universals and a primate legacy (Goodall, 1986; Brown, 1991; Eibl-Eibesfeldt, 1995).

Obtaining high regard and leadership: Self-presentation, threat, being helpful and 'nice' Verbally attracting attention is the most frequent and efficient tactic to obtain high regard. The performer becomes the centre of attention in 21% of all cases and in the long run increases status (over a year; Hold-Cavell & Borsutzky, 1986). There are some other behaviours that are only slightly less frequent and efficacious: ostentatious movements (climbing on a table), gently touching others, and threatening displays. Thus, single acts of self-presentation or threat are not very efficacious, but they add up over long time periods. Moreover, self-presentation items not directed to a specific person, and directed aggressive moves, have additive effects.

Children visually monitor individuals who are frightening and worthy of imitation. The amount of attention paid to an individual has proved to be a valid observational index of social status or group structure. It is related to dominance and popularity, and partially predicts leadership, i.e. initiating and organising games, being imitated, arbitrating, protecting (for a review, see Hold-Cavell, 1992). The fact that threat displays increase rank in attention structure and thus leadership allows prediction of a more frequent and direct involvement of leaders in conflicts, as compared to non-leaders. Actually, Montagner *et al.* (1988) showed that leaders participate much in conflicts, impose themselves, but use gentle forms of aggression, e.g. threat displays. However, they are also very co-operative or 'nice', e.g. they accept objects offered by others or give solicited objects in about 80% of all cases.

Acquisition of social status appears to be an extremely complicated task. In recent years, a number of studies have tried to determine the role of social cognitions associated with this task, particularly with failures to master it. Some conclusions of this research are particularly relevant in the present context (after Dodge & Feldman's, 1990 review). Firstly, there are consistent differences in social intelligence between high and low status children, the latter being less sophisticated. Secondly, children's socio-cognitive intelligence is not a single construct, but a series of distinct social information processing devices. Thirdly, in low-ranking children, the degree of deficiency of their cognitions and behaviour varies across situations and with time. That is, they have no *general* intellectual deficits; rather, they misinterpret and misbehave in particular situations.

Status gain through conflict management: Reciprocity, hawks, mice, bullies, retaliators and supporting others Reciprocal co-operation is associated with gain in social status over the school year (Atzwanger, 1991; sequences of two moves were analyzed; status was measured by position in attention structure). In contrast, reciprocal aggression (an eye for an eye) does not result in status changes (Grammer & Atzwanger, 1992). On the level of three-move sequences, a child, *B*, may immediately counter-attack a charge by *A* and then initiate another attack on *A* (the *hawk* tactic; terminology loosely follows Maynard Smith & Price, 1973). *B* may also persistently take to flight (*mouse*) or first react with a threat and then withdraw when confronted with a new attack (*bully*). Finally, *B* may first show flight and then initiate an attack on *A* (*retaliator*). Only retaliation resulted in long-term status gain (Atzwanger, 1991). The long-term efficiency of *tit-for-tat*, another simple tactic derived from reciprocity, has been shown theoretically in simulation tournaments (Axelrod, 1984).

We want to add an example of status loss through conflict management. Barner-Barry (1986) has described a group of childrens' tacit, non-concerted use of ostracism to control the aggressive and disruptive behaviour of a formerly accepted peer (ROB). The behaviour of all individual group members was as simple and efficient as it could be: they avoided ROB and excluded him from common activity for weeks, until his aggressions almost disappeared (see Chapter 13).

The above interaction and conflict management tactics appear to be cognitively very straightforward and driven by elementary emotions such as the universal anger–retaliation scheme (Russell, 1991) or avoidance of aversive stimuli. This contrasts with supporting others in conflicts, i.e. intervening from an observer position and thus being emotionally less absorbed. Nevertheless, the correlation of long-term status gain with retaliation and supporting are similar (moderately high, around 0.5: Atzwanger, 1991; Grammer, 1992). The following description of the three main supporting tactics illustrates the cognitive demands (Grammer, 1992). Note that in general, both the supporter and the supported gain status. During *ganging-up-on*, a child C backs the high-ranking winner A in a quarrel between A and B. This is a low-cost tactic by which C seems to direct A's attention to itself and to lower B's status. *Despots* are high-ranking and intervene in conflicts between low-ranking B and C. Despots distribute their support among many different children since a repeatedly aided individual may climb the social ladder and become a rival. Despotism thus seems to cement the *status quo* of the group. *Reciprocal supporting among friends* enables both allies to rise in rank. In sum, aid-giving in conflicts may be both a demonstration of a power position and a means to reach it. This conclusion is corroborated by three observations adding to the above. Firstly, most of the time, supporting has no obvious immediate goal. It seems to be 'explorative'. Secondly, high-ranking individuals support and are supported more often than low rankers. Thirdly, friends are helped more often than non-friends.

Very-long-term resource acquisition (life span and beyond)

The ultimate ends of meta-learning It is unclear how the social knowledge children acquire is exactly related to the mastering of adult life. We have already mentioned the influence of early attachment and trust on the later ability to resolve conflicts in the peer group (Suess et al., 1992) and in marriage (Boon & Holmes, 1991). Also, entering a group or making contact with an unknown individual are often needed in adult life. In a general way, many of the behavioural elements and the social dynamics described above are familiar to adults. More specifically, experience with dominance behaviour and tactics used to obtain and maintain high regard, status and power, and the ability to mindread or understand the frame of reference of another may be very useful in mate choice. From a biological viewpoint, mate choice, parental care and altruism towards kin are the most important social tasks adults have to master. Sexual selection theory predicts that all reproductive efforts are fraught with ambivalence and interest conflicts (e.g. since females are the limiting factor in reproduction, males have to compete for females, which in turn choose among males and incite their rivalry; Borgerhoff Mulder, 1991). Men's socio-economic status is an important mate choice criterion of women, who use social position, prestige and wealth as indicators (Buss & Schmitt, 1993). Thus during flirting and courtship, deception attempts are expected to be numerous, e.g. men exaggerate their status and women feign interest in order to discover a man's 'real' attributes. Actually, dates do not often lead to partnership. Success is far below 10% among clients of dating services (Grammer, 1993).

From conditioning to simulating

Some of children's solutions to social problems may be equivalent in terms of success, although they vary much in cognitive and behavioural complexity. Complexity may be used to classify the different arts of social block management. The most simple elements of social 'intelligence' are probably innate (e.g. the maintenance of eye-contact of newborns). Easy to perform behaviours (crying) and reactively mirroring the other's actions (chains of blows during quarrelling, retaliation) need only little more insight. Some understanding of the other is suggested by step-by-step and reactively adapting one's own behaviour to that of the other (obvious when children solicit objects). No more understanding underlies attention-seeking, which is conditioned by glances and looks of others. A broader understanding of the situation and of the available action alternatives, accompanied by some planning, is exemplified in conciliation. Mindreading and simulation may play an important role in supporting others in conflict and in entering groups. This is suggested by the fact that they are often preceded by long observation and by the variability of the behaviours actually performed. Most mindreading and behavioural flexibility is clearly needed in the acquisition of long-term resources such as leadership. In the long run, the 'fittest' tactics may not only survive through mental selection processes (simulation), but also through 'natural' selection (social pressure, success). Heuristics, meta-rules, mindreading and simulation capabilities thus may not only emerge through insightful thinking, but also through conditioning.

A classification like the above, which admittedly is only a first attempt, is one prerequisite (among others such as a similar typology of social problems), to quantitatively test hypotheses derived from Machiavellian intelligence theory. For example, our preliminary analysis does not corroborate the following hypotheses H_1 and H_2 (the reader is asked to imagine how it is related to H_3 and H_4).

H_1: *Successful* solutions to *any* social problem are cognitively and behaviourally *complex*.

H_2: *Complex problems* are better solved by *complex solutions*.

H_3: The more complex a problem, the more potential solutions (intelligence) are required.

H_4: Complexity prevails in the social world, as compared to the non-social world.

An old hat as conclusion: More data and theories needed

We have tried to make clear that social success, and ultimately reproductive success, is mainly determined by the consequences of a behaviour, and less by the cognitive complexity ('intelligence') underlying it. 'Simple' and 'complex' behaviour may be equally adaptive or non-adaptive. What is most needed is a measure for the complexity of problems and solutions. Our description of children's social intelligence showed the diversity of their behavioural repertoire and the successes and failures of their 'social engineering'. We demanded more data, to be collected through naturalistic observation, and an integrative functional theory. The Adapted Mind theory (Barkow *et al.*, 1991) is promising, but since it postulates that our brains are made of separatedly evolved 'modular' entities, its integrative power may not suffice. Indeed, it has no criterion to delimit modules from each other and would postulate distinct modules for each of the resource acquisition strategies identified in children's lives: one for entering groups, for status acquisition, peacemaking etc. In view of the pervasive need for theories, we close with a definitely old epistemological hat, quoting some wearers and champions of it.

- *What I believe was strictly true is that innumerable facts were stored in the minds of naturalists ready to take their proper places as soon as any theory which would receive them was sufficiently explained.* CHARLES DARWIN

- *Theory determines observation.* ALBERT EINSTEIN

- *Nothing is more practical than a good theory.* WINSTON CHURCHILL

- *The above is absolutely true since I have completely imagined it.* BORIS VIAN

Acknowledgements

The authors were supported by the Austrian Science Foundation (FWF, P-9723).

References

Alcock, J. (1993). *Animal Behaviour*, 5th edn. Sunderland, MA: Sinauer Associates.

Anderson, J. A. (1985). *Cognitive Psychology and its Implications*, 2nd edn. New York: W. H. Freeman.

Atzwanger, K. (1991). Tit-for-tat. Strategie in der Kindergruppe? MD thesis, Department of Zoology, University of Vienna, Austria.

Axelrod, R. (1984). *The Evolution of Cooperation*. New York: Basic Books.

Barkow, J., Cosmides, L. & Tooby, J. (eds) (1991). *The Adapted Mind: Evolutionary Psychology and the Generation of Culture*. Oxford: Oxford University Press.

Barner-Barry, C. (1986). Rob: Children's tacit use of peer ostracism to control aggressive behavior. *Ethology and Sociobiology*, 7, 281–93.

Boon, S. D. & Holmes, J. G. (1991). The dynamics of interpersonal trust: Resolving uncertainty in the face of risk. In *Cooperation and Prosocial Behaviour*, ed. R. A. Hinde & J. Groebel, pp. 190–211. Cambridge: Cambridge University Press.

Borgerhoff Mulder, M. (1991). Human behavioural ecology. In *Behavioural Ecology. An Evolutionary Approach*, ed. J. R. Krebs & N. B. Davies, pp. 69–98. London: Blackwell Scientific Publications.

Brown, D. E. (1991). *Human Universals*. New York: McGraw Hill.

Buss, D. M. & Schmitt, D. P. (1993). Sexual strategies theory: An evolutionary perspective on human mating. *Psychological Review*, 100, 204–32.

Bussey, K. (1992). Lying and truthfulness: Children's definitions, standards, and evaluative reactions. *Child Development*, 63, 129–37.

Byrne, R. W. (1993). Do larger brains mean greater intelligence? *Behavioral and Brain Sciences*, 16, 696–7.

Byrne, R. W. (1995). *The Thinking Ape. Evolutionary Origins of Intelligence*. Oxford: Oxford University Press.

Byrne, R. W. & Whiten, A. (1992). Cognitive evolution in primates: Evidence from tactical deception. *Man*, 27, 609–27.

Charlesworth, W. R. (1978). Ethology: Understanding the other half of intelligence. *Social Science Information*, 17, 231–77.

Charlesworth, W. R. & LaFrenière, P. (1983). Dominance, friendship, and resource utilization in preschool children's groups. *Ethology and Sociobiology*, 4, 175–86.

Charlesworth, W. R., Kjeergard, L., Fausch, D., Daniels, S., Binger, K. & Spiker, D. (1976). A method for studying adaptive behaviour in life situations: A study of everyday problem solving in normal and a Down syndrome child. *Developmental Report* (University of Minnesota), 6, 1–20.

Chisholm, J. S. (1976). On the evolution of rules. In *The Social Structure of Attention*, ed. M. R. A. Chance & R. R. Larsen, pp. 325–52. New York: Wiley.

Corsaro, W. A. (1979). "We are friends, right?": Children's use of access rituals in a nursery school. *Language in Society*, 8, 315–36.

Corsaro, W. R. (1981). Friendship in the nursery school: Social organization in a peer environment. In *The Development of Children's Friendships*, ed. S. Asher & J. M. Gottman, pp. 207–41. Cambridge: Cambridge University Press.

Darby, B. W. & Schlenker, B. R. (1989). Children's reactions to transgressions: Effects of the actor's apology, reputation and remorse. *British Journal for Social Psycholology*, **28**, 353–64.

Dawkins, R. & Krebs, J. R. (1978). Animal signals: Information or manipulation? In *Behavioural Ecology: An Evolutionary Approach*, ed. J. R. Krebs & N. B. Davies, pp. 282–309. London: Blackwell Scientific Publications.

Dennett, D. C. (1983). Intentional systems in cognitive ethology: The "Panglossian paradigm" defended. *Brain and Behavioral Sciences*, **6**, 343–90.

Deutsch, M. (1973). *Konfliktregelung. Konstruktive und Destruktive Prozesse*. München: Reinhardt.

Deutsch, M. (1983). The prevention of World War III: A psychological perspective. In *UNESCO Yearbook on Peace and Conflict Studies 1982*, ed. UNESCO, pp. 5–26. Westport, CO: Greenwood.

Deutsch, M. (1991). Subjective features of conflict resolution. In *New Directions in Conflict Theory*, ed. R. Väyrynen, pp. 26–56. London: Sage.

Dodge, K. A. & Feldman, E. (1990). Issues in social cognition and sociometric status. In *Peer Rejection in Childhood*, ed. S. R. Asher & J. D. Coie, pp. 119–55. Cambridge: Cambridge University Press.

Ekman, P. (1989). *Why Kids Lie*. New York: C. Scribner's Sons.

Ekman, P. (1992). *Telling Lies*, 2nd edn. New York: W.W. Norton & Co.

Eibl-Eibesfeldt, I. (1995). *Die Biologie des Menschlichen Verhaltens*, 3rd revised edn. München: Piper (Published in English in 1989 as *Human Ethoogy*).

Eisenberg, A. R. & Garvey, C. (1981). Children's use of verbal strategies in resolving conflicts. *Discourse Processes*, **4**, 149–70.

Erikson, E. H. (1950). *Childhood and Society*. New York: W. W. Norton & Co.

Feldbaum, C. L., Christenson, T. E. & O'Neal, E. C.(1980). An observational study of the assimilation of the newcomer to preschool. *Child Development*, **51**, 497–507.

Fincham, F. D., Bradbury, T. N. & Grych, J. H. (1990). Conflict in close relationships: The role of interpersonal phenomena. In *Attribution Theory: Applications to Achievement, Mental Health and Interpersonal Conflict*, ed. S. Graham & V. S. Folkes, pp. 161–84. Hillsdale, NJ: Lawrence Erlbaum.

Freud, S. (1937). Die endliche und die unendliche Analyse. *Internationale Zeitschrift für Psychoanalyse*, **23**, 209–40.

Ginsburg, H. J. (1980). Playground as laboratory: Naturalistic studies of appeasement, altruism, and the omega child. In *Dominance Relations*, ed. D. R. Omark, F. F. Strayer & D. Freedman, pp. 341–57. New York: Garland.

Goodall, J. (1986). *The Chimpanzees of Gombe: Patterns of Behavior*. Cambridge, MA: The Belknap Press.

Grammer, K. (1988). *Biologische Grundlagen des Sozialverhaltens. Verhaltensforschung in Kindergruppen*. Darmstadt: WBG.

Grammer, K. (1992). Intervention in conflicts among children: Contexts and consequences. In *Coalitions and Alliances in Humans and Other Animals*, ed. A. H. Harcourt & F. B. M. de Waal, pp. 258–3. Oxford: Oxford University Press.

Grammer, K. (1993). *Signale der Liebe*. Hamburg: Hoffmann & Campe.

Grammer, K. & Atzwanger, K. (1992). Wie du mir, so ich dir: Freundschsften, Strategien, Hierarchien und soziale Reziprozität bei Kindern. In *Evolution, Erziehung, Schule*, ed. C. Adick & U. Krebs, pp. 171–94. Erlangen-Nürnberg: Universitätsbund (Erlanger Forschungen, Reihe A, Bd. 63).

Green, E. H. (1933). Friendships and quarrels among preschool children. *Child Development*, 4, 237–52.

Handel, M. I. (1982). Intelligence and deception. *Journal of Strategic Studies*, 5, 122–54.

Harris, P. L. (1991). The work of the imagination. In *Natural Theories of the Mind: Evolution, Development and Simulation of Everyday Mindreading*, ed. A. Whiten, pp. 283–304. Oxford: Basil Blackwell.

Harris, P. L. & Kavanaugh, R. D. (1993). Young children's understanding of pretense. Serial no. 231. *Monographs of the Society for Research in Child Development*, 58, 1–110.

Hartshorne, H. & May, M. A. (1928). *Studies in the Nature of Character. I. Studies in Deceit.* New York, MacMillan.

Hartup, W. W., Laursen, B., Stewart, M. I. & Eastenson, A. (1988). Conflict and the friendship relations of young children. *Child Development*, 59, 1590–600.

Hay, D. F. & Ross, H. S. (1982). The social nature of early conflict. *Child Development*, 53, 105–13.

Heal, J. (1991). Altruism. In *Cooperation and Prosocial Behaviour*, ed. R. A. Hinde & J. Groebel, pp. 159–72. Cambridge: Cambridge University Press.

Hinde, R. A. (1975). The concept of function. In *Function and Evolution in Behaviour*, ed. G. P. Baerends, C. de Beer & A. Manning, pp. 3–15. Oxford: Clarendon Press.

Hinde, R. A. (ed.) (1983). *Primate Social Relationships. An Integrated Approach.* Oxford: Blackwell Scientific Publications.

Hold-Cavell, B. (1992). Attention structure and visual regard as measurement of social status in groups of children. *World Futures*, 35, 115–39.

Hold-Cavell, B. & Borsutzky, D. (1986). Strategies to obtain high regard: Longitudinal study of a group of preschool children. *Ethology and Sociobiology*, 7, 39–56.

Humphrey, N. K. (1976). The social function of intellect. In *Growing Points in Ethology*, ed. P. P. G. Baleson & R. A. Hinde, pp. 303–17. Cambridge: Cambridge University Press

Hymel, S., Wagner, E. & Butler, L. J. (1990). In *Peer Rejection in Childhood*, ed. S. R. Asher & J. D. Coie, pp. 156–86. Cambridge: Cambridge University Press.

Jolly, A. (1966). Lemur social behaviour and primate intelligence. *Science*, 153, 501–6.

Karylowski, J. (1982). Two types of altruistic behavior: Doing good to feel good or to make the other feel good. In *Cooperation and Helping Behavior: Theories and Research*, ed. V. J. Derlega & J. Grzelak, pp. 398–414. New York: Academic Press.

Keating, C. F. & Heltman, K. R. (1994). Dominance and deception in children and adults: Are leaders the best misleaders? *Personality and Social Psychology Bulletin*, 20, 312–21.

Kontar, F. & Soussignan, R. (1987). Les systèmes d'interaction du jeune enfant avec ses pairs. *Biology of Behavior*, 12, 45–59.

Krasnor, L. R. & Rubin, K. H. (1983). Preschool social problem solving: Attempts and outcomes in naturalistic interaction. *Child Development*, 54, 1545–58.

Krebs, J. R. & Davies, N. B. (eds) (1978). *Behavioural Ecology: An Evolutionary Approved*, 1st edn. London: Blackwell Scientific Publications.

Krebs, J. R. & Davies, N. B. (eds) (1984). *Behavioural Ecology: An Evolutionary Approach*, 2nd edn. Oxford: Blackwell Scientific Publications.

Krebs, J. R. & Davies, N. B. (eds) (1991). *Behavioural Ecology: An Evolutionary Approach*, 3rd edn. Oxford: Blackwell Scientific Publications.

Leekam, S. R. (1991). Jokes and lies: Children's understanding of intentional falsehood. In *Natural Theories of the Mind: Evolution, Development and Simulation of Everyday Mindreading*, ed. A. Whiten, pp. 159–74. Oxford: Basil Blackwell.

Lewin, R. (1993). *Human Evolution*, 3rd edn. Oxford: Blackwell Scientific Publications.

Lorenz, K. (1973). *Die Rückseite des Spiegels*. München: Piper.

Marcus, R. F. (1986). Naturalistic observation of cooperation, helping, and sharing and their associations with empathy and affect. In *Altruism and Aggression. Biological and Social Origins*, ed. C. Zahn-Waxler, E. M. Cummings & R. Ianotti, pp. 256–79. Cambridge: Cambridge University Press.

Markl, H. (1985). Manipulation, modulation, information, cognition: Some of the riddles of comunication. *Fortschritte der Zoologie*, 31, 163–94.

Maynard Smith, J. & Price, G. R. (1973). The logic of animal conflict. *Nature*, 246, 15–18.

McGrew, W. C. (1972). *An Ethological Study of Children's Behavior*. New York: Academic Press.

Montagner, H. (1978). *L'enfant et la Communication*. Paris: Stock.

Montagner, H. (1988). *L'attachement, les Débuts de la Tendresse*. Paris: Odile Jacob.

Montagner, H., Restoin, A., Rodriguez, D., Ullmann, V., Viala, M., Laurent, D. & Godard, D. (1988). Social interactions of young children with peers and their modification inrelation to environmental factors. In *Social Fabrics of the Mind*, ed. M. Chance, pp. 237–59. London: Lawrence Erlbaum.

Mosier, C. E. & Rogoff, B. (1994). Infant's intentional use of their mothers to achieve their goals. *Child Development*, 65, 70–9.

Murray, A. (1979). Infant crying as an elicitor of parental behaviour: An examination of two models. *Psychological Bulletin*, 86, 191–215.

Nisbett, R. & Ross, L. (1980). *Human Inference: Strategies and Shortcomings of Social Judgement*. Englewood Cliffs, NJ: Prentice-Hall.

Piaget, J. (1967). *La psychologie de l'intelligence*. Paris: A. Collin.

Popper, K. R. (1989). *Conjectures and Refutations*, 5th edn. London: Routledge.

Putallaz, M. & Gottman, J. M. (1981) An interactional model of children's entry into peer groups. *Child Development*, 52, 986–94.

Putallaz, M. & Wasserman, A. (1990). Children's entry behaviour. In *Peer Rejection in Childhood*, ed. S. R. Asher & J. D. Coie, pp. 60–89. Cambridge: Cambridge University Press.

Rajecki, D. W., Lamb, M. E. & Obmascher, P. (1978). Towards a general theory of infantile attachment: A comparative review of aspects of the social bond. *Behavior and Brain Sciences*, 3, 417–64.

Radke-Yarrow, M., Zahn-Waxler, C. & Chapman, M. (1983). Children's prosocial dispositions and behavior. In *Handbook of Child Psychology: Vol. IV*, ed. P. H. Mussen, pp. 469–544. New York: J. Wiley & Sons.

Radke-Yarrow, M., Zahn-Waxler, C., Barrett, D, Darby, J., King, R., Pickett, M. & Smith, J. (1976). Dimensions and correlates of prosocial behavior in young children. *Child Development*, 47, 118–25.

Russell, J. A. (1991). Culture and categorization of emotions. *Psychological Bulletin*, 110, 426–50.

Sackin, S. & Thelen, E. (1984). An ethological study of peaceful associative outcomes to conflict in preschool children. *Child Development*, 55, 1098–02.

Schropp, R. (1986). Interaction "objectified": The exchange of play-material in a preschool-group. In *Ethology and Psychology*, ed. J. Le Camus & J. Cosnier, pp. 77–88. Proceedings of the Xth International Ethological Conference. Toulouse: Privat.

Shantz, C. U. (1987). Conflicts in children. *Child Development*, 58, 283–305.

Smith, P. K. (1988).The cognitive demands of children's social interactions with peers. In *Machiavellian Intelligence: Social Expertise and the Evolution of Intellect in Monkeys, Apes and Humans*, ed. R. W. Byrne & A. Whiten, pp. 94–110. Cambridge: Cambridge University Press.

Strayer, F. F. & Trudel, M. (1984). Developmental changes in the nature and function of social dominance among young children. *Ethology and Sociobiology*, 5, 279–95.

Suess, G., Grossmann, K. E. & Sroufe, A. L. (1992). Effects of infant attachment to mother and father on quality of adaptation in preschool: From dyadic to individual organization of self. *International Journal of Behaviour Development*, 15, 43–65.

Tversky, A. & Kahneman, D. (1974). Judgement under uncertainty: Heuristics and biases. *Science*, 185, 1124–31.

Verba, M. (1994). The beginnings of collaboration in peer interaction. *Human Development*, 37, 125–39.

Watzlawick, P., Beavin, J. H. & Jackson, D. D. (1967). *Pragmatics of Human Communication*. New York: W. W. Norton & Co.

Weiner, B. (1991). On perceiving the other as responsible. *Nebraska Symposium on Motivation*, 38, 165–98.

Whiten, A. & Byrne, R. (1988). Taking (Machiavellian) intelligence apart: Editorial. In *Machiavellian Intelligence: Social Expertise and the Evolution of Intellect in Monkeys, Apes and Humans*, ed. R. W. Byrne & A. Whiten, pp. 50–65. Cambridge: Cambridge University Press

Youniss, J. (1986). Development in reciprocity through friendship. In *Altruism and Aggression. Biological and Social Origins*, ed. C. Zahn-Waxler, E. Cummings & R. Ianotti, pp. 88–106. Cambridge: Cambridge University Press.

Zahn-Waxler, C., Friedman, S. L. & Cummings, E. M. (1983). Children's emotions and behaviors in response to infants' cries. *Child Development*, 54, 1522–28.

Zahn-Waxler, C., Radke-Yarrow, M., Wagner, E. & Chapman, M. (1992). Development of concern for others. *Developmental Psychology*, 28, 126–36.

5 Minding the behaviour of deception

MARC D. HAUSER

Introduction

In the pain of his passion, Cyrano de Bergerac fed Christian a suite of elegantly crafted lines designed to capture Roxanne's heart. Cyrano's act was clearly deceptive. Christian knew that he was being deceptive, but did not know the basis for Cyrano's apparent act of generosity. And then there is Roxanne, who believes that the handsome Christian is a poetic spirit able to weave verse that strikes at the heart. She is, of course, deceived. Here then, in one triadic interaction, we have Cyrano who knowingly deceives and does so on the basis of his knowledge of what Christian and Roxanne believe and desire. We have Christian who deceives by both withholding information about his lack of eloquence and actively falsifies information by making Roxanne believe that what emerges from his lips are true inspirations from the heart. And Roxanne is our gullible recipient, swept off her feet by Christian's ersatz performance.

Humans perform such complex mental acrobatics all the time, at least those humans who are over the age of about 4 years old and have all of their species-typical neural faculties intact. Is it even reasonable to contemplate the possibility that non-human animals are similarly endowed, to lie, cheat and conceal valuable information from other group members? In this chapter, I wish to accomplish at least three things along the way to answering this question. Firstly, I will discuss several conceptual issues that are relevant to thinking about the origins and subsequent evolution of not only deceptive behaviour, but a mental capacity for deception. Secondly, I will review what is currently known about deception in non-human animals. This review will be highly selective for I will restrict my discussion to cases of deception observed under natural conditions, thereby skipping several fascinating laboratory experiments (e.g. Menzel, 1974; Premack & Woodruff, 1978; Povinelli *et al.*, 1990, 1991) that have focused on extracting some of the cognitive primitives underlying deception; the reason for this selective review will become clear as the chapter progresses. Additionally, I will follow in the footsteps of others (Byrne & Whiten, 1985; Mitchell, 1986, 1993; Whiten & Byrne, 1988; Cheney & Seyfarth, 1990) and draw a distinction between cases of *functional deception*, where an individual's behaviour has been selected to mislead the actions of others, and *intentional deception*, where an individual's behaviour is guided by intentional states such as beliefs and desires (see Dennett 1983; Bennett 1991 for a discussion of some of these issues as they apply to non-human animal behaviour), with the outcome being misrepresentation of belief states.[1] Lastly, I will develop the argument that research on non-human animal deception requires a methodological overhaul, and especially, one that makes use of a rich observational data base to generate novel experimental approaches to the problem.

Conceptual issues in the study of deception

Let me start with three questions: Firstly, how do members of a given species detect cheaters, i.e. acts of deception? Secondly, how can we, as observers, detect deception in other species? Thirdly, what is the adaptive significance of deception? The third question is, relatively, the easiest, so let me give you an answer that emerges from a behavioural ecological perspective. Like humans, non-human animals commonly engage in interactions that are competitive, and thus, there are losers and winners. Winners represent individuals with better strategies, and selection will favour any feature associated with winning, including anatomical traits used for fighting, neural computations associated with planning, and behavioural manoeuvres that maximise the probability of gaining access to resources. It is easy to imagine then that selection might, occasionally, favour dishonesty, especially when it leads to fitness pay-offs (for an early discussion of this logic, see Dawkins & Krebs, 1978; Krebs & Dawkins, 1984). Thus, if two individuals are competing over access to a valued food resource, it will sometimes benefit one individual to signal a level of

---

[1] In Byrne & Whiten's (1990, 1992) analyses of tactical deception in primates, functional deception is classified as 'level-1' and intentional deception as 'level-2'. In Mitchell's (1986, 1993) account, functional deception is generally associated with levels 1–3 whereas intentional deception is associated with levels 4–6.

fighting strength beyond what he can actually defend – the Pee-Wee Herman wimp threatening the Arnold Schwartzenager thug. The sense of dishonesty captured here is that there is a mismatch between the signal's usual or most common message (i.e. 'I gonna pummel you') and what the signaller is actually capable of doing. This mismatch captures part of the answer to the second and third question. In the case described, if Pee-Wee kept up his charade, Arnold would clearly pummel him. The important empirical problem then is what to consider the 'usual' or 'common' message. The problem is particularly severe for the study of non-human animals (also, human infants), for we lack the ability to use language as a device for plucking meaning from a signal. In several studies now, ethologists and behavioural ecologists have provided comprehensive accounts of the frequency with which signals are given in particular socio-ecological contexts (e.g. von Frisch, 1950; Stokes, 1962; Struhsaker, 1967; Caryl, 1979). These kinds of data provide us with some of the requisite information for stating what the 'typical message' is likely to be, as when a call with a specific acoustic structure is *only* heard in the context of predator encounters. Here, suppose we conclude that the signal means something like 'There is a predator' or 'There is danger' or 'Danger! Run for cover'. Dishonest or deceptive signalling might then occur when individuals take advantage of the statistical association between sound and context, and produce the same sounding signal in a completely different context (Byrne & Whiten, 1985; Whiten & Byrne, 1988; see definition below). This would be deception in the form of actively falsifying information.

Animals might be deceptive in yet another way. They could withhold information about valuable resources or danger and, as such, increase their fitness relative to others in the population. Thus, for example, in several avian and mammalian species, individuals produce distinctive vocalisations upon discovering food (for reviews see Hauser & Marler, 1993a; Hauser, 1996) and apparently as a result, recruit group members to the food source. Consequently, food-associated calls increase competition over food. But in some of these species, the probability of calling in the context of food is less than 100%, suggesting the possibility that individuals sometimes suppress their calls, thereby reducing feeding competition. The failure to call in contexts that are apparently expected would represent a second form of deception – withholding information – and is likely to be more prevalent than active falsification because it is relatively more difficult to detect cheaters. For example, an individual who failed to signal the presence of food might have done so out of selfishness, or because he or she made a mistake about the amount of food available to share.

The distinction between active falsification and withholding information is important[2] because it tells us about the kinds of behaviours we might look for with regard to deceptive acts. To formalise these issues, therefore, let me provide a working definition of *functional deception*, leaving the notion of *intentional deception* for the later sections of the chapter. To set my own definition in its appropriate historical context, consider the following definitions[3]:

> *Tactical Deception*: 'Acts from the normal repertoire of the agent, deployed such that another individual is likely to misinterpret what the acts signify, to the advantage of the agent'.
>
> *(Byrne & Whiten, 1992, p. 611).*

> *Deception*: 'Deception occurs when the victim registers or perceives, from the deceiver, something (the 'prop') which simulates or represents something else (the 'sign'); the sign influences (or would influence) the victim to do or believe something, which is an appropriate response to the sign for the victim; the victim responds to the prop as to the sign; the function of the sign for the deceiver is to influence the victim to do or believe; and such a response by the victim is inappropriate given what is actually the case.'
>
> *(Mitchell, 1993, p. 65).*

Although both of these definitions encompass what are clearly important ingredients of deception, I see two shortcomings. Firstly, they do not accommodate cases of concealment that, in some situations at least, are characterised by the absence of an act, as in the failure to produce a food call upon discovering a resource bonanza. In such cases, it is not simply that the animal substitutes one act (e.g. resting but not calling) for another (e.g. resting and calling), but that failure to produce a certain type of behaviour (e.g. calling) allows the individual to go undetected. Authors of both definitions clearly acknowledge these issues, but generally

---

[2] In Byrne & Whiten's (1992) classification of *tactical deception* (see their Table 1, p. 614), active falsification is described under the broad categories of 'Distraction', 'Attraction', or 'Creating an Image', whereas withholding information falls under the heading of 'Concealment'.

[3] For further discussions of deception, and some of its componential features, see essays within the edited volume by Mitchell & Thompson (1986), and in particular, Mitchell's piece which provides a characterisation of different form of deception.

wish to leave them outside of their operational definitions. Secondly, both definitions use terms that, I believe, make strong implications about higher level cognitive processes, thereby mixing functional and intentional issues. I would therefore like to provide a definition that is closer to Mitchell's (1986, 1993) six-tiered hierarchy of deceptive actions, and includes active falsification and withholding information, specifies more precisely what kinds of data are necessary for claiming that a given act is functionally deceptive, and keeps functional and intentional issues more distinct. Additionally, the definition I offer for functional deception can be used as a template to carve out a structurally parallel definition of *intentional deception*.

> *Functional deception:* For an animal's action to be considered
> functionally deceptive, the following conditions must hold:
> (a) There must exist a context, C, in which individuals typically
> (high probability) produce a signal, S_c, which causes other group
> members to respond with behaviour, B; (b) Occasionally, individuals
> produce S in a different context C' ($S_{c'}$) which causes other group
> members to respond with behaviour B, and consequently, enables
> the signaller to experience a relative increase in fitness (*active
> falsification*); (c) Occasionally, individuals fail to produce S in
> context C, consequently enabling them to experience a relative
> increase in fitness (*withholding information*); (d) The fitness increase
> comes from the fact that the functionally deceptive act allows
> deceivers to gain some benefit whereas those who are deceived
> obtain some cost.

This definition requires some elaboration. Part (a) sets up the typical condition for the species. I envisage something like an alarm call (signal S) that is typically given when a predator has been spotted (context C); group members that hear the alarm call respond by running for cover (behaviour B). To set up the importance of parts (b)–(d) it is necessary to establish what 'typical condition' means. Although it is impossible to specify a precise number, and my suspicion is that the value will depend considerably on the species, the most appropriate way to think about the problem is in the light of probability theory. Specifically, for a signal to be designed for a particular function, it must consistently predict a particular situation (e.g. the presence of a predator). Thus, imagine how difficult life would be for a prey species if 50% of all alarm calls were given in the absence of a predator or to a non-predator (i.e. false alarms). This signal represents a poor predictor of predator threat and presumably, selection would either fine tune the association between calling and predator detection, or would favour the evolution of other escape strategies. In many of the early ethological analyses of threat displays, including re-analyses by Caryl (1979), signals accurately predicted subsequent behaviour in 60–80% of all occurrences.

For part (b), alarm calls (signal S) are occasionally produced in the absence of a predator (context C′). In order for this alarm call to function properly (i.e. cause other group members to run for cover), it must have the same structural features as when the call is given in the presence of a predator. Any perceptually salient difference in structure would enable receivers to detect a difference between predator absent *versus* present, and therefore, enable them to avoid functionally useless responses. For part (c), an individual detects a predator, but occasionally fails to produce an alarm call. As with our discussion of 'typical' contexts for signal production, the idea that functionally deceptive acts occur only 'occasionally' is also based on both statistical and evolutionary considerations. Specifically, the frequency with which deceptive acts can be successfully implemented depends on the probability and costs of being detected, as well as the relative costs incurred by those who are deceived. The latter constraint is what ultimately fuels the signalling arms race by selecting for mechanisms that can detect acts of deception. Though several theoretical discussions have concluded that stable social structures can only tolerate infrequent acts of deception (Zahavi, 1975, 1993; Dawkins & Krebs, 1978; Krebs & Dawkins, 1984; Grafen, 1990), it has not yet been possible to specify a precise level of deception, nor the socio-ecological conditions that would favour relatively higher or lower levels. We will revisit this problem throughout the remaining sections of the chapter.

Parts (b) and (c) are each associated with methodological difficulties. Concerning (b), one would ideally like to run a set of quantitative acoustic analyses to determine whether signal S given in contexts C and C′ differs. If it does, then playback experiments should be implemented to assess whether measured differences in acoustic morphology are perceptually salient to the animals under study. Part (c) presents a tougher problem, requiring some assurance that the failure to produce a signal (i.e. the absence of an overt response) is not because the relevant eliciting stimuli are absent. For example, in the case of alarm calls, one must ascertain that the predator was, in fact, clearly detected. Having done this, it is then important to assess the different sorts of factors that might favour silence, but have little to do with withholding information. Thus, for example, if an individual fails to give an alarm call when it is alone, this may not represent a case of deception, but rather, a context that is never associated with calling (i.e. alarm calls are only given in the presence of at least one other group member).

Given the details of our definition, what conditions would favour the evolution of deceptive behaviour? For one, it seems unlikely that deception would evolve within a social system where individuals simply respond to a particular situation in a stereotyped fashion. Rather, deceptive behaviour requires an environment where individuals can co-ordinate their actions with subtle nuances in the socio-ecological conditions. Quite simply, therefore, deception will only evolve where there is some degree of behavioural plasticity (Whiten, 1994; Byrne, 1995), and as cached out in some of the earliest treatments of this problem (de Waal, 1982, 1986; see Whiten & Byrne, 1988 and accompanying commentaries), this will involve organisms that are both capable of learning from their experiences and of inventing novel solutions to old problems. Some relevant questions then, are: do individuals alter their behaviour as a function of those who are around, who is watching them and the relative benefits of the resource at stake? If so, can such behavioural responses be explained by relatively simple rules (e.g. if alone, don't call; if with at least one other group member, then call) or, are more complex cognitive processes at play, suggesting perhaps, intentional manipulation of beliefs and desires, and sensitivity to the fact that seeing is knowing (Gómez, 1991; Povinelli & Eddy, 1996)? When a signal is given, what kinds of statistical calculations do receivers compute in order to assess the probability of behavioural sequelae? Are individuals ever skeptical of the information derived from a signal? To address these problems, let us now turn to the problem of functional deception. Although there are numerous cases of functional deception in the literature, covering a broad range of species (insects, fish, frogs, birds, mammals) and socio-ecological contexts (predator detection, food competition, access to mates), I concentrate in this section on Caldwell's work with the mantis shrimp or stomatopod. I focus on this research, and use it as a test case, for it is unquestionably the most elegant work in the area and covers many of the points I wish to make.

Functional deception: Stomatopods as an exemplary case

The stomatopod exhibits a diversity of mating systems, including promiscuity and life-long pair bonds. After the juvenile molt, individuals attempt to obtain 'homes' — cavities in the substrate. Due to the fact that they continue to grow throughout their lives, with molts occurring once every few months, individuals repeatedly confront the problem of finding a new cavity suitable for their size. Nest cavities, however, represent a limited and highly valued resource. For defending their cavities and fighting off intruders, the stomatopod has evolved a hard exoskeleton and an extremely powerful claw (raptorial appendage); during the molt, it's soft body is extremely vulnerable to attack. When an intruder approaches a cavity, the resident initiates a series of displays, starting with a mild approach and escalating to the meral spread and strike; the latter is associated with heightened aggressiveness and involves spreading the claw and then striking the ground or intruder (Caldwell & Dingle, 1975).

Where does deception fit in? To answer this question, let us look at the research efforts of Caldwell and his colleagues (Caldwell & Dingle, 1975; Steger & Caldwell, 1983; Caldwell, 1986, 1987; Adams & Caldwell, 1990) on *Gonodactylus bredini*, a species of stomatopod found in the Caribbean. Because of a life history trajectory that must take into account indeterminate growth, competitive interactions over nest cavities often involve residents and intruders that differ in size. When residents were larger or equal in size to intruders, they were more likely to retain their nest cavities than when they were smaller. This pattern fits well with the relatively common finding that larger animals outcompete smaller animals for access to valued resources. A more unexpected pattern, however, was uncovered by considering the relationship between size and the molt–inter-molt cycle. Based on the stomatopod's vulnerability during the molt, one would expect individuals in this state to avoid producing the meral spread since even large residents cannot back up their display with an aggressive attack. In fact, Caldwell and colleagues (Steger & Caldwell, 1983; Caldwell, 1986; Adams & Caldwell, 1990) have found the converse. During the inter-molt, individuals shift from low to high intensity displays as a function of changes in intruder pressure. For example, when an intruder probes a cavity to assess availability, the resident will first approach the entrance and then, if the intruder probes further, will gradually escalate the aggressive intensity of the display, culminating in a strike with the claw. The pattern of displays used during the inter-molt is not, however, consistent with the pattern exhibited during the molt. Individuals in molt by-pass the lowest intensity display, moving right into lunges and meral spreads. In fact, most residents in molt produce the meral spread display after the first probe by the intruder. But recall that the resident is incapable of defending the message of his display (i.e. 'attack if intruder probes again'). Thus, it appears that stomatopods are actively falsifying information, or in the words of Caldwell and colleagues (Steger & Caldwell, 1983; Caldwell, 1986), residents are 'bluffing'. Moreover, as the published literature suggests, all stomatopods are capable of this sort of bluffing and do so under the appropriate conditions. It thus appears to be an innately specified conditional[4] strategy that is part of the species-typical repertoire.

Further support for the hypothesis that stomatopods actively falsify information about their aggressive state comes from observations of the frequency and timing of use of the meral spread display, relative to differences in size between resident and intruder (Caldwell, 1986). Experimental results reveal that during the inter-molt phase, the meral spread and meral spread plus strike displays (two of the more aggressive signals) occur at a fairly low rate. Three to four days prior to the molt, however, individuals produce these displays at high rates. In this situation, the resident appears to be signalling a heightened state of aggressiveness. Due to the high costs of probing (possibly death following a strike from the claw), residents are generally able to maintain their cavities. Size asymmetries between resident and intruder do, nonetheless, have a significant effect on the proportion of newly molted individuals using the meral spread as a bluff. A greater proportion of new molts produce the meral spread display during encounters with same-sized intruders than during encounters with intruders who are 15% larger, or when residents are in the inter-molt phase.

The stomatopod data generate three points relevant to our working definition of functional deception: (a) The meral spread display (signal S) is typically given by a resident when challenged over access to the cavity (context C); most often, the cavity resident is in an inter-molt phase, and can vigorously back up this display with a potentially costly strike. Thus, the honesty of the signal is established by the consistent association (i.e. predictability) between type of display and intensity of aggression that ensues. (b) During the molt, individuals use the meral spread when challenged by intruders, but because of their soft exoskeleton (context C'), are not able to back up the display with additional

---

[4] The strategy is conditional in the sense that the particular type of behavioural routine selected depends on the physical condition of the resident and the intruder, as well as the relative value of the cavity.

aggression. Consequently, when newly molted individuals produce a meral spread, they are actively falsifying the information conveyed (i.e. 'if you continue to approach, I will physically attack you'). (c) In general, this functionally deceptive system works because the costs associated with continued probing (i.e. death or severe injury as a result of being struck by the claw) far surpass the benefits (i.e. gaining access to a cavity). The probability of detection is low, for bluffs occur infrequently (a few days per month) and questioning the veridicality of the display is an extremely risky affair, given the possibility of receiving a strike from the resident's claw.

The question I turn to next is: given that functionally deceptive actions such as those observed in stomatopods are guided by cost–benefit assessments, what are the mechanisms that guide such actions? Specifically, do animals simply engage probabilistic rules to determine their behaviour or, are more complex cognitive processes responsible? Do animals intend to falsify or suppress information?

Intentional deception

Introductory comments

Many of the authors in this volume have discussed the topic of intentionality at length, and thus I provide only a few comments here in order to introduce the empirical cases. For purposes of discussion, the notion of *intentional deception* implies that an individual recognises its own intentional states (beliefs, goals, desires), can act on these, and understands that the folk psychological states of other individuals can be similar or different, but crucially, can be altered by means of a suite of events in the world. Thus, in order for an individual to intentionally deceive another, it must have the capacity to represent its own beliefs, to understand that by engaging in some action it can alter someone else's beliefs, and as a result of such actions, that individual will be misled into believing something that is not true (i.e. that deviates from some notion of reality). The functional advantage of an individual with such representational capacities is that they can model the world without directly experiencing how the world, both animate and inanimate, will respond. This ability provides an extraordinarily powerful engine for predicting how others will act in certain situations.

To make this issue more concrete,[5] I would like to offer a working definition of intentional deception that parallels the definition of functional definition provided earlier on.

> *Intentional deception*: For an animal's action to be considered intentionally deceptive, the following conditions must hold:
> (a) There must exist a context C for which individuals typically (high probability) produce a signal S_c from their species-typical repertoire because they know that S_c causes a change in the beliefs of group members and thus, causes them to respond with behaviour B;
> (b) Because of their understanding of the relationship between S_c and B, individuals occasionally produce signal S in a different context C' ($S_{c'}$) knowing that other group members are likely to believe that context C, rather than C' holds, and thus, are likely to respond with behaviour B. As a result, the signaller experiences a relative increase in fitness (active falsification); (c) Because of their understanding of the relationship between S_c and B, individuals occasionally suppress S_c, knowing that this will allow them to maintain private access to information concerning C, and thereby experience an increase in fitness relative to those who lack information about C (withholding information); (d) The fitness increase comes from the fact that the intentionally deceptive act allows deceivers to gain some benefit whereas those who are deceived obtain some cost.

The primary difference between our definitions of functional and intentional deception is that for the latter, individuals must not only *know that* certain acts lead to certain responses, but *know why* (Ryle, 1949) this is true – they must have a kind of theory of mind that is based on an understanding of the mechanisms underlying misrepresentation (e.g. altering belief states). Let us now take a look at two studies that have attempted to explore the topography of intentional deception. Although neither study, in my opinion, is completely satisfactory with regard to attributing intentional states to the putative deceivers, they provide some important boundary conditions or constraints, and raise important questions for future research.

---

[5] As discussed by Whiten (1994), the difference between functional and intentional deception (level 1 *versus* level 2) is more accurately characterised as two ends of a graded continuum of mindreading abilities rather than as two dichotomous states.

Food calling in domestic chickens

Male domestic chickens produce distinctive vocalisations upon discovering food and, in general, call rate is positively correlated with individual food preference (Marler *et al.*, 1986a). In response to such calls, hens typically approach, and are more likely to do so when males call at high rates than when they call at low rates. Moreover, a set of observations and experiments indicate that the chicken's food-associated calls are functionally referential (Marler *et al.*, 1992), providing information about food quality, in addition to information about the caller's affective state. In terms of setting up the problem of intentional deception, three observations (Marler *et al.*, 1986b, 1991; Gyger & Marler, 1988; Evans & Marler, 1994, 1995), detailed more completely below, make the chicken system of interest: (a) the production of food calls depends upon the social composition of the audience; (b) sometimes when an individual finds food, they remain silent; (c) sometimes when an individual finds a non-food item, they produce food calls. The first observation is important because it reveals plasticity in the system. That is, food calling is not simply a reflexive response to seeing food. The second observation suggests that individuals may occasionally withhold information. And the third observation suggests that individuals sometimes actively falsify information. I focus now on the third claim, deception in the form of active falsification.

To examine the possibility of active falsification of information, Gyger & Marler (1988) observed the natural food calling behaviour of males in a free-ranging situation, focusing on the stimuli eliciting such calls in addition to the behaviour of the male and female following call production. In 45% of all vocal utterances scored – where the vocalisation sounded like a food call – no food item was detected by the observer. When the male called and a food item was identified, females approached in 53–86% of all cases; a significant proportion of the variation in female approach could be accounted for by the type of food encountered by the male, with the highest proportion of approaches occurring in the presence of insects (relatively high quality food) and the lowest in the presence of mash (relatively low quality food); recall that there is a positive correlation between food call rate and food preference. When males called in the absence of food, females only approached 29% of the time. Interestingly, males were more likely to approach females when they called in the absence of food than when they called in the presence of food.

To succeed with their apparent bouts of deceptive calling – assuming for the moment that their goal is to bring females within close proximity and thereby increase mating opportunities – then one would expect males to be sensitive to what the female can see with respect to the feeding environment. Specifically, if a female can see that a male lacks food when he calls, then he will be caught red handed. In contrast, if the female is sufficiently far away, then a call produced in the absence of food is not immediately detectable as deceptive. In this situation, females will have to approach in order to see what the male is calling about. Analyses revealed that males were more likely to call to food when females were close and to call in the absence of food when females were far. Although these data do not demonstrate that males intend to deceive females with their calls, they at least show that males are sensitive to the fact that distant females are more likely to be recruited then near females.

What can we say about the cognitive mechanisms underlying the male's food calling behaviour, in addition to the female's response to such calls? First, if food-associated calls given in the presence of food differ from those given in the absence of food, then a mechanism is in place for detecting deceptive calls. To investigate this question, Gyger and Marler looked at differences in call rate for food present and food absent calls. There were no differences. As the authors point out, however, this of course does not rule out the possibility that other acoustic features differ across calling contexts. Such analyses have yet to be conducted, but are critical for establishing the claim that the signal is used, in one sense, to distort the truth. Specifically, and recalling our working definition of intentional deception, active falsification occurs when a signal S that is typically given in context C is now given in context C', thereby misleading a potential pool of receivers into believing that context C holds. Secondly, what are the consequences of putatively deceptive as opposed to honest calling? For example, does the relationship between the male and female change depending upon some critical number of false as opposed to honest calls? Is the female less likely to mate if she is repeatedly deceived (i.e. a form of punishment by means of mating rejections; Clutton-Brock & Parker, 1995)? Stated in more intentional terms, does a female's beliefs about a male change as a function of how often she has been deceived? Clearly, as a female experiences repeated acts of calling in the absence of food, she will build up expectations regarding the veridicality of a male's call. In this sense, changes in behaviour toward the male might indicate changes in her beliefs. Thirdly, given that non-food items elicit food-associated calls approximately 50% of the time, is it even reasonable to treat these as deceptive? This question returns us to the statistical problem raised in our previous discussion. Specifically, for deceptive behaviour to evolve it must be relatively rare. Calling to non-food items is not rare. Consequently, when females approach, perhaps they are not being deceived at all. Perhaps they respond because half the time food is present and the benefit of obtaining the food outweighs the energetic cost of approach. Although these questions have not yet been addressed, some of the methodological tools seem to be in place. Until such questions have been addressed, however, this case provides only suggestive evidence of an intentional act of active falsification.

Food calling in rhesus monkeys

Rhesus monkeys living on the island of Cayo Santiago, Puerto Rico produce five acoustically distinct vocalisations in the context of food (Figure 5.1). For this population, approximately 50% of the diet consists of provisioned monkey chow and the remaining proportion of the diet is made up of fruits (coconut), flowers, grass, and nutrient-rich soil. Although a significant proportion of the diet comes from provisioning, there is, nonetheless, significant competition for food. Moreover, some of the non-chow food items are relatively rare and, when discovered, provide fuel for intense aggressive competition. Let us now turn to some of the sources of variation in food calling behaviour.

Natural observations reveal that females produce food calls at a significantly higher rate than males, and this is generally true for all call types and all contexts. As Figure 5.1 illustrates, the vocalisations produced are acoustically variable, due in part to the eliciting contexts. Specifically, warbles, harmonic arches and chirps are only given in the context of food and, typically, the discovery of high quality food (e.g. coconut). In contrast, coos and grunts are given in both food and non-food contexts (e.g. mother–infant separation, dominant–subordinate interactions, group movement), and in general, the quality of food eliciting these calls is lower (e.g. chow) than what has been observed for warbles, harmonic arches and chirps.

To more directly assess some of the factors associated with call production, Hauser & Marler (1993a,b) used observational data to determine how hunger level and food quality influence calling behaviour. As one measure of relative hunger, analyses of changes in food consumption were calculated during the day for a large sample of adult males and adult

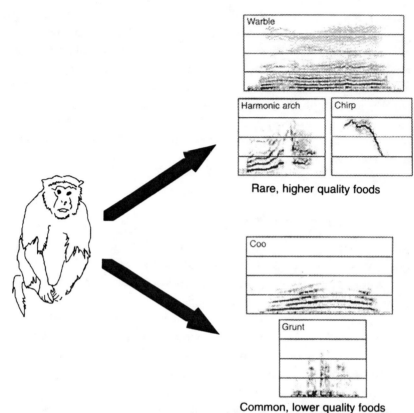

FIGURE 5.1 Sound spectrograms of rhesus monkey food-associated calls, classified according to the quality of food discovered. For the sound spectrograms, the x-axis represents time (milliseconds) and the y-axis represents frequency (kilohertz).

females. Results showed that the rate of food call production was highest when subjects were likely to be most hungry and declined to a low rate when they were relatively satiated. This pattern suggests that call rate is correlated with hunger level. In contrast, call rate was not associated with the type of food discovered, though call type was. These observational data suggest that call rate potentially encodes information about the individual's hunger level whereas call type potentially encodes information about food quality.

The natural observations summarised thus far suggest that rhesus monkeys do not always call when they discover food. Calling in rhesus monkeys is thus not a simple reflexive response to encountering food. An experiment was designed to assess whether the absence of food calling can be considered a case of withholding information, and to determine whether food discoverers who are silent are treated differently from discoverers who vocalise. Three variables were explicitly examined: the food discoverer's gender and hunger level, together with the quality of food discovered. The procedure for the experiment involved firstly, locating a solitary individual (i.e. visually out of sight from other group members) — the discoverer — and secondly, presenting this individual with equivalent amounts of one of two food items: chow and coconut. Discoverers were all permanent residents in a social group. The potential contribution of hunger level to vocal behaviour was assessed by testing some individuals early in the morning before chow was placed in the dispensers, whereas other individuals were tested late in the afternoon when approximately 85% of the foraging for the day has been completed.

When discoverers first sighted the food, they typically spent from a few seconds to a few minutes scanning their immediate environment. This once again emphasises the point made earlier that encountering food is not an automatic food call-releaser. Following a period of scanning, individuals then either called, approached silently and fed, or approached, fed on a few pieces of food, and then called. Discoverers called at least once in 45% of trials, and females called in significantly more trials than males. When discoverers called, they produced warbles, harmonic arches and chirps in response to coconut, but never in response to chow; chow elicited coos and grunts. In addition, discoverers called at higher rates in morning tests with coconut than in afternoon tests with chow. In parallel with natural observations, then, these results indicate that hunger level co-varies with call rate, whereas food quality co-varies with the spectro-temporal structure of the call (i.e. call type). Moreover, although females call more often than males, both males and females sometimes find food and simply fail to call. This case therefore satisfies criteria (a) and (b) for withholding information from a functional perspective. But before we can assess the evidence for intentional deception, we must determine the specific costs and benefits to deceiver and deceived.

As pointed out above, discoverers never bee-lined to the food source upon detecting it, but rather, scanned the environment first. Although it is not possible to identify what or whom they were looking for, such scanning behaviour at least suggests that before they approached the food, discoverers first assessed the situation. Observations following food discovery provide hints with regard to potential targets for scanning.

Depending upon the density of animals nearby, and whether or not the discoverer called, other group members quickly approached the food source and discoverer on 90% of food trials. Upon detection, some discoverers were aggressively attacked and injured whereas other discoverers either stayed and fed with group members, or were peacefully supplanted by dominants, but allowed to keep the food they had collected. Only one factor appeared to determine whether discoverers received aggression, or escaped unharmed: whether or not they called when they found food. Independently of dominance rank, vocal discoverers received significantly less aggression than silent discoverers, and for females, those who called were able to eat more food than those who were silent. In the 10% of trials where discoverers were silent and avoided being detected by other group members, these individuals consumed more food than discoverer's in any other trial. Lastly, individuals who failed to call under experimental conditions, were observed calling under natural conditions. This suggests that the food call system is relatively plastic: rather than a population characterised by a modal distribution of callers and non-callers, individuals within the population appear to have the option to call or abstain on each food discovery. It further suggests that discoverers who fail to call are punished, in much the same way that retaliatory behaviour has been observed in other organisms, including honeybees, birds, horses, and a variety of primates (for a recent review, see by Clutton-Brock & Parker, 1995).

Observations of targeted aggression suggest that prior to food consumption, discoverers may have been scanning for both allies and enemies. Depending upon the results of their scanning, individuals either call or remain silent. Are silent discoverers withholding information? Returning to the criteria laid out earlier, rhesus monkeys (a) fail to signal in a context that typically elicits a signal and (b) as a result of their failure to signal, they sometimes experience a relative increase in fitness (i.e. those who are silent and remain undetected, obtain more food than those who call and are detected). This clearly shows some level of assessment, as opposed to a purely reflexive response. But does it imply that those who fail to signal are intentionally suppressing such information from competitors and that those who signal are intentionally communicating to others about the presence of food? Do rhesus monkeys actually understand the beliefs of others and the sequence of events that are likely to transpire when a call is either produced or withheld? I do not believe that the data presented thus far warrant such interpretations, especially since rhesus monkeys often remain silent in the presence of food. As such, if silence represents a form of deception, it, like active falsification of information in chickens, is not rare — and rarity of occurrence is one of the important components of our defintion of functional and intentional deception. But before we cast our votes, let me briefly describe one last observation that complicates the picture.

Recall that in the experiments just described, all focal subjects were members of a social group. In Clutton-Brock & Parker's (1995) recent theoretical treatment of punishment, they point out that two important conditions for the evolution of targeted/retaliatory aggression are (a) repeated social interactions with the same individuals (some form of stable social relationship; Trivers, 1971) and (b) the costs of aggression toward the punished individual are outweighed by the benefits of reducing what appear to be inappropriate behaviours, perhaps violating some convention or social rule. To more directly assess the importance of punishment in maintaining social conventions, we (M. D. Hauser *et al.*, unpublished results) therefore replicated the first experiments on food calling in rhesus monkeys, but tested adult males who were peripheral to the social groups, and thus lacked stable social relationships. On each of 30 trials, a different peripheral male was presented with a small amount of high quality food. For 24 males, the food pieces were placed in a pile whereas the remaining 6 males received food spread out in a wide circle. In contrast to the pile, more food calling, and therefore sharing was expected under the dispersed condition.

Results showed that peripheral males never called upon food discovery, nor did they receive aggression when detected by other peripheral males or by social group members. Upon detection, discoverers either left the food source or were supplanted in the absence of physical aggression. Thus, and in contrast to individuals within a social group, peripheral males who fail to announce their food discoveries do not receive targeted aggression — they are not punished. This observation provides empirical support for several assumptions and theoretical predictions generated by Clutton-Brock and Parker. Specifically, punishment cannot be an evolutionarily stable strategy unless individuals have the opportunity for repeated social interactions. The probability of repeated social interactions with peripheral males is low and, thus, the relative costs of punishment in the form of aggression far outweigh the relative benefits. Importantly, the absence of calling by peripheral males does not represent a case of deception, for this *non-response* is the norm rather than an uncommon or

Food is encountered

Am I a member of a social group?

NO / YES

Eat food, don't call

Is there anyone nearby?

NO / YES

Eat food and/ or call at low rate

Is the individual a conspecific?

NO / YES

Eat food and/ or call at low rate

Is the individual an enemy?

NO / YES

Eat food and/ or call at low rate

Eat some food + call

Hunger level of discoverer
Quality of discovered food

FIGURE 5.2 A decision tree for rhesus monkeys finding food. Each branch point illustrates a set of possible behaviours, contingent upon such factors as the food discoverer's sex, dominance rank, motivational state and group status. See the text for further description.

rare event. Before leaving rhesus monkeys, and turning to the problem of skeptical receivers, let us briefly construct a decision tree (Figure 5.2) that may help clarify some of the putative calculations made by individuals under the described feeding conditions.

In the depiction above, the discoverer is faced with a suite of decisions, contingent upon its own motivational state, dominance rank, sex, group status (i.e. resident *versus* peripheral) and the quality /quantity of food, together with similar parameters for group members who might be nearby. As studies of chickens (Marler *et al.*, 1991) have revealed, the relationship between discoverer and putative audience is critically related to calling behaviour. The added layer of complexity in the rhesus monkey system appears to be the relative group status of male discoverers. Thus, whereas males who are resident in a social group sometimes call to food, peripheral males apparently never do, at least under the experimental conditions set up. Also whereas silent resident males are attacked if they are caught with food, silent peripheral males are not. As in the proposed case of active falsification described for chickens, we have a situation here with rhesus monkeys where some kind of expectation appears to have been constructed, but the content of the expectation differs, at least for males, depending upon group status. Based on their vocal behaviour, peripheral males seem to know that they can remain silent upon food discovery, and incur relatively minimal costs. Resident males, however, must set up different expectations, including the fact that the costs of being caught are relatively high.

Although expectations of the sort described above suggest that rhesus monkeys form beliefs about the feeding situation, we are forced to entertain a somewhat simpler interpretation. A few decision rules, requiring, I guess, limited computational power, would seem to suffice: (a) What is my group status? (b) If peripheral, don't call. (c) If resident, and enemies are nearby, and I am not that hungry, call. (d) If resident, and no enemies are detected, remain silent. At present, the empirical evidence does not allow us to distinguish between an explanation that is based on a set of rules as opposed to a cognitively richer and more representational account. Let us now complete the empirical path and turn to skepticism, an ability that is clearly relevant to the problem of expectations, and thus, beliefs.

Skeptical receivers

The notion of an evolutionary arms race informs us that in most competitive interactions, there will be oscillations in the successes of each competitive strategy. Such oscillations are due in part to differential selection regimes operating to fine tune each strategy under a set of constraints. In the context of deception, selection will often operate to make signallers ultimately sneaky and perceivers ultimately skeptical (Krebs & Dawkins, 1984). What evidence is there for skepticism? In less loaded terminology, what evidence is there that individuals ignore, fail to respond to, or respond counter to the information content of the signal conveyed? Two experiments, one on honeybees and one on vervet monkeys, have shed some light on this problem.

An extensive body of research shows that honeybees use their dance to convey extraordinarily precise information about the location and

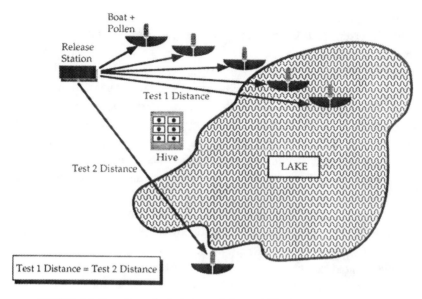

FIGURE 5.3 Experimental design used by Gould (1990) to assess whether honeybees might respond skeptically to the information conveyed in a dance by a returning forager. See the text for further description.

quality of food in the environment (von Frisch, 1967; Dyer & Seeley, 1989; reviewed in Gould & Gould, 1988; Hauser, 1996). Gould (1990) wondered whether honeybees might ever treat such information skeptically, doubting the accuracy of the dancer's assessment of food location or quality. Figure 5.3 provides a schematic illustration of the set-up and experimental procedure.

The first experimental step involved taking a group of foragers away from their hive and allowing them to move from a station on land to a nearby boat on land; the boat contained high quality pollen-substitute. Because this hive had been functioning for a long time in the same location, Gould made the reasonable assumption that individual foragers were well acquainted with the foraging environment. The second step involved moving the boat further and further from the departure station, causing the foragers to travel greater distances. During these forays, the foragers were never allowed to return to the hive. The final position of the boat was at the centre of a lake. Once the foragers reliably visited and returned from the boat on the lake, Gould allowed them to return to their hive and dance. When these foragers danced, however, virtually no recruits were observed at the boat. Thus, although the trained foragers were conveying information about the location of high quality food, hive members appeared to ignore the information conveyed. In contrast, when the boat was placed on land, but at the same distance from the departure station as the boat located at the centre of the lake, foragers actively recruited bees to the food source. Gould's working hypothesis at this point was that although the foragers were saying 'There's great food out in the middle of the lake', hive members were responding 'I don't believe it. There has never been, and will likely never be, food out in the middle of the lake. I know, I fly around that area all the time'. Thus, skepticism seems possible in honeybees[6] because of their ability to compare the information conveyed in a dance with their spatial map or representation of the environment (for reviews, see Gould & Gould, 1988; Seeley, 1989; Gould, 1990; Dyer, 1991; Gallistel, 1992; for evidence against the notion of a cognitive map, see Kirchner & Braun, 1994). However, such skepticism is domain-specific (i.e. restricted to the feeding context) and there is, as yet, no evidence that a honeybee providing misleading information about pollen would be treated skeptically when it announced, for example, a source of danger to the hive.

Cheney & Seyfarth's (1988, 1990) research on vervet monkeys represents the only experimental attempt to address the problem of skepticism in a non-human primate. The experiment relied on a procedure known as habituation–dishabituation, commonly used by developmental psychologists to assess what preverbal human infants know about the salience of different objects and events in the world. The following is a distillation of Cheney & Seyfarth's (1990) logic. If a vocalisation refers to a particular event in the environment, then when an individual produces such a vocalisation, others should expect to detect or observe the event. For example, when an 'inter-group encounter call' is given, individuals should expect to see a neighbouring group, positioned in a relatively threatening spatial location. It then follows that if an individual repeatedly produces an inter-group encounter call in the absence of a neighbouring group, that individual should be considered unreliable.

Two sets of experiments were conducted, one with inter-group encounter calls ('wrrs' and 'chutters') and one with predator alarm calls ('leopard' and 'eagle'). Wrrs and chutters are generally given in the same

---

[6] There may be alternative explanations for this result. For example, the absence of recruits to the boat on the lake may be partially explained by the observation that bees generally avoid flying over large bodies of water (F. Dyer, personal communication).

context (i.e. threat from a neighbouring group) whereas leopard and eagle alarm calls are both given to predators, but ones whose hunting strategies differ, thereby selecting for different escape responses (Struhsaker, 1967; Seyfarth et al., 1980); wrrs and chutters are acoustically different, as are leopard and eagle alarm calls. For both sets of experiments, subjects consistently habituated to repeated playbacks of the same call type from the same individual. Differences emerged, however, in the test trial, involving either a different call type or the same call type but from a different individual. Thus, for example, following habituation to Borgia's wrr, subjects remained in a habituated state (i.e. either a low level of response or no response at all) when Borgia's chutter was played. However, following habituation to Borgia's wrr, subjects dishabituated (i.e. showed a significant rebound in response) in response to Leslie's wrr or chutter. For the second set of experiments, habituation to one alarm call type resulted in dishabituation to the other call type, independently of caller identity (i.e. the same or a different caller).

Cheney and Seyfarth offer the following interpretation. Wrrs and chutters share the same meaning. Thus, if Borgia repeatedly wrrs in the absence of a neighbouring group, then changing to chutters doesn't alter the situation: she is still unreliable when it comes to announcing the presence of a threatening neighbour. But simply because Borgia is unreliable about inter-group encounters does not mean that Leslie is unreliable. Consequently, subjects respond to Leslie's wrr or chutter even after they have stopped responding to Borgia. With alarm calls, the story is quite different. Cheney and Seyfarth suggest that because eagle and leopard alarm calls have different meaning, habituation to one fails to result in habituation to the other, independently of caller identity. That is, Borgia may be unreliable about leopards, but she is not necessarily unreliable about eagles. Cheney and Seyfarth's conclusion, therefore, is that for vervet monkeys, individuals are treated as if they are unreliable if calls (S) typically associated with particular environmental features (C) are produced in the absence of such features. Thus, as in the case of honeybees, the potential for skepticism exists. These results are silent, however, when it comes to the more difficult question of whether vervet monkeys sometimes think that callers intend to mislead them into believing that a neighboring group or predator is present when it is not. Additional experiments are necessary to address this problem head on.

Knowing how and why to deceive: Some conclusions

I would like to conclude this chapter by briefly summarising the main points and by making a few comments with regard to future research on non-human animal deception. I, like others (e.g. Byrne & Whiten, 1985, 1992; Mitchell, 1986, 1993; Cheney & Seyfarth, 1990) have attempted to draw a distinction between functional deception and intentional deception. As in several areas of behavioural biology, this distinction plays an important heuristic role for it allows researchers to firstly isolate behaviours that function in a particular way (e.g. signals that function to refer to objects in the environment (Cheney & Seyfarth, 1985,1990; Marler *et al.*, 1992), behaviours that are functionally pedagogical (Caro & Hauser, 1992)) and secondly, to examine the underlying cognitive mechanisms (e.g. do individuals intend to produce functionally referential signals? (Dennett, 1983; Cheney & Seyfarth, 1990)). As the section on Conceptual Issues revealed, there is evidence from a wide diversity of species that individuals are capable of functionally deceiving other group members, either by means of actively falsifying information or by means of withholding information. Although considerably more work on functional deception is needed, especially in terms of the social and ecological consequences of deception (e.g. punishing cheaters; Hauser, 1992; Clutton-Brock & Parker, 1995), it is reasonable to conclude that animals are capable of such acts, perform them with sufficient frequency that studies can be fruitfully conducted, and perhaps most importantly, provide the requisite empirical foundation for research on intentional deception.

The studies of intentional deception that we have reviewed fall short of the kinds of evidence that would be necessary to show that individuals intend to deceive, either through active falsification of information or through concealment of information. There are two main reasons for this. Firstly, none of the studies have identified, even crudely, what non-human animals believe about other individuals and consequently, have failed to establish whether they form expectations about how other individuals might act in certain situations. Secondly, although several observations indicate that non-human animals are more than simple reflex-response machines, appearing to sample from a suite of alternative responses for any given situation, there is only weak evidence that animals intentionally control their behavioural responses – that they have precise goals in mind and use their signalling skills to achieve such goals. Though an individual's production of communicative signals may be contingent upon particular aspects of the socio-ecological environment, this does not allow us to say whether we have an organism with knowledge *that* signals produce responses in other individuals as opposed to an organism with knowledge of *why* signals produce such responses (Ryle, 1949). Yet, knowing *why* is critically involved in forming a theory about beliefs, both one's own and those formed by other group members. Furthermore, having a theory about beliefs, what changes them, who has them, and why, is an important component of having a theory of mind. Let me now turn to a few brief thoughts on how future work on deception might proceed from a methodological perspective, aimed at providing a richer description of the kinds of expectations animals form about other individuals and how such expectations potentially guide their intentional actions.

As humans, we constantly, and often unconsciously form expectations about how the world works, and we tend to form different expectations about the animate world than we do about the inanimate world. In the domain of human social interactions, such expectations are foundationally related to our ability to reason and make decisions about other individuals, and as Cosmides & Tooby (1992) have suggested, to both cheat and detect cheaters who have violated rules of social exchange. But, for organisms lacking language, how might we determine the content of their expectations? And further, how might we assess how such expectations fuel intentional behaviour? Developmental psychologists working with preverbal infants have developed a very simple, yet elegant technique, aimed precisely at these problems (Baillargeon, 1994; Spelke, 1994; Spelke, *et al.*, 1995). The technique involves setting up visual presentations that are either consistent or inconsistent with how the animate or inanimate world works. If the viewer sets up expectations about the world, then violations should elicit surprise, and in the world of the preverbal infant, surprise translates into relatively prolonged looking at the unanticipated event. For example, if infants understand that human bodies represent cohesive entities that cannot be taken apart and reconstituted into functional wholes, then they, like human adults, should be surprised when a magician (the ultimate deceiver) saws through a body, throws one half on one side of the room, and then brings the pieces back together, and releases an intact human. As I have argued elsewhere (Hauser *et al.*, 1996), the logic underlying this preferential looking paradigm is ideally suited for testing nonhuman organisms for it will enable us to directly assess the kinds of expectations they form and the extent to which such expectations can be altered by specific experiences. But let us be more specific, and use the logic of this approach to look at the relationship between an individual's expectations and intentions. This is important because an organism capable of intentional deception must be able to manipulate the expectations of other individuals.

En route to a full-blown theory of mind, the human child must acquire the ability to distinguish animate from inanimate objects, and most importantly, determine which objects have intentions (Gelman, 1990). Recently, David Premack (1990) and Alan Leslie (1994) have argued that a key insight for the developing child is the realisation that a fundamental difference exists between objects that are self-propelled and those that are not. In contrast to objects that require an external force to move, self-propelled objects have the potential to move on their own and consequently, can act in certain ways toward other objects. When we see an object moving on its own, we typically assume that there is some internal mechanism and when the object is animate, we assume that the mechanism is a brain. Premack & Premack (1995) have developed a simple test that uses the logic underlying the perception of self-propelled objects to assess whether preverbal infants understand the notion of false beliefs. In essence, their design represents a looking time version of the classic false belief test used to assess whether 3–4 year old children have a theory of mind (Wimmer & Perner, 1983). Because the test employs preferential looking, rather than a verbal response assay (though see observations of gaze direction in Clements & Perner's (1994) modified false belief test), it can readily be used with human infants and non-human animals. But before this experiment is carried out, I would like to briefly suggest an even simpler one, that might be run as a kind of litmus test for assessing the likelihood of uncovering a capacity for false belief attribution. Briefly, set up a two-chambered box with an opaque partition in the middle; the partition has a hole at its centre. Allow the test organism – let us say a non-human primate – to have some experience with the chamber, and in particular, to explore the hole in the partition. Now run a series of familiarisation trials, using one object that is self-propelled (e.g. a mouse) and one that is not (e.g. an apple). The familiarisation trials involve placing an object in one chamber (through the top) and filming the amount of time the subject looks at the object in a 10 second period; the object never passes through the hole in the partition. Now repeat this familiarisation trial, but with the object placed in the second chamber. This shows the subject that each object can be placed in either chamber. There are two test trials. The first involves placing an object in one chamber. Subsequently, an occluder is set up to block the subject's ability to see the object. A few seconds later, the occluder is taken away, revealing the object in the same chamber. The second test trial is identical to the first, but when the occluder is taken away, the object is in the opposite chamber. If our non-human primate subject understands the difference between objects that are self-propelled and those that are not, then when the self-propelled object appears in the opposite chamber (second test trial), this should come as no surprise — although subjects might expect to see the object in the starting chamber (i.e. pre-occluder), its capacity for self-generated motion means that it could enter the other chamber through the partition. Conversely, the subject should be surprised to see the non-self-propelled object in the opposite chamber — in the absence of some external force, this object should not move. If this preliminary experiment works, then there are several interesting permutations, involving manipulations of both the non-self-propelled object (e.g. a stuffed toy mouse) and the self-propelled object (e.g. a wind-up mouse that only moves in circles and thus, would not be expected to cross through the partition, even though it is self-propelled). If these tests succeed, we are in an ideal position to run the Premacks' experiment on false belief attribution. Our lab is currently in the process of running these experiments with cotton-top tamarins, a small New World monkey.

The research programme sketched above will shed some light on the expectations non-human animals form about the animate and inanimate world. Moreover, the empirical observations obtained can provide insights into what non-human animals understand about intentional actions, a critical feature of our more humanistic notion of deception. These experiments should, however, be designed in the light of the kinds of deception that appear feasible in non-human animal societies, and in this sense, the rich observational data-set collected for primates (Byrne & Whiten, 1990) provides an extraordinary empirical springboard.

In conclusion, although non-human animals may not be capable of working through the mental acrobatics of a Cyrano de Bergerac, much of their behaviour appears designed to respond to the intricacies of their social relationships, including functionally deceptive acts that mislead others by misrepresenting reality. Whether or not individuals in any species other than humans are actually aware of their actions, in that they think about their own beliefs and the beliefs of other group members, remains to be convincingly demonstrated. But there are methodological tools and intriguing empirical observations that should facilitate future experimentation, thereby paving the way to an understanding of how the minds of other animals work to solve the complex social and ecological problems they face in the natural world. This should ameliorate our understanding of whether the apparent ease with which humans both deceive and detect cheaters represents an evolutionarily ancient mental faculty or, a more recently evolved ability, dating back to the early hominids (Cosmides & Tooby, 1994).

Acknowledgements

I would like to thank Hilary Farmer for considerable help in compiling many of the references. For running food call experiments on peripheral rhesus monkey males, I thank Bethany Leeman, Roland Davis and Kate Clark-Schmidt. For logistical support and access to the long-term records, I thank the Caribbean Primate Research Center (USPHS Core Grant no. RR03640), and especially Drs J. Berard and M. Kessler. Issues discussed in this manuscript received the critical comments of R. Byrne, L. Cosmides, A. Harcourt, P. Marler, K. Stewart, J. Tooby and A. Whiten. The author's research was supported by grants from the Leakey Foundation, National Science Foundation (Young Investigator Award), and Wenner–Gren Foundation.

References

Adams, E. S. & Caldwell, R. L. (1990). Deceptive communication in asymmetric fights of the stomatopod crustacean *Gonodactylus bredini*. *Animal Behaviour*, 39, 706–16.

Baillargeon, R. (1994). A model of physical reasoning in infancy. In *Advances in Infancy Research*, ed. C. Rovee-Collier & L. Lipsitt, vol. 9, pp. 124–68. Norwood, NJ: Ablex.

Bennett, J. (1991). How is cognitive ethology possible? In *Cognitive Ethology: The Minds of Other Animals*, ed. C. A. Ristau, pp. 35–49. Hillsdale, NJ: Lawrence Erlbaum Associates.

Byrne, R. W. (1995). *The Thinking Ape: Evolutionary Origin of Intelligence*. Oxford: Oxford University Press.

Byrne, R. & Whiten, A. (1990). Tactical deception in primates: The 1990 database. *Primate Report*, 27, 1–101.

Byrne, R. W. & Whiten, A. (1985). Tactical deception of familiar individuals in baboons. *Animal Behaviour*, 33, 669 72.

Byrne, R. W. & Whiten, A. (1992). Cognitive evolution in primates: Evidence from tactical deception. *Man*, 27, 609–27.

Caldwell, R. L. (1986). The deceptive use of reputation by stomatopods. In
    Deception: Perspectives on Human and Nonhuman Deceit, ed. R. W. Mitchell &
    N. S. Thompson, pp. 129–46. New York: SUNY Press.
Caldwell, R. L. (1987). Assessment strategies in stomatopods. *Bulletin of Marine
    Science*, 41, 135–50.
Caldwell, R. L. & Dingle, H. (1975). Ecology and evolution of agonistic behavior in
    the stomatopods. *Naturwissenshaften*, 62, 214–22.
Caro, T. M. & Hauser, M. D. (1992). Is there teaching in nonhuman animals?
    Quarterly Review of Biology, 67, 151–74.
Caryl, P. G. (1979). Communication by agonistic displays: What can games theory
    contribute to ethology? *Behaviour*, 68, 136–69.
Cheney, D. L. & Seyfarth, R. M. (1985). Social and non-social knowledge in vervet
    monkeys. *Philosophical Transactions of the Royal Society of London, Series B*,
    308, 187–201.
Cheney, D. L. & Seyfarth, R. M. (1988). Assessment of meaning and the detection of
    unreliable signals by vervet monkeys. *Animal Behaviour*, 36, 477–86.
Cheney, D. L. & Seyfarth, R. M. (1990). *How Monkeys See the World: Inside the Mind
    of Another Species*. Chicago: University of Chicago Press.
Clements, W. A. & Perner, J. (1994). Implicit understanding of belief. *Cognitive
    Development*, 9, 377–95.
Clutton-Brock, T. H. & Parker, G. A. (1995). Punishment in animal societies. *Nature*,
    373, 209–16.
Cosmides, L. & Tooby, J. (1992). Cognitive adaptations for social exchange. In *The
    Adapted Mind: Evolutionary Psychology and the Generation of Culture*, ed.
    J. Barkow, L. Cosmides & J. Tooby, pp. 163–228. New York: Oxford
    University Press.
Cosmides, L. & Tooby, J. (1994). Origins of domain specificity: the evolution of
    functional organization. In *Mapping the Mind: Domain Specificity in Cognition
    and Culture*, ed. L. A. Hirschfield & S. A. Gelman, pp. 85–116. Cambridge:
    Cambridge University Press.
Dawkins, R. & Krebs, J. R. (1978). Animal signals: Information or manipulation. In
    Behavioural Ecology: An Evolutionary Approach, ed. J. R. Krebs & N. B.
    Davies, pp. 282–309. Oxford: Blackwell Scientific Publications.
de Waal, F. B. M. (1982). *Chimpanzee Politics: Power and Sex Among Apes*. London:
    Jonathan Cape.
de Waal, F. B. M. (1986). Deception in the natural communication of chimpanzees.
    In *Deception: Perspectives on Human and Nonhuman Deceit*, ed. R. W.
    Mitchell & N. S. Thompson, pp.129–46. New York: SUNY Press.
Dennett, D. C. (1983). Intentional systems in cognitive ethology: The 'Panglossian
    paradigm' defended. *Behavioral and Brain Sciences*, 6, 343–90.
Dyer, F. C. (1991). Comparative studies of dance communication: Analysis of
    phylogeny and function. In *Diversity in the Genus* Apis, ed. D. R. Smith,
    pp. 177–98. Boulder, CO: Westview Press.
Dyer, F. C. & Seeley, T. D. (1989). On the evolution of the dance language.
    American Naturalist, 133, 580–90.
Evans, C. S. & Marler, P. (1994). Food-calling and audience effects in male chickens,
    Gallus gallus: Their relationships to food availability, courtship and social
    facilitation. *Animal Behaviour*, 47, 1159–70.

Evans, C. S. & Marler, P. (1995). Language and animal communication: Parallels and contrasts. In *Comparative Approaches to Cognitive Science*, ed. H. Roitblatt, pp. 341–82. Cambridge, MA: MIT Press.

Gallistel, C. R. (1992). *The Organization of Learning*. Cambridge, MA: MIT Press.

Gelman, R. (1990). First principles organize attention to and learning about relevant data: Number and the animate-inanimate distinction as examples. *Cognitive Science*, 14, 79–106.

Gómez, J. C. (1991). Visual behaviour as a window for reading the mind of others in primates. In *Natural Theories of Mind: Evolution, Development and Simulation of Everyday Mindreading*, ed. A. Whiten, pp. 195–208. Oxford: Basil Blackwell.

Gould, J. L. (1990). Honey bee cognition. *Cognition*, 37, 83–103.

Gould, J. L. & Gould, C. G. (1988). *The Honey Bee*. New York: Freeman Press.

Grafen, A. (1990). Biological signals as handicaps. *Journal of Theoretical Biology*, 144, 475–546.

Gyger, M. & Marler, P. (1988). Food calling in the domestic fowl (*Gallus gallus*): The role of external referents and deception. *Animal Behaviour*, 36, 358–65.

Hauser, M. D. (1992). Costs of deception: Cheaters are punished in rhesus monkeys. *Proceedings of the National Academy of Sciences of the USA*, 89, 12137–9.

Hauser, M. D. (1996). *The Evolution of Communication*. Cambridge, MA: Bradford/MIT Press.

Hauser, M. D. & Marler, P. (1993a). Food-associated calls in rhesus macaques (*Macaca mulatta*). I. Socioecological factors influencing call production. *Behavioral Ecology*, 4, 194–205.

Hauser, M. D. & Marler, P. (1993b). Food-associated calls in rhesus macaques (*Macaca mulatta*). II. Costs and benefits of call production and suppression. *Behavioral Ecology*, 4, 206–12.

Kirchner, W. H. & Braun, U. (1994). Dancing honey bees indicate the location of food sources using path integration rather than cognitive maps. *Animal Behaviour*, 48, 1437–41.

Krebs, J. R. & Dawkins, R. (1984). Animal signals: Mind-reading and manipulation. In *Behavioural Ecology: An Evolutionary Approach*, 2nd edn, ed. J. R. Krebs & N. B. Davies, pp. 380–402. Sunderland, MA: Sinauer Associates Inc.

Leslie, A. M. (1994). ToMM, ToBY, and Agency: Core architecture and domain specificity. In *Mapping the Mind: Domain Specificity in Cognition and Culture*, ed. L. A. Hirschfeld & S. A. Gelman, pp. 119–48, New York: Cambridge University Press.

Marler, P., Dufty, A. & Pickert, R. (1986a). Vocal communication in the domestic chicken. I. Does a sender communicate information about the quality of a food referent to a receiver? *Animal Behaviour*, 34, 188–93.

Marler, P., Dufty, A. & Pickert, R. (1986b). Vocal communication in the domestic chicken. II. Is a sender sensitive to the presence and nature of a receiver? *Animal Behaviour*, 34, 194–8.

Marler, P., Karakashian, S. & Gyger, M. (1991). Do animals have the option of withholding signals when communication is inappropriate? The audience effect. In *Cognitive Ethology: The Minds of Other Animals*, ed. C. Ristau, pp. 135–86. Hillsdale, NJ: Lawrence Erlbaum Associates.

Marler, P., Evans, C. S. & Hauser, M. D. (1992). Animal signals? Reference, motivation or both? In *Nonverbal Vocal Communication: Comparative and Developmental Approaches*, ed. H. Papoucek, U. Jürgens & M. Papoucek, pp. 66–86. Cambridge: Cambridge University Press.

Menzel, E. W. (1974). A group of young chimpanzees in a one-acre field: Leadership and communication. In *Behaviour of Nonhuman Primates*, ed. A. M. Schrier & F. Stollnitz, pp. 130–50. New York: Academic Press.

Mitchell, R. W. (1986). A framework for discussing deception. In *Deception: Perspectives on Human and Nonhuman Deceit*, ed. R. W. Mitchell & N. S. Thompson, pp. 3–40. New York: SUNY Press.

Mitchell, R. W. (1993). Animals as liars: The human face of nonhuman duplicity. In *Lying and Deception in Everyday Life*, ed. M. Lewis & C. Saarni, pp. 59–89. New York: The Guilford Press.

Mitchell, R. W. & Thompson, N. S. (eds) (1986). *Deception: Perspectives on Human and Nonhuman Deceit*. New York: SUNY Press.

Nelson, D. A. (1984). Communication of intentions in agonistic contexts by the pigeon guillemot, *Cepphus columba*. *Behaviour*, 88, 145–89.

Povinelli, D. J. & Eddy, T. J. (1996). What young chimpanzees know about seeing. *Monographs of the Society for Research in Child Development*, vol. 61, no. 2. Serial number 247.

Povinelli, D. J., Nelson, K. E. & Boysen, S. T. (1990). Inferences about guessing and knowing by chimpanzees (*Pan troglodytes*). *Journal of Comparative Psychology*, 104, 203–10.

Povinelli, D. J., Parks, K. A. & Novak, M. A. (1991). Do rhesus monkeys (*Macaca mulatta*) attribute knowledge and ignorance to others? *Journal of Comparative Psychology*, 105, 318–25.

Premack, D. (1990). The infant's theory of self-propelled objects. *Cognition*, 36, 1–16.

Premack, D. & Premack, A. J. (1995). Intention as psychological cause. In *Causal Cognition: A Multidisciplinary Debate*, ed. D. Sperber, D. Premack & A. J. Premack, pp. 85–199. Oxford: Clarendon Press.

Premack, D. & Woodruff, G. (1978). Does the chimpanzee have a theory of mind? *Behavioral and Brain Sciences*, 4, 515–26.

Ryle, G. (1949). *The Concept of Mind*. New York: Barnes and Noble.

Seeley, T. D. (1989). The honey bee colony as a superorganism. *American Scientist*, 77, 546–53.

Seyfarth, R. M., Cheney, D. L. & Marler, P. (1980). Vervet monkey alarm calls: Semantic communication in a free-ranging primate. *Animal Behaviour*, 28, 1070–94.

Spelke, E. S. (1994). Initial knowledge: Six suggestions. *Cognition*, 50, 431–45.

Spelke, E. S., Vishton, P. & von Hofsten, C. (1995). Object perception, object-directed action, and physical knowledge in infancy. In *The Cognitive Neurosciences*, ed. M. Gazzaniga, pp. 165–79. Cambridge, MA: MIT Press.

Steger, R. & Caldwell, R. L. (1983). Intraspecific deception by bluffing: A defense strategy of newly molted stomatopods (Arthropods: Crustacea). *Science*, 221, 558–60.

Struhsaker, T. T. (1967). Auditory communication among vervet monkeys (*Cercopithecus aethiops*). In *Social Communication Among Primates*, ed. S. A. Altmann, pp. 281–324. Chicago: University of Chicago Press.

Trivers, R. L. (1971). The evolution of reciprocal altruism. *Quarterly Review of Biology*, 46, 35–57.

von Frisch, K. (1950). *Bees: Their Vision, Chemical Senses and Language*. Ithaca, NY: Cornell University Press.

von Frisch, K. (1967). *The Dance Language and Orientation of Bees*. Cambridge, MA: The Belknap Press.

Whiten, A. (1994). Grades of mindreading. In *Children's Early Understanding of Mind: Origins and Development*, ed. C. Lewis & P. Mitchell, pp. 47–70. Hove: Lawrence Erlbaum Associates.

Whiten, A. & Byrne, R. W. (1988). Tactical deception in primates. *Behavioral and Brain Sciences*, 11, 233–73.

Wimmer, H. & Perner, J. (1983). Beliefs about beliefs: Representation and constraining function of wrong beliefs in young children's understanding of deception. *Cognition*, 13, 103–28.

Zahavi, A. (1975). Mate selection: A selection for a handicap. *Journal of Theoretical Biology*, 53, 205–14.

Zahavi, A. (1993). The fallacy of conventional signalling. *Proceedings of the Royal Society of London*, 340, 227–30.

6 The Machiavellian mindreader

ANDREW WHITEN

Introduction

In 1988, one section of *Machiavellian Intelligence* asked 'are primates mind-readers?'. There seemed an obvious logic for posing the question. One of the most powerful ways to succeed in a complex social world is to read the very minds of one's companions, and get one step ahead in whatever competitive or co-operative games are at stake. We know this most clearly from our own human Machiavellianism, but we also know that the complexities of primate social life suggest niches for the ability and we know that primates have advanced social cognition: thus, the distribution of mindreading mechanisms in the primate order clearly begs investigation. Unfortunately, despite the years that had elapsed since Premack & Woodruff (1978) first tried experimentally to answer the question, 'Does the chimpanzee have a theory of mind?' (see Chapter 1), relevant empirical studies were still few in 1988 and mostly restricted to our own species: those on non-human primates could be counted on the fingers of one hand.

The situation has changed dramatically since 1988. Growth in the study of mindreading has blossomed, perhaps more than any other subject dealt with in the predecessor to this volume. To be sure, this has principally focused on the development of the capacity in humans. Developmental psychologists were the first to pick up on the potential of Premack & Woodruff's ideas, and more specifically on suggestions in the peer commentary on the article, that testing whether an individual can discriminate another's false *belief* would be the most convincing way to demonstrate a true reading of 'mind'. Premack and Woodruff had focused on a chimpanzee's ability to read, in a person's frustrated striving behaviour (e.g. trying to get some out-of-reach bananas), what the individual *wants* or *intends*. Some critics suggested that since the chimpanzee would probably have the same want if put in the same situation, she might be able to act 'as if' mindreading through knowing merely what *she* would *do* in that situation, and thus what the person would also be predicted to *do* in the circumstances. By contrast, attributing false belief requires the mindreader to recognise a mental state in another individual (e.g. thinking 'the banana is behind the bush') that is *different* to the mindreader's own state of mind (knowing the banana is *not* behind the bush — perhaps it is behind the mindreader's back, for example).

Wimmer & Perner (1983) devised tests for this level of mindreading in children, which also nicely highlighted one reason — perhaps the main reason — why members of our species have evolved as mentalists rather than behaviourists. In one test the child subjects heard and watched an illustrated story in which Maxi puts chocolate in a drawer. While Maxi is out, his mother uses a bit of the chocolate for cooking, and then puts the bar somewhere else and herself goes out. Then Maxi comes back and the child watching all this is asked, 'where will Maxi look for the chocolate?' Children older than five usually made the right prediction that Maxi will look in the original drawer, but younger children were equally likely to predict he will look in the place the mother has moved it to. The older children could also predict where Maxi will say the chocolate is in two very different situations: one in which he needs his grandpa's help to reach the drawer; and a second in which he wants to get his elder brother to look in the wrong place. In this part of the test, these children showed the pragmatic power of mentalism: having diagnosed Maxi's state of mind, they could make very different, but correct and socially adaptive predictions about how he will act in these two quite different circumstances, of helping or hindering another.

In the wake of this study, others have gone on to replicate the basic finding of a 'watershed' for this sophisticated step in mindreading in the preschool years. However, a 'second wave' of studies has gone on to conclude that an appreciation of misrepresentation is starting to function even earlier in childhood, although its operation is easily masked by various aspects of the earlier methodologies that do not fully engage the abilities of fledgling 3 year old mindreaders (see Mitchell, 1994, for a review). Equally importantly, further studies have mapped out the developing child's ability to discriminate several other states of mind, not only after, but also well before the putative pre-school watershed for belief attribution and these studies now go right back to infancy. This has important implications for our expectations of non-human primates, because even apes' highest cognitive achievements map mostly to those of the 2 year old, at best the 3 year old: Premack (1988) expressed the rule of thumb that 'if the $3\frac{1}{2}$ year old child cannot do it, neither can the chimpanzee'. It is thus also of interest that attention has shifted most recently to *how* the human mindreading system begins and develops in infancy (see Baron-Cohen, 1995, for a theory of particular interest to evolutionary psychologists, and a review of others). Some idea of the productivity of the field, as well as a useful guide to its content, is given by edited collections that track the state of the art from 1988 onwards (Astington *et al.*, 1988; Butterworth *et al.*, 1991; Frye & Moore, 1991; Whiten, 1991b; Baron-Cohen *et al.*, 1993; Lewis & Mitchell, 1994; Moore & Dunham, 1994; Davies & Stone, 1995; Stone & Davies, 1995; Carruthers & Smith, 1996).

The development of the evolutionary and comparative perspective

When we turn from the development of mindreading to its evolution, we find that progress has lagged behind. Indeed, in the decade following Premack and Woodruff's beginning, the *only* empirical studies published were on children. Nevertheless, in this period influential theoretical papers appeared in the discipline of ethology, which complemented the Premack and Woodruff achievement by suggesting *why* mindreading might evolve in animals. Krebs & Dawkins (1984) built their analysis on an earlier paper (Dawkins & Krebs, 1978) in which they had argued that the traditional view that communication amongst animals is about transmitting good, honest information to others, was fundamentally flawed in that it appeared to suggest that behaviour could evolve because it benefited others, rather than the communicator. Instead, we should expect natural selection to mould animals' communicative repertoires to evolve to *manipulate* the world — including their companions — in ways that ultimately make the communicator reproductively succesful. Krebs and Dawkins went on to argue that this manipulative function could in turn create a selection pressure for animals on the receiving end of the manipulation to evolve a retaliatory strategy, and in effect see through the manipulative behaviour to the protagonist's true state of mind. If animal *A* intends to attack *B*, but lures them forward with a false appeasement gesture, there exists a selective pressure for any ability in *B* to see through the gesture to the true state of *A*'s intent.

This is a quite general argument for why mindreading might evolve in animals, particularly with respect to the reading of (false) intent. It does, of course, assume a certain cognitive potential on which the proposed selection pressure can act to create a mindreader — an individual capable of discriminating true intent from misleading surface behaviour. Humphrey (1980, 1986) suggested that primate societies would represent a potential hotbed for such 'natural psychology'. In primates we find both a high level of the kind of selection pressures Krebs and Dawkins suggest — complex and shifting mixes of antagonistic and affiliative intentions — and advanced mental and neural attributes likely to support relatively sophisticated social discriminations of the kind suggested by the ideas of 'mindreading' or 'natural psychology'.

Thus, when Richard Byrne and I began to collate records of tactical deception in primates, based on our own and others' observations (Whiten & Byrne, 1986, 1988a), we started to wonder if in some of these we were seeing manifestations of the kinds of mindreading abilities the theories were suggesting would be most likely to emerge in exactly these types of social situation. Although our central goal was simply to map the range of functions served by tactical deception (Whiten & Byrne, 1988a; Byrne & Whiten, 1990: see also Chapter 5), we also suggested that a subset of records was worth highlighting with the working hypothesis, 'if primates mindread, these are the kind of features we might expect to see, and *can* see in social interactions in natural societies'. Among the features that impressed us were careful adjustment to the attentional states of others, and apparently novel retaliatory responses to being deceived (counterdeception) — phenomena we shall return to later (see Whiten & Byrne, 1988a; Byrne & Whiten, 1991).

This is perhaps the major contribution of this ethological approach: to describe what is distinctive in the natural social interactions of candidate mindreaders, in the wild. This functional analysis of what mindreading is naturally *about* — what it is used for — is something that laboratory experiments are clearly less reliably equipped to do. Conversely, naturalistic observations are restricted in their ability to provide convincing evidence of cause and effect — in this case, that the actions observed rest on the reading of mental states rather than behaviours. This is something more powerfully done in experiments, in which control conditions can be used to reject alternative causal explanations. Thus field observations and laboratory experiments complement each other, each contributing methods and results the other cannot. In the tactical deception research, we have simply aimed to emulate the success of the ethological tradition perhaps best exemplified in the work of Niko Tinbergen, in which the natural history comes first: only then are the appropriate experiments designed, so they are well-informed and appropriate to the nature and ecology of the phenomenon.

In fact, more empirical primate studies, including many experiments, have emerged in the 1990s than in the period before, so much so that there is not the space to review them all fully here: Table 6.1 thus shows a summary list of these studies and the principal claims they make. Given the focus of this volume, I shall instead concentrate on the operation of mindreading in those functional contexts that are most relevant to Machiavellian manouevring, doing so first with respect to the case of the human child, in whom mindreading is well documented. From this perspective I shall then in each case consider relevant evidence in primates,

Table 6.1. *The Study of Mindreading in Animals: A Summary History* (Modified and extended after Whiten, 1996b.

Italicised phrases here summarise the claims made by the authors.)

Early speculations on the possibility of animal mindreading
* Thorndike, 1911
* Lloyd-Morgan, 1930
* Menzel & Johnson, 1976

Theoretical analyses of the functional plausibility of animal mindreading
* Humphrey, 1980
  – *skilled social gamesmanship would be enhanced by 'natural psychology'*
* Krebs & Dawkins, 1984
  – *communication should evolve to be manipulative and in turn select for mindreading*

Empirical studies
* Premack & Woodruff, 1978
  – *chimpanzee attributes wants, intentions*
* Savage-Rumbaugh, 1986
  – *chimpanzees recognise ignorance (need for information)*
* Whiten & Byrne, 1988a, b
  – *chimpanzees distinguish true and apparent intention: baboons discriminate what others can see*

* Premack 1988
  - *chimpanzees recognise seeing-knowing linkage, fail to attribute false belief*
* Cheney & Seyfarth, 1990
  - *macaque monkeys do not discriminate knowledge versus ignorance*
* Byrne & Whiten, 1990, 1991, 1992
  - *great apes distinguish true and apparent intention: baboons, macaques discriminate what others can see*
* Boesch, 1991
  - *chimpanzee recognises need for information*
* Gómez, 1991
  - *gorilla understands perception-action linkage*
* Povinelli *et al.*, 1990, 1992b
  - *chimpanzees and 4 year olds discriminate knowledge and ignorance: macaques and 3 year olds do not*
* Povinelli, 1991
  - *chimpanzee discriminates intentional from accidental acts*
* Povinelli *et al.*, 1992a, c
  - *chimpanzees show empathy in role reversal: macaques do not*
* Gómez & Teixidor, 1992 (see also Gómez, 1996)
  - *orangutan recognises ignorance*
* Povinelli *et al.*, 1994
  - *young chimpanzees fail to discriminate knowledge (through seeing) and ignorance*
* Call & Tomasello, 1994
  - *enculturated orangutan (but not non-enculturated one) signals when recipient's eyes open*
* Gómez, Teixidor & Laa (see Gómez 1995; see also Gómez 1996)
  - *enculturated chimpanzees attract attention if others' gaze is diverted or occluded*
* Povinelli & Eddy, 1996a
  - *young chimpanzees fail to discriminate all but the crudest aspects of seeing: fail to understand seeing as the mental state of attention*
* Povinelli & Eddy, 1996b
  - *chimpanzee gaze-following shows understanding of visual occlusion by opaque barrier*
* A. Whiten, unpublished results
  - *language-trained chimpanzees label objects a human questioner visually attends to*

supplementing earlier attempts to sketch where the similarities and differences lie (Whiten, 1991a, 1993a). Throughout I shall attempt to consider mindreading as a skill hypothesised to serve particularly useful ends for the Machiavellian primate, whether human or non-human. First, however, we should recognise some fundamental features of our subject matter.

Just what is mindreading?

Whiten (1994) listed 18 different expressions and concepts used by various authors to refer to versions of the basic idea of the everyday reading of other minds. Some of these are used interchangeably in the literature; others have subtle, or even grossly different meanings; and some are used in different ways by different workers. Aside from the potential confusion that can be caused by the latter, there are important and interesting reasons why there is not a single term, nor a single meaning, we can appeal to: essentially, mindreading is *not* an all-or-none idea. It is more interesting than that. Two points about this are worth spelling out a little here.

Firstly, the most obviously crucial question of whether an organism is reading mind or reading behaviour is not a simple one to answer, for the simple reason — as I have remarked before — that we are not talking of telepathy. No mindreader looks 'directly' into another's mind. Mind must be read in some combination of another individual's behaviour patterns and the situation they face: so one might say that mindreading must be some particular kind of behaviour-reading that we can't write off as 'just' behaviour-reading. What kind might that be? Whiten (1996a) considered four candidates. (a) *Implicit mindreading*, in which an individual's appreciation of the linkage between, for example, another invidual's perception and their consequent actions suggests some recognition of what implicitly comes between the perception and the action (*viz.*, the mind) (Gómez, 1991). (b) *Counter-deception*, in which an individual is able to discriminate the true state of mind (e.g. intentions) of a protagonist from its overt, 'false' behaviour (e.g. Krebs & Dawkins, 1984). (c) *Recognition of intervening variables*, the insight that certain arrays of behaviour, and/or circumstances, generate states in other individuals that in turn predict arrays of future actions: such 'intervening variables' lying at the centre of causal webs amount to states of mind (Whiten, 1993a, 1994, 1996a). (d) *Experience projection*, in which an individual is able to use its own experience (for example of being ignorant in a particular circumstance) to predict how another will act in similar circumstances (e.g. Harris, 1991). Whiten (1996a) argued that the last two of these can provide the strongest bases for ascribing mindreading to an individual, the first two being more prone to redescription as behaviour-reading. However, mindreading not being telepathy, such judgements are not of an all-or-none nature.

The second point about such gradations is that even where there is agreement that the assumption of mindreading is appropriate, there are many shades to contemplate (Whiten, 1994). Developmental psychologists have begun to trace mindreading capacities, and the nature of changes in these capacities, from early infancy right up through every stage of childhood (see Lewis & Mitchell, 1994; Bråten (1997), for wide ranging surveys). At each age, we can find limitations in the extent to which the child really appreciates 'the mental', and instead relies on a more literal reading of actions and situations: Perner (1991), for example, allows the 4 year old a 'representational theory of mind' (in which the child at last grasps that the mind represents, and can therefore misrepresent, reality) and younger children only a 'mentalistic theory of behaviour'. Although debates about such stages sometimes veer towards the rather fruitless question of when the child 'is *really* a mentalist', they are best seen as steps towards the mapping of progressions through different *grades* of mindreading ability, from the primitive to the sophisticated (e.g. Perner, 1991; Wellman, 1991, Whiten 1991b; Baron-Cohen, 1995). Bearing this in mind, we can begin to discuss the more recent data on the 'Machiavellian mindreader'.

Machiavelli and the social context of mindreading in childhood

In looking at mindreading in the context of Machiavellian intelligence I continue to focus first on children, because the empirical basis for ascribing mindreading to children is well established. From this foundation I venture to the more uncertain case of non-human primates.

However, much of the achievement in the developmental psychology of mindreading has been in simply charting what children of different ages can do, and beginning to sketch what might be involved in the building of the child's theory of mind. Relative to this effort, less attention has been paid to questions about functional significance, such as 'what is mindreading used for?' and 'what benefits does it offer (over behaviour-reading)?', which are of equal interest to those concerned with the central issues of the present volume. One exception is the work of

Judy Dunn and her colleagues, who have taken the ethological approach and studied children in their own homes, interacting with others, particularly their parents and siblings. Relevant findings from these studies will be summarised next, bringing us naturally to a subject that has always been prominent in the study of Machiavellian intelligence: deception.

Children's everyday talk about causality

The most general point to be made at the outset of discussing this topic comes from a study of 2 to 3 year old children's everyday talk about causality when observed in their homes (Bloom & Capatides, 1987). These children are surrounded by potentially mysterious objects, machines and devices, so that one might expect that most of their conversations about 'what causes what' would involve the workings of this elaborate physical world. Instead, and in line with the Machiavellian intellect hypothesis outlined in Chapter 1, their talk about causal relations was chiefly about *explaining people's behaviour*, and this drew on reference to *internal states* as well as social practices.

A study by Dunn & Brown (1993) paints in more detail at two particular ages of assessement, 33 and 40 months. This is clearly an interesting age, because over the period, talk about parents'and siblings' internal states as causes of action increased approximately fourfold, by which time it was more common than reference to other behaviour as a causal factor. At 40 months, the respective percentages of reference to various causes of people's behaviour were (averaging the authors' figures over talk with mother and sibling): internal states, including knowledge, 48; actions, 29; social practices (e.g. conventions), 15; and physical reality, 8. Thus, these young 3 year olds are already operating in a social world where a theory of mind is used in a major way to explain why people act as they do. In what social contexts is this particularly important?

Dunn and Brown distinguished a number of pragmatic categories that cast light on this. Percentages of the different functional contexts in which reference to mental states was utilised at 33 months were: self-interest, 46; commentary, 44; shared positive acts, 3; other, 7. With respect to the narrow sense of 'Machiavellian' as self-interested social manipulation, the swamping of 'shared positive' acts by 'self-interest' is of obvious interest. Self-interest included cases where the child was trying to satisfy its own wants ("Give it me first because I *need* it"), or to excuse or extract itself from trouble ("I only stood there 'cause I was *trying to* turn it off")

(Dunn & Brown, 1993, p. 122). Shared positive uses of mental state words, which included friendly sharing of humour, comforting or assisting the other, were by contrast rare in this early hotbed of mindreading.

A related emphasis on self-oriented acts occurred as theory of mind developed, in the particular contexts of disputes. Dunn (1994) notes that such episodes of conflict are common in families with small children, as illustrated by the figure of 11 disputes per hour between 33 month olds and their mothers. From 33 to 47 months, there was a substantial increase in the proportion of such conflicts in which children reasoned with their protagonists. However, 'perhaps sadly' remarks Dunn, 'we found that the growth of children's ability to use reasoned argument . . . was reflected only in an increase in *self-oriented* argument . . . The rapidly growing ability of children to understand other's feelings and goals was not reflected, that is, in increased harmony between the children and the other family members' (Dunn, 1994, p. 303).

This narrowly Machiavellian phase in 3 year olds' use of their budding theory of mind may contrast with its earlier roots in infancy, which is perhaps nurtured by more co-operative social processes, an issue we shall return to below. Still, when Dunn and Brown searched for correlations between the categories of childrens' causal talk described above and later tests of competence in theory of mind, the two categories yielding significant results were *self-interest*, and *disputes* with mother and siblings: it was children who scored highly particularly on these who had the more advanced theory of mind 7 months later. This emphasis on narrow Machiavellianism on the child's part was balanced to some extent by the finding that the best predictor of the child's later theory of mind competence in the *mother's* behaviour was the 'shared positive' category.

Deception and the appreciation of false beliefs

Deception is of obvious relevance to the hypothesis of a Machiavellian origin of intellect, and so it is of interest that Dunn's ethological studies in the home found that one of the earliest signs of understanding mental states lies in deceitful episodes reported during the child's second year and increasingly during their third (Dunn, 1988, 1991). 'Among the variety of strategies used we found for instance denial of future possible psychological states, reference to what other people would like, or would be upset by, and reference to transgressions made in pretend, as an excuse' (Dunn, 1991, p. 55).

Perhaps an earlier precursor to these episodes is the teasing practised even by infants (Reddy, 1991). Teasing may achieve its effect by creating uncertainty or even false beliefs in others. However, any suggestion that the young perpetrators observed by Dunn and by Reddy appreciate that a false belief may be being created comes into conflict with much of the carefully controlled experimental evidence that has accumulated on the child's theory of mind. Not only have many studies supported the idea of a 4 to 5 years old watershed in passing tests of false belief understanding on the lines of Wimmer and Perner's 'Maxi test' described earlier, but a correlated difference has been found in studies of deception.

This may be thought unsurprising given that so many tests of false belief understanding can be thought of as implicit exercises in deception in any case. Three tests have become the stock-in-trade of developmental psychologists. One, the descendant of the Maxi experiment, has Sally putting her marble in a basket, then while she is out for a while, Anne moves the marble to a box: and the subject is asked where the returning Sally will look for her marble. Although the motives of Anne are usually not specified, she can be seen as 'playing a trick' on Sally. In the second type of test, the subject is shown a well-known box of sweets, and having said what will be inside (obvious from the wrapper), is shown that in fact there is something else there, such as pencils. They are then asked what the next person to see the box will say is in it. Again, a deceptive trick is played on the subject and others who may see the box. A third approach often distinguished (although logically it seems quite similar to the second) is to present a trick object, such as a sponge that resembles a rock, and investigate the subject's ability to discriminate how people will react to its appearance *versus* reality: again, an explicit deception.

Not only young normal children, but autistic children with mental ages beyond the 'watershed', have failed to make correct predictions on such tests (e.g. see Baron-Cohen *et al.*, 1985, for the Sally–Anne test; Perner *et al.*, 1989, for the deceptive box test; Baron-Cohen, 1989, for appearance versus reality; and Happe, 1994, for a recent review). Baron-Cohen (1995) has thus described such autistic children as 'mindblind', and he, Happe (1994), Frith (1989) and colleagues have argued that this blindness is probably at the root of the severe impairments in social functioning that define the condition. This possibility is of considerable relevance to the subject of Machiavellian intelligence, because it suggests that with a deficit in mindreading, one primate at least is severely *disabled* in social competence. Given that so many non-human primates are highly socially *competent*, engaging, for example, in the manipulation of coalitions and negotiation of sexual partnerships described elsewhere in this volume, one must ask how this might be managed without mindreading, when the case of autism appears to demonstrate that mindblind social behaviour is so limited? (Or to put this the other way round, if primates lack a theory of mind, yet are so socially expert, why need mindblind people be so severely constrained in their social abilities?)

The weight of evidence that even in normal children, false belief attribution is not common until about 5 years, may appear to put this ability out of reach of non-human primates. Recalling Premack's rule of thumb that the chimpanzee is unlikely to surpass the mentality of the $3\frac{1}{2}$ year old, it becomes of interest that a corpus of more recent and quite diverse studies argues for a much earlier onset in children. One of the first involved an experiment by Chandler *et al.*, (1989). Consistent with Dunn's data on early signs of deceit in children's everyday social life, this experiment picked out the deceit element in the Maxi task, but put the child subject itself in the role of potential deceiver. Chandler *et al.* found that $2\frac{1}{2}$ to 3 year old children would remove tell-tale cues, and even lay false trails, to mislead a protagonist about the location of some hidden reward. Moreover, if 3 year olds are *actively involved* in the deceiving role, a majority may make correct predictions in tasks of both the Sally–Anne and Deceptive Sweet Box type described earlier (Chandler & Hala, 1994). A variety of other studies are consistent with the idea that 3 year olds do have some grasp of misrepresentation, but that this is relatively specific or sensitive to particular contexts and modes of expression (e.g. reviewed by Mitchell, 1994). That these demonstrations tend to rely on deception as the cause of false beliefs (not an inevitable link – witness Maxi's mother's actions), together with the data of Dunn, Chandler and colleagues, suggests that the Machiavellian context of deceit may be a potent early context for childen's emerging grasp of the way the mind (mis)represents.

The other side of this coin is that 3 year olds' first attempts at deception express an intriguing, often imperfect appreciation of the mental consequences of their actions. In experiments that introduce a variety of controls to check how well children of this age adjust their behaviour specifically so as to change other's beliefs, much contradictory evidence emerges. For example, 3 year olds are likely to lay false trails even in situations where they could benefit from correctly informing a partner, and in a situation where they can be shown to be good at directly sabotaging the actions of a protagonist (e.g. by locking a box), they are much poorer – unlike older children – at deception (e.g. directing the protagonist to the wrong box: Sodian, 1991, 1994). Perner *et al.* (1994) argue that children at this age do not have a differentiated concept of belief, but instead act on the basis of an undifferentiated concept of belief/pretence ('prelief'), and Sodian (1994) suggests this may be the level on which 3 year old deception operates. They may thus 'create an as-if scenario and invite others to join in with them' (Sodian, 1994, p. 398), without necessarily intending to make the person believe something *false* about reality. At first sight this seems an extremely subtle distinction but it may help to resolve the puzzle of why the 2 year old can indulge in pretend play, yet not grasp false belief until later, despite the fact that these two states of mind share the fundamental characteristic of discriminating the not-real from the real. It also makes the evidence for true pretence in apes (Whiten & Byrne, 1991; Whiten, 1996b) relevant to their deception and putative mindreading, the subjects of the next section.

Deception and the reading of false beliefs and other epistemic states in primates

The above account illustrates the prominence of false belief understanding and deception in the analysis of children's developing theories of mind. While early studies tended to equate the two as late developments, more recent studies on deception in early childhood raise the possibility that this deception is where we find the most precocious beginnings of an appreciation of false belief, and/or that the Machiavellian context of deception in everyday life provides a particularly influential training ground for important precursors of the robust ability to attribute false beliefs that is manifested a year or two later.

Both of these possibilities are of interest when we turn to the 'political' manoeuvring of primates and the cognitive processes that underlie it. We already know that deception is widespread and expressed in a great variety of forms and functions in monkeys and apes, even if naturally constrained by the 'cry-wolf' problem to low frequencies in the daily life of each individual (Whiten & Byrne, 1988a; Byrne & Whiten, 1990). The child research suggests that our original conjecture that such interactions would be amongst the most likely to manifest the highest levels of mindreading the animals are capable of, and encourage their further refinement, were well-founded.

However, as the above-reviewed debates about young children illustrate, and as was always well acknowledged in our primate analyses,
deception does not of itself support direct inferences about particular
levels of mindreading (see also Chapter 5). Deceptive actions have been
described in many vertebrate and invertebrate species (Whiten, 1993b),
which can usually be explained in terms of the operation of rules for
reacting to particular situations, derived from some mix of inheritance and
learning about what are effective ways to influence others' behaviours. It
is possible that some of the deceptive and counterdeceptive tactics we
have described are adjusted to certain states of mind in the protagonists,
and indeed a range of behavioural indicators support this (Whiten &
Byrne, 1988a,b, Byrne & Whiten, 1991); but field observations do not
permit us confidently to rule out the possibility that the acts are tuned
to others' actions rather than their states of mind (Whiten, 1996a). Thus
the catalogue of largely field observations was presented as a naturalistic
jumping off point for further investigations, such as thorough experimentation, and we will turn to these for further insights.

Learned tactics and the inhibition of actions

One of the most obvious alternative explanations that one might generate
to explain a deceptive act without recourse to mindreading is some
straightforward process of trial-and-error learning. Monkeys and apes have
long childhoods and have plenty of time to learn social routines. However,
a variety of studies indicates that such learning may not be as easy as it
sounds. In one study with human children by Russell *et al.* (1991), children could gain a reward if they misled a protagonist by pointing to an
empty box, and not the baited one. Not only did young children fail to
do this, but many continued to do so over all 20 trials. Thus it is not the
case that in the absence of false belief attribution, deceptive tactics can
be easily learned at the behavioural level, even in such sophisticated
learners as human children.

Perhaps the most likely reason for the children's difficulty was that
they, unlike their protagonist, could actually *see* where the reward was,
and they had difficulty ignoring this reality 'staring them in the face'.
Mitchell (1994) points out that an apparent parallel occured in a study
of chimpanzees by Boysen & Berntson (1995), in which one chimpanzee
watched the hiding from another of a large and a small pile of rewards.
The first chimpanzee could then indicate one of the two locations, and

the second chimp was allowed to search at this location. The first animal finally received the remaining reward. The best strategy would be to point towards the location with the small pile, but typically subjects appeared unable to resist pointing to the large pile they wanted. By contrast, when the task became more divorced from perceived reality through a replacement of the rewards with symbols for small and large amounts, chimpanzee subjects were able to switch to the optimal strategy.

However, some primates can inhibit their indication of the locations of desirable hidden items. Our tactical deception data-base contains episodes in which an observer sees an ape first spot a desirable but at least half-hidden food item: but then when a competitor comes on the scene, the first ape inhibits attention to the item, usually indulging in some alternative activity such as grooming their arm. As soon as the competitor leaves, the first individual making a bee-line for the food reconfirms they had not merely forgotten its whereabouts, but were inhibiting the action (visual attention) that would have immediately drawn the competitor's gaze to the food. In one famous sequence of such ploys between the same two chimpanzees, the one who knew the location went further than mere inhibition of gaze, and led the competitor away towards a false location before quickly doubling back to snatch the food (Menzel, 1974: record no. 252 in Byrne & Whiten, 1990, p. 98).

Given the 'reality bias' apparent in the responses of children and chimpanzees in the experiments described earlier, the ability of the subjects in these episodes to detach themselves from reality may have depended on a certain physical or perceptual distancing from the desirable object. However, some primates appear more capable of the required inhibition than others. Goodall (1986), for example, drew a contrast between two young chimpanzees who had worked out how to break into some provisioning boxes by unscrewing a nut and bolt. One could not contain his excitement and having released the catch, ran to the box making food grunts, at which point he was displaced by alert adult males. But a second chimpanzee *was* able to inhibit such giveaway behaviour, in a way that suggested he was sensitive to the possibility of restricted perceptual access by the more dominant competitors, with respect to what he was up to:

> 'Very nonchalantly, and with an apparent lack of purpose, he
> wandered to a handle. There he sat and performed the entire
> unscrewing operation with one hand, never so much as glancing at

what he was doing. Thereafter he simply sat, gazing anywhere but at the box, one hand or one foot resting on the handle so that the lid remained shut. There he outwaited the big males, sometimes for as long as thirty minutes. Only when the last one had gone did he release the handle and (silently) run to claim his well-earned reward'

(*Goodall, 1986, p. 578: record no. 217 in Byrne & Whiten, 1990*).

Do primates attribute false beliefs?

Did the chimpanzee observed by Menzel aim to make its protagonist falsely believe the food was at a different location? Did the chimpanzee observed by Goodall aim to keep others ignorant of what he was achieving? How could we tell from such observations? The most convincing evidence would be the employing of novel tactics that would create the same false belief, in cases where a first tactic is somehow blocked. Perhaps this was what Menzel's chimp was doing in leading the other away, because her usual strategy of waiting for him to leave did not work? But it is difficult to discount the alternative explanation that, perhaps frustrated, she wandered away, and discovered the tactic in this way. If she had pretended to begin digging in the wrong place the case would be more convincing, and it is this kind of novel elaboration that is what makes naturalistic observations like those of Dunn on children as suggestive of manipulating others mental states as they are. With wild primates judgements of novelty are often diffcult to make with any confidence. Nevertheless, the naturalistic observations, coupled with the recent data on early false belief attribution in very young children noted above, suggest that novel experimental tests of such attribution are worth making, particularly with great apes. The execution of such tests with non-verbal subjects, however, is difficult, and few attempts have been published.

The first, reported in outline by Premack (1988), involved arranging that a chimpanzee would see a human partner repeatedly stocking, and later sharing food from one side of a cabinet, while avoiding disgusting objects on the other side. The chimpanzee had control of opening the doors for the partner to do this. On the critical test, a masked third party broke into the cabinet and reversed the nice and nasty contents before the usual partner entered. The question then became whether the chimpanzee would now hesitate in opening the door, which might result in the partner dipping into the disgusting objects. Premack could report only the unimpressive result that the chimpanzee opened the door as usual, her only unusual behaviour being to manipulate the lever again once the partner opened the door.

More recently Gómez & Teixidor (1992: see Gómez, 1996) followed a somewhat similar logic, aiming to create a scenario like the Sally–Anne task. An orangutan learned a familiar routine in which she would indicate to a human partner which of two boxes had been stocked with food, whereupon the partner would take a key from a nearby container, open the box and offer the food. In the critical trials interpersed with these, another human intervened, moving the key to a novel position, such that the usual partner would have a false belief about its location. The test was whether the orangutan would now attempt to compensate for this changed epistemic state in the partner, by pointing to the new location, instead of the usual routine of pointing to the box. She did not do this on the first trial, but began to do so on the second trial: however, this was only after the partner failed to find the keys in the usual place and gave behavioural cues of a need for help. On the seventh trial the orangutan started to point to the new location *first*, and thereafter continued to do so quite consistently. It may be significant that this more sophisticated action began when the key was hidden by a stranger, to whom the orangutan was both hostile and attentive. It is possible that such a condition could have produced pointing out the new location earlier, but as things stand, the orangutan's performance in the first six trials does not support the idea that she was attuned to the person's state of mind. Nevertheless, as Gómez (1996) remarks, this quite brief exposure to the situation led to appropriate understanding of what was required: it does not seem to conform to slow, blind, trial-and-error learning, so much as to some faster insight into the needs of the partner who could not find the missing key.

As Gómez also acknowledges, even if the orangutan had pointed to the new location from the outset, it would not necessarily have demonstrated attribution of *false belief*, but perhaps only recognition of the *ignorance* of the partner; ignorance can be corrected by pointing out the new true location, whereas in the Sally–Anne test, the subject is required to point to the location where the object *is no longer* (where Sally should be expected to search, given her false belief). Experiments by Povinelli *et al.* (1990) attempted directly to assess this ability to distinguish states of knowledge and ignorance by having chimpanzees choose between two humans to advise them where to search for food, one of the humans having watched the hiding of the food, and another having been absent from the room and so not witnessed the hiding. Critical transfer trials were administered in which ignorance was maintained not by leaving the room, but by placing a bag over the person's head. Povinelli *et al.* found a significant preference for the knowledgeable adviser, but as with the Gómez and Teixidor study outlined above, the effect was not apparent in the first critical test trials (Heyes, 1993; Povinelli, 1994). Apes do not appear to bring to these types of experiment the kind of theory of mind that allows the average 4 year old child to succeed on their first attempt (Povinelli & deBlois, 1992).

However, the chimpanzees in these experiments did quickly pick up on discriminations of the conditions of ignorance *versus* knowledge, and the orangutan's grasp of the distinction appeared particularly rapid and competent. This contrasts with the performance of younger chimpanzees (Povinelli *et al.*, 1994) and macaque monkeys (Povinelli *et al.*, 1992b), who did not 'tune in' in this fashion. Thus the adult apes, whilst not demonstrating a grasp of seeing–knowing relationships that smoothly generalises to new situations, express a sensitivity to the signs of such relationships that allows them quickly to learn relevant discriminations and thus use others as social tools in a sophisticated way. Gómez (1991, 1996) suggests that the ability to take into account such ignorance/knowledge differences as some apes come to do is evidence of an intermediate level of social understanding, which he calls an implicit theory of mind. The idea is that the apes may not evidence a theory of mind in which a mental state such as ignorance is explicitly represented; rather, fundamental features of mind are implicit in the connections between seeing (watching) and acting to which the apes are sensitive.

The origins of mindreading? – reading attention

As the results of tests of ape theory of mind increasingly focus interest on such intermediate levels of mindreading, work in developmental psychology has also extended to attempting to trace the origins of the preschool child's theory of mind in earlier grades of mindreading. These can often be characterised as lying in the grey area between sophisticated behaviour-reading and fledgling appreciation of mental phenomena (Whiten, 1994). In this respect one mental state has been of particular interest to both camps – the state of *attention* (particularly visual attention). Attention is a state of mind insofar as it can be considered a mental attitude — at the simplest level, interested *versus* not interested — taken with respect to some external phenomenon. However, visual attention can often be read rather directly in such cues as gaze direction. Accordingly, developmental psychologists have proposed that the infant's ability to tune in to others' attention marks an important step in the development of mindreading. This is evidenced by such phenomena as joint attention to objects in the environment, social referencing (in which the infant assimilates an adult's evaluative reaction to something) and early language acquisition (e.g. see Baldwin & Moses, 1994). Baron-Cohen (1991, 1995) has shown that one of the earliest signs of the mindreading deficits of autism is a failure to recognise others' visual attention. He has suggested that what may be damaged is a specific 'shared attention mechanism' that normally comes into play in the second year, later supporting the development of a full 'theory of mind mechanism'. Whether such a sensitivity is available to primates as embryonic mindreaders is thus a question of obvious interest.

A second, converging reason for interest in attention-reading is that in classifying different types of tactical deception amongst primates. Whiten & Byrne (1988b) found that the bulk of the episodes described were concerned with the manipulation and monitoring of visual attention. Thus, common categories include concealment (of objects, or body parts, for example) from the visual and auditory attention of others, inhibiting one's own attention to prized hidden items, and distracting others by a variety of methods such as gazing intently into the distance. To a Machiavellian primate, an entry-level approach to mindreading through sensitivity to attention makes functional sense, insofar as reading the attention of others affords information on those aspects of the environment that will most probably affect their decision-making, and thence determine future behaviour.

These observations raise a number of questions for further experimental investigation. Perhaps the most basic is whether the perception of ethologists that primates track others' attention at the level of gaze-following, is accurate. Surprisingly, this has only recently been investigated. Povinelli & Eddy (1996a) showed that chimpanzees would follow the gaze of a human towards a locus above and behind them, either as the human shifted their gaze, or when the chimpanzee first saw the human intently staring up. Confirming this ability, I have recently shown that language-trained chimpanzees are able to name objects when the superficially simple, verbal question 'what's that?' is accompanied merely by gaze at a particular object (A. Whiten, unpublished results). Emery *et al.* (1996) have shown that a rhesus macaque will follow the gaze of a conspecific to one side rather than the other.

However, other recent studies have provided conflicting evidence on aspects of the sensitivity of chimpanzees to visual attention. Povinelli & Eddy (1996a) used a paradigm in which a young chimpanzee could choose one of two human partners to help offer it food, with the visual access of one partner restricted compared to the other. When one faced towards the chimpanzee and another away, the chimpanzee chose the one facing them. However, the subjects did not discriminate between a human with a blindfold over their eyes, and one with the blindfold over their mouth. Moreover, they were also initially indiscriminate with respect to a range of other conditions in which one partner could not see them because of screens over the face or head, hands over eyes, eyes shut, or looking distractedly away. Although Povinelli and Eddy note that it remains possible that older chimpanzees are more discriminating, these young chimpanzees expressed very little appreciation of the conditions of 'seeing'. However, the Povinelli and Eddy tests may be harder than they appear at first sight. It is surprising that a comparison sample of children just under 3 years of age failed to discriminate the person looking at them to another holding a screen over their eyes, given that other experiments show such children have a good grasp of the conditions of 'seeing' (Flavell *et al.*, 1981). The children did, however, discriminate Povinelli and Eddy's hands-over-eyes condition, which the chimpanzees did not.

Gómez, Teixidor and Laa (reported in Gómez, 1995; see also Gómez, 1996), using a different approach with six young chimpanzees, obtained some apparently contrary results.[1] They recorded attempts by the ape to attract the attention of a human partner to help obtain food, in different conditions of attention. For three chimpanzees who already had extensive human contact, attention-getting behaviour (mostly touching, and vocalising) was scarcely seen when the human was looking at the chimpanzee, but it occurred on most occasions when the human was looking away to the side (82%), looking up (100%) had eyes closed (60%), or looked at an object (75%). Povinelli and Eddy report that their chimpanzees' performance improved in later trials, so it may be that, not implausiby, the sensitivity shown by these three chimpanzees in the experiment of Gómez

---

[1] Preliminary data reported in Gómez (1996) differ slightly from the final figures described by Gómez (1995): I am grateful to the author for the latter figures, reported here.

et al. has been refined through repeated everyday interactions with humans. A convergent result comes from an experiment incorporating a similar design by Call & Tomasello (1994). A hand-reared orangutan gestured to a human for aid preferentially when the person looked towards them, compared to a condition in which the eyes were closed: whereas another orangutan lacking this human rearing experience discriminated only the cruder contrast of a person looking at them *versus* turning away.

It is easy to appreciate that reading of attention could be a bridge to deeper mindreading, as Baron-Cohen suggests with respect to human development, and the same could be true in evolution: but is attention-reading really any level of mindreading in its own right? The positive results described above could all be interpreted as a facility in just reading a particular aspect of behaviour, namely the relative positions of the head and eyes. Povinelli & Eddy (1996a) argue that although their results show chimpanzees can follow gaze, the negative findings on visual occlusion suggest that chimpanzees do not read into that gaze any intentional significance – that attention is *about* something. Two experiments begin to address this issue. In one (Povinelli & Eddy, 1996b), a chimpanzee faced a human through an open window, so that when the human gazed intently somewhat to the side, their attention would be focused on a part of the dividing wall that the chimpanzee could not see from its own side. Inside the chimpanzee's room a target was placed on the wall, at a point that would have been the terminus of the human's gaze if the wall were transparent. When the human stared along this line, the chimpanzee did not look at the target in its room, but attempted to peer round the side of the window at the true locus of the human's attention. This shows that the chimpanzee can take the visual perspective of another, as suggested earlier by observations of spontaneous social interactions (de Waal, 1986; and see Tanner & Byrne, 1993, for gorillas), and can also appreciate the significance of visual occlusion in this context. In addition it suggests that when chimpanzees see overt visual attention, they expect this to be about something with a specific and realistic location in space.

This last interpretation is consistent with results of the second relevant experiment, that by A. Whiten (unpublished results) outlined earlier, with language-trained chimpanzees. In this experiment, the chimpanzee subject faced a human, who then looked at one of several objects arranged in an arc around them and asked the question, 'what's that?'. This is a question normally asked only by a person holding up an object in their hand or tapping one, so that it was not known if the question would have any meaning for the apes. In fact it did, both subjects performing near-perfectly on their first trials of four objects each. This reinforces the conclusion that chimpanzees do in fact see visual attention as 'about' something. Similar reasoning has been applied to the tendency of 18 month old infants to learn the name of an object that their parent names whilst visually attending to it (Baldwin & Moses, 1994). Baldwin and Moses conclude that this can only occur if the infant sees the parent's attention as a kind of psychological spotlight that makes sense of referential communication. For the Machiavellian primate, the advantage of perceiving attention as 'about things' could lead to more sophisticated strategies to search for the objects of another's attention, or attempt to control or shift it from one focus to another more to one's advantage.

Reading volition

Wellman (1991) showed that 2 year old children have some (verbal) apprecation of the state of desire and its implications for emotions and actions. Gergely et al. (1995) have shown that preverbal 1 year olds perceive goal-directedness even in quite abstract movements, and Baron-Cohen (1995) has argued on the basis of this and related evidence that an 'intentionality detector' is operating at a very early stage in the ontogeny of the human mindreading system.

Reading of comparable aspects of intention by non-human primates is plausible but remains uninvestigated in any formal manner. Of course, primates are able to read the intentions of others in many contexts: an infant may read its mother's intent to leave, for example, and jump onto her; and an ally may read the intent of their partner to attack a third party. However, this sense of reading intent probably applies to many other animals, such as a female gull assessing whether a male intends to attack or court her.

Assessment of true intent becomes a major issue in the case of deception, and episodes of counter-deception, particularly in apes, suggest a sophisticated ability to discriminate real from apparent intentions, as noted earlier. D. J. Povinelli, H. K. Perilloux, J. E. Reaux and D. Bierschwale (unpublished results) have examined a related, but different discrimination, between intended and unintended, accidental actions. If in Machiavellian society it is important to discriminate who really means you harm, it could be important to be able to discount negative incidents not intended by particular individuals. In these experiments, young mpanzees were denied food and drink through what were actually staged incidents. In some of these, the food and drink appeared to be lost through accident, and in others it was caused by intentionally withholding the supply or by deliberate third party interventions in the supply process. None of these differences were found to affect the subjects' subsequent attitude to the various actors in a later preference test, suggesting that the distinctions are not as relevant to chimpanzees as the hypothesis of mindreading would predict. However, the chimpanzees also did not discriminate these conditions from one in which they received the resources as usual, indicating that the losses they suffered in the experimental conditions were not of sufficient consequence to powerfully test the intentional/accidental contrast.

Summary and conclusions

The empirical study of mindreading has expanded enormously in the period since *Machiavellian Intelligence* was published.[2] Principally this has concerned child development, but it is also the case that much more work has been done on non-human primates than in the period before. However, investigators of primate mindreading remain few and the studies can still be fitted into one table (see Table 6.1), such that the field is still in its infancy, grappling with fundamental conceptual issues about what shall count as mindreading and how it can properly be tested in non-verbal subjects. In addition most studies of both children and non-humans have been experimental 'laboratory' investigations, so that conclusions about the functional context of mindreading, whether Machiavellian or not, are frustratingly difficult to draw.

Nevertheless, there are a few such studies and I have used these to sketch the picture that begins to emerge. In the development of the child, early signs of an appreciation of states of mind emerges in the case of reading attention, and this is now being proposed by several theorists as a key developmental step. The contexts in which these early steps are taken may be relatively co-operative, such as enjoyable games establishing the beginnings of joint prelinguistic and early linguistic communication.

---

[2] The study of mindreading may yet be in its infancy, but several issues are nevertheless beyond the scope of this chapter, which has focused on mindreading in the context of complex social interaction. For a discussion of relationships between mindreading and other aspects of social cognition including imitation, pretence and self-recogntion, the reader is referred to Gallup (1982), Whiten & Byrne (1991), Povinelli (1993), Byrne (1995) and Whiten (1996b).

By contrast, a year or two later in childhood, there is evidence that further refinements in theory of mind are honed by more narrowly Machiavellian interactions involving self-interested social manipulaton of others, disputes and the beginnings of deception.

In non-human primates, the context appears in general more Machiavellian. The most altruistic context for putative mindreading is probably teaching in wild chimpanzees (Boesch, 1991), but such observations seem much rarer than those concerning manipulation and deception (Goodall, 1986; Byrne & Whiten, 1990). Neither the observations nor experiments to date offer evidence that such deception is based on an intention to create false beliefs, although many records of tactical deception remain consistent with that possibility and anything approaching a full 'Sally–Anne' test still remains to be published. What the observations of tactical deception do portray is a quite rich sensitivity to the conditions of informational access and their implications for others' likely actions, which is aptly termed 'mindreading'; this is a conclusion supported by some of the experimental tests with chimpanzees, but in conflict with other experiments showing a failure to appreciate all but the crudest aspects of 'seeing' (Povinelli, 1996).

Evidence that visual attention is monitored and manipulated in self and others during primates' social manouevring is of particular interest given the role currently ascribed to a capacity for shared attention in the ontogeny of the human mindreading system. Although gaze monitoring can operate at the level of behaviour-reading, some lines of evidence, parallel to those appealed to in the case of human infants, support the hypothesis that some primates perceive visual attention in a mentalistic way, as being 'about' something in the world and thus linking with actions in principled ways, as recognised in humans' theory of mind.

The subject of Premack and Woodruff's original experiments, recognition of volitional states, has been relatively little studied, although like the reading of attention it has been proposed as an early achievement in the ontogeny of the human mindreading system, and it is central to Krebs and Dawkins' ideas about the evolution of mindreading. Reading others' intentions may be an accomplishment much more widespread in the animal kingdom than in primates alone. What is of more interest, both in its cognitive implications and the context of Machiavellian behaviour, is the capacity suggested by observations and experiments to discriminate true states of mind from overt behaviour in the case of false intent (deception and counter-deception).

So are monkeys and apes Machiavellian mindreaders? Some appear clearly to be so: young human children. By the age of 2–3 years children are clearly developing a theory of mind, and evidence was reviewed suggesting that a key context for such development is Machiavellian social interactions. Whether we give an affirmative answer for other taxa depends very much on how we define mindreading and the criteria we emphasise amongst the several distinguished on page 150 (Whiten, 1996a,b). Despite the increase in numbers of studies since 1988, they remain small in absolute number. No systematic experiments have yet appealed to the stronger criteria for the non-verbal reading of states of mind (intervening variables and experience projection): instead they tend to rely on counter-deception and implicit mindreading. Positive results using these criteria are more vulnerable to interpretation as 'just sophisticated behaviour reading' (Whiten & Perner, 1991). But to the extent that even human mindreading *is* sophisticated behaviour-reading, the study of mindreading even by these criteria has been valuable in demonstrating primates' sensitivities to some of those manifestations of mind – such as attention – which are crucial to the functioning of our own thorough-going mentalism.

Acknowledgements

For comments on an earlier version of this paper I am grateful to Richard Byrne, Judy Dunn, Juan-Carlos Gómez, Daniel Povinelli and Iain Wallace.

References

Astington, J. W., Harris, P. L. & Olson, D. (eds) (1988) *Developing Theories of Mind.* Cambridge: Cambridge University Press.

Baldwin, D. A. & Moses, L. J. (1994). Early understanding of referential intent and attentional focus: Evidence from language and emotion. In *Children's Early Understanding of Mind: Origins and Development,* ed. C. Lewis & P. Mitchell, pp. 133–56. Hillsdale, NJ: Lawrence Erlbaum Associates.

Baron-Cohen, S. (1989). The autistic child's theory of mind: A case of specific developmental delay. *Journal of Child Psychology and Psychiatry,* 30, 285–98.

Baron-Cohen, S. (1991). Precursors to a theory of mind: understanding attention in others. In *Natural Theories of Mind: Evolution, Development and Simulation in Everyday Mindreading,* ed. A. Whiten, pp. 233–51. Oxford: Basil Blackwell.

Baron-Cohen, S. (1995). *Mindblindness: An Essay on Autism and Theory of Mind.* Cambridge, MA: Bradford/MIT Press.

Baron-Cohen, S., Leslie, A. M. & Frith, U. (1985). Does the autistic child have a 'theory of mind'? Cognition, 21, 37–46.

Baron-Cohen, S., Tager-Flusberg, H. & Cohen, D. J. (eds) (1993) Understanding Other Minds: Perspectives from Autism. Oxford: Oxford University Press.

Boesch, C. (1991) Teaching among wild chimpanzees. Animal Behaviour, 41, 530–2.

Bloom, L. & Capatides, J. B. (1987). Sources of meaning in the acquisition of complex syntax: The sample case of causality. Journal of Experimental Child Psychology, 43, 112–28.

Boysen, S. T. & Berntson, G. G. (1995). Responses to quantity versus cognitive mechanisms in chimpanzees (Pan troglodytes). Journal of Experimental Psychology: Animal Behaviour Processes, 21, 82–6.

Bråten, S. (1997). Intersubjective Communication and Emotion in Ontogeny: A Sourcebook. New York: Cambridge University Press. (In press.)

Butterworth, G., Harris, P. L., Leslie, A. M. & Wellman, H. M. (eds) (1991). Perspectives on the Child's Theory of Mind. Oxford: Oxford University Press.

Byrne, R. W. (1995) The Thinking Ape: Evolutionary Origins of Intelligence Oxford: Oxford University Press.

Byrne, R. W. & Whiten, A. (1990). Tactical deception in primates: The 1990 database. Primate Report, 27, 1–101.

Byrne, R. W. & Whiten, A. (1991). Computation and mindreading in primate tactical deception. In Natural Theories of Mind: Evolution, Development and Simulation in Everyday Mindreading, ed. A. Whiten, pp. 127–41. Oxford: Basil Blackwell.

Byrne, R. W. & Whiten, A. (1992). Cognitive evolution in primates: Evidence from tactical deception. Man, 27, 609–27.

Call, J. & Tomasello, M. (1994). Production and comprehension of referential pointing by orangutans (Pongo pygmaeus). Journal of Comparative Psychology, 108, 307–17.

Carruthers, P. & Smith, P. K. (eds) (1996). Theories of Theories of Mind. Cambridge: Cambridge University Press.

Chandler, M. & Hala, S. (1994). The role of personal involvement in the assessment of early false belief skills. In Children's Early Understanding of Mind: Origins and Development, ed. C. Lewis & P. Mitchell, pp. 403–25. Hillsdale, NJ: Lawrence Erlbaum Associates.

Chandler, M., Fritz, A. S. & Hala, S. (1989). Small scale deceit: Deception as a marker of 2, 3 and 4 year olds' early theories of mind. Child Development, 60, 1263–77.

Cheney, D. L. & Seyfarth, R. M. (1990). How Monkeys See the World: Inside the Mind of Another Species. Chicago: University of Chicago Press.

Davies, M. & Stone, T. (1995). Folk Psychology and the Theory of Mind Debate. Oxford: Basil Blackwell.

Dawkins, R. & Krebs, J. R. (1978). Animal signals: Information or manipulation? In Behavoural Ecology: An Evolutionary Approach, ed. J. R. Krebs & N. B. Davies, pp. 282–308. Oxford: Blackwell Scientific Publications.

de Waal, F. B. M. (1986). Deception in the natural communication of chimpanzees. In Deception: Perspectives on Human and Non-Human Deceit, ed. R. W. Mitchell & N. S. Thompson, pp. 221–44. Albany, NY: SUNY Press.

Dunn, J. (1988). The Beginnings of Social Understanding. Oxford: Basil Blackwell.

Dunn, J. (1991). Understanding others: evidence from naturalistic studies of children. In *Natural Theories of Mind: Evolution, Development and Simulation in Everyday Mindreading*, ed. A. Whiten, pp. 51–61. Oxford: Basil Blackwell.

Dunn, J. (1994). Changing minds and changing relationships. In *Children's Early Understanding of Mind: Origins and Development*, ed. C. Lewis & P. Mitchell, pp. 297–310. Hillsdale, NJ: Lawrence Erlbaum Associates.

Dunn, J. & Brown, J. R. (1993). Early conversations about causality: Content, pragmatics and developmental change. *British Journal of Developmental Psychology*, 11(2), 107–23.

Emery, N. J., Lorincz, E. N., Perrett, D. I., Oram, M. W. & Baker, C. I. (1996). Shared visual attention in the rhesus monkey. Paper presented at the 3rd Annual Cognitive Neuroscience Society Meeting, San Francisco, CA, 31 March–2 April.

Flavell, J. H., Everett, B. A., Croft, K. & Flavell, E. R. (1981). Young children's knowledge about visual perception: Further evidence for the Level 1–Level 2 distinction. *Developmental Psychology*, 17, 99–103.

Frith, U. (1989a). *Autism: Explaining the Enigma*. Oxford: Oxford University Press.

Frye, D. & Moore, C. (1991). *Children's Theories of Mind*. Hove, U.K.: Lawrence Erlbaum Associates.

Gallup, G. G. (1982). Self-awareness and the emergence of mind in primates. *American Journal of Primatology*, 2, 237–48.

Gergeley, G., Nadasdy, Z., Csibra, G. & Biro, S. (1995). Taking the intentional stance at 12 months of age. *Cognition*, 56, 165–93.

Gómez, J.-C. (1991). Visual behaviour as a window for reading the mind of others in primates. In *Natural Theories of Mind: Evolution, Development and Simulation of Everyday Mindreading*, ed. A. Whiten, pp. 195–207. Oxford: Basil Blackwell.

Gómez, J.-C. (1995). Eye gaze, attention and the evolution of mindreading in primates. Paper presented at the Annual Conference of the Jean Piaget Society, 'Piaget, Evolution and Development', Berkeley, CA, 1–3 June.

Gómez, J.-C. (1996). Nonhuman primate theories of (nonhuman primate) minds: Some issues concerning the origins of mindreading. In *Theories of Theories of Mind*, ed. P. Carruthers & P. K. Smith, pp. 330–343. Cambridge: Cambridge University Press.

Gómez, J.-C. & Teixidor, P. (1992). Theory of mind in an orangutan: A nonverbal test of false-belief appreciation? Paper presented at the XIV Congress of the International Primatological Society, Strasbourg, 16–21 August.

Goodall, J. (1986). *The Chimpanzees of Gombe: Patterns of Behavior*. Cambridge, MA: The Belknap Press.

Happe, F. (1994). *Autism*. London: UCL.

Harris, P. L. (1991). The work of the imagination. In *Natural Theories of Mind: Evolution, Development and Simulation of Everyday Mindreading*, ed. A. Whitten, pp. 283–304. Oxford: Basil Blackwell.

Heyes, C. M. (1993). Anecdotes, training, trapping and triangulating: Do animals attribute mental states? *Animal Behaviour*, 46, 177–88.

Humphrey, N. K. (1980). Nature's psychologists. In *Consciousness and the Physical World*, ed. B. Josephson & V. Ramachandran, pp. 57–80. Oxford: Pergammon Press.

Humphrey, N. K. (1986). *The Inner Eye.* London: Faber and Faber.

Krebs, J. R. & Dawkins, R. (1984). Animal signals: Mind reading and manipulation. In *Behavioural Ecology: An Evolutionary Approach,* ed. J. R. Krebs & N. B. Davies, pp. 380–401. Oxford: Blackwell Scientific Publications.

Lewis, C. & Mitchell, P. (eds) (1994). *Children's Early Understanding of Mind: Origins and Development.* Hillsdale, NJ: Lawrence Erlbaum Associates.

Lloyd-Morgan, C. (1930). *The Animal Mind.* London: Edward Arnold.

Menzel, E. (1974). A group of young chimpanzees in a one-acre field. In *Behaviour of Non-human Primates,* ed. M. Schrier & F. Stolnitz, vol. 5, pp. 83–153. New York: Academic Press.

Menzel, E. W. & Johnson, M. K. (1976). Communication and cognitive organisation in humans and other animals. *Annals of the New York Academy of Sciences,* 280, 131–42.

Mitchell, P. (1994). Realism and early conception of mind: A synthesis of phylogenetic and ontogenetic issues. In *Children's Early Understanding of Mind: Origins and Development,* ed. C. Lewis & P. Mitchell, pp. 19–45. Hillsdale, NJ: Lawrence Erlbaum Associates.

Moore, C. & Dunham, P. (1994). *Joint Attention: Its Origin and Role in Development.* Hillsdale, NJ: Lawrence Erlbaum Associates.

Perner, J. (1991). *Understanding the Representational Mind.* Cambridge, MA: Bradford/MIT.

Perner, J., Baker, S. & Hutton, D. (1994). Prelief: The conceptual origins of belief and pretence. In *Children's Early Understanding of Mind: Origins and Development,* ed. C. Lewis & P. Mitchell, pp. 261–86. Hillsdale, NJ: Lawrence Erlbaum Associates.

Perner, J., Frith, U., Leslie, A. M. & Leekam, S. (1989). Exploration of the autistic child's theory of mind: Knowledge, belief and communication. *Child Development,* 60, 689–700.

Povinelli, D. J. (1991). Social Intelligence in Monkeys and Apes. PhD thesis, Yale University, New Haven, CT.

Povinelli, D. J. (1993). Reconstructing the evolution of mind. *American Psychologist,* 48, 493–509.

Povinelli, D. J. (1994). Comparative studies of animal mental state attribution: A reply to Heyes. *Animal Behaviour,* 48, 239–41.

Povinelli, D. J. (1996). Chimpanzee theory of mind: The long road to strong inference. In *Theories of Theories of Mind,* ed. P. Carruthers & P. K. Smith, pp. 293–329. Cambridge: Cambridge University Press.

Povinelli, D. J. & deBlois, S. (1992). Young children's understanding of knowledge formation in themselves and others. *Journal of Comparitive Psychology,* 106, 228–38.

Povinelli, D. J. & Eddy, T. J. (1996a). What young chimpanzees know about seeing. *Monographs of the Society for Research in Child Development,* vol. 61, no. 2, Serial No. 247.

Povinelli, D.J. & Eddy, T.J. (1996b). Chimpanzees: Joint visual attention. *Psychological Science,* 7, 129–35.

Povinelli, D. J., Nelson, K. E. & Boysen, S. T. (1990). Inferences about guessing and knowing by chimpanzees (*Pan troglodytes*). *Journal of Comparative Psychology,* 104, 203–10.

Povinelli, D. J., Nelson, K. E. & Boysen, S. T. (1992a). Comprehension of role reversal in chimpanzees: Evidence of empathy? *Animal Behaviour*, **43**, 633–40.

Povinelli, D. J., Parks, K. A. & Novak, M. A. (1992b). Do rhesus monkeys (*Macaca mulatta*) attribute knowledge and ignorance to others? *Journal of Comparative Psychology*, **105**, 318–25.

Povinelli, D. J., Parks, K. A. & Novak, M. A. (1992c). Role reversal by rhesus monkeys; but no evidence of empathy. *Animal Behaviour*, **44**, 269–81.

Povinelli, D. J., Rulf, A. B. & Bierschwale, D. T. (1994). Absence of knowledge attribution and self-recognition in young chimpanzees (*Pan troglodytes*). *Journal of Comparative Psychology*, **108**, 74–80.

Premack, D. (1988). Does the chimpanzee have a theory of mind? revisited. In *Machiavellian Intelligence: Social Expertise and the Evolution of Intellect in Monkeys, Apes and Humans*, ed. R. W. Byrne & A. Whiten, pp. 160–79. Oxford: Clarendon Press.

Premack, D. & Woodruff, G. (1978). Does the chimpanzee have a theory of mind? *Behavioral and Brain Sciences*, **1**, 515–26.

Reddy, V. (1991). Playing with other's expectations?: Teasing and mucking about in the first year. In *Natural Theories of Mind: Evolution, Development and Simulation of Everyday Mindreading*, ed. A. Whiten, pp. 143–58. Oxford: Basil Blackwell.

Russell, J., Mauthner, N., Sharpe, S. & Tidswell, T. (1991). The "windows task" as a measure of strategic deception in pre-schoolers and autistic subjects. *British Journal of Developmental Psychology*, **9**, 331–49.

Savage-Rumbaugh, E. S. (1986). *Ape Language: From Conditioned Response to Symbol*. New York: Columbian University Press.

Sodian, B. (1991). The development of deception in young children. *British Journal of Developmental Psychology*, **9**, 173–88.

Sodian, B. (1994). Early deception and the conceptual continuity claim. In *Children's Early Understanding of Mind: Origins and Development*, ed. C. Lewis & P. Mitchell, pp. 385–401. Hillsdale, NJ: Lawrence Erlbaum Associates.

Stone, T. & Davies, M. (1995). *Mental Simulation: Evaluation and Applications*. Oxford: Basil Blackwell.

Tanner, J. E. & Byrne, R. W. (1993). Concealing facial evidence of mood: Perspective-taking in a captive gorilla? *Primates*, **34**, 451–7.

Thorndike, E. L. (1911). *Animal Intelligence*. New York: Macmillan.

Wellman, H. M. (1991). From desires to beliefs: Acquisition of a theory of mind. In *Natural Theories of Mind: Evolution, Development and Simulation of Everyday Mindreading*, ed. A. Whiten, pp. 19–38. Oxford: Basil Blackwell.

Whiten, A. (1991a). The emergence of mindreading: Steps towards an interdisciplinary enterprise. In *Natural Theories of Mind: Evolution, Development and Stimulation of Everyday Mindreading*, ed. A. Whiten, pp. 319–31. Oxford: Basil Blackwell.

Whiten, A. (ed.) (1991b). *Natural Theories of Mind: Evolution, Development and Simulation of Everyday Mindreading*. Oxford: Basil Blackwell.

Whiten, A. (1993a). Evolving a theory of mind: The nature of non-verbal mentalism in other primates. In *Understanding Other Minds: Perspectives from Autism*, ed. S. Baron-Cohen, H. Tager-Flusberg & D. J. Cohen, pp. 367–96. Oxford: Oxford University Press.

Whiten, A. (1993b). Deception in animal communication. In *The Pergamon Encyclopedia of Language and Linguistics*, ed. R. E. Asher, pp. 829–32. Oxford: Pergamon Press.

Whiten, A. (1994). Grades of mindreading. In *Origins of an Understanding of Mind*, ed. C. Lewis & P. Mitchell, pp. 47–70. Hillsdale, NJ: Lawrence Erlbaum Associates.

Whiten, A. (1996a). When does smart behaviour-reading become mind-reading? In *Theories of Theories of Mind*, ed. P. Carruthers & P. K. Smith, pp. 227–92. Cambridge: Cambridge University Press.

Whiten, A. (1996b) Imitation, pretence and mindreading: Secondary representation in comparative primatology and developmental psychology? In *Reaching Into Thought: The Minds of the Great Apes*, ed. A. E. Russon, K. A. Bard & S. T. Parker, pp. 300–24. Cambridge: Cambridge University Press.

Whiten, A. & Byrne, R. W. (1986). The St. Andrews catalogue of tactical deception in primates. *St. Andrews' Psychological Reports*, 10, 1–47.

Whiten, A. & Byrne, R. W. (1988a). Tactical deception in primates. *Behavioral and Brain Sciences*, 11, 233–73.

Whiten, A. & Byrne, R. W. (1988b). The manipulation of attention in primate tactical deception. In *Machiavellian Intelligence: Social Expertise and the Evolution of Intellect in Monkeys, Apes and Humans*, ed. R. W. Byrne & A. Whiten, pp. 211–23. Oxford: Clarendon Press.

Whiten, A. & Byrne, R. W. (1991). The emergence of metarepresentation in human ontogeny and primate phylogeny. In *Natural Theories of Mind: Evolution, Development and Simulation in Everyday Mindreading*, ed. A. Whiten, pp. 267–81. Oxford: Basil Blackwell.

Whiten, A. & Perner, J. (1991). Fundamental issues in the multidisciplinary study of mindreading. In *Natural Theories of Mind: Evolution, Development and Simulation in Everyday Mindreading*, ed. A. Whiten, pp. 1–17. Oxford: Basil Blackwell.

Wimmer, H. & Perner, J. (1983). Beliefs about beliefs: Representation and constraining function of wrong beliefs in young children's understanding of deception. *Cognition*, 13, 103–28.

7 Exploiting the expertise of others

ANNE E. RUSSON

In 1988, Byrne and Whiten coined the phrase *Machiavellian intelligence* to portray primate intelligence as geared primarily to the sorts of conniving we ascribe to Machiavelli – deceit, cunning, and other manipulative, self-serving tactics – in short, to navigating the social, not the physical world. As they point out in this second edition (Chapter 1), intelligence honed for sociality may employ strategies for gaining social advantage beyond self-serving social manoeuvres, such as exploiting others' expertise. Exploiting expertise has many faces, for many reasons. It can aim at varied targets – expertise itself, such as *knowledge* or *skills*, or the products of expertise, especially *resources* such as food. There are two sides to the story of exploitation, as there are with most social stories – the exploiter's and the exploited's. Exploiters come in many guises, from learners and partners to bullies and thieves. So do the exploited, from co-operative, supportive teachers, sharing partners and tolerant mothers, to unwilling, niggardly hoarders or even neutral, naive dupes; and their responses can affect the nature and success of the ploys exploiters use. All these sides of the story suggest a number of broad factors behind primates' efforts at exploiting others (see Table 7.1). Exploitation may also vary within the primates because of differences in intellectual capacity between primate species, notably between monkeys and great apes. This chapter explores some of the ways in which non-human primates exploit one another's expertise and how various tactical roles come into play when they do.

Exploiting others' expertise

Exploiting others' knowledge entails the social transfer of knowledge and skills. This occurs in many species, including many mammals and birds

Table 7.1 *Machiavellian primate tactics in the game of social exploitation*

Gained or lost	Exploiters' tactics	Tactics of the exploited		
		Defend	Tolerate	Donate
Knowledge	Social learning (imitation)	Lie	Vary or grade tolerance	Teach
'Fruits' of knowledge	Scrounge	Fight, hide	Tolerate scrounging	Share

(e.g. Boyd & Richerson, 1988; Zentall & Galef, 1988). The primate order should be prominent among them because primates characteristically rely on intricate forms of *sociality* for survival (e.g. Jolly, 1966; Fedigan, 1982; Smuts *et al.*, 1987) and on *life-long learning* for acquiring much essential expertise (e.g. Fobes & King, 1982; Parker & Gibson, 1990; King, 1994a, b).

Evidence that non-human primates acquire important expertise socially has been proffered since the earliest days of scientific primatology. Over 40 years ago, Japanese primatologists traced the spread of food handling techniques such as sweet potato washing and 'placer mining' for separating wheat grains from sand within troops of Japanese macaques (e.g. Imanishi, 1952, 1957; Itani, 1954, 1958/1965; Kawamura, 1954; Kawai, 1965). Research into the 1970s confirmed the centrality of social experience in forming non-human primates' skills and knowledge: the black period of social deprivation studies showed the devastating effects that lack of social experience has on non-human primate abilities (e.g. Rogers, 1973); communication studies showed the elaborate signal systems used by non-human primates to transfer information socially (e.g. Altmann, 1967; van Hooff, 1967); studies on social structures traced the social channels along which information travels in primate societies (e.g. Kummer, 1967; Itani & Nishimura, 1973); and a few studies suggested primates' abilities to glean information about external events from subtle cues in the behaviour of knowledgeable individuals (e.g. Menzel, 1973).

The Machiavellian intelligence hypothesis marked growing interest in the mechanisms underlying these capacities – precisely how, mentally, non-human primates were transferring information socially and what sorts of information they were exchanging. At the time, little was known. It was not known, for instance, whether the mechanisms that govern learning from social partners differ from those that govern learning from direct experience with problems. Since then much effort has been devoted to these very issues, as well as to exploring the relations between social and ecological intelligence. The range and sophistication of these mechanisms govern what expertise non-human primates can exploit from one another, so these mechanisms are the first issues to address.

Exploiting knowledge: Social learning

The mechanisms nonhuman primates use to exploit others' expertise have been studied under the rubric of *social learning*, the general term for learning that takes some input from other individuals. Learning refers to relatively permanent but modifiable changes in an individual that can be detected in its behaviour and that are caused by specific experiences (e.g. Rescorla, 1988). Social learning is then distinguished from *individual learning*, also called ecological or asocial learning, which derives from experiences with the physical world alone (Box, 1984; Heyes, 1994).

Social learning then concerns not *what* expertise is acquired, but *how* expertise is acquired. It is also a mere extension of individual learning — it is individual learning to which some social influences have been added. This formulation is partially a product of the way history unfolded. The concept of social learning is a recent one; it was introduced in 1984, by Box, who pointed out that learning can result from social *as well as* asocial experiences. To fit it into the existing conceptual and theoretical structures of animal learning theory, the contemporary rendition of association and instrumental learning used by many comparative psychologists, it was conceived of in relation to individual learning.

The mechanisms of social learning could then be a very mixed bag because they include mechanisms that handle social *in addition to* physical input. Some comparative psychologists have argued recently, however, that non-human social learning is really no different from individual learning (e.g. Heyes, 1994). What happens is learning, period. Social learning accepts some different input than individual learning does — stimuli and reinforcers can be social as well as ecological, but the same mechanisms are employed — linking old behaviour with new circumstances (association or classical learning) and modifying old behaviour to fit new circumstances (instrumental or operant learning).

There are several reasons to think that non-human primates, at least, use additional mechanisms in their social learning. The animal learning view entails two presumptions that may not hold for some primates: (a) animal learning results from experiences, primarily physical, asocial ones; and (b) animal learning is limited to associative and instrumental mechanisms, so sophisticated mechanisms such as imitation and cultural learning are not available (Boyd & Richerson, 1988). However, social partners generate experiences too and their input is qualitatively different from physical input. Social partners are animate, not inanimate; they are active agents, not passive respondants; and they produce stimuli designed to activate conspecifics, for example ritualised displays. Learners from social species may have special sensitivities to social input; for instance, they may attend preferentially to social over non-social stimuli and they may be predisposed to respond in predetermined ways to social signals. In addition, some primates, the great apes at least, are capable of mental operations beyond associative and instrumental learning (e.g. Byrne, 1995; Russon et al., 1996); this opens the possibility of sophisticated social learning mechanisms. Good candidates for special social mechanisms in primate social learning are then *priming* and *imitation*.

Byrne (1994) argues that *priming*, increasing the accessibility or retrievability of mental records a learner has already created and stored, may play a major role in social learning. Observing social partners use particular items or actions can prime the observer's brain records of the same items or actions, and these primed records tend to become the key factors in the observer's subsequent learning. Byrne suggests that what comparative psychologists have considered to be several different social learning mechanisms may all reflect priming: stimulus enhancement (partners draw observers' attention to particular stimuli), contagion (partners' unlearned reactions, especially emotional ones, trigger similar reactions in observers), emulation (partners draw observers' attention to their goals or outcomes), and response facilitation (partners' learned behaviours elicit similar behaviour in observers) (for current views, see Galef, 1988; Tomasello, 1990; Moore, 1992; Whiten & Ham, 1992; Byrne, 1994). The role of priming in primate social learning may vary according to partners' relationships with observers because primate social exchanges tend to be channelled along lines defined by long-term relationships (e.g. parent–offspring, friendship, dominance: e.g. Huffman, 1984; Huffman & Quiatt, 1986). Friends or parents, for instance, may more strongly influence observers' learning than others do. Priming influences on learning are indirect – priming does not bring about learning itself, it merely orientates learning – but its effects can be nonetheless profound. Some primates have learned new behaviour only after observing a preferred partner perform it (e.g. Sumita *et al.*, 1985).

Imitation, also called imitative learning or true imitation, is an elite form of social learning that involves 'learning to do an act by seeing it done' (Thorndike, 1898, p. 50). Much of the newer understanding of social learning mechanisms in non-human primates is due to renewed interest in imitation. The simple definition is deceptive; on investigation, it entails great complexity. It implies that the behaviour learned is a *copy* of that observed; the copy matches the observed behaviour *by design*; observation is *necessary* and *sufficient* for learning to occur; the copy is learned *without practice* – so, by mechanisms beyond individual learning; the behaviour's *form* is copied, not merely its orientation or outcomes; and *new* behaviour for which learners have *no instinctive tendency* can be acquired (e.g. Thorpe, 1963; Mitchell, 1987; Galef, 1988; Visalberghi & Fragaszy, 1990; Moore, 1992; Whiten & Ham, 1992).

Imitation is considered special for many reasons. Any mechanism that generates copies is valuable because it enhances the social co-ordination needed for effective communication and harmonious group operation. As a form of learning, imitation is seen as a great leap forward because it is an exceptionally rapid and error-free way of acquiring new expertise – at least, in comparison with tedious, error-plagued individual learning. Imitation has the unusual capacity to translate information about behaviour that was input in one modality (in primates, usually the visual) into output in a different modality (the kinesthetic) so that the resulting behaviour matches the original (Mitchell, 1993). Imitation is considered to reflect symbolic mental processes because it generates behaviour from mental images created by observation, without direct experience; such mental images are considered rudimentary symbols (e.g. Piaget, 1952, 1962). Finally, imitation is considered a cornerstone of culture (e.g. Bonner, 1980; Donald, 1991; Tomasello *et al.*, 1993a; Parker & Russon, 1996).

How then does imitation, this outstanding achievement, figure as Machiavellian? Machiavelli's own work offers an answer. His notorious book, *The Prince*, promotes the use of imitation for social power and suggests who to take as the best models for seizing and keeping political power. Machiavelli even practised what he preached. He copied many of the book's ideas as well as its structure from other works popular at the

Table 7.2 *A brief history of primate imitation*

Belief (1950s–1980s)	*Non-human primates imitate*

*Field studies find imitation (e.g. pre-culture, tool use)
*Captive studies find imitation (Yerkes, 1916; Kohts, 1921, 1928; Kohler, 1925; Yerkes & Yerkes, 1929; Hayes & Hayes, 1952).

Demolition (late 1980s)   *Non-human primates can't imitate*
*Existing evidence rejected for standard methodological reasons
*Great apes re-invent tool use independently
*Monkey traditions spread too slowly, human influence likely

Reinstatement (mid 1990s)   *Apes can imitate*
*Tighter empirical methods devised
*New studies conducted
*Critics converted

Deconstruction (emerging)   *How do apes imitate?*
*Puzzling discrepancies between experimental (weak) and spontaneous (rich and complex) imitation
*Great ape imitation seems fragile and weak
*Imitation may be non-homogeneous, a mixed bag

time (e.g. see Gilbert, 1938; Whitfield, 1965). Imitation is then a strategy *par excellence* for expropriating others' expertise.

Scientists' considered opinions on whether non-human primates can imitate have fluctuated drastically, even recently (see Table 7.2). Non-human primates were believed for many years to imitate because imitative behaviour is prominent in many species. In the late 1980s, when Machiavellian manoeuvres such as imitation came under serious scrutiny as to their intellectual sophistication, this belief was challenged. Challenges stem primarily from beliefs that the symbolic and cultural capacities linked with imitation are intellectual adaptations that evolved uniquely with the human line. That any non-human species might imitate then has serious fallout for these beliefs. But whether primates, or any species, can imitate turns out to be devilishly difficult to prove because many other mechanisms can generate copies.

Firstly, many of the mechanisms that 'mimic' imitation are simple attentional and sensorimotor ones typical of non-human social learning. The proposed list of simple imitative mechanisms is lengthy and it continues to grow (those interested in the excruciating details can consult Galef, 1988; Moore, 1992; Whiten & Ham, 1992). It does seem probable that this list reflects a smaller set of generic social processes, such as priming (which orientates behaviour) and social reinforcement (which effects learning), combined with individual learning (after Whiten & Ham, 1992; Byrne, 1994). For instance, an observer's behaviour can come to match a model's by priming combined with individual learning: the model's behaviour primes the observer to orientate to a subset of stimuli and/or known actions; the observer's behaviour comes to match the model's through individual learning, because in focusing on this subset the observer then undergoes trial-and-error experiences that are similar to those that shaped the model's behaviour. Social partners can also influence learning by reinforcing others' behaviour; if partners favour conformity, their reactions can shape others' behaviour to match a standard. If the behaviours involved are communicative signals, the process has been called *conventionalisation* or, more recently, *ontogenetic ritualisation* (Tomasello, 1990, 1996).

Secondly, developmental and motivational variables have gained little input into this work although both are known to affect imitation in humans (e.g. Piaget, 1962; Yando et al., 1978) and they are likely to be equally significant in non-human primates (e.g. Parker & Gibson, 1990; Russon & Galdikas, 1995). Development may be a particularly important consideration because it is through prolonged development that primates' intellectual abilities are constructed (e.g. Antinucci, 1989; Parker & Gibson, 1990). The ability to imitate develops in humans only near the end of infancy, as symbolic abilities begin to emerge (e.g. see Mitchell, 1987, 1994 for recent reviews). In non-human primates, intellectual development proceeds more slowly than this. Great apes, for instance, achieve symbolic abilities only after 3–4 years of age (e.g. Chevalier-Skolnikoff, 1983; Doré & Dumas, 1987; Langer, 1996; Parker, 1996). An important consideration in testing for non-human primate imitation may then be the ages at which it could be expected to emerge.

Thirdly, even with these theoretical improvements, empirically identifying imitation is problematic. Comparative psychologists consider that imitative behaviour does not clearly point to the mechanisms that produced it, so they use experimental tests of imitation designed to control against intrusions from simpler mechanisms that 'mimic' imitation (e.g.

Thorpe, 1963; Dawson & Foss, 1965; Galef, 1988; Lefebvre & Palameta, 1988; Moore, 1992; Custance & Bard, 1994; Whiten et al., 1966). Examples of controls are: demonstrating only novel behaviour (precluding prior learning), offering observers only a few attempts at imitation (precluding ongoing individual learning), and 'baseline' sessions with the task pre-demonstration (precluding observers' spontaneously producing the demonstrated behaviour). Designs gaining support are Dawson & Foss' (1965) two-action method and Hayes & Hayes' (1952) 'do what I do' method. In the first, subjects observe only one of several techniques for doing a task; if they enact the alternative they observed, evidence is strong for imitation. In the second, subjects are initially trained to follow the general rule, 'copy the action demonstrated'; once they grasp the rule, novel actions are demonstrated; if they copy many of these novel actions, evidence grows against chance resemblance and for imitation. Others consider that experimental tests inevitably lack ecological validity and opt instead to use non-intrusive, naturalistic observational techniques to study spontaneous imitative behaviour. In response to criticisms that spontaneous imitative behaviour is always influenced by other mechanisms, newer procedures collect data on conditions that render mechanisms other than imitation implausible – the imitative behaviour is arbitrary or improbable, it is novel and rapidly acquired, it was not tutored, it could not have been learned individually, etc. (Hauser, 1988; Boesch, 1996; Russon, 1996).

When interest in primate imitation rekindled in the late 1980s, one of the first things scholars did was re-examine the existing claims for primate imitation in the light of these various considerations (e.g. Mitchell, 1987; Galef, 1988; Tomasello, 1990; Visalberghi & Fragaszy, 1990; Moore, 1992; Whiten & Ham, 1992). Consistently, they found most of the existing evidence wanting. As a typical example, Whiten and Ham's review of the last 100 years' research on imitation concluded that all the putative evidence for imitation in monkeys and prosimians (approximately 30 incidents) and a sizable proportion of that for great apes could be explained by mechanisms such as stimulus enhancement and individual learning. These evaluations generated a whole new wave of empirical studies on primate imitation.

Results from this new wave of studies restored faith in at least part of the traditional view: all the great apes can imitate, after 3–4 years of age and under appropriate social and physical rearing and testing conditions (e.g. Byrne & Byrne, 1991, 1993; Russon & Galdikas, 1993, 1995;

Tomasello *et al.*, 1993b; Custance & Bard, 1994; Custance *et al.*, 1994, 1996; Call & Tomasello, 1996; Miles *et al.*, 1996; Visalberghi & Limong-elli, 1996; Whiten *et al.*, 1996). The conclusion that monkeys and prosimians are not capable of imitation, even under propitious conditions, has stood in the face of newer work (e.g. Mitchell & Anderson, 1993; Visalberghi & Limongelli, 1996). Even capuchins, the 'cognitive champions' of monkeys, perform poorly. For example, Brahms, a 5 year old female capuchin, observed Carlotta, another capuchin, get food from a transparent tube by pushing it out with a stick – 57 times; Brahms did retrieve the stick Carlotta left inside the tube but she never tried to use it as a tool (Visalberghi & Limongelli, 1996). In the same test, a 5 year old chimpanzee who had not discovered the stick technique independently started to use it immediately after watching *one* demonstration, 3 and 4 year old chimpanzees acquired it more rapidly after observing demonstrations, and 2 year old chimpanzees did not benefit from demonstrations.

This work does not close the book on imitation in non-human primates. Concerning monkeys, some point out that absence of evidence is not evidence of absence and caution that the jury is still out (e.g. Anderson, 1996). Concerning great apes, it remains puzzling that the imitation experimenters have elicited is fragile and weak – it is very difficult to elicit and it generates only minute changes in behaviour – while the purported imitation in free-ranging great apes entails elaborate, multi-levelled behavioural concoctions such as multi-stage manual preparation of food, nut-cracking with stone hammer-anvil-wedge tool sets, and making fires (e.g. Byrne & Byrne, 1991, 1993; Russon & Galdikas, 1993; Matsuzawa, 1994). Some of the discrepancy probably stems from differences in the living and testing conditions used with experimental *versus* free-living subjects. However, some of the limitations to great ape imitation found experimentally are probably 'real'. Researchers are now searching for explanations.

Several hypotheses have been proposed – one, that great apes can imitate only at the level of *emulation*, reproducing the outcomes but not the behavioural techniques observed (e.g. Tomasello *et al.*, 1987; Tomasello, 1990; Call & Tomasello, 1994); another, that only *enculturated* great apes, those who have been steeped in the trappings of a human culture, achieve imitation (e.g. Tomasello *et al.*, 1993a,b). Neither is holding up. We now have evidence of imitation in non-enculturated great apes (e.g. Whiten *et al.*, 1996; Meinel & Russon, 1996) and of their imitating demonstrated techniques (e.g. Miles *et al.*, 1996; Whiten *et al.*, 1996). A promising alternative stems from our understanding that great apes acquire complex behavioural routines painstakingly, bit by bit, over many years. The contribution of imitation may be various small advances that cumulatively, and in conjunction with other social and individual learning mechanisms, build complex routines (e.g. McGrew, 1977; Nishida, 1987). If great apes do not achieve the ability to imitate until later stages in the acquisition of complex routines, after 3–4 years of age, imitation probably contributes to facets of complex routines that require sophisticated understanding — possibly, the physical relations involved in object or tool manipulations (e.g. Parker & Russon, 1996; Russon, 1996; Visalberghi & Limongelli, 1996). This alternative is consistent with both findings — the experimental ones, that great apes' imitation supports only minute advances per attempt, and the field ones, that imitation is most evident in highly complex routines. But the precise story of how great apes imitate awaits the next round of research.

How non-human primates use social learning

Work on mechanisms addresses the range of expertise that non-human primates *can* exploit socially. What expertise they actually *do* exploit this way is an empirical question. The relevant evidence comes from field observations, not laboratory experiments — the concern is how primates *themselves* use social learning, not how clever experimenters can induce them to use it. It is then unrealistic to expect to identify expertise that is acquired by social mechanisms *alone* because non-human primates acquire much of their expertise gradually, even over many years, using a mixed bag of learning mechanisms. Scholars have therefore looked for circumstantial evidence of *some* social influence in learning — for instance, that a technique is common in one social group but not a neighbouring one, that it spreads faster than individual learning affords, that those who acquire an innovative technique can be predicted from the social relationships of those who already know it, etc. (e.g. Huffman, 1984; Nishida, 1987; McGrew, 1992; Boesch, 1996). It is only in a few special circumstances, such as captive colonies living in 'semi-natural' conditions, that the roles of social learning mechanisms in acquiring expertise can be clearly traced (e.g. Chapais & Gauthier, 1993; Pereira, 1993). For these reasons, evidence about what expertise is socially exploited is often found in discussions of topics such as 'pre-' or 'proto-' cultures, behaviour traditions, gestural 'dialects', and the like.

Social knowledge That non-human primates acquire social expertise by social learning seems almost a truism. This has been demonstrated in several areas.

Non-human primates' social *abilities*, even ones so fundamental to survival that one could expect them to be strongly instinctively governed, are importantly shaped by social learning. For instance, interest in mothering may be instinctively designed, but the expertise must be learned through appropriate social experience. The same tends to be true of other skilled social behaviour such as sexual techniques, age-appropriate behaviour and aggression (e.g. Itani & Nishimura, 1973; Rogers, 1973; Pereira & Fairbanks, 1993). In great apes, some social abilities may be acquired by imitation. For instance, a female chimpanzee attempted an innovative attack technique after observing another chimpanzee use it (de Waal, 1982).

Social learning may play a key role in the *communicative repertoire*, where standardised signals can be essential to effective communication (e.g. Seyfarth *et al.*, 1980; Tomasello *et al.*, 1985; Tanner & Byrne, 1996). Many primate signals appear to originate in functional or innately guided species-typical patterns, but they may be varied or refined by social learning. When chimpanzees groom, for instance, partners may groom one another's underarm area. Grooming patterns that may be functional are an upraised arm, a posture that invites grooming that particular area, and holding a bough overhead during the underarm grooming. In some, but not all, chimpanzee communities, however, a more elaborate, stereotyped pattern is used, the 'grooming handclasp': each partner simultaneously raises one arm overhead then one or both grasps the other's hand or wrist; the other hand grooms the underarm area so revealed (McGrew & Tutin, 1978; Ghiglieri, 1984). Evidence suggests that this stereotyped pattern is most likely a variant created through social learning. Some signals may be due largely to social learning. Bonobos at the San Diego Zoo, for instance, locally created a hand-clapping gesture to communicate pleasurable activities (Ingmanson, 1987) and an adult male lowland gorilla at the San Francisco Zoo developed a whole suite of iconic gestures, including requesting a particular action from his partner by 'drawing' the action through space or on his partner's body (Tanner & Byrne, 1996). Social reinforcement could be one of the mechanisms responsible, shaping signals to the precise forms and uses that elicit desired social effects. This is the process that Tomasello *et al.*(1985) termed conventionalisation. Tomasello (1990) suggested it may contribute to two well-known chimpanzee signals, leaf-clipping and grooming handclasp traditions (McGrew & Tutin, 1978; Nishida, 1980). Boesch (1996), however, reported that the uses of leaf-clipping in Taï chimpanzees changed abruptly and one of the new uses sometimes involved new leaf-clipping techniques. Change this fast is consistent with imitation rather than conventionalisation.

Non-human primates' social *relations* and *roles* are viewed as products of many social interactions (Hinde, 1979) so they too are affected by social learning. Dominance offers a good example. It is widespread in living species – interest originated through the 'pecking orders' of chickens – and it is prominent in many primate species. Dominance is defined generally by asymmetry in the outcomes of social encounters, such that outcomes are systematically more favourable for one partner than the other (for recent discussions of primate dominance, see Smuts *et al.*, 1987; de Waal, 1989; Harcourt & de Waal, 1992; Silverberg & Gray, 1992). In some Old World monkeys that live in matrilineal societies, such as macaques, infant females 'inherit' their mother's dominance rank; they must, however, learn it. Infants learn dominance-related expertise from their own experiences in social conflicts but more importantly from *tripartite encounters*, encounters in which a third party intervenes as an ally of one opponent in order to influence outcomes (Kummer, 1967). In Japanese macaques, for instance, mothers, female kin, and even non-kin systematically intervene in favour of infants from high-ranking over low-ranking families. Infants can learn to identify high- from low-born foes even if they never interacted with these foes themselves (Chapais & Gauthier, 1993). Their learning must be social, stemming from interventions. An interesting contrast is Pereira's (1993) finding of virtually no comparable intervention in the dominance experiences of infant ringtailed lemurs: their dominance expertise was due almost entirely to direct dyadic experience. Pereira suggested cognitive limitations as a plausible explanation for the lack of systematic third party input.

Ecological knowledge Much less obvious is whether non-human primates exploit others' ecological expertise. Behavioural ecologists and animal learning theorists maintain that individual learning is the main process for acquiring physical world expertise in non-human species. Some point out that ecological expertise acquired socially is rapidly outdated when environmental conditions are changeable (see Rogers, 1988; Galef, 1992) so reliance on social sources of expertise is a poor and improbable strategy.

Against these arguments sits 40 years' accumulated evidence of non-human primate *behavioural traditions* of ecological expertise, behaviours for handling ecological problems that spread through members of a social group (e.g. see overviews by Itani & Nishimura, 1973; Nishida, 1987; Galef, 1990; McGrew, 1992). Included are observations like this: A. Zeller (personal communication) offered prunes to a provisioned Gibralter macaque group (*Macaca sylvanus*). Youngsters gobbled them up so the adult male, the group's leader, came to investigate. He picked up a prune, sniffed it, then dropped it. The youngsters immediately stopped eating and picking up the prunes even though the male left. A few days later Zeller offered prunes again; not one individual even looked at them.

Most ecological traditions have been reported in macaques and chimpanzees. Japanese macaque traditions have been studied since the early 1950s; chimpanzee traditions, since the mid-1980s, when long-term evidence from several communities had sufficiently accumulated. Categories of ecological expertise that appear to transfer socially include how space is used (e.g. ranging patterns), attitudes to other creatures (e.g. fear of predators, tolerance or avoidance of humans), identifying food (accepting, rejecting, or preferring items as food), procuring food (extracting or processing food to render it edible), self-medication (ingesting items for medicinal *versus* nutritional purposes) and complex object manipulation (e.g. Itani & Nishimura, 1973; Nishida, 1987; Mineka & Cook, 1988; King, 1991, 1994a,b). The most contentious are procuring food, self-medication and complex object manipulation, because these involve complex techniques that *must* be fine-tuned to ecological contingencies. It seems unlikely that social learning mechanisms such as priming and social reinforcement could generate them because these mechanisms influence ecological techniques only indirectly.

Nonetheless, evidence has been presented for a whole array of traditions of complex techniques for *procuring food*. The Japanese macaque traditions are among the most complex reported for monkeys; classic examples are 'placer mining' to separate wheat from sand and washing sweet potatoes in ocean water (for a review, see Itani & Nishimura, 1973). Examples have also been reported for macaques, baboons and capuchins (for reviews, see Nishida, 1987; Whiten & Ham, 1992). Great apes' traditions include manipulative and tool assisted food processing techniques (e.g. Nishida, 1987; Byrne & Byrne, 1991, 1993; McGrew, 1992; Matsuzawa, 1994; Boesch, 1996; Matsuzawa & Yamakoshi, 1996). Byrne & Byrne (1991, 1993) proposed several mountain gorilla manipul-

ative food processing techniques as behavioural traditions, based on standardisation of the technique at the program-level and their distribution
among residents but not newcomers. Classic tool-using traditions are
stylistic variants of termite fishing between chimpanzee communities.
While chimpanzees in both Assirik and Gombe use vines and twigs to
make probe tools, for example, the Assirik chimpanzees mostly make
probes of the vine or twig peeled of its bark (and discard the bark) but
the Gombe chimpanzees mostly make probes of the bark (and throw away
the twig or vine). Gombe chimpanzees also usually use both ends of their
twig/vine probes while Assirik chimpanzees almost never do (McGrew,
1977; McGrew et al., 1979). McGrew singled out the double-ended use
because it makes no ecological sense – changing ends does not improve
the catch; it looks more like the sort of useless habit that is socially
acquired. Boesch (1996) argued that chimpanzees' stone nut-cracking technique is a food processing tradition, based on its distribution and acquisition patterns. Its distribution is compatible with social, but not ecological or genetic, explanations; and mothers have been observed teaching
their offspring aspects of the technique (Boesch, 1991).

Some *object manipulations* beyond tool use appear to be socially transmitted. A striking example is a stone play tradition that was innovated
in the Arashiyama troop of Japanese macaques in 1979 and subsequently
spread through the troop along kinship and peer playmate lines
(Huffman, 1984; Huffman & Quiatt, 1986). Object manipulation traditions are again more complex and extensive in great apes than in other
non-human primates. In chimpanzees, candidates include various techniques for reaching lower branches of trees, leaf clipping, leaf grooming,
ectoparasite squashing and knuckle knocking (Sugiyama & Koman, 1979;
Nishida, 1987; Boesch, 1996). In leaf clipping, for example, Mahale chimpanzees pick a stiff leaf then, holding petioles between thumb and index
finger, repeatedly pull the leaf from side to side and bite the leaf blade
off; when only the midrib with bits of blade remain, this leaf is dropped,
another picked, and the sequence repeated (Nishida, 1987). Taï chimpanzees also leaf clip but they take both sides of the leaf blade in their teeth
at once and remove them in one movement, rather than repeatedly biting
off little bits (Boesch, 1996).

A recently discovered possibility is self-medication, or *zoopharmacognosy* (Wrangham & Nishida, 1983; Huffman & Seifu, 1989; Glander,
1994; Rodriguez & Wrangham, 1994). Chimpanzees, for instance, consume at least 13 medicinal plant species, apparently expressly for

medicinal purposes (Huffman & Wrangham, 1994). Self-medication is not necessarily complex. Many species use medicinal plants, including other non-human primates, and they may be predisposed to recognise them from typical properties such as taste and smell (e.g. Etkin, 1994; Glander, 1994). However, chimpanzees are conservative in their food choice so they are unlikely to chance upon medicinal plants by trial-and-error sampling of vegetation. Their self-medication also requires precise timing, precise dosage and specific techniques to extract and activate medicinal agents. For instance, they consume *Aspilia* spp. plants with known medicinal properties by selecting one leaf at a time, holding it by the stalk, and placing it in the mouth; they apparently don't chew it but hold it with the tongue against the inside of the mouth for about 5 seconds then swallow it whole; and they tend to swallow *Aspilia* leaves this way within a hour of dawn (Huffman & Wrangham, 1994; Nishida, 1994). Available evidence suggests this expertise is probably a behavioural tradition in chimpanzees (Huffman & Wrangham, 1994).

Although this evidence for non-human primate traditions of ecological expertise looks impressive at first sight, it is the sum total from over 40 years' research from all of primatology, very few species are involved, and the incidence is very low (e.g. Whiten & Ham, 1992). The evidence has also been challenged on the grounds that the real causes of these traditions could be environmental; for instance, differences between localities in the availability of tool construction materials or foods could explain why chimpanzee food procurement techniques differ between communities (e.g. McGrew *et al.* 1979; Nishida & Uehara, 1980; Tomasello, 1990). Careful digging into the classic cases, Japanese macaque sweet potato washing and chimpanzee termite fishing, uncovered ecological circumstances that make individual learning a plausible source of the expertise (e.g. Green, 1990, 1992; Tomasello, 1990). Group members or humans may have created facilitatory opportunities to wash sweet potatoes, but the technique itself could have been acquired by trial-and-error experiences with sweet potatoes and ocean water, and human reinforcement (Green, 1975; Galef, 1992). Likewise, chimpanzees have acquired termite-fishing techniques without benefit of social input (Paquette, 1992). Responses to these challenges lead in two directions.

Supporting the view that individual learning builds ecological expertise are two recent reports where ecological skills that could or 'should' be socially transmitted were acquired without expert social input. Milton (1993) followed a motley crew of ex-captive juvenile spider monkeys after their release to free forest life. Despite atypical rearing experiences, including no access to experienced conspecifics whose forest expertise they could exploit, these monkeys acquired ecological expertise much like that of normal spider monkeys. Similar reports come from rehabilitant orangutans (personal observations). A typical case is a juvenile female who was orphaned as a young infant, raised in Taiwan by humans until 3–4 years of age, rehabilitated for 18 months in Borneo, then released into the forest. Rehabilitation provided no forest experience and no experienced orangutans lived in the release forest. Instead of a struggling individual, however, staff who sighted her 2 years after her release saw a sleek, healthy and carefree one.

Supporting the social exploitation view, even the most convincing ecological explanations of the classic cases of ecological traditions do not eliminate social input: they merely relegate it to the role of some sort of optional or facilitatory process like social enhancement (e.g. Galef, 1992; Whiten & Ham, 1992). In every category, some traditions of ecological expertise remain for which plausible ecological explanations have not been found, and not for lack of trying, or for which ecological explanations have themselves been challenged with counter evidence (McGrew, 1992; Wrangham et al., 1994; Boesch, 1996). For these cases, social exploitation remains the prime candidate. Whether primates can acquire ecological expertise independently may also depend in part on their ecological niches. Both spider monkeys and orangutans are classified as frugivores (Galdikas, 1978; Milton, 1993). Frugivorous diets are relatively benign compared to folivorous and herbivorous ones, which involve a high risk of toxicity. Frugivores could rely on individual trial-and-error learning to acquire feeding expertise with relative impunity, whereas this would have much more dangerous consequences for herbivores or folivores. Evidence also indicates that non-human primates vary their use of social exploitation as a function of ecological conditions. Infant howler monkeys and baboons, for instance, may exploit others' expertise for foods that are difficult or dangerous to process, but not necessarily for foods that are easy to process (Whitehead, 1986; King, 1991, 1994a,b). That non-human primates *can* gain ecological expertise by individual learning, then, does not guarantee that they normally *do*.

Overview of gains from social learning Evidence nonetheless leaves the sense that non-human primates, other than the great apes, use social exploitation extensively to gain social expertise but as a minor and peripheral way of gaining ecological expertise. This may be a consequence of the social learning mechanisms available. Priming seems to be a major mechanism, and it adds only a certain 'feed forward' to individual learning (it marks the significance of particular stimuli or particular responses). Social reinforcement may contribute substantially to social expertise but little to ecological expertise (King, 1991, 1994b; Caro & Hauser, 1992). Imitation, apparently available only to great apes, can be applied to both social and ecological expertise. Because of developmental constraints on its emergence and its limited power, however, it probably fits a narrow range of problems – perhaps relational or organisational dimensions of complex tool-based or manipulative extractive food processing techniques. In both ecological and social domains, this adds up to suggest that social exploitation constitutes an efficiency device that channels or pre-focuses behaviour more finely than it would have been independently. It offers a sort of 'value added' component, but not the main substance (e.g. Pereira & Fairbanks, 1993).

Exploiting the fruits of others' expertise

Ernie & Bibi: Part I. Ernie and Bibi were gorillas at the Denver zoo. Ernie was an accomplished nest builder. Bibi wasn't but she loved nests, especially Ernie's. Bibi was dominant over Ernie, so she could expropriate his nests. She did.

(Woods, 1992)

A second, perhaps baser, Machiavellian ploy is to exploit the fruits of others' expertise rather than the expertise itself. We call those who do it *scroungers* and beggars (Barnard & Sibley, 1981; Barnard, 1984). Scrounging is probably common in socially-living species; full-time scrounging may emerge in large groups (Blurton-Jones, 1984, 1987).

Non-human primates scrounge a number of resources from one another – prominent among them is food. Food scrounging is the exploiter's eye view of what has been more generously labelled *food sharing* (e.g. Isaac, 1978; Feistner & McGrew, 1989; King, 1994b). Non-human primates also scrounge other resources. Great apes, for instance, scounge the tools of the trade as well as its fruits. Young chimpanzees scrounge stone tool sets their mothers assemble, sometimes to their mothers' clear disadvantage (Boesch, 1991). The advantage in both cases is clear. Scroungers get the goods with less work.

Indeed, why exploit social partners' expertise if you can exploit their products? Scrounging can apparently be so lucrative that scroungers may even refine their scrounging skills at the expense of their foraging expertise. In long-tailed macaques (*Macaca fascicularis*), when a skilled forager produced food, others in the group turned to scrounging and stopped foraging themselves – although they did begin to treat the forager more positively (Stammbach, 1988). As one hunter-gatherer explained it, 'some people like to hunt, other people just like to eat' (Blurton-Jones, 1987).

Despite this tendency, scrounging could facilitate acquiring foraging expertise. A study by Aisner & Terkel (1992) on tree rats suggests how. They found that tree rats used a special technique for procuring pine nuts, removing pinecone scales in a spiral pattern from the base, only if their mothers also did. Their study suggested that the rats acquire this technique by social learning, as a side-effect of scrounging. Offspring probably scrounge partly processed pinecones, so their experiences are influenced by their mothers' *behavioral after-effects*; or, they may co-feed with their mothers, so joining in her expert processing through *co-action* (Visalberghi & Fragaszy, 1990). Both experiences could channel their own scale removing along the pattern their mothers started.

This scenario could well apply to non-human primate immatures, who are dedicated food scroungers well into the juvenile period (e.g. McGrew, 1975; Galdikas, 1978; Rijksen, 1978; Goodall, 1986; McGrew & Feistner, 1992; King, 1994a,b). Their scrounging occurs in a similar context of behavioural after-effects and co-action that could, in like fashion, expose them to items they might not otherwise identify as edible, the forms of food items in various stages of processing, the techniques used to process them, and how manipulations are organised (Visalberghi & Fragaszy, 1990). Primate mothers may then facilitate acquisition of foraging expertise, if only as a side-effect of satisfying their own needs. In great apes, this may partially 'subsidise', or compensate for, the prolonged apprenticeship involved in acquiring complex foraging expertise. Scrounging may also assist rather than inhibit acquiring foraging expertise in non-human primate immatures because they are dedicated learners, perhaps more motivated than adults to acquire independent skills.

The exploited – the good, the bad, and the ugly

Ernie & Bibi: Part II. Ernie wised up to Bibi's nest scrounging. When he saw her heading for his nest, he would get out of it, pick the whole thing up, and carry it off, bipedally, to a safer spot.

(Woods, 1992).

How experts respond to exploitation is the other face of Machiavellian intelligence. Do Machiavellian primates tolerate being exploited, contribute wholeheartedly to it, or try to foil exploiters? Their responses could transform the intellectual complexity of exploitation itself. Food sharing is our case in point.

The fruits of expertise revisited: Tolerance

Food sharing suggests benevolent donation by the exploited, but close scrutiny of primate food sharing suggests that *toleration of scounging*, tinged with begrudging and hostility, better describes the predominant attitude (Isaac, 1978; Blurton-Jones, 1987; Feistner & McGrew, 1989; McGrew & Feistner, 1992; King, 1994a,b). Although infants regularly beg food from parents, unsolicited offers are rare outside callitrichids, bonobos and chimpanzees (Galdikas & Teleki, 1981; Kuroda, 1984; Watts, 1985; Goodall, 1986; Ferrari, 1987; McGrew & Feister, 1992; King, 1994a,b).

Blurton-Jones (1984) argues that tolerance depends mainly on ecological factors – for example, it should be relatively high for big but not small food items. Of interest to Machiavellian intelligence, or perhaps we should say counter-intelligence, is evidence that social factors also influence the tolerance equation. Blurton-Jones suggests that in groups whose members frequently meet, mutual tolerance makes more sense than fighting – after all, today a producer, tomorrow a hungry scrounger. Some primates use ritualised gestures to beg, which suggests that food scrounging is a species-typical social negotiation involving some mutual consent (Goodall, 1968, 1986; Plooij, 1978; Bard, 1990). Experts' tolerance varies with their relationships to scroungers: greatest tolerance is accorded young infants (by their mothers) but sexual partners and friends also rate indulgence (e.g. McGrew, 1975, 1992; Galdikas & Teleki, 1981; Watts, 1985; Goodall, 1986; McGrew & Feistner, 1992). Maternal tolerance decreases with offspring's development: mothers begin resisting begging as infancy ends, tolerating scrounging on hard to process foods but not foods the youngster can acquire itself (Silk, 1978; McGrew, 1992; King, 1994b). Exploitation negotiations can become complex. Youngsters' whimpering or tantrums, for example, can temporarily revive waning tolerance.

Instructive with respect to the interplay between ecological and social factors in tolerance is chimpanzee meat eating. Blurton-Jones' ecological model suggests scrounging meat should be tolerated: prey can be large (e.g. bushpig weighing 20 kg or more), large prey are hard to find and highly valued, and group members meet frequently (Goodall, 1986). As predicted, chimpanzees commonly share meat (e.g. Teleki, 1973; Goodall, 1986; McGrew & Feistner, 1992). Producers tolerate some scrounging, mostly begging. Begging success does depend on the amount of meat involved and how much the possessor has already consumed, but also on social factors, especially the relationship between beggar and possessor (e.g. relative age, rank, kinship, friendship).

It is probably significant to the social exploitation of ecological expertise that the exploited may grade their tolerance in step with scroungers' expertise, notably between chimpanzee mothers and scrounging offspring. The processing stage at which scroungers get the goods will then systematically vary in a way that could guide their acquiring expertise in a progressive, step-wise fashion. Graded tolerance may then foster the transfer of expertise by the support structures, or 'scaffolding', it provides to partially competent learners. This resembles a scenario proposed by Parker & Gibson (1979), that food sharing arose in early hominids to support the prolonged apprenticehip involved in acquiring complex, tool-assisted extractive foraging skills.

Of interest to Machiavellian counter-intelligence are two other possible responses to exploitation, *defence* and *donation*. Both have implications for the nature of the social commerce between exploiter and exploited.

Closely watched expertise: Defence

Producers don't always tolerate scrounging, they also *defend* themselves against it (Wrangham, 1975). Fighting is one way to rebuff exploiters but it is probably effective only in defending resources. When expertise is targeted, other counterploys are needed. In primates, tactical deception is a prominent one.

Byrne & Whiten (1990) assembled a lengthy catalogue of the tactical deception primates use to defend their resources and expertise. Chimpanzees, for instance, use multiple deceptive ploys: diverting attention, faking tantrums, acting without exploiters' knowledge (quietly, when inattentive), hiding, hiding interest or feigning no interest, suppressing 'giveaway' behaviour such as food vocalisations or an erect penis, and providing false information such as deliberately moving away from food or feigning a limp (Goodall, 1986). Turning this deception around can point to the types of expertise and resources that exploiters can, and want to, exploit. Primate deception also reveals just how devious, complex and layered exploitation negotiations can become. For exemple, Menzel (1973) set up an exploitation caper between Belle and Rock, two members of a captive chimpanzee colony. He hid food in a field, showed its location only to Belle, then let Belle and the other chimpanzees into the field. Belle went straight to the food; Rock et al. simply followed her and took it when she uncovered it. So, Belle began approaching the food more slowly, even sitting on it without uncovering it until Rock left. Rock then shoved her aside to search under where she sat, or he sometimes wandered off without looking back – until 5 m away, at which point he could usually nab her in the act of uncovering the food. So Belle began staying farther from the food spot when Rock watched, even walking away from it. Rock figured out Belle's 'indirect' cues – firstly, increasing his search radius around her, then searching by using increases in her fidgeting to signal when he was getting 'hot'. The ante stopped there, but only because Belle never managed to control her fidgeting.

Donating expertise: Teaching

More surprising than defence is that non-human primates occasionally do voluntarily give their resources away. Chimpanzees with meat have offered some to interested bystanders who were not begging and who were not kin (Goodall, 1986). Offers tended to come at the end of feeding, when the food's value had decreased, but their mere occurrence is intriguing because active donation is uncommon in non-human primates (e.g. King, 1991, 1994b). They suggest there is some pay-off for generosity in non-human primates: satisfied scroungers may leave possessors in peace, or sharing may preserve the social harmony important to long-term social groups (Wrangham, 1975).

Active donation is also significant in transferring expertise. If experts initiate the transfer, without prior request, they would seem to show some capacity to understand others' wants or needs – i.e. others' perspectives. They would also seem to be teaching. Interest in this possibility is currently high because some consider teaching a cornerstone of human culture (e.g. Bonner, 1980; Parker & Russon, 1996).

The commonsense idea of teaching as an intentional activity involving verbal instruction, special pedagogical materials, etc., automatically excludes non-human species, because these techniques have never been found outside humans. Caro & Hauser (1992) proposed opening the door to non-human species by thinking about teaching in functional terms –

i.e. what it is for or what it achieves rather than how it is done. They consider that an individual A *teaches* if (a) A modifies its behaviour only in the presence of a novice B, at some cost or at least without immediate benefit to A; (b) A's behaviour provides B with experience, encourages or punishes B's behaviour, or sets an example for B; and (c) because of A's actions, B acquires knowledge or skills earlier in life, faster, or more efficiently that it might otherwise do, or that it might not learn at all. In other words, teaching generates support structures or *scaffolding* to help novices learn (Wood *et al.*, 1976). Caro and Hauser also suggested three types of teaching non-human species might use, given their learning capacities: *opportunity teaching* (providing opportunities to learn), *coaching* (shaping behaviour through reinforcement), or *demonstration teaching* (modelling behaviour). These three types of teaching reflect increasing cognitive sophistication (see also Parker, 1996).

Under this definition, some non-human primates teach. Many of the cases offered can be explained as opportunity teaching (Caro & Hauser, 1992). Monkey and great ape mothers place their young infants in situations requiring climbing or locomotion (e.g. van de Rijt-Plooij & Plooij, 1987) and chimpanzee mothers provide their offspring with the wherewithal for stone nut-cracking (Boesch, 1991).

Coaching also occurs in both monkeys and great apes, but probably rarely (e.g. Nishida, 1987; Caro & Hauser, 1992). Most common is reinforcement that discourages particular actions. Hauser reported infant vervet monkeys misusing alarm calls, unnecessarily frightening other group members including their mothers. When things calmed down, the mothers returned and bit or slapped their infants. When these infants next used the same type of alarm call, it was in an appropriate context (Caro & Hauser, 1992). Mothers also encourage their infants' locomotory skills, prodding them or gesturing them to move or climb on target objects (e.g. see van de Rijt-Plooj & Plooj, 1987; Caro & Hauser, 1992). Great apes have also used moulding: Koko, a gorilla, moulded her doll's hands to make one of her signs (Patterson & Cohn, 1994); and Washoe, a chimpanzee, similarly moulded her son's hands (Fouts *et al.*, 1989).

Demonstration teaching requires advanced intellectual abilities. It is effective only if learners can learn by imitation and if teachers can take complementary roles in relation to them (Parker, 1996). This seems within the scope of great apes' capacities (e.g. de Waal, 1982; Povinelli *et al.*, 1992; Miles, 1994; Whiten, 1996). A few candidates for great ape demonstration teaching have been offered. A human-enculturated signing orangutan, Chantek, demonstrated signs to human companions (Miles, 1994). Boesch (1991) reported two cases in wild chimpanzees. In one, a mother interrupted her activities to approach her juvenile daughter, who was having difficulty cracking nuts with an awkwardly shaped stone hammer. The mother took the stone from her daughter, and with slow and exaggerated motions demonstrated to her the most effective grip for it, monitoring her daughter's attention throughout. The mother then opened nuts with this hammer. The daughter watched the demonstration attentively, then, when the mother returned to her former activities, retrieved the hammer and painstakingly imitated the grip demonstrated. She had failed to open nuts with this hammer before the demonstration but she succeeded afterwards, using the demonstrated technique (Boesch, 1991). The case is highly contentious (e.g. Caro & Hauser, 1992; Call & Tomasello, 1996) but it is hard to dismiss.

That non-human primate teaching is rare is actually consistent with arguments that teaching should occur only in the most difficult circumstances where learning needs an added boost (e.g. Giraldeau & Lefebre, 1987; Caro & Hauser, 1992). It then makes sense that the most sophisticated non-human primate teaching focuses on difficult or uncommon foraging techniques where independent re-invention is unlikely or learning opportunities are rare. That non-human primates teach at any level suggests that exploiting others' expertise is a built-in feature of non-human primate adaptation. Although this marks them even more strongly as Machiavellian, it also makes them, at least on occasion, good Samaritans.

Conclusion

Returning to our opening question, what can the Machiavellian primate gain from exploiting others' expertise, the answer must be, as it usually is with the primates, that it depends greatly on who you are and who you know. What one individual can exploit from another varies with the intellectual mechanisms involved; this depends on the species, age and experience of both protagonists, and the complexity of the expertise itself. Due to these intellectual constraints, only some sorts of expertise and some exploitation tactics fall within non-human primates' grasp. Here, as elsewhere, there seems to be a cognitive gap between great apes and other non-human primates. Particulars of the problem addressed and the relationship between exploiter and exploited also figure prominently – e.g. what food (fruit or meat *versus* leaves) and who (kin or friends *versus* strangers) are involved can affect whether social exploitation is used to gain foraging expertise. The target of exploitation (resources *versus* expertise) and responses to exploitation (assist *versus* oppose) also affect exploitation ploys. The upshot seems to be that non-human primates apply social exploitation selectively and flexibly.

What non-human primate exploitation appears to serve with respect to social expertise is channelling or levelling for conformity. This is important in communication and co-ordinating group life, where standardisation is more effective than variability. With respect to ecological expertise, the general effect of social exploitation seems to be to boost individual learning by priming mechanisms, which channel and scaffold independent efforts to acquire expertise. In the great apes, imitation affords some extra ability to acquire skills directly from social experts although it appears limited in power. The extra boost available to non-human primates from teaching seems to be rare and limited in scope. Its most complex form, demonstration teaching, has again been claimed only for great apes and it may operate narrowly, on only the most demanding skills.

This leaves the sense that social exploitation is a peripheral or a sometime contributor to non-human primates' acquisition of expertise. Yet even in humans, who are considered the most sophisticated in social transmission and for whom culture is considered the bedrock of our species' adaptation, we have the saying 'experience is the best teacher'. And even if individual experience remains singled out, scholars who have studied the issue seriously point to the special place of Machiavellianism: 'But so far from its being a sign of weakness to depend upon the past, it is rather a mark of genius – certainly indispensible to the exhibition of genius – to make use of earlier work'. (Gilbert, 1938, pp. 231–2.)

References

Aisner, R. & Terkel, J. (1992). Ontogeny of pine cone opening behaviour in the black rat (*Rattus rattus*). *Animal Behaviour*, 44, 327–36.

Altmann, S. (1967). The structure of primate social communication. In *Social Communication among Primates*, ed. S. A. Altmann, pp. 325–62. Chicago: University of Chicago Press.

Anderson, J. R. (1996). Chimpanzees and capuchin monkeys: Comparative cognition. In *Reaching into Thought: The Minds of the Great Apes*, ed. A. E. Russon, K. A. Bard & S. T. Parker, pp. 23–56. Cambridge: Cambridge University Press.

Antinucci, F. (ed.) (1989). *Cognitive Structure and Development in Nonhuman Primates*. Hillsdale, NJ: Lawrence Erlbaum Associates.

Bard, K. A. (1990). 'Social tool use' by free-ranging orang-utans: A Piagetian and developmental perspective on the manipulation of an animate object. In *"Language" and Intelligence in Monkeys and Apes: Comparative Developmental Perspectives*, ed. S. T. Parker & K. R. Gibson, pp. 356–78. Cambridge: Cambridge University Press.

Barnard, C. J. (1984). The evolution of food-scrounging strategies within and between species. In *Producers and Scoungers: Strategies of Exploitation and Parasitism*, ed. C.J. Barnard, pp. 95–125. New York: Chapman & Hall.

Barnard, C. J. & Sibly, R. M. (1981). Producers and scroungers: A general model and its application to captive flocks of house sparrows. *Animal Behaviour*, 29, 543–50.

Blurton-Jones, N. G. (1984). A selfish origin for human food sharing: Tolerated theft. *Ethology and Sociobiology*, 5, 1–3.

Blurton-Jones, N. G. (1987). Tolerated theft, suggestions about the ecology and evolution of sharing, hoarding and scrounging. *Social Sciences Information*, 26, 31–54.

Boesch, C. (1991). Teaching among wild chimpanzees. *Animal Behaviour*, 41, 530–33.

Boesch, C. (1996). Three approaches for assessing chimpanzee culture. In *Reaching into Thought: The Minds of the Great Apes*, ed. A. E. Russon, K. A. Bard & S. T. Parker, pp. 404–29. Cambridge: Cambridge University Press.

Bonner, J. T. (1980). *The Evolution of Culture in Animals*. Princeton, NJ: Princeton University Press.

Boyd, R. & Richerson, P. J. (1988). An evolutionary model of social learning: The effects of spatial and temporal variation. In *Social Learning: Psychological and Biological Perspectives*, ed. T. R. Zentall & B. G. Galef, Jr, pp. 29–48. Hillsdale, NJ: Lawrence Erlbaum Associates.

Box, H. O. (1984). *Primate Behavior and Social Ecology*. London: Chapman & Hall.

Byrne, R. W. (1994). The evolution of intelligence. In *Behaviour and Evolution*, ed. P. J. B. Slater & T. R. Halliday, pp. 223–64. Cambridge: Cambridge University Press.

Byrne, R. W. (1995). *The Thinking Ape: Evolutionary Origins of Intelligence*. Oxford: Oxford University Press.

Byrne, R. W. & Byrne, J. M. E. (1991). Hand preferences in the skilled gathering tasks of mountain gorillas (*Gorilla g. berengei*). *Cortex*, 27, 521–46.

Byrne, R. W. & Byrne, J. M. E. (1993). Complex leaf-gathering skills of mountain gorillas (*Gorilla g. berengei*): Variability and standardization. *American Journal of Primatology*, 31, 241–61.

Byrne, R. W. & Whiten, A. (eds) (1988). *Machiavellian Intelligence: Social Expertise and the Evolution of Intellect in Monkeys, Apes and Humans*. Oxford: Clarendon Press.

Byrne, R. W. & Whiten, A. (1990). Tactical deception in primates: The 1990 data-base. *Primate Report*, 27, 1–101.

Call, J. & Tomasello, M. (1994). The social learning of tool use by orangutans (*Pongo pygmaeus*). *Human evolution*, 9, 297–313.

Call, J. & Tomasello, M. (1996). The effect of humans on the cognitive development of apes. In *Reaching into Thought: The Minds of the Great Apes*, ed. A. E.

Russon, K. A. Bard & S. T. Parker, pp. 371–403. Cambridge: Cambridge University Press.

Caro, T. M. & Hauser, M. D. (1992). Is there teaching in nonhuman animals? *Quarterly Review of Biology*, 67, 151–74.

Chapais, B. & Gauthier, C. (1993). Early agonistic experience and the onset of matrilineal rank acquisition in Japanese macaques. In *Juvenile Primates: Life History, Development, and Behavior*, ed. M. E. Pereira & L. A. Fairbanks, pp. 245–58. New York: Oxford University Press.

Chevalier-Skolnikoff, S. (1983). Sensorimotor development in orang-utans and other primates. *Journal of Human Evolution*, 12, 545–61.

Custance, D. & Bard, K. A. (1994). The comparative and developmental study of self-recognition and imitation: The importance of social factors. In *Self-awareness in Humans and Animals: Developmental Perspectives*, ed. S.T. Parker, R. W. Mitchell & M.L. Boccia, pp. 207–26. New York: Cambridge University Press.

Custance, D. M., Whiten, A. & Bard, K. A. (1994). The development of gestural imitation and self-recognition in chimpanzees (*Pan troglodytes*) and children. In *Current Primatology: Selected Proceedings of the XIVth Congress of the International Primatological Society*, vol. 2: *Social Development, Learning and Behavior*, ed. J. J. Roeder, B. Theirry, J. R. Anderson & N. Herrenschmidt, pp. 381–7. Strasbourg: Université Louis Pasteur.

Custance, D. M., Whiten, A. & Bard, K. A. (1996). Can young chimpanzees (*Pan troglodytes*) imitate arbitrary actions? Hayes and Hayes (1952) revisited. *Behaviour*. 132, 837–59.

Dawson, B. V. & Foss, B. M. (1965). Observational learning in budgerigars. *Animal Behaviour*, 13, 470–4.

de Waal, F. B. M. (1982). *Chimpanzee Politics: Power and Sex Among Apes*. New York: Harper and Row.

de Waal, F. B. M. (1989). *Peacemaking Among Primates*. Cambridge, MA: Harvard University Press.

Donald, M. (1991). *Origins of the Modern Mind: Three Stages in the Evolution of Culture and Cognition*. Cambridge, MA: Harvard University Press.

Doré, F.-Y. & Dumas, C. (1987). Psychology of animal cognition: Piagetian studies. *Psychological Bulletin*, 102, 219–33.

Etkin, N. L. (ed.) (1994). *Eating on the Wild Side: The Pharmacologic, Ecologic, and Social Implications of Using Noncultigens*. Tucson, AZ: University of Arizona Press.

Fedigan, L. M. (1982). *Primate Paradigms: Sex Roles and Social Bonds*. Montreal: Eden Press.

Feistner, A. & McGrew, W. C. (1989). Food-sharing in primates: A critical review. In *Perspectives in Primate Biology*, vol. 3, ed. P. K. Seth & S. Seth, pp. 21–36. New Delhi: Today and Tomorrow's Printers and Publishers.

Ferrari, S. F. (1987). Food transfer in a wild marmoset group. *Folia Primatologica*, 48, 203–6.

Fobes, J. L. & King, J. E. (1982). *Primate Behavior*. New York: Academic Press.

Fouts, R. S., Fouts, D. H. & van Cantfort, T. E. (1989). The infant Loulis learns signs from cross-fostered chimpanzees. In *Teaching Sign Language to*

Chimpanzees, ed. R. A. Gardner, B. T. Gardner & T. E. van Cantfort, pp. 280–92. New York: SUNY Press.

Galdikas, B. M. F. (1978). Orangutan Adaptation at Tanjung Puting Reserve, Central Borneo. PhD thesis, University of California, Los Angeles.

Galdikas, B. M. F. & Teleki, G. (1981). Variations in subsistence activities of female and male pongids: New perspectives on the origins of hominid labor division. *Current Anthropology*, 22, 241–56.

Galef, B. G., Jr (1988). Imitation in animals: History, definition and interpretation of data from the psychological laboratory. In *Social Learning: Psychological and Biological Perspectives*, T. R. Zentall & B.G. Galef, Jr, pp. 3–28. Hillsdale, NJ: Lawrence Erlbaum Associates.

Galef, B. G., Jr. (1990). Tradition in animals: Field observations and laboratory analysis. In *Comparative Perspectives*, ed. M. Bekoff & D. Jamieson, pp. 74–95. Boulder, CO: Westview Press.

Galef, B. G., Jr (1992). The question of animal culture. *Human Nature*, 3, 157–78.

Ghiglieri, M. P. (1984). *The Chimpanzees of Kibale Forest*. New York: Columbia University Press.

Gilbert, A. H. (1938). *Machiavelli's "Prince" and its Forerunners: The Prince as a Typical Book "de Regimine Principum"*. New York: Barnes & Noble.

Giraldeau, L.-A. & Lefebvre, L. (1987). Scrounging prevents cultural transmission of food-finding behaviour in pigeons. *Animal Behaviour*, 35, 387–94.

Glander, K. E. (1994). Nonhuman primate self-medication with wild plant foods. In *Eating on the Wild Side: The Pharmacologic, Ecologic, and Social Implications of Using Noncultigens*, ed. N. L. Etkin, pp. 227–39. Tucson, AZ: University of Arizona Press.

Goodall, J. van Lawick- (1968). The behaviour of free-living chimpanzees in the Gombe Stream Reserve. *Animal Behaviour Monographs*, 1, 161–311.

Goodall, J. (1986). *The Chimpanzees of Gombe: Patterns of Behavior*. Cambridge, MA: The Belknap Press.

Green, S. (1975). Dialects in Japanese monkeys: Vocal learning and cultural transmission of locale-specific vocal behavior? *Zeitschrift fur Tierpsychologie*, 38, 304–14.

Harcourt, A. & de Waal, F. (eds) (1992). *Coalitions and Alliances in Humans and Other Animals*. Oxford: Oxford University Press.

Hauser, M. D. (1988). Invention and social transmission: New data from wild vervet monkeys. In *Machiavellian Intelligence: Social Expertise and the Evolution of Intellect in Monkeys, Apes and Humans*, ed. R. W. Byrne & A. Whiten, pp. 327–43. Oxford: Clarendon Press.

Hayes, K. & Hayes, C. (1952). Imitation in a home-raised chimpanzee. *Journal of Comparative and Physiological Psychology*, 45, 450–9.

Heyes, C. M. (1994). Social learning in animals: Categories and mechanisms. *Biological Reviews*, 69, 207–31.

Hinde, R. A. (1979). *Towards Understanding Relationships*. London: Academic Press.

Huffman, M. (1984). Stone play of *Macaca fuscata* in Arashiyama B troop: Transmission of a nonadaptive behavior. *Journal of Human Evolution*, 13, 725–35.

Huffman, M. A. & Quaitt, D. (1986). Stone handling by Japanese macaques (*Macaca fuscata*): Implications for tool use of stone. *Primates*, 27, 413–23.

Huffman, M. A. & Seifu, M. (1989). Observations on the illness and consumption of a possibly medicinal plant, *Vernonia amygdalina* (Del.), by a wild chimpanzee in the Mahale Mountains National Park, Tanzania. *Primates*, 30, 51–63.

Huffman, M. A. & Wrangham, R. W. (1994). Diversity of medicinal plant use by chimpanzees in the wild. In *Chimpanzee Cultures*, ed. R. W. Wrangham, W. C. McGrew, F. B. M. de Waal & P. G. Heltne, pp. 129–148. Cambridge, MA: Harvard University Press.

Imanishi, K. (1952). Evolution of humanity. In *Man*, ed. K. Imanishi. Tokyo: Mainichi-Shinbunsha. (In Japanese).

Imanishi, K. (1957). Learned behavior of Japanese monkeys. *Japanese Journal of Ethnology*, 21, 185–9. (In Japanese).

Ingmanson, E. J. (1987). Clapping behavior: Non-verbal communication during grooming in a group of captive pygmy chimpanzees (*Pan paniscus*). *American Journal of Physical Anthropology*, 72, 173–4.

Isaac, G. L. (1978). Food sharing and human evolution: Archaeological evidence from the plio-pleistocene of East Africa. *Journal of Anthropological Research*, 34, 311–25.

Itani, J. (1954). Japanese monkeys in Takasakiyama. In *Nihon Dobutsuki*, vol. 2, ed. J. Imanishi, pp. 1–285. Tokyo: Kobunsha. (In Japanese).

Itani, J. (1958/1965). On the acquisition and propagation of a new food habit in the troop of Japanese macaques at Takasakiyama. *Primates*, 1, 84–98. [In Japanese, translated into English in *Japanese Monkeys: A Collection of Translations*, ed. K. Imanishi & S. Altmann, pp. 52–65. Edmonton, Alta: University of Alberta Press.]

Itani, J. & Nishimura, A. (1973). The study of infrahuman culture in Japan. In *Symposium of the Fourth International Congress of Primatology*, vol. 1: *Precultural Primate Behavior*, ed. E. W. Menzel, pp. 26–50. Basel: S. Karger.

Jolly. A. (1966). Lemur social behavior and primate intelligence. *Science*, 153, 501–6.

Kawai, M. (1965). Newly acquired pre-cultural behavior of a natural troop of Japanese monkeys on Koshima Island. *Primates*, 6, 1–30.

Kawamura, S. (1954). On a new type of feeding habit which developed in a group of wild Japanese macaques. *Seibutsu Shinka*, 2, 1–4.

King, B. J. (1991). Social information transfer in monkeys, apes, and hominids. *Yearbook of Physical Anthropology*, 34, 97–115.

King, B. J. (1994a). Primate infants as skilled information gatherers. *Pre- and Perinatal Psychology Journal*, 8, 287–307.

King, B. (1994b). *The Information Continuum*. Santa Fe: School of American Research Press.

Kummer, H. (1967). Tripartite relations in hamadryas baboons. In *Social Communication Among Primates*, ed. S. A. Altmann, pp. 63–72. Chicago: University of Chicago Press.

Kuroda, S. (1984). Interaction over food among pygmy chimpanzees. In *The Pygmy Chimpanzee*, ed. R. L. Susman, pp. 301–24. New York: Plenum Press.

Langer, J. (1996). Heterchrony and the evolution of primate cognitive development. In *Reaching into Thought: The Minds of the Great Apes*, ed. A. E. Russon, K. A. Bard & S. T. Parker, pp. 257–77. Cambridge: Cambridge University Press.

Lefebvre, L. & Palameta, B. (1988). Mechanisms, ecology, and population diffusion of socially learned, food-finding behavior in feral pigeons. In *Social Learning: Psychological and Biological Perspectives*, ed. T. R. Zentall & B. G. Galef Jr, pp. 141–64. Hillsdale, NJ: Lawrence Erlbaum Associates.

Matsuzawa, T. (1994). Field experiments on use of stone tools in the wild. In *Chimpanzee Cultures*, ed. R. W. Wrangham, W. C. McGrew, F. B. M. de Waal, & P.G. Heltne, pp. 351–70. Cambridge, MA: Harvard University Press.

Matsuzawa, T. & Yamakoshi, G. (1996). Comparison of chimpanzee culture between Bossou, Guinea and Nimba, West Africa. In *Reaching into Thought: The Minds of the Great Apes*, ed. A. E. Russon, K. A. Bard & S. T. Parker, pp. 211–32. Cambridge: Cambridge University Press.

McGrew, W. C. (1975). Patterns of plant food sharing by wild chimpanzees. In *Contemporary Primatology*, ed. S. Kondo, M. Kawai & A. Ehara, pp. 304–9. Basel: Karger.

McGrew, W. C. (1977). Socialization and object manipulation by wild chimpanzees. In *Primate Biosocial Behavior: Biological, Social, and Ecological Determinants*, ed. S. Chevalier-Skolnikoff & F. Poirier, pp. 261–88. New York: Garland Press.

McGrew, W. C. (1992). *Chimpanzee Material Culture: Implications for Human Evolution*. Cambridge: Cambridge University Press.

McGrew, W. C. & Feistner, A. T. C. (1992). Two nonhuman primate models for the evolution of human food sharing: Chimpanzees and callitrichids. In *The Adapted Mind: Evolutionary Psychology and the Generation of Culture*, ed. J. H. Barkow, L. Cosmides & J. Tooby, pp. 229–43. Oxford: Oxford University Press.

McGrew, W. C. & Tutin, C. E. G. (1978). Evidence for a social custom in wild chimpanzees? *Man*, 13, 234–51.

McGrew, W. C., Tutin, C. E. G. & Baldwin, P. J. (1979). Chimpanzees, tools and termites: Cross-cultural comparisons of Senegal, Tanzania, and Rio Muni. *Man*, 14, 185–214.

Meinel, M. & Russon, A. (1996). Eliciting true imitation of object use in captive orangutans. Paper presented at the XVth Congress of the International Primatological Society, Madison, WI, 11–17 August.

Menzel, E. W. Jr (1973). Leadership and communication in young chimpanzees. In *Symposium of the Fourth International Congress of Primatology*, vol. 1, *Precultural Primate Behavior*, ed. E. W. Menzel, pp. 192–225. Basel: S. Karger.

Miles, H. L. (1994). ME CHANTEK: The development of self-awareness in a signing orangutan. In *Self-awareness in Animals and Humans: Developmental Perspectives*, ed. S. T. Parker, R. W. Mitchell & M. L. Boccia, pp. 254–72. New York: Cambridge University Press.

Miles, H. L., Mitchell, R. W. & Harper, S. (1996). Simon says: The development of imitation in an enculturated orangutan. In *Reaching into Thought: The Minds of the Great Apes*, ed. A. E. Russon, K. A. Bard & S. T. Parker, pp. 278–99. Cambridge: Cambridge University Press.

Milton, K. (1993). Diet and social organization of a free-ranging spider monkey population: The development of species-typical behavior in the absence of adults. In *Juvenile Primates: Life History, Development, and Behavior*, ed. M. E. Pereira & L. A. Fairbanks, pp. 173–81. Oxford: Oxford University Press.

Mineka, S. & Cook, M. (1988). Social learning and the acquisition of snake fear in monkeys. In *Social Learning: Psychological and Biological Perspectives*, ed. T. R. Zentall & B. G. Galef, Jr (eds), pp. 51–74. Hillsdale, NJ: Lawrence Erlbaum Associates.

Mitchell, R. W. (1987). A comparative-developmental approach to understanding imitation. In *Perspectives in Ethology*, ed. P. P. G. Bateson & P. H. Klopfer, vol. 7, pp. 183–215. New York: Plenum Press.

Mitchell, R. W. (1993). Mental models of mirror self-recognition: Two theories. *New Ideas in Psychology*, 11, 295–325.

Mitchell, R. W. (1994). The evolution of primate cognition: Simulation, self-knowledge, and knowledge of other minds. In *Hominid Culture in Primate Perspective*, ed. D. Quiatt & J. Itani, pp. 177–232. Boulder, CO: University of Colorado Press.

Mitchell, R. W. & Anderson, J. R. (1993). Discrimination learning of scratching, but failure to obtain imitation and self-recognition in a long-tailed macaque. *Primates*, 34, 301–9.

Moore, B. R. (1992). Avian movement imitation and a new form of mimicry: Tracing the evolution of a complex form of learning. *Behaviour*, 122, 231–63.

Nishida, T. (1980). The leaf-clipping display: A newly-discovered expressive gesture in wild chimpanzees. *Journal of Human Evolution*, 9, 117–28.

Nishida, T. (1987). Local traditions and cultural transmission. In *Primate Societies*, ed. B. B. Smuts, D. L. Cheney, R. M. Seyfarth, R. W. Wrangham & T. T. Struhsaker, pp. 462–74. Chicago: University of Chicago Press.

Nishida, T. (1994). Review of recent findings on Mahale chimpanzees: Implications and future research directions. In *Chimpanzee Cultures*, ed. R. W. Wrangham, W. C. McGrew, F. B. M. de Waal & P. G. Heltne, pp. 373–96. Cambridge, MA: Harvard University Press.

Nishida, T. & Uehara, S. (1980). Chimpanzees, tools and termites: Another example from Tanzania. *Current Anthropology*, 21, 671–2.

Paquette, D. (1992). Discovering and learning tool-use for fishing honey by captive chimpanzees. *Human Evolution*, 7, 17–30.

Parker, S. T. (1996). Apprenticeship in tool-mediated extractive foraging: The origins of imitation, teaching and self-awareness in great apes. In *Reaching into Thought: The Minds of the Great Apes*, ed. A. E. Russon, K. A. Bard & S. T. Parker, pp. 348–70. Cambridge: Cambridge University Press.

Parker, S. T. & Gibson, K. R. (1979). A developmental model for the evolution of language and intelligence in early hominids. *Behavioral and Brain Sciences*, 2, 367–408.

Parker, S. T. & Gibson, K. R. (eds) (1990). *"Language" and Intelligence in Monkeys and Apes: Comparative Developmental Perspectives*. Cambridge: Cambridge University Press.

Parker, S. T. & Russon, A. E. (1996). On the wild side of culture and cognition in the great apes. In *Reaching into Thought: The Minds of the Great Apes*, ed. A. E. Russon, K. A. Bard & S. T. Parker, pp. 430–50. Cambridge: Cambridge University Press.

Patterson, F. G. P. & Kohn, R. H. (1994). Self-recognition and self-awareness in lowland gorillas. In *Self-awareness in Animals and Humans: Developmental Perspectives*, ed. S. T. Parker, R. W. Mitchell & M. L. Boccia, pp. 273–90. New York: Cambridge University Press.

Pereira, M. E. (1993). Agonistic interaction, dominance relation, and ontogenetic trajectories in ringtailed lemurs. In *Juvenile Primates: Life History, Development, and Behavior*, ed. M. E. Pereira & L. A. Fairbanks, pp. 285–305. New York: Oxford University Press.

Pereira, M. E. & Fairbanks, L. A. (eds) (1993). *Juvenile Primates: Life History, Development, and Behavior*. New York: Oxford University Press.

Piaget, J. (1952). *The Origins of Intelligence in Children*. New York: Norton.

Piaget, J. (1962). *Play, Dreams and Imitation in Childhood*. New York: Norton.

Plooij, F. X. (1978). Some basic traits of language in wild chimpanzees. In *Action, Gesture, and Symbol: The Emergence of Language*, ed. A. Lock, pp. 111–31. New York: Academic Press.

Povinelli, D. J., Nelson, K. E. & Boysen, S. T. (1992). Inferences about guessing and knowing by chimpanzees (*Pan troglodytes*). *Journal of Comparative Psychology*, 104, 203–10.

Rescorla, R. A. (1988). Behavioral studies of Pavlovian conditioning. *Annual Review of Neuroscience*, 11, 329–52.

Rijksen, H. D. (1978). *A Field Study in Sumatran Orang Utans* (Pongo pygmaeus abelii *Lesson 1827): Ecology Behaviour and Conservation*. Wageningen, The Netherlands: H. Veenman & B. V. Zoren.

Rodriguez, E. & Wrangham, R. W. (1994). Zoopharmacognosy: The use of medicinal plants in animals. In *Recent Advances in Phytochemistry*, ed. K. R. Downum, J. T. Romeo & H. A. Stafford, vol. 27, pp. 89–106. New York: Plenum Press.

Rogers, A. R. (1988). Does biology constrain culture? *American Anthropologist*, 90, 819–31.

Rogers, C. M. (1973). Implications of a primate early rearing experiment for the concept of culture. In *Symposium of the Fourth International Congress of Primatology*, vol. 1, *Precultural Primate Behavior*, ed. E. W. Menzel, pp. 185–91. Basel: S. Karger.

Russon, A. E. (1996). Imitation in everyday use: Matching and rehearsal in the spontaneous imitation of rehabilitant orangutans (*Pongo pygmaeus*). In *Reaching into Thought: The Minds of the Great Apes*, ed. A. E. Russon, K. A. Bard & S. T. Parker, pp. 152–76. Cambridge: Cambridge University Press.

Russon, A. E. & Galdikas, B. M. F. (1993). Imitation in free-ranging rehabilitant orangutans (*Pongo pygmaeus*). *Journal of Comparative Psychology*, 107, 147–61.

Russon, A. E. & Galdikas, B. M. F. (1995). Constraints on great apes' imitation: Model and action selectivity in rehabilitant orangutan (*Pongo pygmaeus*) imitation. *Journal of Comparative Psychology*, 109, 5–17.

Russon, A. E., Bard, K. A. & Parker, S. T. (eds) (1996). *Reaching into Thought: The Minds of the Great Apes*. Cambridge: Cambridge University Press.

Seyfarth, R. W., Cheney, D. L. & Marler, P. (1980). Vervet monkey alarm calls: Semantic communication in a free-ranging primate. *Animal Behaviour*, 28, 1070–94.

Silk, J. B. (1978). Patterns of food sharing among mother and infant chimpanzees at Gombe National Park, Tanzania. *Folia Primatologica*, 29, 129–41.

Silverberg, J. & Gray, P. (eds) (1992). *Aggression and Peacefulness in Humans and Other Primates*. New York: Oxford University Press.

Smuts, B. B., Cheney, D. L., Seyfarth, R. M., Wrangham, R. W. & Struhsaker, T. T. (eds) (1987). *Primate Societies*. Chicago: University of Chicago Press.

Stammbach, E. (1988). An experimental study of social knowledge: Adaptation to the special manipulative skills of single individuals in a *Macaca fascicularis* group. In *Machiavellian Intelligence: Social Expertise and the Evolution of Intellect in Monkeys, Apes and Humans*, ed. R. W. Byrne & A. Whiten, pp. 309–26. Oxford: Clarendon Press.

Sugiyama, Y. & Koman, J. (1979). Tool-using and -making behavior in wild chimpanzees at Bossou, Guinea. *Primates*, 20, 513–24.

Sumita, K., Kitahara-Frisch, J. & Norikoshi, K. (1985). The acquisition of stone tool use in captive chimpanzees. *Primates*, 26, 168–81.

Tanner, J. E. & Byrne, R. W. (1996). Representation of action through iconic gesture in a captive lowland gorilla. *Current Anthropology*, 37, 162–73.

Teleki, G. (1973). *The Predatory Behavior of Wild Chimpanzees*. E. Brunswick, NJ: Bucknell University Press.

Thorndike, E. L. (1898). Animal intelligence: An experimental study of the associative process in animals. *Psychological Review Monographs*, 2, 551–3.

Thorpe, W. H. (1963). *Learning and Instinct in Animals*, 2nd edn. London: Methuen.

Tomasello, M. (1990). Cultural transmission in the tool use and communicatory signalling of chimpanzees? In *"Language" and Intelligence in Monkeys and Apes: Comparative Developmental Perspectives*, ed. S. T. Parker & K. R. Gibson, pp. 271–311. Cambridge: Cambridge University Press.

Tomasello, M. (1996). Do apes ape? In *Social Learning: The Roots of Culture*, ed. C. M. Heyes & B. G. Galef, Jr, pp. 319–46. New York: Academic Press.

Tomasello, M., Kruger, A. C. & Ratner, H. H. (1993a). Cultural learning. *Behavioral and Brain Sciences*, 16, 495–552.

Tomasello, M., Savage-Rumbaugh, S. & Kruger, A. (1993b). Imitative learning of actions on objects by children, chimpanzees, and enculturated chimpanzees. *Child Development*, 64, 1688–705.

Tomasello, M., Davis-Dasilva, M., Camak, L. & Bard, K. (1987). Observational learning of tool use by young chimpanzees. *Human Evolution*, 2, 175–83.

Tomasello, M., George, B., Kruger, A., Farrar, J. & Evans, E. (1985). The development of gestural communication in young chimpanzees. *Journal of Human Evolution*, 14, 175–86.

van de Rijt-Plooj, H. H. C. & Plooij, F. X. (1987). Growing independence, conflict and learning in mother–infant relations in free-ranging chimpanzees. *Behaviour*, 101, 1–86.

van Hooff, J. A. R. A. M. (1967). The facial displays of the catarrhine monkeys and apes. In *Primate Ethology*, ed. D. Morris, pp. 7–68. London: Weidenfeld & Nicholson.

Visalberghi, E. & Fragaszy, D. (1990). Do monkeys ape? In *"Language" and Intelligence in Monkeys and Apes: Comparative Development Perspectives*, ed. S. T. Parker & K. R. Gibson, pp. 247–73. Cambridge: Cambridge University Press.

Visalberghi, E. & Limongelli, L. (1996). Acting and understanding: Tool use revisited through the minds of capuchin monkeys. In *Reaching into Thought: The Minds of the Great Apes*, ed. A. E. Russon, K. A. Bard & S. T. Parker, Cambridge.: Cambridge University Press.

Watts, D. P. (1985). Observations on the ontogeny of feeding behavior in mountain gorillas (*Gorilla gorilla berengei*). *American Journal of Primatology*, 8, 1–10.

Whitehead, J. M. (1986). Development of feeding selectivity in mantled howler monkeys, *Alouatta palliata*. In *Primate Ontogeny, Cognition, and Social Behaviour*, ed. J. Else & P. C. Lee, pp. 105–17. Cambridge: Cambridge University Press.

Whiten, A. (1996). Imitation, pretense and mindreading: Secondary representation in comparative primatology and developmental psychology? In *Reaching into Thought: The Minds of the Great Apes*, ed. A. E. Russon, K. A. Bard & S. T. Parker, pp. 300–24. Cambridge: Cambridge University Press.

Whiten, A., Custance, D. M., Gómez, J.-C., Teixidor, P. & Bard, K. A. (1996). Imitative learning of artificial fruit processing in children (*Homo sapiens*) and chimpanzees (*Pan troglodytes*). *Journal of Comparative Psychology*, 110, 3–14.

Whiten, A. & Ham, R. (1992). On the nature and evolution of imitation in the animal kingdom: Reappraisal of a century of research. In *Advances in the Study of Behavior*, ed. P. J. B. Slater, J. S. Rosenbatt, C. Beer & S. Milinski, vol. 21, pp. 239–83. New York: Academic Press.

Whitfield, J. H. (1965). *Machiavelli*. New York: Russell & Russell.

Wood, D., Bruner, J. & Ross, G. (1976). The role of tutoring in problem solving. *Journal of Child Psychology and Psychiatry*, 17, 89–100.

Woods, S. (1992). Implementation and Evaluation of a Behavioral Enrichment Program for Captive Gorillas, with an Emphasis on Tool Behaviors. PhD thesis, University of Colorado.

Wrangham, R. W. (1975). *The Behavioural Ecology of Chimpanzees in Gombe National Park, Tanzania*. PhD thesis, University of Cambridge.

Wrangham, R. W. & Nishida, T. (1983). *Aspilia* spp. leaves: A puzzle in the feeding behavior of wild chimpanzees. *Primates*, 24, 276–82.

Wrangham, R. W., McGrew, W. C., de Waal, F. B. M. & Heltne, P. G. (eds.). (1994). *Chimpanzee Cultures*. Cambridge, MA: Harvard University Press.

Yando, R., Seitz, V. & Zigler, E. (1978). *Imitation: A Developmental Perspective*. Hillsdale, NJ: Lawrence Erlbaum Associates.

Zentall, T. R. & Galef, B. G., Jr (eds) (1988). *Social Learning: Psychological and Biological Perspectives*. Hillsdale, N J: Lawrence Erlbaum Associates.

8 Primates' knowledge of their natural habitat: As indicated in foraging

CHARLES R. MENZEL

Introduction

Humphrey (1976) suggested that primate information processing skills, as displayed in laboratory learning tasks, exceed the demands of finding food, finding shelter and avoiding danger in the natural habitat, and he hypothesised that the apparent surplus capability evolved in response to the demands posed by life in complex social groups. Other chapters in this book attempt to spell out the empirical predictions of Humphrey's hypothesis, termed the 'social intelligence' or 'Machiavellian intelligence' hypothesis (Byrne & Whiten, 1988; Cheney & Seyfarth, 1992), and to evaluate the evidence from studies of social behaviour and brain size. In 1976 Humphrey had little information available on how primates find food in their natural habitat, and his statement about the relative simplicity of this task was mainly speculation. An alternative to Humphrey's viewpoint is that primates are capable of learning the relative positions and characteristics of a very large number of objects and topographical features in their natural habitat and that they use this stored information, in combination with current cues, to find food, to discriminate food from non-food objects, and to travel efficiently and safely. In this chapter, the questions of what information primates possess about the structure of their habitat and how such information might contribute to their survival and reproductive success are examined.

To form an evolutionary explanation for as complex a phenomenon as primate learning and memory capabilities requires that the capabilities of interest be well described and that a reasonable guess can be made about their biological value in the animals' evolutionarily relevant environment. To date, however, only a modest number of primate studies have analysed learning and memory experimentally in tasks that require locomotion (E. Menzel, 1971, 1973, 1974, 1978, 1984; Fragaszy, 1980; Andrews, 1986, 1988a, 1988b; Joubert & Vauclair, 1986; C. Menzel 1991, 1996a,b; Mac-Donald et al., 1994; Hemmi & Menzel, 1995). Furthermore, there are still few experimental studies of any kind on wild primates (Tsumori, 1966; E. Menzel, 1966, 1969; Cheney & Seyfarth, 1990), and even fewer on the operation of learning and memory capabilities in the animal's natural habitat in the context of foraging and travel (C. Menzel, 1991; for detailed descriptive studies see Sigg, 1980; Sigg & Stolba, 1981; Boesch & Boesch, 1984; Garber, 1989). The idea that spatial orientation and food finding in the natural habitat are less demanding tasks than living in a social group is therefore based on limited data.

There is no single, accepted definition of animal intelligence (Macphail, 1987 and commentary), and few current researchers would suggest that intelligence is a unitary, general capacity that increases progressively in vertebrate phylogeny (Warren, 1973). Authors generally agree, however, that the methods used to study intelligence should permit one to compare species and age classes, to measure the contribution of perceptual, motivational and situational factors to differences in performance, and to determine the information that animals acquire on their own without human training. My aim in this chapter is not to formulate a single hypothesis that stands in opposition to the Machiavellian intelligence hypothesis, but rather to draw attention to the diversity of information handling problems that primates face in their foraging and to the ways that these problems might vary across species. I review concepts pertaining to the discrimination of object categories and recent studies of learning and foraging in macaques. I then discuss some similarities between information processing in the foraging and social contexts. I do not review studies of diet per se (e.g. Izawa & Nishida, 1963; Suzuki, 1965; Maruhashi, 1980), of food handling techniques (Janson & Boinski, 1992 and see Chapter 11), or of tool use (Beck, 1980).

Questions about animals' knowledge of the natural habitat include the following (Robinson, 1986). Does an animal know what kinds of plants and topographical features are in its habitat? Does it know the relative positions of these objects? By what processes does an animal gather, organise, store and retrieve this information? How do the underlying mechanisms develop in the individual? What is the phyletic distribution of these mechanisms? What is their evolutionary history?

Categorisation of food items and their natural settings

The idea that organisms classify objects and events in their environment is of course not new. Classification activities are fundamental to biology and to information processing systems in general. Simpson (1961, pp. 2–3) states:

> If each of the many things in the world were taken as distinct,
> unique, a thing in itself unrelated to any other thing, perception of
> the world would disintegrate into complete meaninglessness . . .
> The necessity for aggregating things into classes is a completely
> general characteristic of living things . . . Such generalization, such
> classification . . . is an absolute, minimal requirement of adaptation,
> which in turn is an absolute and minimal requirement of being or
> staying alive.

The relationships among objects and events that primates might take into account are of many different kinds and include associations based on spatial or temporal proximity, as well as those based on similarity (Simpson, 1961; Rescorla, 1985; Kummer, 1995a). Relationships among objects are potentially informative to foragers, and discrimination of similarities and differences is often regarded as a basic way of predicting the properties of objects. Trees of the same species often produce fruit at the same time of year; most branches larger than a certain diameter can support a monkey's weight; stones along a river cover invertebrates, and so on. Identification of kinds of objects 'is made possible because the diversity of nature is not continuous but consists of discrete entities, separated from each other by discontinuities. One finds in nature not merely individuals but also "species", that is, groups of individuals that share certain characteristics with each other' (Mayr, 1982, p. 252; see also Berlin, 1978, p. 17). The survival value to an animal of detecting and responding to discontinuities and natural groupings is potentially enormous. One could ask what types of patterns and associations exist in an organism's natural environment, which objects and events the organism treats as equivalent or differentiates, through what processes this categorisation is achieved, and to what degree the categories of different animals are co-extensive. With respect to the first issue, types of similarities existing in nature, it is important to recognise that the similarity among the individuals of a plant species is very different from the similarity that exists among members of a set of non-living objects. Shared evolutionary origin is responsible for complex, multi-dimensional similarities and internal cohesiveness and organisation of species (Mayr, 1988).

Simpson (1961, p. 11) says 'The basic or . . . primitive step in classification is simply the grouping together of individual objects . . . by some system of relationships (or associations) among them'. Bruner *et al.* (1956, p. 1) state, 'To categorize is to render discriminably different things equivalent, to group the objects and events . . . around us into classes and to respond to them in terms of their class membership rather than their uniqueness' (see also Smith & Medin, 1981; Shepard, 1987; Snowdon, 1987 for discussions of definitions and criteria). Of course few, if any, non-human primates in the wild literally collect objects and sort them into piles for study (captive chimpanzees show spontaneous sorting of objects, Matsuzawa, 1990); they encounter objects during their travel and feeding and presumably learn something about the classes of objects present and where the members of these classes are located (E. Menzel, 1978).

Sorting rules

Herrnstein (1982, 1984) argues that sorting rules for natural objects by animals are often polymorphous; that is, that no single feature is necessary for sorting and that many features contribute in combination to the discrimination of categories. In other instances, a key feature reliably indicates (e.g. is highly correlated with) the properties of an object and is responded to by the animal much more than other perceived and equally reliable cues (Tinbergen, 1976; see also Schrier *et al.*, 1984). In evolutionary systematics, groupings are often formed by visual inspection, on the basis of a large number of characteristics, and only then are specific, reliable features sought (Mayr, 1982). A systematist does not classify a given living organism solely from a pre-established list of 20 or 30 characters, but instead follows a gestalt in which 'a virtually endless number of characters are interwoven' (Lorenz, 1971, vol. 2, p. 199). The grouping of organisms into named classes by preliterate humans appears to be based largely on overall perceived similarity, presumably as judged from gross morphological and behavioural characteristics (Berlin, 1978). The

stimulus features and processes by which non-human primates discriminate the relevant properties of new objects in the field is largely an open
question. Differences among species, and differences from humans are
obviously to be expected.

General benefits of categorisation

The proposed general benefits of categorisation are that the animal can
ignore irrelevant detail and respond quickly without having to learn each
situation independently (Herrnstein, 1984), that the same object can be
recognised despite variations in lighting, orientation, etc (Lorenz, 1971),
and that the animal is required to process a limited and manageable
amount of information (Marler, 1982). 'Categorising serves to cut down
the diversity of objects and events that must be dealt with uniquely by
an organism of limited capacities' (Bruner et al., 1956, p. 245; cited in
Rosch & Lloyd, 1978, p. 1). Bruner et al. (1956, p. 11–15) distinguish
five biological functions of categorization. According to them, categorisation (a) reduces the complexity of the animal's environment, (b) is the
means by which objects in the environment are identified, (c) 'reduces
the necessity of constant learning', (d) provides direction for instrumental
activity (i.e. provides a goal for exploration), and (e) provides an opportunity for 'ordering and relating classes of events'. The authors stress that
the anticipatory nature of much of categorising has biological significance.
'It is not simply that organisms code the events of their environment into
equivalence classes, but that they utilise cues for doing so that allow an
opportunity for prior adjustment to the event identified' (Bruner et al.,
1956, p. 14). Gilmour (1951, cited in Warburton, 1967) regards summar-
isation, retrieval of information and, especially, formation of classes for
making inductive generalisations as the primary general functions of classification systems; for example, given that a proposition is true of items a,
b, c, . . . , x, a biologist might predict that the proposition is also true of
other members of the smallest taxon from which the initial items are
drawn (Warburton, 1967). Plant taxonomists face the problem of gen-
eralising 'from a limited set of data to conclusions about populations that
are generally too large to be studied in individual detail' (Cronquist, 1988,
p. 97). Consolidation of information about the locations and phenological
characteristics of plants is often regarded as a problem for primates that
utilise patchily distributed, seasonally available food sources (Altmann,
1974; Milton, 1988; Garber, 1989).

Costs of categorization

There are potential costs involved in categorisation. One obvious draw-back to treating different objects as equivalent is that important variations within categories might be ignored (Lorenz, 1962; Marler, 1982; Herrnstein, 1984). Ripe fruits that appear at the same time of year can vary in physical composition (Van Roosmalen, 1984), in spatial distribution, or in whether they are produced synchronously or asynchronously (Terborgh, 1983). Serious costs can be incurred with misidentification of toxic items. Another risk proposed for categorisation is that the wrong features might be used in the animal's sorting rule, as when incorrect categories are formed prematurely after experience with only one or two cases (Herrnstein, 1984). Animals are presumably capable of revising categories and of classifying the same food item in more than one way.

In general, animals might be expected to discriminate the smallest relevant category. Nevertheless, if perceptual learning takes time that could be spent in other activities, it may not always be cost-effective for an organism to recognise the individual members of every category of natural objects or even every available food species (Stephens & Krebs, 1986). There are possibly limits to how finely animals distinguish categories in a new situation. Pigeons trained on one exemplar of a silhouette of a white oak leaf generalised to all other silhouettes of white oak leaves and discriminated these from silhouettes of leaves of other non-oak species. In contrast, the pigeons failed to learn to discriminate specific individual exemplars within the white oak species (Cerella, 1979).

Experimentally naive rhesus macaques spontaneously distinguished between slides of individual monkeys. They habituated quickly to repeated presentations of slides of the same individual, but showed renewed visual attention whenever a slide of a new individual was shown. By contrast, the subjects showed no 'dishabituation' to slides of new individual domestic animals, as if individual members of these species were perceived as equivalent. With mere visual exposure to slides of additional animal species, however, the subjects came to treat slides of all individual animals as different (Humphrey, 1974). Humphrey suggested that the subjects initially attended to gross, salient, species-specific features of the domestic animals but came to attend to subtler details that distinguished individuals. Humphrey (1974) termed the phenomenon 'bias in perceptual acuity'.

Given the difficulty of field identification of plants to the species level in the tropics (Leighton, 1993), it would not be surprising if there are genera of food plants in which at least young wild primates do not normally differentiate species, and there are presumably species of plants in which primates do not care to distinguish individuals. At the same time, certain other plant genera in the same habitat might be differentiated finely by species, by the temporal and spatial settings in which the individuals are found, or by aspects of the individual's momentary appearance (Real et al., 1984; Bulmer & Healey, 1993); human classifications of animals based on such aspects of appearance as the life-stage of the individual or polymorphisms can cut across closely related species (Bulmer & Healey, 1993). The upper limit, if any, in the ability of long-lived nonhuman primates to differentiate categories perceptually (Gibson & Gibson, 1955; Gibson, 1969) is an open question. Comparisons of the extent or speed of perceptual learning and comparisons of features of plant parts that attract visual attention in sympatric primate species (e.g. frugivorous orangutans and macaques, folivorous *Presbytis*) would be of interest. A question here is what things are the most different about the categories formed by two different animals.

Human folk taxonomies

Studies on the folk taxonomies of preliterate human groups raise additional issues. These examples from the area of language and communication illustrate how the environment can be divided into categories. Folk taxonomies usually include about 250–800 named 'generic' level distinctions for plant forms and a similar number for animal forms. The typical number is less than 500, even in species-rich habitats (Berlin, 1992). Named categorical distinctions within higher and lower taxonomic ranks are much more limited in number (Raven et al., 1971). Berlin (1978, p. 17) suggests why categorical distinctions in folk taxonomies are primarily at the so-called 'generic' level. 'Generic taxa appear to correspond rather closely with the species in . . . biology as the fundamental taxonomic unit. That this should be so is not surprising in that the species in any one restricted geographic region, especially the species of vertebrates and major flowering plants, tend to represent highly perceptually distinct discontinuities in nature' (see also Gould, 1979). Perhaps the biological species – or the biological genus (Berlin, 1992) – is usually the highest rank of category in which constituent elements are both (a) easily discriminated by their appearance without requiring intensive study

(Cain, 1958, cited in Berlin, 1992) and (b) share important properties in common (e.g. the categories predict the properties of their elements). Named groups of plants at higher levels in folk taxonomies often have poor agreement with biological classifications. It is generally more difficult for biologists to construct higher taxa of flowering plants than higher taxa of vertebrates (e.g. Carnivora), due to less morphological integration and a lower correlation with habitat and lifestyle (Cronquist, 1988; Stuessy, 1990).

One might expect human and non-human primates to categorise natural objects in a largely pragmatic fashion. For example, a forager might be expected to differentiate into refined categories the food items that it normally consumes (or perhaps specifically avoids) but categorise in only a gross manner the surrounding inedible items and food items that are unfamiliar, or that are not normally consumed or avoided. This pattern approximately characterises the classification schemes of preliterate groups (Raven et al., 1971; Berlin et al., 1974; Gould, 1979; Mayr, 1982). Nevertheless, categorisation of natural items by humans does not always bear a close relation to their nutritional content. Preliterate humans name many plants that appear to have no cultural significance and that are not specifically avoided due to their poisonous content or other negative qualities (Berlin, 1978). 'Most of the recognized plant and animal groupings in folk systems of classification represent perceptually distinct discontinuities in the biological world that appear to "cry out to be named" ' (Berlin, 1978, p. 11), and there are instances of close agreement between the independently developed taxonomies of indigenous peoples and those of western biologists (Mayr, 1969). The taxonomic distinctiveness or phenotypic salience of the animal or plant, its size in relation to human beings, and its prevalence and ease of observation in the environment appear to influence whether humans will name an organism. The level of biological classification (e.g. species, genus, family) that is most perceptually salient to humans is not fixed and varies with the group of organisms being classified (Berlin, 1992).

Challenges to categorisation in primate habitats

Discriminating differences and recognising similarities among living objects can be a challenging task. At least six potential problems can be distinguished. Firstly, there is a striking degree of variability within tropical habitats. All living individuals are biologically unique, and uniqueness implies diversity (Mayr, 1982). The number of individual food items in the home range of most primate groups is uncountable, and species diversity can be high. In the Kutai National Park in East Kalimantan, for example, 781 species of woody plants produced fruits during a 2 year period; orangutans ate the pulp or seeds of at least 89 species (Leighton, 1993). The number of plant species eaten by a group of Japanese macaques can be as high as 209 (Clark, 1979; Maruhashi, 1980; Koganezawa, 1983). There are presumably limits to how far animals can go, or care to go, in short timespans in discriminating individual leaves, flowers and fruits and limits to how far they can go in memorising the exact positions of these items. It must be emphasised that the upper limits for the number of individual objects and locations that primates can learn within their home range are unknown.

Secondly, no single aspect of morphological organisation or spatial distribution is constant for all plant species in general (Cronquist, 1988, p. 11). 'The rapidity with which a single character can undergo phylogenetic alteration can vary greatly between closely related animal and plant types. The result is a continuous variability in the taxonomic reliability of each individual character' (Lorenz, 1971, vol. 2, p. 199). For example: (a) morphological characters (e.g. leaf shape) that discriminate species within one plant genus may not be sufficient in another genus; (b) species X may occur near other species that share the same narrow soil requirements, whereas species Y may tolerate a much broader range of soil types and have no reliable spatial association with other species. The degree of variability of a character within a species is itself variable. For example, whether an animal can treat one ripe fruit as a signal that the same fruit is now widely available in the habitat depends on the species of fruit and degree of synchrony of fruit production. The probability that an additional tree will contain ripe fruit given that N out of a sample of M other individual trees of the same species now contain ripe fruit varies by species. The above facts would seem to be of importance for dietary generalists.

Thirdly, discriminating the spatial limits of individual plants or of the topographical structures that are correlated with certain plants may not be a simple matter. The precise boundaries between a vine and the trees on which the vine grows may be hard to see; the transition from one plant community or soil type to another may be gradual. There is little information on the perception of environmental borders and gradients, such as gradients in plant colour, density or height, by non-human primates.

Fourthly, objects that appear similar to one another can differ in important ways. Vervets eat some species of *Acacia* gum but avoid others that contain high amounts of condensed tannin (gum colour is an available cue, but it is not known whether vervets use colour to make their discriminations: Wrangham & Waterman, 1981). Orangutans select systematically from among 31 species of figs that vary in important ways in chemical content (Leighton, 1993). When several chemical and nutritional variables are included together in a food content analysis, many of the fig species appear to the ecologist to have a unique combination of chemical features and patch size (Leighton, 1993). Complex, multi-dimensional similarity due to common evolutionary origin (e.g. among the individual members of a fig species) is very different biologically, and much richer, than the sort of class membership that exists among inanimate objects (Mayr, 1988). Little testing has been done on whether primates discriminate species of plants differently than sets of non-living objects, but it seems likely that dietary generalists use more than a single cue and revise their initial categorisations based on an integration of criteria (Leighton, 1993). After an animal has determined the relevant properties of objects, then its ability to use distal visual cues might be important in saving time. How many intrinsic and extrinsic (e.g. spatial, seasonal) features of natural objects a wild primate integrates is unknown. Baboons select the corms of just one of three species of *Hypoxis* that are very similar to the human eye but that differ in lipid, protein and phenolics content (Whiten *et al.*, 1991). It is not simply the mean or modal value of a category that an animal must know, but what the limits of the category are and how to distinguish between two overlapping categories with very different properties (Altmann, 1967; Rosch, 1978; Medin & Dewey, 1984).

A fifth problem for animals is that objects that are different in appearance, or that occur in widely separated locations, or that occur at different points in time, can nevertheless stand in a useful predictive relationship. For example, two plant species might produce ripe fruits at the same time of year. Whether primates can use the presence of ripe fruits on species A as a cue that species B simultaneously contains different-looking ripe fruits (and *vice versa*) is unknown. Whether they use the unripe fruits of particular individuals of species B as a cue that these individuals will contain ripe fruits several days later, or use the phenological state of woody plant species C in location X as a cue that mushrooms are currently available on the ground in location Y are unknown. The question of whether wild primates respond to predictive relations between two unrelated and visually dissimilar species departs from a biologically based concept of grouping by similarity, and it is relevant from a psychological and ecological standpoint. The question is what stimulus factors enable primates to overcome gaps in space (Jarvik, 1953; Meyer et al., 1965; Rumbaugh et al., 1989), in time and in the appearance of objects to make valid inductive generalisations. What constitutes contiguity or connection between any two objects? Do animals generalise their search primarily within, rather than across synchronously fruiting species, as the Gestalt principle of grouping by similar form would suggest (C. Menzel, 1996b)?

To take a concrete example, wild Japanese macaques that find experimentally introduced, ripe, *Akebia trifoliata* fruit subsequently inspect naturally occurring vines of both species of the genus (*A. trifoliata* and *A. quinata*) that are present in the animals' habitat, rather than species of non-*Akebia* plants that produce fruits at the same time of year (C. Menzel, 1991; see below). The two *Akebia* vines are easily distinguishable by humans because they have markedly different leaf configurations; and to an uninformed person the two vine species can appear no more similar to one another than either is to other vine species in the macaques' home range. However, these two species of *Akebia* produce nearly identical looking fruits at precisely the same time of year, and with additional study a human can see that the vines share subtle features, such as similar silhouettes on a tree. In principle, not only the high degree of synchrony of ripe fruit production but also the specific, detailed similarity of the fruits might be a significant feature of the learning situation for macaques.

These findings show that the degree of similarity of two plant species depends on the particular characters selected, and a question arising again is what specific characters, or combinations of characters, limit how far primates generalise their search across plant species. Component stimuli that merit study include the degree of similarity of the food items produced by the available species, the similarity of the source plants aside from the food items (for an experimental example see C. Menzel, 1996b and below), the degree of synchrony in the production of food items by the different species, and the similarity in the height level and habitat in which the food items occur. The method described above could be used to determine the relative importance of different dimensions of plant similarity for learning, and it could be used to identify significant features of the component stimuli. In this manner, an animal's process of delimiting a particular plant type from other plants in the habitat could be clarified and its use of visual, tactile, gustatory and other stimuli could be put into perspective. It should be added that performance typically underestimates knowledge (Marler & Terrace, 1984) and that animals might possess more precise information about species boundaries than they reveal in any one foraging situation.

Sixthly, and most basically, an animal may not be able to detect directly the properties of an object that are of long range importance. From an evolutionary perspective the importance of objects and events depends on their effect on the animal's lifetime reproductive success, a judgement that can be made only in retrospect. Over the short-term, however, individuals are capable of using reliable cues that predict the long-range effects of objects and of revising their assessment of cues based on the immediate consequences of contact with objects. An issue is therefore how organisms extend their categories under novel circumstances (Bulmer & Healey, 1993). *Macaca fuscata* transplanted from their native habitat in Japan to Texas consumed unfamiliar and unusual plant items, such as cactus, almost immediately, despite the fact that they had provisioned food available (Clark & Mano, 1975; Clark, 1979). *M.mulatta* that were transplanted from Cayo Santiago, Puerto Rico, to Desecheo (a small, semi-arid island), fed almost immediately on a great variety of plants. Species that had been common foods on Cayo Santiago were not selected in greater proportion than unfamiliar species (Morrison & Menzel 1972). These findings suggest that macaques are prepared in some manner to discriminate new potential food items. Macaques do not, however, simply accept unfamiliar foods under all conditions. Japanese macaques from one newly provisioned group – that was not transplanted – readily consumed provisioned sweet potatoes and wheat, which they had previously obtained from nearby crop fields, but initially ignored unfamiliar items including apples, tangerines and soybeans (Itani, 1965; Itani & Nishimura, 1973). Similarly, wild chimpanzees do not always consume eggs or other experimentally introduced, unfamiliar foods (Kortlandt, 1967).

These considerations suggest that primates, like other dietary generalists, face a conflict between exploring new opportunities that have potentially dangerous consequences and using only familiar options that may be of lower quality or that may be limited by future environmental change (Rozin's, 1976, 1977, 1982 'omnivore's paradox'). This conflict is illustrated by howling monkeys (*Alouatta palliata*) and their food supply. Howlers in Costa Rica prefer leaves that have low rather than high concentrations of alkaloids and tannins. Such leaves are not always easy to find, because the concentration of the compounds in leaves varies across individual trees of the same species and across seasons for the same tree and is apparently difficult to judge by the visual appearance of the leaves alone. A primary means by which howlers track such environmental changes is by cautiously tasting leaves in new potential source trees (Glander, 1981, 1982). To my knowledge, no study has been conducted on how howlers decide which new trees to sample.

Keeping track of individual items of a category over a larger area

Thus far I have said little about spatial aspects of primate foraging. The movements of chimpanzees in relation to previously seen objects indicate that animals keep track of the locations of many different individual items over a sizeable area. Chimpanzees transport stone hammers to still-invisible tree-root anvils for cracking nuts and appear to take into account both the weight of the stone and its distance from an available anvil so as to minimise their overall travel effort (Boesch & Boesch, 1984). E. Menzel (1978, 1984) reviewed studies of spatial memory in captive chimpanzees in tasks that entail locomotion. In one study, a single chimpanzee from a group of six was carried and could watch as an experimenter hid up to 18 piles of food in natural cover in a 1 acre enclosure. When the animal was released several minutes later, it recovered most of the hidden food; its path of travel connecting the food piles approximated a least-distance routing. When the animal was shown two food piles on one side of the enclosure and three piles on the other side, it usually travelled first to the side containing the larger amount of food. The animals appeared to perceive the relative positions of the hidden food piles and their own position within this scaled frame of reference (E. Menzel, 1973; see also Tinklepaugh, 1932). Furthermore, young chimpanzees could convey information to social partners about the direction, approximate distance, relative desirability and quantity of food items (E. Menzel, 1974).

Neotropical monkeys can travel among the individual trees of a particular species that currently bear ripe fruit (Terborgh, 1983; Milton, 1988). Garber (1989) has argued that travel patterns of saddle-back and moustached tamarins (genus *Saguinus*) imply the use of spatial memory and 'detailed knowledge of the distribution of particular plant species'. Garber examined the distribution of feeding bouts by tamarins to a sample of 192 individual trees of 20 fruit- and exudate-producing species. For 15 of the 20 species there was a high degree of intraspecific synchrony among individual trees in the production of fruits or exudates. Only trees that the tamarins visited during a longer 12 month study were considered as potential feeding choices. When the tamarins fed in a tree, their next feeding bout was in the nearest individual tree of the same species in 70% of 385 total occasions.

The foraging pattern that distinguishes *Saguinus* from other non-*Saguinus* species in the same region is their use of fruits that occur in small, spatially discrete patches that ripen gradually over a period of several weeks. This pattern of ripening ensures that tamarins can obtain a small but reliable amount of fruit on each visit (Terborgh, 1983; E. Menzel & Juno, 1985). When saddle-back tamarins are tested in captivity with methods suited to their behavioural organisation, they possess excellent memories for the location, visual appearance and orientation of objects in their living area. They show exceptionally rapid learning of objects that contain food and strong 'win–stay' strategies with respect to these objects (Menzel & Menzel, 1979; E. Menzel & Juno, 1982, 1985).

Hamadryas baboons appear to orientate toward waterholes that are hidden behind hills. Males establish a shared travel direction with the other males of the same band when they leave their sleeping cliff in the morning. Their initial departure movement points in the direction of one of about eight distant, still invisible, water holes. After departing from the cliff in this cohesive manner, however, the band eventually splits into separate units (clans) for foraging, and the clans lose visual and auditory contact with one another. At midday, the clans of a band reassemble at the waterhole toward which the band had orientated earlier. The baboons' behaviour suggests that the direction of the morning departure from the cliff communicates and establishes the specific waterhole to be visited later in the day (Stolba, 1979; Sigg & Stolba, 1981; Kummer, 1995b).

Empirical examples from a particular genus: Macaque foraging

How far ahead do animals need to plan their route?

To determine whether long-tailed macaques, *M. fascicularis*, plan their foraging route more than one step ahead, I analysed the sequence of moves by which animals harvested multiple visible food items. Seven adult males were tested individually on variations of the classic Travelling Salesman problem (E. Menzel, 1973; Anderson, 1983); an animal's task was to choose the shortest route from its starting location to all the individual food items. Interest was in the efficiency of the animal's chosen route and in the decision rules that it followed. An animal was confined to an indoor cage and could not observe the experimenter while the experimenter positioned up to 21 food items in an 880 m² field. The animal was released into a holding cage, from where it could look out at the still-visible food items. After 1 min the animal was released into the field and could harvest the items.

In the initial experiment, the visible food items were distributed at random. In this situation, the macaques' overall path was much shorter than a random sequence, and it approximated to an optimal (least-distance) routing, as estimated by computer algorithm. Subsequent experiments were conducted to determine whether animals were attempting to minimise their overall distance (a global strategy) or were actually following a more local strategy, such as that of always moving to the next closest available item (termed the 'nearest-neighbour' strategy). Visible food items were rearranged in space, such that the strategy of minimising overall distance was now pitted directly against the use of the nearest-neighbour strategy. In order for an animal to minimise its overall travel distance, it now had to forego a nearby food item on its initial movement, in favour of a more distant item. Under these particular spatial arrangements, which would rarely occur in nature, an animal typically went for one of the closest available items rather than for a distant item and thereby failed to minimise its overall distance. Thus, the animals did not appear to plan their foraging routes at a high level, despite the fact that they were very sensitive to small differences in distance. Additional experiments showed that this behaviour was effective in obtaining food quickly in the presence of a social competitor. In sum, by using a relatively simple movement rule animals were able to harvest dispersed food items in a highly efficient sequence; only in especially arranged conditions did the rule lead to large departures from the shortest possible path.

Discrimination of novel and familiar fruits

In another series of tests, I have asked what are all the things a macaque can deduce from one object. The amount of information that an animal can gain by examining an object is potentially unlimited. It is an oversimplification to regard a focal object as the sole source of information, or to assume that the animal's interests are limited to identifying and appraising only that object. That is, to what other environmental structures is the object connected? What is the logic of these connections from the standpoint of the animal? What does the presence of the object imply to an animal about the state of the environment?

I examined the extent to which free-ranging Japanese macaques, *Macaca fuscata*, responded differentially to familiar and novel fruits within a natural feeding context, to assess in a preliminary manner how well they knew their environment (see E. Menzel, 1966, 1969 for background). I conducted tests during Autumn at the Osaka Prefectural Park, Minoo, Japan. I presented novel fruits 1 m from undisturbed natural fruits on the ground in the forest before animals had arrived in the area. The undisturbed natural fruits were those that had previously fallen from an overhead tree. I used different combinations of novel fruits and familiar wild fruits in the test. For example, on several trials I placed a novel New Zealand passion fruit next to a fallen persimmon (*Diaspyros*), underneath a large persimmon tree that the group frequently visited. Thirty-seven animals sniffed or made physical contact with one or both of the fruits. All 37 initial responses were directed toward the novel fruit rather than toward the familiar fruit. Animals rarely consumed the novel fruit. Thus, animals clearly distinguished novel foods from familiar foods when they encountered these items under routine feeding conditions.

Responses to dummy fruits

I also examined whether Japanese macaques responded differentially to model fruits and non-representational objects, to assess approximately how well they could discriminate potential foods. I presented animals with novel artificial models of fruit at the Okayama Prefectural Park, Katsuyama. I placed test objects along a mountain trail that the group commonly used for travel. Ten trials were conducted over 17 days. Insofar as possible, I avoided scoring an individual animal more than once per trial. On each trial two objects were presented on the trail: an artificial model fruit and a brightly colored novel object that was approximately matched for size and visual complexity and that did not resemble fruit in its details. For example, on one trial a red plastic tomato and a red rubber ball with a black band were used. The model and the novel object were located 1.5 m apart; I swapped their locations across trials and used a different pair of objects for each trial.

Sixty animals per trial came within 8 m of the objects. More than 80% of 115 instances of sniffing (without touching) – and all instances of carrying and tasting – were directed toward the model fruit rather than toward the brightly coloured object. Both juveniles and adults showed this pattern. The findings will be reported in detail elsewhere, but the data suggest that Japanese macaques react to the visual appearance of unfamiliar potential food items. The animals are more apt to approach, sniff, handle and taste objects that bear a generic visual resemblance to actual categories of plant foods than to do the same with objects that do not resemble food.

Learning and long-term memory

In another study (C. Menzel, 1991; described briefly above) I attempted to assess the macaques' knowledge of relationships between food items and their natural sources. I addressed the following questions. If an animal detects one food item, how does it go about finding more of the same item? Where does it go? What does its behaviour suggest about its knowledge and 'inferences' about its feeding environment (E. Menzel & Johnson, 1976; Premack, 1976; Cheney & Seyfarth, 1985)? I presented *M. fuscata* at the Osaka Prefectural Park with either ripe akebi (*Akebia trifoliata*) fruit, chocolate, or no experimental food (control), from about 1 month before until about 1.5 months after the time when ripe akebi fruit were available in the home range. I obtained ripe akebi fruits out of season from a commercial distributor. Native akebi fruit is a good food for tests of memory, because it is highly preferred, relatively rare and hard for monkeys to detect from a distance. Chocolate is also a seldom-encountered, highly preferred food; it was included in the study to test the macaques' readiness to form new search patterns for novel occurrences of food.

In each trial I placed a small amount of food near the edge of a path within the home range of the group of animals, well before the group arrived in the area. In control trials I moved to a location, knelt as if placing out food but actually left nothing, then withdrew to a distance. The first animal that found and ate the food (experimental conditions) or that came within 5 m of the predetermined location (control condition) became the focal animal. I followed this animal for at least 20 min and recorded its path of travel and manual manipulations of the environment.

Behaviour varied according to the type of food item found (Figure 8.1). Animals that found a piece of experimentally introduced akebi fruit stared upwards and entered distant trees that contained naturally occurring akebi vines. They did so even at times of year when the naturally

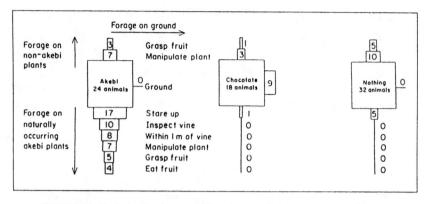

FIGURE 8.1 Variation in the spatial locations and plants investigated by Japanese macaques, according to the type of experimentally introduced food discovered. The three central squares show the numbers of different focal animals who ate akebi fruit, chocolate or nothing (control). Scores are the numbers of different focal animals who showed a response at least once. Cell width is proportional to the percentage of focal animals responding. Arrows point along three foraging dimensions: down is foraging on naturally occurring akebi plants; up is on non-akebi plants, to the right of the square is on the surface of the ground near the test location. A particular individual could search along more than one dimension. Reprinted with permission from Menzel (1991) *Animal Behaviour*, 41, 397–402.

occurring akebi fruits were not ripe. Animals that found chocolate returned to the food site at later times and restricted much of their searching to a small area of ground. Animals that ate 'nothing' seldom stared upwards and did not inspect akebi plants or the ground near their starting location. Figure 8.1 shows the proportion of animals that searched along three dimensions of the environment: on akebi plants, on non-akebi plants and on the ground. The macaques' behaviour suggested detailed knowledge of the feeding environment, adjustment of search method to the type of food found, and the use of long-term memory.

Structure-guided foraging

In additional field experiments, Japanese macaques that found chocolate in one location sometimes searched along the stream-bed, path edge or tree grove that had contained the food. Stream- and path-following suggested that animals organised their search, in part, by the spatial proximity of food to visible environmental structures or gestalts (E. Menzel,

(a)

Visible border, straight or curved

(b)

Visible matching object

(c)

Invisible straight line

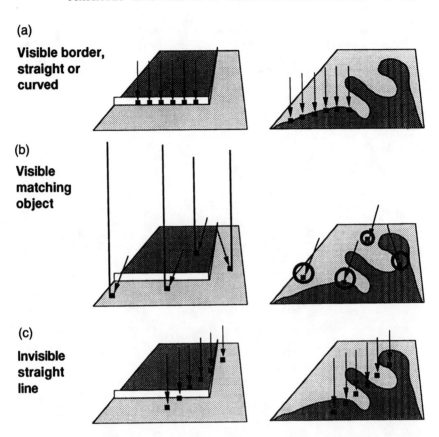

FIGURE 8.2 Sample layouts of hidden food in three experimental conditions. (a) Visible environmental border: the food (black squares) lies along either a low cement wall between a grass field and a sand field (left); or along the border between a stone field and a grass field (right). (b) Visible matching objects: food next to bases of vertical poles (left); or next to wooden crates (right). (c) Invisible line: the line cuts across grass and sand fields (left); it cuts across stone and grass fields (right). Based on photographs in Menzel (1996b) *American Journal of Primatology*, 38, 117–32, with permission.

1969; Brown & Gass, 1993; Brown, 1994). I subsequently studied whether captive long-tailed macaques used visual cues to predict the location of new potential food sites in trial-unique learning situations (C. Menzel, 1996b). A group of 37 macaques was confined to a holding cage while an experimenter concealed food in an outdoor enclosure according to one of four rules (Figure 8.2): (a) at intervals of 1 m along a visible, straight or curved border between fields of grass, gravel or stones,

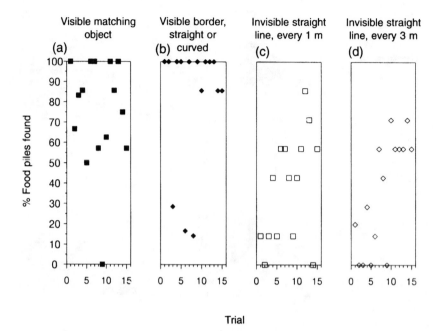

FIGURE 8.3 Percentage of available food piles found during a 30 min trial, as a function of experimental conditions and problem (trial) number. (a) Visible matching object. (b) Visible border, straight or curved. (c) Invisible straight line, every 1 m. (d) Invisible straight line, every 3 m. Reprinted with permission from Menzel (1996b) *American Journal of Primatology*, 38, 117–32.

(b) next to objects that were all of the same general type, (c) at intervals of 1 m along an ecologically irrelevant, arbitrarily oriented, invisible straight line, or (d) at intervals of 3 m along an arbitrarily oriented, invisible straight line. To provide the animals with a cue for detecting the rule, three piles of visible food were also presented according to the rule. Each of the 60 trials used a different location in the 880 m² enclosure. Only one pattern was presented in a trial.

The macaques appeared to use the first two rules from the outset of testing and the last two rules after about five trials. Animals found food along environmental borders and within matching objects more quickly than along invisible lines. They also showed a rapid improvement in food finding on the invisible lines (Figure 8.3). The results suggested that the macaques extended their search for food from one location to another based on the spatial proximity of food to a particular class of environmental structure, rather than entirely by spatial gradients. That is, prospective

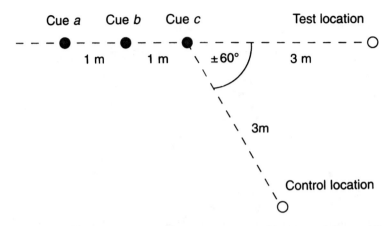

FIGURE 8.4 Experimental design. Cue *a* was a piece of banana and five visible raisins; cue *b* was eight visible raisins; cue c was four visible and four hidden raisins; at both the test and control locations, two or three visible and five hidden raisins were placed. Reprinted with permission from Hemmi & Menzel (1995) *Animal Behaviour*, 49, 457–64.

foraging 'space' was the layout of structures, surfaces and food items, rather than an empty, homogeneous area around a single reinforcer.

Directional extrapolation

The macaques' improvement in food finding in the invisible line condition (above) was surprising, because the pattern was a relatively abstract, 'unnatural' one and the background terrain varied along the invisible line. In a subsequent experiment Jan Hemmi and I examined in more detail whether macaques could use purely spatial characteristics of a food distribution as cues to organise their search (Hemmi & Menzel, 1995).

We tested five male long-tailed macaques individually. Each animal was given 14 trial-unique experimental tests (Figure 8.4). Three visible food piles (cues) were presented to the monkeys at 1 m intervals along an invisible directional line. The three cues differed mainly in the degree of visibility, which decreased in the direction of the third cue (cue c). The decreasing visibility potentially prepared the animals to expect additional food that was difficult to find. The line changed its location and orientation in space on each trial. After the macaques had found the cues, they inspected other places that were on the extension of the invisible line through the three cues and in the direction in which the visibility of the

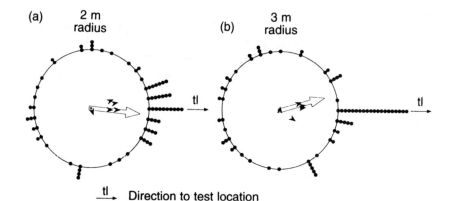

FIGURE 8.5 Directions in which the monkeys started searching, defined as the direction from the last cue taken to the point where the animal first crossed an imaginary circle of (a) 2 m or (b) 3 m radius around this last cue. Each trial is represented by a dot ($n = 70$; all animals combined). Arrow heads within the circle represent the first-order vector (mean direction) of each animal. The large open arrow (second-order vector) represents the mean direction of the combined group. Vector length is a measure of the concentrations of the crossings. Reprinted with permission from Hemmi & Menzel (1995) *Animal Behaviour*, 49, 457–64.

cues decreased (Figure 8.5). Thus, the macaques appeared to extrapolate from the decreasing visibility of the cues and from the position of the cues relative to one another to new potential food sites. This study suggested a close connection between foraging tendencies and event perception in macaques.

General discussion

Few current researchers would attempt to rank-order species as to their general intelligence, much less construct a ranking on the basis of any single measure (Warren, 1973). From an ecological viewpoint, every animal faces a different set of tasks and possesses a different set of strategies for solving them (E. Menzel & Juno, 1985). The studies reviewed in this chapter illustrate some of this diversity. The experimental findings on tamarins, macaques and chimpanzees demonstrate that animals acquire information about the nature and relative positions of objects in their environment and use many different types of cues to improve their foraging efficiency. Macaques that encounter a few initial food items vary their search according to the type of food item found, the spatial layout of the new food items, the food's proximity to visible environmental features, and the types of locations that contained the same food in past seasons. Results from descriptive studies of tamarins, baboons and chimpanzees are also consistent with the hypothesis that the use of long-term memory and detailed knowledge are not restricted to the social domain (Cheney & Seyfarth 1985; Kummer & Goodall, 1985) and underlie adaptation to the inanimate environment. A question is how findings on primates' taxonomy of objects and knowledge of spatial relations can be related to the topic of social complexity. I will briefly discuss five broad aspects of primate information processing that seem pertinent to both foraging and social behaviour.

Firstly, evolutionary modifications of the visual system, including forward directed eyes, the evolution of an area centralis or fovea, multiple map areas in visual cortex, stereopsis, and eye–hand co-ordination at near distances are distinctive adaptations of primates (Allman & McGuinness, 1988). Other authors suggest that these traits originally arose in the context of grasping locomotion or manual predation in an arboreal environment (for a review, see Martin, 1990) and provide the foundations for differentiated central representation of space, for differentiated movements in space, and, in a few species, for refinements of planned movements of the organism or of environmental objects in space (Lorenz, 1971, vol. 2, p. 220–3). Almost all the studies of 'natural concepts' to date are on visually dominant animals, i.e. birds and primates. With respect to communication and eye–hand co-ordination, a distinctive feature of primate social behaviour is manual contact, notably manual grooming of other individuals. Similarly, a distinctive feature of primate foraging and investigation is handling of food items and moving objects with the hand while examining them visually (Glickman & Sroges, 1966; Torigoe, 1985). The use and control of the hand differs markedly across primate species, and there may be co-variation across species in hand use and in the organisation of near space in the social and non-social realms.

Secondly, for primates available space is determined by the layout of environmental objects. A titi monkey will move three times farther to obtain a visible food item if it can walk along a stick that lies flat on the ground rather than walk across the open ground (e.g. C. Menzel, 1986). Long-tailed macaques find food along visible environmental borders more quickly than along invisible lines (C. Menzel, 1996b). Rhesus macaques approach unfamiliar objects from overhead or from the side rather than from underneath (E. Menzel, 1969). In the social realm, animals face choices about when, how closely, and along which route to approach other animals (de Waal, 1993). Hamadryas males tolerate the close proximity of other males to their females on the sleeping cliff (Kummer, 1995b). If an infant macaque screams a nearby animal is likely to receive aggression from the group, even if it did not provoke the scream (Kummer & Cords, 1991). Whether the 'area of responsibility' around an infant extends uniformly in all directions, including across visual barriers and gaps between trees is unknown but is a testable question. Analysis of the metrics of available space in primates can be expected to reveal substantial species differences and interesting departures from human-like performances.

Thirdly, animals learn the nature and relative positions of stationary objects in their environment without food reinforcement (Menzel & Menzel, 1979). A question of current interest is the extent to which primates learn about the spatial relationships and movements of other pairs of animals in their group. Dasser (1988) tested two long-tailed macaque females using slides of known group members as stimuli. The females discriminated between slides of mother–offspring pairs and pairs of unrelated animals. The precise basis and origin of their discriminations is presently unknown, but they did not appear simply to use the relative ages of the animals as a cue, and they correctly classified some older mother–offspring pairs that they had never observed nursing. Dasser hypothesised that the females used information about which animals were often seen together in the group. This raises the question of whether animals assign different weights to social proximity according to context. Thus, for primate researchers, the average distance between two animals over a day or month, or the number of times they are in physical contact, often provides only a crude measure of the animals' social relationship and potential actions together. Close proximity can be incidental if animals have similar location preferences. Among macaques, sitting in contact at night or feeding in close proximity is probably a more reliable sign of an intimate relationship than sitting in contact under the only available shelter during the rain (also see Chapter 2). Current studies of primate cognition often dismiss the perception and learning of associations as mechanistic and trivial, but to do so takes a narrow view of the issue. The broader issue is how animals detect that certain sets of things go together. The importance of similarity of food items and of environmental structures in the generalisation of search patterns has been discussed above, and as long ago as 1935 Koffka argued that discrimination of social groups also involved basic perceptual grouping principles, including similar form and common direction.

Fourthly, from a developmental perspective, it is not obvious that primates come to know their social and non-social environments in fundamentally different ways. (a) So-called 'social' behaviour patterns can be directed toward inanimate objects. Rhesus macaque infants form attachments to cloth-covered surrogate mothers; tamarins will groom a fur-covered object; an infant chimpanzee might threaten an unfamiliar piece of food. (b) Broad, unspecific stimulus attributes of a surrogate mother, such as its mobility, influence later behaviour and learning in rhesus macaques in a wide range of situations (Mason, 1978). (c) An animal's ability to predict whether and how an object will move in space is highly relevant to social behaviour. The ability to discriminate that objects (e.g. insects) move in different ways, and that certain classes of objects do not move unless they fall or are carried by another animal, is also important for foraging and for decisions about whether to return later to a particular food source. The development of such capabilities is not automatic: chimpanzees reared for 2 years in social isolation showed impaired ability to cope with objects in space in novel situations and seemed unable to predict the path and adjust to the approach of a rolling ball, human being or another chimpanzee (Davenport & Rogers, 1970; E. Menzel, 1978). (d) From a cross-species perspective, the development of self-control (i.e. the ability to forego a small amount of available food to obtain a larger amount later, or to withold responding to food in the presence of a higher ranking animal) may prove to be similar in the social and non-social realms. It would be surprising if primates do not find such tasks easier than do rats and pigeons (Logue, 1988).

Fifthly, primates are long-lived and each individual presumably builds up detailed information about the structure and changes of its home range over years. The upper limits for the number of individual plants that primates can learn in their habitat, and the extent to which long-term memory and perceptual learning improve a primate's ability to pick up subtle cues of food in new situations is unknown, but it is a safe bet that this capacity is very substantial and vastly greater than was thought at the time Humphrey posed his question. Individual recognition of group members and the ability to keep track of other animals' locations is important in the contexts of foraging and travel; an animal's choice of where to go and of whether to follow is influenced by the momentary travel directions of group members in relation to resources and pathways. Furthermore, choices are influenced by where social events have occurred in the past, and this is a subset of all possible locations; the sleeping sites toward which an individual titi monkey orientates are those in which the entire group has retired in the past, not all possible shelters (C. Menzel, 1993).

Historically, research on primate social intelligence has been based on naturalistic observations of how animals interact spontaneously; considerable effort has been devoted to the construction of ethograms of behaviours that are directed toward group members and toward unfamiliar conspecifics. Thus, with some exceptions, studies of primate social behaviour have adapted their procedures to take advantage of pre-existing activities. In contrast, research on primate learning and problem-solving has not traditionally been derived from observations or descriptions of naturally occurring behaviour patterns; it has been based to a larger extent on *a priori* criteria of mental capabilities and on ideas about what humans do, and the tasks presented to animals have frequently not been adjusted to an animal's particular preferences. This approach can substantially underestimate an animal's learning and memory capabilities (Olton, 1978) and also leaves open questions about the relation of these capabilities to behaviour in the field. Thus, differences in traditional procedure seem to be partly reponsible for the current perception of differences in primate social and non-social intelligence.

Although the Machiavellian intelligence hypothesis is sometimes stated as 'primate intelligence evolved in response to pressure for social sophistication', intelligence is not a unitary phenomenon, and it seems doubtful that a single factor explanation can be expected to account for the variety of ways in which learning and memory capabilities operate in free-living primates. This chapter is not intended to criticise the concepts of intelligence or of social behaviour, but rather to suggest additional ways of researching these issues.

Acknowledgements

Research on macaques was conducted at the Department of Comparative and Ethological Studies of Behavior, Osaka University, and at the University of Zürich. I thank N. Itoigawa, H. Kummer and T. Minami for their discussions and support. Research was supported by grant no.

INT-8603379 from the NSF U.S. Industrialized Countries Program for the Exchange of Scientists and Engineers, NRSA no. NS07973 from the NINDS, U.S. Public Health Service, a Sigma-Xi Grant-in-Aid, and Swiss National Science Foundation Grant 31.27721.89. Manuscript preparation supported by HD06016.

References

Allman, J. & McGuinness, E. (1988). Visual cortex in primates. *Comparative Primate Biology: Neurosciences*, 4, 279–326.

Altmann, S. A. (1967). *Social Communication Among Primates*. Chicago: University of Chicago Press.

Altmann, S. A. (1974). Baboons, space, time and energy. *American Zoologist*, 14, 221–48.

Anderson, D. J. (1983). Optimal foraging and the travelling salesman. *Theoretical Population Biology*, 24, 145–59.

Andrews, M. W. (1986). Contrasting approaches to spatially distributed resources by *Saimiri* and *Callicebus*. In *Primate Ontogeny, Cognition and Social Behaviour*, ed. J. G. Else & P. C. Lee, pp. 79–86. Cambridge: Cambridge University Press.

Andrews, M. W. (1988a). Selection of food sites by *Callicebus moloch* and *Saimiri sciureus* under spatially and temporally varying food distribution. *Learning and Motivation*, 19, 254–68.

Andrews, M. W. (1988b). Spatial strategies of oriented travel in *Callicebus moloch* and *Saimiri sciureus*. *Animal Learning and Behavior*, 16, 429–35.

Beck, B. B. (1980). *Animal Tool Behavior*. New York: Garland Press.

Berlin, B. (1978). Ethnobiological classification. In *Cognition and Categorization*, ed. E. Rosch & B. B. Lloyd, pp. 9–26. Hillsdale, NJ: Lawrence Erlbaum Associates.

Berlin, B. (1992). *Ethnobiological Classification*. Princeton, NJ: Princeton University Press.

Berlin, B., Breedlove, D. E. & Raven, P. H. (1974). *Principles of Tzeltal Plant Classification*. New York: Academic Press.

Boesch, C. & Boesch, H. (1984). Mental map in wild chimpanzees: An analysis of hammer transports for nut cracking. *Primates*, 25, 160–70.

Brown, G. S. (1994). Spatial association learning by rufous hummingbirds *Selasphorus rufus*: Effects of relative spacing among stimuli. *Journal of Comparative Psychology*, 108, 29–35.

Brown, G. & Gass, C. L. (1993). Spatial association learning by hummingbirds. *Animal Behaviour*, 46, 487–97.

Bruner, J. S., Goodnow, J. J. & Austin, G. A. (1956). *A Study of Thinking*. New York: John Wiley & Sons, Inc.

Bulmer, R. & Healey, C. (1993). Field methods in ethnozoology. In *Traditional Ecological Knowledge*, ed. N. M. Williams & G. Baines, pp. 43–55. Canberra: Centre for Resource & Environmental Studies, Australian National University.

Byrne, R. & Whiten, A. (eds) (1988). *Machiavellian Intelligence: Social Expertise and the Evolution of Intellect in Monkeys, Apes and Humans*. Oxford: Clarendon Press.

Cerella, J. (1979). Visual classes and natural categories in the pigeon. *Journal of Experimental Psychology: Human Perception and Performance*, 5, 68–77.

Cheney, D. L. & Seyfarth, R. M. (1985). Social and nonsocial knowledge in vervet monkeys. *Philosophical Transactions of the Royal Society of London, Series B*, 308, 187–201.

Cheney, D. L. & Seyfarth, R. M. (1990). *How Monkeys See The World: Inside the Mind of Another Species*. Chicago: University of Chicago Press.

Cheney, D. L. & Seyfarth, R. M. (1992). Precis of *How Monkeys See The World*. *Behavioral and Brain Sciences*, 15, 135–82.

Clark, T. W. (1979). Food adaptations of a transplanted Japanese macaque troop (Arashiyama West). *Primates*, 20, 399–410.

Clark, T. W. & Mano, T. (1975). Transplantation and adaptation of a troop of Japanese macaques to a Texas brushland habitat. In *Contemporary Primatology: Proceedings of the Vth International Congress of Primatology*, ed. S. Kondo, M. Kawai & A. Ehara, pp. 358–61. Basel: S. Karger.

Cronquist, A. (1988). *The Evolution and Classification of Flowering Plants*. Bronx, New York: The New York Botanical Garden.

Dasser, V. (1988). A social concept in Java monkeys. *Animal Behaviour*, 36, 225–30.

Davenport, R. K. & Rogers, C. M. (1970). Differential rearing of the chimpanzee. In *The Chimpanzee*, vol. 3, ed. G. Bourne, pp. 337–60. Basel: S. Karger.

dede Waal, F. B. M. (1993). Reconciliation among primates: A review of empirical evidence and unresolved issues. In *Primate Social Conflict*, ed. W. A. Mason & S. P. Mendoza, pp. 111–44. Albany, NY: State University of New York Press.

Fragaszy, D. M. (1980). Comparative studies of squirrel monkeys (*Saimiri*) and titi monkeys (*Callicebus*) in travel tasks. *Zeitschrift fur Tierpsychologie*, 54, 1–36.

Garber, P. A. (1989). Role of spatial memory in primate foraging patterns: *Saguinus mystax* and *Saguinus fuscicollis*. *American Journal of Primatology*, 19, 203–16.

Gibson, E. J. (1969). *Principles of Perceptual Learning and Development*. New York: Appleton-Century-Crofts.

Gibson, J. J. & Gibson, E. J. (1955). Perceptual learning: Differentiation or enrichment? *Psychological Review*, 62, 32–41.

Glander, K. E. (1981). Feeding patterns in mantled howling monkeys. In *Foraging Behavior: Ecological, Ethological and Psychological Approaches*, ed. A. C. Kamil & T. D. Sargent, pp. 231–57. New York: Garland Press.

Glander, K. E. (1982). The impact of plant secondary compounds on primate feeding behavior. *Yearbook of Physical Anthropology*, 25, 1–18.

Glickman, S. E. & Sroges, R. W. (1966). Curiosity in zoo animals. *Behaviour*, 26, 151–88.

Gould, S. J. (1979). A quahog is a quahog. *Natural History*, 88, 18–26.

Hemmi, J. M. & Menzel, C. R. (1995). Foraging strategies of long-tailed macaques, *Macaca fascicularis*: Directional extrapolation. *Animal Behaviour*, 49, 457–64.

Herrnstein, R. J. (1982). Stimuli and the texture of experience. *Neuroscience and Biobehavioral Reviews*, 6, 105–17.

Herrnstein, R. J. (1984). Objects, categories, and discriminative stimuli. In *Animal Cognition*, ed. H. L. Roitblat, T. G. Bever & H. S. Terrace, pp. 233–61. Hillsale, NJ: Lawrence Erlbaum Associates.

Humphrey, N. K. (1974). Species and individuals in the perceptual world of monkeys. *Perception*, 3, 105–14.

Humphrey, N. K. (1976). The social function of intellect. In *Growing Points in Ethology*, ed. P. P. G. Bateson & R. A. Hinde, pp. 303–317. Cambridge: Cambridge University Press.

Itani, J. (1965). On the acquisition and propagation of a new food habit in the troop of Japanese monkeys at Takasakiyama. In *Japanese Monkeys: A Collection of Translations*, ed. K. Imanishi & S. A. Altmann, pp. 52–65. Edmonton, Alta: University of Alberta Press.

Itani, J. & Nishimura, A. (1973). The study of infrahuman culture in Japan. A review. In *Symposium of the IVth International Congress of Primatology*, vol. 1: *Precultural Primate Behavior*, ed. E. W. Menzel, Jr, pp. 26–50. Basel: S. Karger.

Izawa, K. & Nishida, T. (1963). Monkeys living in the northern limits of their distribution. *Primates*, 4, 67–88.

Janson, C. H. & Boinski, S. (1992). Morphological and behavioral adaptations for foraging in generalist primates: The case of the cebines. *American Journal of Physical Anthropology*, 88, 483–98.

Jarvik, M. E. (1953). Discrimination of colored food and food signs by primates. *Journal of Comparative Psychology*, 46, 390–2.

Joubert, A. & Vauclair, J. (1986). Reaction to novel objects in a troop of guinea baboons: Approach and manipulation. *Behaviour*, 96, 92–104.

Koganezawa, M. (1983). Seasonal changes in food habits of Japanese monkeys *Macaca fuscata* in Nikko, Tochigi prefecture. *Memoirs of Tochigi Prefectural Museum*, 1, 83–94. (In Japanese, English summary).

Koffka, K. (1935). *Principles of Gestalt Psychology*. New York: Harcourt Brace.

Kortlandt, A. (1967). Experimentation with chimpanzees in the wild. In *Progress in Primatology*, ed. D. Starck, R. Schneider & H-J. Kuhn, pp. 203–24. Stuttgart: Gustav, Fischer, Verlag.

Kummer, H. (1995a). Causal knowledge in animals. In *Causal Cognition. A Multidisciplinary Debate*, ed. D. Sperber, D. Premack & A. J. Premack, pp. 26–36. Oxford: Clarendon Press.

Kummer, H. (1995b). *In Quest of the Sacred Baboon*. Princeton, NJ: Princeton University Press.

Kummer, H. & Cords, M. (1991). Cues of ownership in long-tailed macaques, *Macaca fascicularis*. *Animal Behaviour*, 42, 529–49.

Kummer, H. & Goodall, J. (1985). Conditions of innovative behaviour in primates. *Philosophical Transactions of the Royal Society of London, Series B*, 308 203–14.

Leighton, M. (1993). Modeling dietary selectivity by Bornean orangutans: Evidence for integration of multiple criteria in fruit selection. *International Journal of Primatology*, 14, 257–313.

Logue, A. W. (1988). Models of self-control: Toward an integration. *Behavioral and Brain Sciences*, 11, 665–709.

Lorenz, K. (1962). Kant's doctrine of the *a priori* in the light of contemporary biology. *General Systems*, 7, 23–35.

Lorenz, K. (1971). *Studies in Animal and Human Behaviour*. Cambridge, MA: Harvard University Press.

MacDonald, S. E., Pang, J. C. & Gibeault, S. (1994). Marmoset (*Callithrix jacchus jacchus*) spatial memory in a foraging task: Win-stay versus win-shift strategies. *Journal of Comparative Psychology*, 108, 328–34.

Macphail, E. M. (1987). The comparative psychology of intelligence. *Behavioral and Brain Sciences*, 10, 645–95.

Marler, P. R. (1982). Avian and primate communication: The problem of natural categories. *Neuroscience and Biobehavioral Reviews*, 6, 87–94.

Marler, P. & Terrace, H. S. (1984). Introduction. In *The Biology of Learning*, ed. P. Marler & H. S. Terrace, pp. 1–13. Dahlem Konferenzen. Berlin: Springer-Verlag.

Martin, R. (1990). *Primate Origins and Evolution: A Phylogenetic Reconstruction.* London: Chapman and Hall.

Maruhashi, T. (1980). Feeding behavior and diet of the Japanese monkey *(Macaca fuscata yakui)* on Yakushima Island, Japan. *Primates*, 21, 141–60.

Mason, W. A. (1978). Social experience and primate cognitive development. In *The Development of Behavior: Comparative and Evolutionary Aspects*, ed. G. M. Burghardt & M. Bekoff, pp. 233–51. New York: Garland Press.

Matsuzawa, T. (1990). Spontaneous sorting in human and chimpanzee. In *'Language' and Intelligence in Monkeys and Apes: Comparative Developmental Perspectives*, ed. S. T. Parker & K. R. Gibson, pp. 451–68. Cambridge: Cambridge University Press.

Mayr, E. (1969). The biological meaning of species. *Biological Journal of the Linnean Society*, 1, 311–20.

Mayr, E. (1982). *The Growth of Biological Thought.* Cambridge, MA: The Belknap Press.

Mayr, E. (1988). *Towards A New Philosophy of Biology.* Cambridge, MA: Harvard University Press.

Medin, D. L. & Dewey, G. I. (1984). Learning of ill-defined categories by monkeys. *Canadian Journal of Psychology*, 38, 285–303.

Menzel, C. R. (1986). Structural aspects of arboreality in titi monkeys *(Callicebus moloch)*. *American Journal of Physical Anthropology*, 70, 167–76.

Menzel, C. R. (1991). Cognitive aspects of foraging in Japanese monkeys. *Animal Behaviour*, 41, 397–402.

Menzel, C. R. (1993). Coordination and conflict in *Callicebus* social groups. In *Primate Social Conflict*, ed. W. A. Mason & S. P. Mendoza, pp. 253–90. Albany: State University of New York Press.

Menzel, C. R. (1996a). Spontaneous use of matching visual cues during foraging by long-tailed macaques *(Macaca fascicularis)*. *Journal of Comparative Psychology*, 110, 370–6.

Menzel, C. R. (1996b). Structure-guided foraging in long-tailed macaques. *American Journal of Primatology*, 38, 117–32.

Menzel, E. W. (1966). Responsiveness to objects in free-ranging Japanese monkeys. *Behaviour*, 26, 130–50.

Menzel, E. W. (1969). Naturalistic and experimental approaches to primate behavior. In *Naturalistic Viewpoints in Psychological Research*, ed. E. P. Willems & H. L. Raush, pp. 78–121. New York: Holt, Rinehart & Winston, Inc.

Menzel, E. W. (1971). Group behavior in young chimpanzees: Responsiveness to cumulative novel changes in a large outdoor enclosure. *Journal of Comparative and Physiological Psychology*, 74, 46–51.

Menzel, E. W. (1973). Chimpanzee spatial memory organization. *Science*, 182, 943–5.

Menzel, E. W. (1974). A group of young chimpanzees in a one-acre field. In *Behavior of Nonhuman Primates*, vol. 5, ed. A. M. Schrier & F. Stollnitz, pp. 83–153. New York: Academic Press.

Menzel, E. W. (1978). Cognitive mapping in chimpanzees. In *Cognitive Processes in Animal Behavior*, ed. S. H. Hulse, H. Fowler & W. K. Honig, pp. 375–422. Hillsdale, NJ: Lawrence Erlbaum Associates.

Menzel, E. W. (1984). Spatial cognition and memory in captive chimpanzees. In *The Biology of Learning*, ed. P. Marler & H. S. Terrace, pp. 509–31. Dahlem Konferenzen. Berlin: Springer-Verlag.

Menzel, E. W. & Johnson, M. K. (1976). Communication and cognitive organization in humans and other animals. *Annals of the New York Academy of Sciences*, 280, 131–42.

Menzel, E. W. & Juno, C. (1982). Marmosets (*Saguinus fuscicollis*): Are learning sets learned? *Science*, 217, 750–2.

Menzel, E. W. & Juno, C. (1985). Social foraging in marmoset monkeys and the question of intelligence. *Philosophical Transactions of the Royal Society of London Series B*, 308, 145–58.

Menzel, E. W. & Menzel, C. R. (1979). Cognitive, developmental and social aspects of responsiveness to novel objects in a family group of marmosets (*Saguinus fuscicollis*). *Behaviour*, 70, 251–79.

Meyer, D. R., Treichler, F. R. & Meyer, P. M. (1965). Discrete-trials training techniques and stimulus variables. In *Behavior of Nonhuman Primates*, vol. 1, ed. A.M. Schrier, H. F. Harlow & F. Stollnitz, pp. 1–49. New York: Academic Press.

Milton, K. (1988). Foraging behaviour and the evolution of primate intelligence. In *Machiavellian Intelligence: Social Expertise and the Evolution of Intellect in Monkeys, Apes and Humans*, ed. R. W. Byrne & A. Whiten, pp. 285–305. Oxford: Clarendon Press.

Morrison, J. A. & Menzel, E. W. (1972). Adaptation of a free-ranging rhesus monkey group to division and transplantation. *Wildlife Monographs*, 31, 3–78.

Olton, D. S. (1978). Characteristics of spatial memory. In *Cognitive Processes in Animal Behavior*, ed. S. H. Hulse, H. Fowler & W. K. Honig, pp. 341–373. Hillsdale, NJ: Lawrence Erlbaum Associates.

Premack, D. (1976). *Intelligence in Ape and Man*. Hillsdale, NJ: Lawrence Erlbaum Associates.

Raven, P. H., Berlin, B. & Breedlove, D. E. (1971). The origins of taxonomy. *Science*, 174, 1210–13.

Real, P. G., Iannazzi, R., Kamil, A. C. & Heinrich, B. (1984). Discrimination and generalization of leaf damage by blue jays (*Cyanocitta cristata*). *Animal Learning and Behavior*, 12, 202–8.

Rescorla, R. A. (1985). Pavlovian conditioning analogues to gestalt perceptual principles. In *Affect, Conditioning and Cognition*, ed. F. R. Brush & J. B. Overmier, pp. 113–30. Hillsdale, NJ: Lawrence Erlbaum Associates.

Robinson, J. G. (1986). Seasonal variation in the use of time and space by the wedge-capped capuchin monkey, *Cebus olivaceus*: Implications for foraging theory. *Smithsonian Contributions to Zoology*, 431, 1–60.

Rosch, E. (1978). Principles of categorization. In *Cognition and Categorization*, ed. E. Rosch & B. B. Lloyd, pp. 9–26. Hillsdale, NJ: Lawrence Erlbaum Associates.

Rosch, E. & Lloyd, B. B. (eds) (1978). *Cognition and Categorization*. Hillsdale, NJ: Lawrence Erlbaum Associates.

Rozin, P. (1976). Psychobiological and cultural determinants of food choice. In *Appetite and Food Intake*, ed. T. Silverstone, pp. 285–312. Berlin: Abakon Verlagsgesellschaft.

Rozin, P. (1977). The significance of learning mechanisms in food selection: Some biology, psychology and sociology of science. In *Learning Mechanisms in Food Selection*, ed. L. M. Barker, M. R. Best & M. Domjan, pp. 557–89. Waco, TX: Baylor University Press.

Rozin, P. (1982). Human food selection: The interaction of biology, culture and individual experience. In *The Psychobiology of Human Food Selection*, ed. L. M. Lewis, pp. 225–55. Westport, CT: Avi Publishing Co.

Rumbaugh, D. M., Richardson, W. K. & Washburn, D. A. (1989). Rhesus monkeys (*Macaca mulatta*), video tasks, and implications for stimulus-response spatial contiguity. *Journal of Comparative Psychology*, 103, 32–8.

Schrier, A. M., Angarella, R. & Povar, M. L. (1984). Studies of concept formation by stumptailed monkeys: Concepts humans, monkeys, and letter A. *Journal of Experimental Psychology: Animal Behavior Processes*, 10, 564–84.

Shepard, R.N. (1987). Toward a universal law of generalization for psychological science. *Science*, 237, 1317–23.

Sigg, H. (1980). Differentiation of female positions in hamadryas one-male-units. *Zeitschrift fur Tierpsychologie*, 53, 265–302.

Sigg, H. & Stolba, A. (1981). Home range and daily march in a Hamadryas baboon troop. *Folia Primatologica*, 36, 40–75.

Simpson, G. G. (1961). *Principles of Animal Taxonomy*. New York: Columbia University Press.

Smith, E. E. & Medin, D. L. (1981). *Categories and Concepts*. Cambridge, MA: Harvard University Press.

Snowdon, C. T. (1987). A naturalistic view of categorical perception. In *Categorical Perception*, ed. S. Harnad, pp. 332–54. Cambridge: Cambridge University Press.

Stephens, D. W. & Krebs, J. R. (1986). *Foraging Theory*. Princeton, NJ: Princeton University Press.

Stolba, A. (1979). Entscheidungsfindung in Verbanden von *Papio hamadryas*. Ph.D. thesis, University of Zürich.

Stuessy, T. P. (1990). *Plant Taxonomy*. New York: Columbia University Press.

Suzuki, A. (1965). An ecological study of wild Japanese monkeys in snowy areas – focused on their food habits. *Primates*, 6, 31–72.

Terborgh, J. (1983). *Five New World Primates: A Study in Comparative Ecology*. Princeton, NJ: Princeton University Press.

Tinbergen, N. (1976). *The Study of Instinct*. Oxford: Oxford University Press.

Tinklepaugh, O. L. (1932). Multiple delayed reaction with chimpanzees and monkeys. *Journal of Comparative Psychology*, 13, 207–43.

Torigoe, T. (1985). Comparison of object manipulation among 74 species of nonhuman primates. *Primates*, 26, 182–94.

Tsumori, A. (1966). Delayed response of wild Japanese monkeys by the sand-digging method. II. Cases of the Takasakiyama troops and the Ohirayama troop. *Primates*, 7, 363–80.

Van Roosmalen, M. G. M. (1984). Subcategorizing foods in primates. In *Food Acquisition and Processing in Primates*, ed. D. J. Chivers, B. A. Wood & A. Bilsborough, pp. 167–75. New York: Plenum Press.

Warburton, F. E. (1967). The purposes of classification. *Systematic Zoology*, 16, 241–5.

Warren, J. M. (1973). Learning in vertebrates. In *Comparative Psychology: A Modern Survey*, ed. D. A. Dewsbury & D. A. Rethlingshafer, pp. 471–509. New York: McGraw-Hill.

Whiten, A., Byrne, R. W., Barton, R. A., Waterman, P. G. & Henzi, S. P. (1991). Dietary and foraging strategies of baboons. *Philosophical Transactions of the Royal Society of London, Series B*, 334, 187–97.

Wrangham, R. W. & Waterman, P. G. (1981). Feeding behaviour of vervet monkeys on *Acacia tortilis* and *Acacia xanthophloea*: With special reference tò reproductive strategies and tannin production. *Journal of Animal Ecology*, 50, 715–31.

9 Evolution of the social brain

ROBERT A. BARTON AND ROBIN I. M. DUNBAR

Introduction

The social intelligence hypothesis posits that the large brains and distinctive cognitive abilities of primates (in particular, anthropoid primates) evolved *via* a spiralling arms race in which social competitors developed increasingly sophisticated 'Machiavellian' strategies (Byrne & Whiten, 1988). The idea stemmed originally from observations suggesting that the polyadic interactions and relationships typical of anthropoid societies place exceptional demands on the ability of individuals to process and integrate social information. This hypothesis has been contrasted with foraging niche hypotheses, which propose that it is the need to find food in patchy, unpredictable environments, or even to extract it from awkward substrates, that required large brains and cognitive specialisation (e.g. Gibson, 1986; Milton, 1988). A major task in the study of primate cognition is to devise tests of these hypotheses.

In trying to establish the nature of cognitive adaptation, studies of the behaviour of individual species (whether experimental or based on field observations) are inevitably of limited value. While such studies may suggest what cognitive skills are used in meeting the demands of a particular lifestyle (e.g. Milton, 1988; Cheney & Seyfarth, 1990; Chapter 8), they do not in themselves provide tests of the evolutionary hypotheses. Indeed, they occasionally lead to the circular logic that primate species are good at the things that primatologists have chosen to study (such as complex sociality, or difficult foraging). This problem may also be compounded by 'primatocentric' reasoning, in which primate behaviour is automatically assumed to be more complex and clever, and more demanding of evolutionary explanation, than is non-primate behaviour. Attempts to show that primates are better at solving problems in the social domain than roughly equivalent problems in the ecological domain (see Cheney & Sey-farth, 1990) are also problematic as tests of the hypotheses; they may reveal as much about motivation, learning and immediate salience to the animals as they do about intrinsic cognitive abilities.

Comparative methods are useful for testing hypotheses about adaptation (Harvey & Pagel, 1991). One could, for example, test whether species differences in the use of strategic behaviour, such as coalition formation, are associated with differences in social complexity. The problem here, of course, is once again circularity; coalition formation is itself an aspect of social complexity, and it would not be clear whether coalitions are absent from some species' recorded repertoire because of a cognitive constraint or only because the relevant circumstances do not arise (the extreme case being solitary species). In order to break this sort of circularity, we need to look more directly at the site of cognitive adaptation, the brain. In principle, we can use comparative data to assess which features of lifestyle have been responsible for the evolutionary differentiation of the neural systems underpinning cognitive abilities. In practice, this approach is not straightforward, and results are sometimes ambiguous, but it remains the most direct way of testing the hypotheses.

Comparative brain studies: What to measure

Relative brain size and ecology

Comparative studies of the brain have begun to provide a convergence point for the interests of evolutionary biologists and neuroscientists. Since Jerison's landmark survey more than 20 years ago (Jerison, 1973), studies of brain size and its correlates have been carried out in a wide range of animal taxa, including primates, bats, insectivores, rodents, carnivores, marsupials and birds (see Harvey & Krebs, 1990 for a review). These studies have tried to establish connections between the size of a species' brain and its ecological niche. Nearly all such research has been based on the notion of relative brain size, or encephalisation — the size of the brain corrected according to body size. Primates have large brains relative to body size. The finding that those with a frugivorous diet and large home range tend to have the largest brains has been taken as evidence for the foraging niche hypothesis (Clutton-Brock & Harvey, 1977; Milton, 1988).

Unfortunately, as studies on different taxa have proliferated the picture has become less and less clear. One problem is that different ecological correlates of encephalisation have been found within different taxa. Harvey & Pagel (1988) and Harvey & Krebs (1990), reviewing several studies, note that large brains relative to body size are also correlated with diet in bats and rodents, but not in carnivores (despite substantial interspecific differences in diet). In small mammals, burrowing species are generally less encephalised than terrestrial species, while among didelphid marsupials, arboreal species are more encephalised than terrestrial species. To some extent it may be posssible to integrate these different correlates of large brain size under the catch-all concept of 'environmental complexity', but this is vague and smacks of *post-hoc* reasoning. In some taxa even this level of explanation will not work. In birds, the correlations are with patterns of development rather than with behavioural ecology; there is a strong and consistent association between large brain size and altriciality (Bennet & Harvey, 1985). Taking an overview, we are left with a rather perplexing array of statistical associations, making it hard to infer any general adaptive principle.

More fundamental problems arise from the theoretical significance of relative brain size. Firstly, brain size is very crude as a neurobiological variable; the brain is, to say the least, a structurally and functionally heterogenous organ, so the significance of its overall size (and hence of correlates of overall size) is unclear. Different correlates in different taxa could reflect selection on different neural systems within the brain. Secondly, measures of relative brain size may confound selection on brain size and selection on body size. A species' relative brain size is measured as the deviation between its actual brain size and that predicted from an interspecific regression on body size. The measure assumes that such deviations reflect selection on brain size. Some researchers, however, claim that body size is evolutionarily more labile than brain size, so that species that increased in body size in recent evolutionary history are less 'encephalised' than their relatives, simply because brain size has not caught up (Gould, 1975; Lande, 1979; Shea, 1983; Willner & Martin, 1985; Deacon, 1990). Part of what we are seeing in measures of encephalisation, it is argued, is in fact 'somatisation' (selection for increased body size, with brain size lagging behind). The so-called taxon-level effect, which refers to the tendency for the brain to scale against body weight with lower exponents among closely related taxa than among more distantly related taxa has been taken as evidence for such evolutionary lags. A possible reason why folivorous primates are generally less 'encephalised' than their frugivorous relatives is that folivory tends to go with large body size. Thus, for example, gorillas may be more somatised than chimpanzees, rather than less encephalised (see Byrne, 1994). According to this view, measures of relative brain size cannot distinguish between the effects of selection on brains and selection on body size. The cognitive implications of brain size lagging behind body size in this way remain unclear, but there may be none, if the number of 'extra' neurones (Jerison, 1973), devoted to non-vegetative functions, is somehow maintained. On the other hand, it is possible that the reason for the brain size 'lag' is ultimately ecological: larger-bodied species eating more folivorous diets don't need such big brains! Pagel & Harvey (1989) have shown how the taxon-level effect in mammals can be explained as the result of greater ecological differences among distantly related than among closely related taxa. Thus we are back full circle. The unpalatable fact is that these and other considerations render the significance of relative brain size, at best, opaque.

Other explanations of relative brain size: Lifespan and energy constraints

Sacher (1959) noted that brain size is more highly correlated with lifespan than with body weight, and concluded that there is a fundamental relationship between lifespan and brain size. Subsequently, Economos (1980) pointed out that the reason for the better correlation with lifespan than with body weight may be an artefact, due to the error with which body weight estimates the 'true' size of a species; the adrenal gland, with no putatative life history significance, also correlates more strongly with lifespan than with body weight. Brain size is likely to correlate more strongly with any size-related variable that is subject to less error than body weight. Correlating lifespan with brain size after removing the effects of weight statistically from each (Allman et al., 1993) does not solve the problem; if lifespan and brain size estimate true body size more accurately than does body weight, then residual values from regressions of lifespan and brain size on body weight will inevitably be correlated with one another. This problem bedevils all similar analyses where the 'reference' variable is measured with relatively great error, a point not widely appreciated. A partial solution is to remove size effects from each variable of interest using two independent sets of size estimates, taken from different individuals, since the error variance in the two data sets is less likely to be correlated.

The observation that the brain uses up a lot of energy and that both brain size and basal metabolic rate scale to body size with the same 0.75 exponent, has led to the suggestion that metabolic rate constrains adult brain size, either because maternal metabolic rate constains neonatal brain size, which, in turn, dictates adult brain size (Martin, 1981), or because brain size is directly tied to metabolic turnover in adults (Armstrong, 1983). An attractive feature of these ideas is that they potentially explain at one stroke both the scaling of brain size and ecological correlates of relative brain size: the reason why folivorous primates are less encephalised than frugivore–omnivores might be because they have lower basal metabolic rates and hence less energy to support the development and running of the brain. However, folivores do not have lower basal metabolic rates than frugivores (Elgar & Harvey, 1987; Ross, 1992), and relative basal metabolic rate is not correlated with either adult brain size (McNab & Eisenberg, 1989), or neonatal brain size (Pagel & Harvey, 1988). Furthermore, as Harvey & Krebs (1990) and Harvey & Pagel (1988) point out, there are unexplained assumptions in these ideas; why, for example, should the proportion of metabolic turnover devoted to the brain, of either adult or neonate, be constant? The metabolic hypothesis, therefore, does not appear to work.

Evolutionary cognitive neuroscience

The most popular variant of the foraging niche hypothesis is, in fact, implicitly a 'spatial cognition' hypothesis; it is based on the idea that frugivores require a good memory for the location of food patches, and perhaps an ability to optimise travel routes between them. We should therefore perhaps be looking at the specific brain systems that mediate spatial cognition. One obvious candidate would be a small structure in the limbic system, the hippocampus – whether one believes it stores spatial maps of the environment (e.g. O'Keefe & Nadel, 1979) or mediates working memory in tasks such as foraging route optimisation (Olton et al., 1979). It is therefore of great interest that correlations have been found between hippocampus size and foraging habits in birds (see Krebs, 1990 for a review) and in rodents (Jacobs et al., 1990); species that store food and have to remember the location of many hidden caches have larger hippocampi than those that do not, but do not have larger brains overall. In arboreal primates, there is a suggestive though weak relationship between hippocampus size and home range size (Barton & Purvis,

1994). Thus, selection may have operated on spatial cognition, but we shouldn't necessarily expect this to be reflected in overall brain size. The general inference to be drawn here is that understanding brain evolution requires that we look beneath the surface of brain size measures, and examine species differences in functionally distinct neural systems. Recent developments in this area are leading to the emergence of a new field, evolutionary cognitive neuroscience (e.g. Krebs, 1990; Barton & Dean, 1993; Devoogd et al., 1993; Kaas, 1995; Barton et al., 1995).

A key task of evolutionary cognitive neuroscience is to decide what are the relevant features of brain morphology to relate to putative selection presures. This is not necessarily a straightforward task, but if we are interested in high-level cognitive integration in mammals, we should almost certainly be looking at the neocortex (and perhaps also parts of the limbic system, with which we will deal later). The neocortex is commonly, if rather cavalierly, thought of as the 'intelligent' part of the mammalian brain. It processes and integrates diverse streams of sensory information, controls voluntary motor output and deals with the planning of behaviour. It constitutes 41–76% of the brain in non-human primates, and is generally agreed to have been the focus of brain evolution in mammals (Allman, 1987, 1990; Kaas, 1995). It is in the light of these facts that primatologists have begun to examine species differences in the neocortex.

The question to be considered is, what selection pressures have led to the evolutionary diversification of the neocortex in primates? Perhaps because of the 'somatisation' process referred to above, differences in brain size relative to body size are by no means only a product of differences in the 'intelligent' neural hardware, but reflect size differences throughout the brain, including structures involved in basic functions, such as the medulla (Barton & Purvis, 1994). Thus, controlling only for body size may not tell us much about neocortical adaptive variation or the evolution of higher cognitive functions, and the most relevant index of 'corticalisation' is probably neocortex size relative to overall brain size. Deciding how to control for overall brain size raises its own problems. For example, measuring the size of a brain structure relative to the size of a different portion of the brain, assumes that the 'other' bit has not itself been systematically affected by selection in a way that confounds the analysis. An example of this problem was noted by Barton et al. (1995) in their analysis of sensory systems in bats; frugivorous species have larger visual and olfactory structures relative to the size of the rest of the brain than do predatory species, suggesting that selection for the ability to identify ripe, palatable fruit by sight and smell has influenced brain evolution in this group. It is, however, theoretically possible that the elaboration of sonar brain systems in predatory species caused expansion of 'the rest of the brain', so that visual and olfactory structures only appear smaller in those species. In fact visual and olfactory structures are also larger relative to body size in the frugivores, so in this case the conclusion that vision and olfaction have co-evolved with frugivory seems to be justified. One useful approach is to use a part of the nervous system that processes very basic sensorimotor information, such as the hindbrain or spinal cord, on the assumption that these are evolutionarily conservative and so provide a good baseline against which to assess the development of the more 'intelligent' neural hardware. Even here caution is necessary; Barton & Dean (1993) showed that the descending pathway from the tectum to the spinal cord, which mediates simple orienting, tracking and biting responses, has been subject to differential selection in mammals, according to their predatoriness. It is apparent, then, that there is no single, perfect, unbiased reference variable against which to determine the development of specific brain systems. This does not mean that we cannot make any progress in understanding the evolution of species differences in the brain; we must interpret measures cautiously and triangulate using different measures that have their own particular imperfections, but which together give reason for confidence.

Neocortex size in primates

Which species are the most corticalised? Sawaguchi & Kudo (1990) and Dunbar (1992, 1995) have provided evidence that species with large average group sizes are the most corticalised. For example, Dunbar (1992) found that a 'neocortex ratio' (neocortex volume divided by the volume of the rest of the brain) was positively correlated with average group sizes of primate genera. Here, group size is taken as a proxy for social complexity. This makes sense, because as group size increases, not only do individuals have to remember more details about their dyadic interactions and relationships, but there is an exponential increase in the strategic possibilities within polyadic interactions and relationships.

   In primates, neocortex size increases more rapidly relative to body size than does the size of other brain parts. Because of this, simple ratios between neocortex size and the size of other brain parts are correlated with body size. Larger neocortex ratios in bigger-bodied species might reflect increased selection on cognitive abilities (if, for example, body size is correlated with group size), but it is also possible that it simply reflects some basic scaling law for brain parts. A more conservative method would be to control for other brain parts using regression, so as to make no *a priori* assumption about the scaling of neocortex size.

There is also a potential problem with analyses that treat individual taxa (such as species or genera) as independent data points; the logic of the comparative method is that common regimes of selection produce similar adaptive solutions in separate taxa (Harvey & Pagel, 1991). Thus, in order to infer adaptive associations, it is necessary to demonstrate that traits have evolved together repeatedly in separate lineages. Individual taxa cannot be treated as independent because traits are shared through common inheritance as well as through independent evolution. For example, there is a strong statistical association between relative brain size and activity timing in the primates; nocturnal species are smaller-brained than diurnal species. This, however, is not a general evolutionary association, but one simply reflecting the split between the mainly nocturnal strepsirhines and the mainly diurnal haplorhines (R. Barton, unpublished results). In order to show a general association, we would have to demonstrate that diurnality and large brain size, or nocturnality and small brain size, had co-evolved repeatedly (which they have not). In evaluating the apparent relationship between neocortex size and group size, it is important to rule out this problem of phylogenetic non-independence.

Finally, group size may be confounded with other ecological variables, such as diet, home range size and activity timing, so it is also important to make sure that none of these is the 'real' correlate of neocortex size. For example, Barton et al. (1995) showed that the primary visual area of the neocortex (area V1), which is involved in early stages of visual processing, is larger (relative to the size of the rest of the brain) in diurnal than in nocturnal primate lineages, and, amongst the former, is larger in frugivore—omnivores than in folivores. These ecological associations may reflect quite basic visual adaptations, such as colour vision for distinguishing between ripe, palatable fruits and unripe or toxic fruits. In fact, about half of the neocortex of diurnal anthropoids is involved in visual processing, and since group size, like visual cortex size, is smallest in nocturnal species and largest in diurnal frugivore—omnivores, it is theoretically possible that the apparent association between neocortex size and group size is actually due to the evolution of quite basic visual processes associated with diurnality and frugivory.

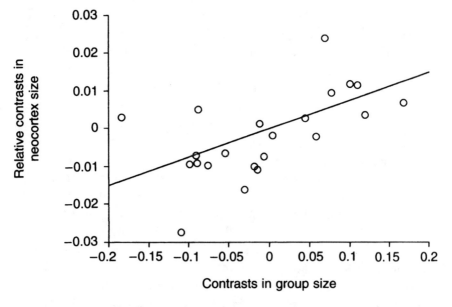

FIGURE 9.1 Correlation between relative neocortex size and group size among diurnal haplorhine primates, based on independent contrasts generated using the C.A.I.C. package (Purvis & Rambaut, 1995). $r^2 = 0.35$, $p < 0.01$.

New analysis taking these factors into account suggest that the group size–neocortex size correlation is genuine. The method of independent contrasts (Felsenstein, 1985) allows one to identify cases of correlated evolution across independent evolutionary events, thereby controlling for phylogenetic bias in comparative data (see Harvey & Pagel, 1991). The following results all use this basic method.[1] Firstly, across all primates, contrasts in neocortex size (relative to contrasts in the size of the rest of the brain) are correlated with contrasts in group size (Barton, 1996). Secondly, the association holds within diurnal haplorhines (Figure 9.1), ruling out activity timing as the critical ecological variable. No association could be found within the strepsirhines, and there is a clear grade-shift in neocortex size between haplorhine and strepsirhine primates (Figure 9.2). Next, multiple regression analysis shows that degree of frugivory and group size are each independently related to neocortex size in diurnal haplorhines (Barton, 1996). Following the results of Barton et al. (1995),

[1] The C.A.I.C. programme developed by A. Purvis (Purvis & Rambaut, 1995) was used in our analyses. This implements Felsenstein's method with modifications by Pagel (1992). The primate phylogeny used in analyses was taken from Purvis (1995).

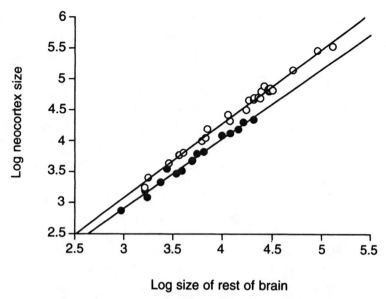

FIGURE 9.2 Grade-shift between strepsirhine (filled circles) and haplorhine (open circles) primates in neocortex size relative to the size of the rest of the brain. Slopes are similar (1.1 and 1.2, respectively), while intercepts differ ($F = 66.2$, $df = 1.39$, $p < 0.0001$).

we interpret these two correlates as reflecting selection on basic visual abilities for selecting fruit, and on social cognition, respectively. It should not surprise us that corticalisation in primates is a complex of more than one type of neural adaptation, given the functional specialisation of different cortical areas. Across all primates, however, neocortex size and home range size are not correlated once group size has been taken into account (Barton & Purvis, 1994, and recent unpublished re-analysis), ruling out the ecological cognition hypothesis (for the neocortex, if not for other brain structures such as the hippocampus). Finally, these findings are not altered if the medulla (part of the hindbrain associated with basic regulatory functions), rather than the whole of the rest of the brain, is used as the reference variable, nor if body weight is partialled out. In summary, the correlation between neocortex size and group size in primates cannot easily be explained as the result of some artefact or confounding ecological variable, but does appear to reflect selection on social cognition.

Further analyses indicate that more direct measures of social complexity than group size are also correlated with neocortex size. Firstly, H. Kudo, S. Lowen & R. I. M. Dunbar (unpublished results) found that independent contrasts in grooming clique size were positively correlated with contrasts in neocortex size. Secondly, Byrne (1993) found a positive correlation between neocortex size and the rates with which tactical deception occurs. An important question is whether these measures of social complexity correlate with neocortex size independently of the correlation with group size, or simply reflect some common underlying property of social groups that is equally well estimated by group size. An analysis by B. Pawlowski, S. Lowen & R. I. M. Dunbar (unpublished results) suggests the former; in polygamous anthropoid primates, independent contrasts in the coefficient of correlation between male rank and reproductive success (a measure of the extent to which high-ranking males monopolise matings) are negatively correlated with contrasts in neocortex size, and this pattern is found independently in small, medium and large sized groups. It may be, therefore, that in species with large neocortices, low-ranking animals are able to deploy social strategies that undermine high-ranking males' dominance-based monopolisation of access to females.

Neocortex size in other groups

The conclusion that variation in primate neocortex size reflects selection on social intelligence would be strengthened if it could be shown that the neocortex has responded to selection in similar ways in other taxa with marked interspecific variance in social complexity. In some carnivores, stable groups with long-term dominance hierarchies and polyadic interactions are seen, and preliminary analysis suggests a link between group size and neocortex size (Figure 9.3). Similarly, in bats that have stable social groups, neocortex size is greater than in those that do not (Figure 9.4). One of the two species with stable groups is the vampire bat, for which anthropoid-like grooming and reciprocity have been recorded (Wilkinson 1990). The bat data in particular emphasise that the relevant information is still rather lacking for many taxa, and properly controlled analyses have yet to be done. The cetaceans are another obvious group to look at when appropriate data become available.

The primate amygdala

The amygdala, a part of the limbic system, is involved in the emotional modulation of social perception and interaction; damage to the amygdala

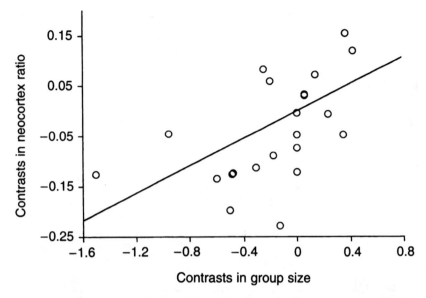

FIGURE 9.3 Correlation between neocortex ratio and group size in carnivores, based on independent contrasts. $r^2 = 0.33$, $p < 0.01$. Because actual neocortex volumes were available for only a restricted subsample, relative neocortex sizes could not be computed in the same way as for the primate analyses. Instead, following the procedure described by Aiello & Dunbar (1993) the subsample was used to generate a regression equation predicting neocortex ratios from overall brain size, enabling neocortex ratios to be estimated for the whole sample. Data from R. I. M. Dunbar and J. Bever (unpublished results).

can result in inappropriate social responses, a lack of fear when threatened or a lack of ability to discriminate fearful expressions, and impairments of face recognition (Kling & Steklis, 1976; Brothers et al., 1990; Aggleton, 1993; Adolphs et al., 1994). Electrophysiological work has revealed neurons responsive to faces and to social interaction (Leonard et al., 1985; Brothers et al., 1990). The amygdala also has complex connections with the neocortex (Aggleton, 1993), and Brothers et al. (1990) have argued that, together, the amygdala and certain regions of the neocortex comprise a 'social cognition' brain module (see below). If this is true, then we might expect to find evidence that the amygdala and neocortex have co-evolved as parts of a unitary system. There is some such evidence; the relative size of the amygdala and neocortex are correlated when medulla size is used as the reference variable. There is a particularly strong correlation for the cortico–basolateral group of amygdaloid nuclei (Figure 9.5(a)), which has relatively strong neocortical

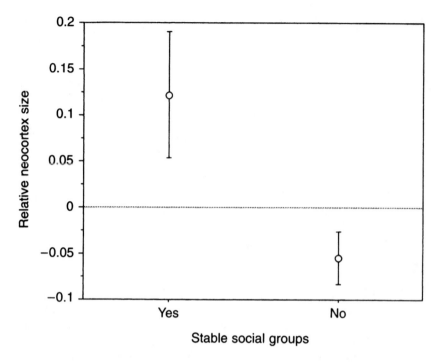

FIGURE 9.4 Neocortex size and social stability in bats: species with unstable ($n = 9$) *versus* stable social group ($n = 2$). Note that the latter two species (*Desmodus rotundus* and *Phyllostomus discolor*) are not closely related nor ecologically similar (a microchiropteran vampire and a megachiropteran frugivore, respectively). Relative neocortex size computed as the residual from the regression of neocortex size on size of the rest of the brain. Brain data from Stephan *et al.*(1974) and Stephan & Pirlot (1970).

connections, but no correlation for the centromedial nucleus, which does not (Stephan *et al.*, 1986; Aggleton, 1993). Furthermore, the cortico–basolateral group, like the neocortex, shows a grade-shift in the primates, being significantly larger in haplorhines than in strepsirhines (Figure 9.5(b)). On the negative side, the amygdala–neocortex correlation does not hold when the whole of the rest of the brain is used as the reference variable, and in neither case is the amygdala or its constituent nuclei correlated with group size. It may be that a clearer pattern would emerge if the individual amygdaloid nuclei were analysed separately – since the anatomical data provided by Stephan *et al.* (1986) group somewhat heterogenous elements together (Aggleton, 1993), and also if the relevant regions of the neocortex were analysed separately.

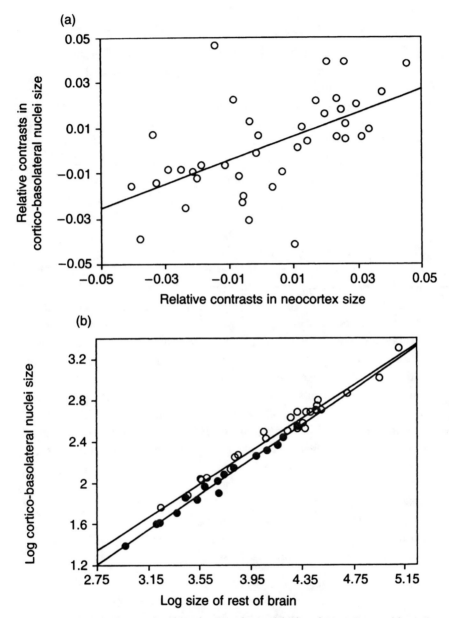

FIGURE 9.5 Cortico–basolateral group of amygdaloid nuclei in primates: (a) correlation between relative nuclei size and relative neocortex size ($r^2 = 0.33$, df = 1.39, p = 0.001); (b) grade-shift between strepsirhine (filled circles) and haplorhine (open circles) primates in size of cortico–basolateral nuclei relative to the size of the rest of the brain. The two groups are significantly different ($F = 18.9$, df = 1.39, $p < 0.0001$).

Towards an evolutionary neuroscience of social cognition

So far we have shown that there are some interesting correlations between brain measures and social behaviour, and we have presented limited evidence for co-evolution of neocortical and limbic components of a putative social intelligence module in primates. We have said very little about what information is actually processed by these brain systems or why the correlations might make neurobiological sense. Here we encounter a general problem for the understanding of brain evolution: determining the relationship between brain structure and cognitive attributes.

What is social cognition?

The title of our chapter is partly plagiarised from Brothers et al. (1990), who made the first attempt to specify 'the social brain' as a primate neural adaptation (see Karmiloff-Smith et al., 1995 for development of these ideas as applied to humans). Brothers (1990, p. 28) defined social cognition as 'the processing of any information which culminates in the accurate perception of the dispositions and intentions of other individuals'. To this might be added; the computation of strategic alternatives and their consequences, according to social constraints such as relative power. Brothers details which brain areas, notably the temporal lobe and orbital frontal cortex, handle social information. But what is this information exactly, and how is it processed? We need to provide answers to those questions in order to establish a clearer understanding of how social cognition has evolved and what species differences in brain structure mean.

Social information is multi-faceted. On an immediate level, it is made up of a diverse range of sensory input: auditory, tactile, olfactory, and, in diurnal species, especially visual. As Brothers (1990, p. 29) states, the evolutionary switch to a diurnal lifestyle

> was probably accompanied by two developments, one, a greater
> reliance on visual social communication, and two, more complex
> social structures. That these two developments should go together
> is not surprising, given that vision permits a high degree of
> temporal sequencing and brevity of signals compared to olfaction.

Group-living primates co-ordinate information on the identity of other individuals, their attributes (age–sex class, kinship, relative power, etc), their past behaviour, their current 'dispositions and intentions' as judged by facial expression, vocalisations, posture and movements with respect to the individual concerned and other group members. This stream of information ebbs and flows according to the immediate context; it is at its peak during high-intensity polyadic interactions, but even during quiet foraging with little apparent interaction occurring, there is probably always subtle socio-spatial manouevring and monitoring going on. How does the brain manage the co-ordination of all this information?

At present we can only give fairly general answers to the last question, but they are answers that may lay the groundwork for understanding the neurobiology and evolution of social cognition. Perhaps the most general of all answers is that the brain handles the information in parallel. The revolution in cognitive neuroscience wrought by the concept of parallel distributed processing (Rumelhart, McLelland and the PDP Research Group, 1986) and neural network models has to some extent superceded the old 'symbol manipulation' approach, together with its top-down models based on black boxes and abstract definitions of cognitive processes that give no hint as to what a brain area is actually doing or how its size might be related to its functioning. Neural network models show how perceptual or cognitive tasks can be solved by the parallel processing of information by many individual processing units, or neurones; this approach implies that the size of a neural network (the number of its processing units) determines the amount of information processed in parallel, and hence the complexity of the computation carried out. But brains are not, of course, amorphous neural networks; different regions are specialised for handling particular aspects of the input. Even a single sensory modality, such as vision, is carried out by a range of functionally specialised subsystems, probably, as Marr (1982) pointed out, because complex computational tasks are most economically handled by breaking them down into separate subroutines. Social cognition would seem to be a prime example of this, given the multi-faceted nature of social information. The notion of social cognition as a large array of perceptual–cognitive operations occurring in parallel fits in with what is known about the structure of the visual system in primates; in the macaque there are 305 pathways connecting 32 cortical visual areas, comprising 10 levels of visual processing, and visual areas make up about half of the neocortex (van Essen et al., 1992). Each level involves increasing computational specialisation and essentially comprises a map of the visual scene based on particular aspects of it, such as movement, form and colour. Allman

(1982) and Allman & McGuinness (1988) have pointed out that the number of cortical visual areas in primates varies between species, with additional areas seemingly evolved by a kind of simple duplication and subsequent functional divergence. Indeed, Crick argues that:

> The secret of the neocortex, if it has one, is probably its ability to evolve additional layers to its hierarchies of processing, especially at the upper levels of those hierarchies. Such extra layers of processing are probably what distinguishes higher mammals, like man, from lower mammals, such as the hedgehog.
>
> Crick (1994, p. 159)

These layers of processing are not physically arranged one on top of the other, but comprise functionally distinct interconnected areas spread out across the surface of the cortex. Differences in neocortex size are almost entirely due to differences in surface area (cortical thickness is quite invariant), with increases in size occurring by lateral expansion, accompanied by parcellation into new functional areas (Rakic, 1995). Presumably, the observed variation within primates in the number of distinct cortical visual areas or maps corresponds to variation in the number of layers in the 'processing hierarchy' and the overall computational complexity. In fact sensory maps are a fundamental feature of neocortical organisation in general, and the parallel processing of topographically organised visual, tactile and auditory information allows the neocortex to 'resolve the structure within the noisy sensory array' (Allman, 1990). It is known that, amongst the visual pathways, there are systems dealing specifically with social stimuli, such as faces and bodily interaction between subject and object (Brothers, 1990; Perrett et al., 1992). These processes constitute a large parallel load that could only be managed by extensive neural networks, and correspondingly involve large amounts of brain tissue. This is why it makes sense that neocortex size and social complexity should have co-evolved; it also helps to explain why the anthropoid brain is so large overall, given that the neocortex makes up such a large proportion of it.

Social versus ecological cognition

Primates do of course face a range of ecological problems that must be solved each day in order to survive, and evidence for the evolution of social cognitive adaptations does not in itself refute the idea of ecological cognitive adaptations. Can ecological problems explain the evolution of sophisticated cognitive mechanisms or large brains in primates? As we mentioned, home range size and neocortex size are uncorrelated once group size is taken into account. The correlation between frugivory and primary visual cortex size (and hence overall neocortex size) probably reflects the evolution of relatively basic visual mechanisms for locating and selecting fruit. Much has been made of the idea that anthropoid primates may have 'cognitive maps' of their home range (e.g. Sigg & Stolba, 1981; Milton, 1988; Garber & Hannon, 1993), but this is mostly based on observational data, which cannot easily distinguish between alternative explanations for non-random foraging routes. Furthermore, attributing cognitive mapping as a special primate skill ignores similar evidence in rodents (e.g. Leonard & McNaughton, 1990; Jacobs & Liman, 1991), birds (e.g. Sherry et al., 1981), fish (Noda et al., 1994) and even, though more controversially, insects (Gould, 1986). Differences among primates in hippocampus size are slight and, as the work on birds shows, even where there has been intense selection for spatial memory, this does not necessarily have any implications for overall brain size. The large anthropoid brain is therefore unlikely to have a specific connection with cognitive mapping. The reason is probably that geo-spatial information is just not as multi-faceted and complex as social information, constituting a much lighter parallel load. We suggest that it is the massively parallel nature of social information that requires so much brain tissue; social interactions and relationships are in a constant state of flux, demanding continuous on-line processing of rapidly changing information. The only comparable ecological processing would be the computation of optimal foraging routes simultaneously taking into account a range of resources and hazards at varying distances and trajectories relative to the individual's current position; experimental work would be required to establish to what extent primates and other animals actually solve this kind of problem. In fact, there is little, if any, evidence suggesting that the ecological problems faced by primates are particularly complex, or that primates have especially sophisticated foraging strategies. As for the idea that the processing of foods, in extractive foraging for example, could have selected for large brains, it is hard to see why these tasks, in which the complexity is largely of a serial, rather than a parallel kind, should require big neural networks, and it has yet to be convincingly shown that primates' mastery of such tasks is unique. The use of tools in foraging by chimpanzees and perhaps capuchin monkeys may be unusually sophisticated (see Gibson,

1986). However, these instances cannot explain the wider variance in brain or neocortex size among primates. Dunbar (1992, 1995) found no evidence for an association between extractive foraging and neocortex size. In conclusion, while ecological cognition is an interesting area of study in its own right, and questions about what strategies primates use remain to be answered (see Chapter 8), we do not believe it is what distinguishes the primate brain and cognition, nor what has selected for major neural differences within the primates.

Cognition, perception and evolution

The brain is fundamentally an organ for performing sensorimotor transformations. The transformations are often extremely complex and may involve long time-lags and other systems, such as the endocrine system, but what we think of as cognition is really just an aspect of this general process, and as such is intimately tied to perceptual operations. Here, for example, we have argued that social cognition in diurnal primates involves the parallel processing and integration of diverse streams of sensory (primarily visual) information, involving large areas of neocortex and related systems. We therefore see no justification for any firm distinction between perceptual and cognitive evolution. Indeed, it is probably this distinction that has been responsible for a great deal of confusion over the issue of the evolution of intelligence. In a superb survey of comparative psychology, Macphail (1982) demolished the idea that vertebrates can be ranked in a linear scale of intelligence, corresponding broadly to the *scala naturae* (fish and reptiles at the bottom, mammals, and especially primates, at the top). Hodos & Cambell (1969) had already drawn attention to the problems of the *scala naturae* as the pervasive if implicit evolutionary model in comparative psychology. Macphail went further in arguing that, not only is there no linear scale of intelligence, but that there are no species differences in intelligence at all (or at least, no evidence for them). This conclusion was based on the reasoning that, if one controls for 'contextual variables', such as motivation and sensory and motor specialisations, there are no differences, humans apart, in basic learning abilities. Macphail's argument is provocative and important in forcing us to think about what is meant by intelligence in a comparative context. The concept of intelligence does tend to imply a general-purpose mechanism for problem-solving. For that reason alone it should probably be rejected as a comparative concept:

Learning is accomplished not by some single general-purpose device
but by different modules, each keyed to the peculiar logic and laws
of one domain

Pinker (1994)

A brain does not look even a little bit like a general-purpose
computer.

Crick (1994)

The basic neural mechanisms for learning are present in even the simplest
nervous systems (some of the most interesting work in this area has been
conducted on sea slugs), and in the sense that these are fundamentally
the same in complex nervous systems, there may be little or no species
differences in the underlying general capacity to learn. But these basic
mechanisms are merely the building blocks of specialised neural circuits,
or modules (Fodor, 1983), that have been put together in particular evolutionary contexts and which solve particular types of problem (e.g.
Barkow et al., 1992; Pinker, 1994). It is therefore an unecessary distraction to search for a general property – intelligence – that is unconnected
with specialisations for particular ways of life. If we control for all contextual variables then, insofar as these include sensory specialisations, we
control out what is interesting from an evolutionary point of view. The
inescapable conclusion of contemporary neuroscience is that brain modules cut across the arbitrary distinction between perception and cognition
(e.g. Marr, 1982; Brothers, 1990; Jackendoff, 1992; Zeki, 1993; Crick,
1994; Damasio, 1995). Because of this, analyses of general 'intelligence'
as distinct from specific sensoricognitive adaptations are misguided. A key
task for future research into social cognition is to establish whether it has
the evolutionary history, distinctive ontogeny, neurophysiological cohesiveness and functional integrity to qualify it as such an adaptation.

References

Adolphs, R., Tranel, D., Damasio, H. & Damasio, A. (1994). Impaired recognition of
emotion in facial expressions following bilateral damage to the human
amygdala. Nature, 372, 669–72

Aggleton, J. P. (1993). The contribution of the amygdala to normal and abnormal
emotional states. Trends in Neuroscience, 16, 328–33.

Aiello, L. C. & Dunbar, R. I. M. (1993) Neocortex size, group size and the evolution
of language. Behavioral and Brain Sciences, 34, 184–93.

Allman, J. (1982). Reconstructing the evolution of the brain in primates through the
use of comparative neurophysiological and neuroanatomical data. In Primate

Brain Evolution, ed. E. Armstrong & D. Falk, pp. 13–28. New York: Plenum Press.

Allman, J. (1987). Evolution of the brain in primates. In *The Oxford Companion to the Mind*, ed. R. L. Gregory, pp. 633–9. Oxford: Oxford University Press.

Allman, J. (1990). The origin of the neocortex. *Seminars in the Neurosciences*, 2, 257–62.

Allman, J. & McGuinness, E. (1988). Visual cortex in primates. In *Comparative Primate Biology*, ed. H. D. Steklis & J. Erwin, vol. 4, pp. 279–326. New York: Alan R. Liss Inc.

Allman, J., McLaughlin, T. & Hakeem, A. (1993). Brain weight and life-span in primate species. *Proceedings of the National Acadamy of Sciences of the U.S.A.*, 90, 118–22.

Armstrong, E. (1983). Relative brain size and metabolism in mammals. *Science*, 220, 1302–4.

Barkow, J., Cosmides, L. & Tooby, J. (eds) (1992). *The Adapted Mind: Evolutionary Psychology and the Generation of Culture*. Oxford: Oxford University Press.

Barton, R. A. (1996). Neocortex size and behavioural ecology in primates. *Proceedings of the Royal Society, Series B*, 263, 173–7.

Barton, R. A. & Dean, P. (1993). Comparative evidence indicating neural specialization for predatory behaviour in mammals. *Proceedings of the Royal Society, Series B*, 254, 63–8.

Barton, R. A. & Purvis, A. (1994). Primate brains and ecology: Looking beneath the surface. In *Current Primatology: Proceedings of the XIVth Congress of the International Primatological Society*, ed. J. R. Anderson, B. Thierry & N. Herrenschmidt, pp. 1–11. Strasbourg: Université Louis Pasteur.

Barton, R. A., Purvis, A. & Harvey, P. H. (1995). Evolutionary radiation of visual and olfactory brain systems in primates, bats and insectivores. *Philosphical Transactions of Royal Society, Series B*, 348, 381–92.

Bennet, P. M. & Harvey, P. H. (1985). Brain size, development and metabolism in birds and mammals. *Journal of Zoology*, 207, 491–509.

Brothers, L. (1990). The social brain: A project for integrating primate behavior and neurophysiology in a new domain. *Concepts in Neuroscience*, 1, 27–51.

Brothers, L., Ring, B. & Kling, A. (1990). Response of neurons in the macaque amygdala to complex social stimuli. *Behavioural Brain Research*, 41, 199–213.

Byrne, R. W. (1993). Do larger brains mean greater intelligence? *Behavioral and Brain Sciences*, 16, 696–7.

Byrne, R. W. (1994). *The Thinking Ape: Evolutionary Origins of Intelligence*. Oxford: Oxford University Press.

Byrne, R. W. & Whiten, A. (eds) (1988). *Machiavellian Intelligence: Social Expertise and the Evolution of Intellect in Monkeys, Apes and Humans*. Oxford: Clarendon Press.

Cheney, D. L. & Seyfarth, R. M. (1990). *How Monkeys See The World: Inside the Mind of Another Species*. Chicago: University of Chicago Press.

Clutton-Brock, T. H. & Harvey, P. H. (1980) Primates, brains and ecology. *Journal of Zoology*, 207, 151–69.

Crick, F. H. C. (1994). *The Astonishing Hypothesis*. London: Simon and Schuster.

Damasio, A. R. (1995) *Descartes Error: Emotion, Reason and the Human Brain*. London: Picador.

Deacon, T. W. (1990) Fallacies of progression in theories of brain size evolution. *International Journal of Primatology*, 11, 193–236.

Devoogd, T. J., Krebs, J. R., Healy, S. D. & Purvis, A. (1993). Relations between song repertoire size and the volume of brain nuclei related to song: Comparative evolutionary analyses amongst oscine birds. *Proceedings of the Royal Society of London, Series B*, 254, 75–82.

Dunbar, R. I. M. (1992). Neocortex size as a constraint on group size in primates. *Journal of Human Evolution*, 20, 469–93

Dunbar, R. I. M. (1995). Neocortex size and group size in primates: A test of the hypothesis. *Journal of Human Evolution*, 28, 287–96.

Economos, A. C. (1980). Brain-life span conjecture: A re-evaluation of the evidence. *Gerontology*, 26, 82–9.

Elgar, M. A. & Harvey, P. H. (1987). Basal metabolic rates in mammals: Allometry, phylogeny and ecology. *Functional Ecology*, 1, 25–36.

Felsenstein, J. (1985). Phylogenies and the comparative method. *American Naturalist*, 125, 1–15.

Fodor, J. A. (1983). *The Modularity of Mind*. Cambridge, MA: MIT Press.

Garber, P. A. & Hannon, B. (1993). Modeling monkeys: A comparison of computer-generated and naturally ocurring foraging patterns in two species of neotropical primates. *International Journal of Primatology*, 14, 827–52.

Gibson, K. R. (1986). Cognition, brain size and the extraction of embedded food resources. In *Primate Ontogeny, Cognition and Social Behaviour*, ed. J. G. Else & P. C. Lee, pp. 93–104. Cambridge: Cambridge University Press.

Gould, S. J. (1975). Allometry in primates, with emphasis on scaling and the evolution of the brain. *Contributions to Primatology*, 5, 244–92.

Gould, J. L. (1986). The locale map of honeybees: Do insects have cognitive maps? *Science*, 232, 861–3.

Harvey, P. H. & Krebs, J. R. (1990). Comparing brains. *Science*, 249, 140–6.

Harvey, P. H. & Pagel, M. D. (1988). The allometric approach to species differences in brain size. *Journal of Human Evolution*, 3, 461–72.

Harvey, P. H. & Pagel, M. D. (1991) *The Comparative Method in Evolutionary Biology*. Oxford: Oxford University Press.

Hodos, W. & Cambell, C. B. G. (1969). The scala naturae: Why there is no theory in comparative psychology. *Psychological Review*, 76, 337–50.

Jackendoff, R. (1992). *Consciousness and the Computational Mind*. Cambridge, MA: MIT Press.

Jacobs, L. F. & Liman, E. R. (1991). Grey squirrels remember the location of buried nuts. *Animal Behaviour*, 41, 103–10.

Jacobs, L. F., Gaulin, S. C., Sherry, D. F. & Hoffman, G. E. (1990). Evolution of spatial cognition: Sex-specific patterns of spatial behaviour predict hippocampal size. *Proceedings of the National Academy of Sciences of the U.S.A.*, 87, 6349–52.

Jerison, H. J. (1973). *Evolution of the Brain and Intelligence*. New York: Academic Press.

Kaas, J. H. (1995). The evolution of isocortex. *Brain, Behavior and Evolution*, 46, 187–96.

Karmiloff-Smith, A., Klima, E. Bellugi, U., Grant, J. & Baron-Cohen, S. (1995). Is there a social module? Language, face processing and theory of mind in individuals with Williams syndrome. *Journal of Cognitive Neuroscience*, 7, 196–208.

Kling, A. & Brothers, L. (1992). The amygdala and social behaviour. In *Neurobiological Aspects of Emotion, Memory and Mental Dysfunction*, ed. J. Aggleton. New York: Wiley-Liss, Inc.

Krebs, J. R. (1990). Food-storing birds: Adaptive specialization in brain and behaviour? *Philosophical Transactions of the Royal Society, Series B*, 329, 153–60.

Lande, R. (1979). Quantitative genetic analysis of multivariate evolution, applied to brain:body size allometry. *Evolution*, 33, 402–16

Leonard, B. & McNaughton, B. L. (1990). Spatial representation in the rat: Conceptual, behavioural and neurophysiological perspectives. In *Neurobiology of Comparative Cognition*, ed. R. P. Kesner & D. S. Olton, pp. 363–422. London: Lawrence Erlbaum Associates.

Leonard, C. M., Rolls, E. T., Wilson, F. A. W. & Baylis, G. C. (1985). Neurons in the amygdala of the monkey with responses selective for faces. *Behavioural Brain Research*, 15, 159–76.

Macphail, E. M. (1982). *Brain and Intelligence in Vertebrates*. Oxford: Clarendon Press.

Marr, D. (1982). *Vision*. San Francisco: Freeman.

Martin, R. D. (1981). Relative brain size and basal metabolic rate in terrestrial vertebrates. *Nature*, 293, 57–60.

McNab, B. K. & Eisenberg, J. F. (1989). Brain size and its relation to the rate of metabolism in mammals. *American Naturalist*, 133, 157–67.

Milton, K. (1988). Foraging behaviour and the evolution of primate intelligence. In *Machiavellian Intelligence: Social Expertise and the Evolution of Intellect in Monkeys, Apes and Humans*, ed. R. W. Byrne & A. Whiten, pp 285–306. Oxford: Clarendon Press.

Noda, M., Gushima, K. & Kakuda, S. (1994). Local prey search based on spatial memory and expectation in the planktivorous reef fish, *Chromis chrysurus*. *Animal Behaviour*, 47, 1413–22.

O'Keefe, J. & Nadel, L. (1979). *The Hippocampus as a Cognitive Map*. Oxford: Clarendon Press.

Olton, D. S., Becker, J. T. & Handleman, G. E. (1979). Hippocampus, space and memory. *Behavioral and Brain Sciences*, 2, 313–22.

Pagel, M. D. (1992). A method for the analysis of comparative data. *Journal of Theoretical Biology*, 156, 434–42.

Pagel, M. D. & Harvey, P. H. (1988). How mammals produce large-brained offspring. *Evolution*, 42, 948–57.

Pagel, M. D. & Harvey, P. H. (1989). Taxonomic differences in the scaling of brain on body weight among mammals. *Science*, 244, 1589–93.

Perrett, D. I., Hietanen, J. K., Oram, M. W. & Benson, P. J. (1992). Organization and function of cells responsive to faces in the temporal cortex. *Philosophical Transactions of the Royal Society of London, Series B*, 335, 23–30.

Pinker, S. (1994). *The Language Instinct*. London: Penguin Books.

Purvis, A. (1995). A composite estimate of primate phylogeny. *Philosophical Transactions of the Royal Society of London, Series B*, 348, 405–21.

Purvis, A. & Rambaut, A. (1995). Comparative analysis by independent contrasts (CAIC): An Apple Macintosh application for analysing comparative data. *Computer Applications in the Biosciences*, 11, 247–251.

Rakic, P. (1995). Evolution of neocortical parcellation: The perspective from experimental neuroembryology. In *Origins of the Human Brain*, ed. J. P. Changeux & J. Chavaillon, pp. 84–100. Oxford: Oxford University Press.

Ross, C. (1992). Basal metabolic rate, body weight and diet in primates: An evaluation of the evidence. *Folia Primatologica*, 58, 7–23.

Rumelhart, D. E., McLelland, J. L., & the PDP Research Group (1986). *Parallel Distributed Processing: Explorations in the Microstructure of Cognition*, vol. 1. Cambridge, MA: MIT Press.

Sacher, G. A. (1959). Relationship of lifespan to brain weight and body weight in mammals. In *C.I.B.A. Foundation Symposium on the Lifespan of Animals*, ed. G. E. W. Wolstenholme & M. O'Connor, pp. 115–33. Boston, MA: Little and Brown.

Sawaguchi, T. & Kudo, H. (1990). Neocortical development and social structure in primates. *Primates*, 31 283–90.

Shea, B. T. (1983). Phyletic size change and brain/body allometry: A consideration based on the African pongids and other primates. *International Journal of Primatology*, 4, 33–60.

Sherry, D. F, Krebs, J. R. & Cowie, R. J. (1981). Memory for the location of stored food in marsh tits. *Animal Behaviour*, 29, 1260–6.

Sigg, H. & Stolba, A. (1981). Home range and daily march in a hamadryas baboon troop. *Folia Primatologica*, 36, 40–75.

Stephan, H. & Pirlot, P. (1970). Volumetric comparisons of brain structures in bats. *Zeitschrift fur Zodogisches Systematik und Evolutions-forschung*, 8, 200–36.

Stephan, H., Pirlot, P. & Schneider, R. (1974). Volumetric analysis of pteropid brains. *Acta Anatomica*, 87, 161–92.

Stephan, H., Frahm, H. D. & Baron, G. (1981). New and revised data on volumes of brain structures in insectivores and primates. *Folia Primatologica*, 35, 1–29.

Stephan, H., Frahm, H. D. & Baron, G. (1986). Comparison of brain structure volumes in insectivora and primates VII. Amygdaloid components. *J. Hirnforschung*, 28, 571–84.

van Essen, D. C., Anderson, C. H. & Felleman, D. J. (1992). Information processing in the primate visual system: An integrated systems perspective. *Science*, 255, 419–23.

Wilkinson, G. S. (1990). Food sharing in vampire bats. *Science*, 262, 76–82.

Willner, L. & Martin, R. D. (1985). Some basic principles of mammalian sexual dimorphism. In *Human Sexual Dimorphism*, ed. J. Ghesquiere, R. D. Martin & F. Newcombe, pp. 1–19. London: Taylor and Francis.

Zeki, S. (1993). *A Vision of the Brain*. Oxford: Blackwell Scientific Publications.

10 The modularity of social intelligence

GERD GIGERENZER

In a 'protected threat', a baboon induces a dominant member of its group to attack a third one. The baboon appeases the dominant member whom it uses as a tool to threaten the target and manoeuvres to prevent the target from doing the same (Kummer, 1988). This 'social tool use' is mastered by baboons at puberty, whereas chimpanzees are adult before they learn to use a stone as a tool for cracking hard nuts (Boesch & Boesch, 1984). Primates appear to manipulate social objects with more ease and sophistication than physical tools.

Observations such as these have suggested that primate intelligence is designed primarily for the social rather than the physical and have led to the *Machiavellian intelligence* hypothesis (Whiten & Byrne, 1988a) or *social intelligence* hypothesis (Kummer *et al.*, 1997). The term Machiavellian intelligence emphasises the besting of rivals for personal gain over co-operation, whereas the term social intelligence (which is the more general term) is neutral on the balance between exploitation and co-operation.

The social intelligence hypothesis is both stimulating and vague. It is stimulating because it reminds us that whenever psychologists study intelligence and learning in humans or animals, it is almost invariably about inanimate objects: symbols, sticks and bananas. It is vague because the nature of the intelligence it invokes is largely unclear, and as a consequence, the mechanisms of social intelligence have not yet been specified. This combination of exciting and imprecise should be an alarming signal. The social intelligence hypothesis has the seductive power of a political party with no precise programme that allows everyone unhappy with the established system to project his or her own values on it. At the risk of losing votes, I will argue in this chapter that some of the vague but seductive propositions of the social intelligence hypothesis are most likely empirically empty and should be dropped. To get some votes back, I will subsequently propose a specific theory about the mechanisms of social intelligence: a 'modular' version of the social intelligence hypothesis.

What does the social intelligence hypothesis say?

The social intelligence hypothesis is at present a collection of loosely related assertions about the special role of the social (i.e. intraspecific) in the intellectual life of humans and other primates. Here is my reconstruction from the collection of papers in Byrne & Whiten (1988) and the review by Kummer et al. (1997):

(1) *Social intelligence is qualitatively different from non-social intelligence.* This is because:
   (i) The social environment of a species that lives in groups is *more complex* than its ecological environment;
   (ii) The social environment is *less predictable* than the ecological environment;
   (iii) The social environment is *more challenging* than the ecological environment.
(2) *Social intelligence preceded non-social intelligence.* This evolutionary headstart is because:
   (i) There were selective pressures for sociality *per se,* and in addition for a form of intelligence designed to manage sociality;
   (ii) Sexual selection led to the development of intelligent strategies to outwit competitors and to attract mates.
(3) *Social intelligence influences non-social intelligence.* This transfer occurs because:
   (i) Social intelligence preceded non-social intelligence (Assumption 2);
   (ii) Prior adaptations characteristically become 'exaptations' for new adaptations (Gould & Vrba, 1982), and social intelligence is thus generatively entrenched relative to non-social intelligence (Wimsatt, 1986).

Other versions of the social intelligence hypothesis are possible (see Kummer et al., 1997). For instance, a weaker form is to drop Assumption 1, which leaves us with only one kind of intelligence, but to maintain

Assumption 2 (and 3), that is, to assume that the selective pressures for this general intelligence stem from the social context rather than from our ancestors' use of tools (Wynn, 1988) or from foraging for hyper-dispersed and patchy foods in tropical forests (Milton, 1988). An illustration of this weaker form is the hypothesis that transitive inference is a universal cognitive process that originally evolved in the context of constructing a social dominance hierarchy: not all dyadic interactions need be observed directly; some can be inferred (Smith, 1988).

In this chapter, I will focus on the nature of social intelligence, ignore the issue of whether it preceded non-social intelligence (on this see Todd & Miller, 1995; Miller, 1997), and discuss some implications for its influence on non-social intelligence.

Is social intelligence qualitatively different from non-social intelligence?

The distinction between social and non-social intelligence is often motivated by the claim that social environments are qualitatively different from non-social environments. The social environment 'is special because it is reactive' (Chance & Mead, 1953; Whiten & Byrne, 1988a, p. 5); it 'contrasts with the physical world in that it is more challenging' (Whiten & Byrne, 1988a, p. 2); it is 'more intellectually demanding' (Humphrey, 1988, p. 15 (originally published in 1976)), and so on. I agree that social intelligence is special and cannot be subsumed with non-social intelligence under one general intelligence, but not for these reasons. These claims about the difference between the social and the physical world strike me as either untestable, false, or both. I propose to get rid of these mystical, vague justifications for a special social intelligence and to replace them with a more secure foundation: the modular view of intelligence.

Is the social environment more 'complex'?

Can we say that social environments are more 'complex' than non-social environments? Whiten & Byrne (1988b, p. 59) attempt to spell out what the vague term 'social complexity' could mean. Assume a primate distinguishes five conditions of social interaction with two possible states each, such as whether the interactant is of higher or lower rank and whether its own mother is present or not. The resulting number of possible social interactions (in our example $2^5 = 32$) is, according to Whiten and Byrne, a measure of social complexity. It is clear that this definition is one of the *perceived* complexity of a social environment, not of the environment itself that supposedly motivates a special social intelligence. Whatever the complexity of an environment *per se* is (if there is such a thing), not every species perceives and acts upon that complexity. For instance, termites vary individually, but the members of a termite colony do not seem to recognise this variation. The social intelligence of primates, in contrast, exploits individual variations among their conspecifics, although not of plants, predators and prey (Kummer *et al.*, 1997). Thus, even if one could measure the complexity of a social environment in one number, a hope for which we have no evidence, such a number would be irrelevant because what counts is the perceived complexity (or 'relational' complexity: the complexity in an environment to which an organism responds). The degree of perceived complexity, however, can hardly 'explain' why there is a particular level of social intelligence in a species, because the perceived complexity is itself dependent on, or even part of, social intelligence. Add to this the unresolved – and I believe, unresolvable – problem of finding a common denominator for measuring the complexity of social and non-social environments. Such a common denominator would be necessary to turn the statement that the social environment is more 'complex' than the physical environment into an empirically meaningful one. To illustrate this problem of comparability, can we say that triadic interactions in primates, which are said to be complex, are more complex than triadic interactions between heavenly bodies (the Three Body problem, which so far has been too complex for human minds to solve)? How could we? Complexity comparisons drive us into a conceptual cul-de-sac. I do not believe that the complexity argument is of any scientific promise for justifying a special social intelligence.

Is the social environment less predictable?

Complexity does not necessarily entail unpredictability and *vice versa*. Thus instead of complexity, one might consider the 'role of unpredictability in social interaction generating social intelligence' (Whiten & Byrne, 1988a, p. 8). Unpredictability is a particularly interesting feature of certain types of behaviour, such as Protean behaviour in predator–prey encounters (e.g. the rabbit that tries to escape the fox by running in a quasi-random pattern; Driver & Humphries, 1988). The evolution of adaptive unpredictability is an important and neglected topic (see Chapter 12). However, to propose that unpredictability is larger in interactions with the social than with the physical world seems to me empirically meaningless. What is the evidence that the social world has been less predictable than the rest of nature during primate and human evolution? I do not know of any common yardstick that would allow such a comparison. Thus, this line of justifying a special social intelligence seems to be, like the complexity argument, empirically empty, or possibly, false.

It may be false because the argument projects our 20th-century view of nature — tamed by technology, medicine and science — into the past. Until recently, nature used to be seen as fickle and unstable, willing to inflict unpredictable hazards: sudden death by plague, lightening, and flood; the permanent gamble of early infant death; unknown diseases killing livestock; famine caused by weather hazards, drought and millions of grasshoppers that surface without warning, among others. For instance, 16th-century insurers rejected the use of statistical information for calculating insurance premiums as impractical because they did not believe that the world was stable enough for the use of statistics (Daston, 1987). Why then do 20th-century researchers tend to see nature as more predictable than society? Nature may have indeed become more stable, or it may be our scientific idealisations that have made it appear to be so. Galileo's law of falling bodies is one illustration of the successful strategy of physicists to look for strong regularity and ignore the unpredictable parts of nature, such as air currents, surface area and a myriad of intervening factors. Any actual case of a falling leaf remains unpredictable by the law of falling bodies. More generally, 20th-century physics has replaced the deterministic world view of classical physics by a probabilistic view: Brownian motion and radioactive decay exemplify the unpredictability of individual particles, which become predictable only by statistical laws. Unpredictability and probability seems to be rooted not only in the human mind, but also in the constitution of the universe (Gigerenzer *et al.*, 1989).

To summarise, the claim that social interaction was once less predictable than encounters with nature, artefacts and the rest of the non-social world does not seem to be built on solid evidence. Therefore, it does not provide a foundation for a special social intelligence.

Is the social environment more intellectually challenging?

Humphrey (1988, p. 19) asserted that social systems create and maintain 'calculating beings' who 'must be able to calculate the consequence of their own behaviour, to calculate the likely behaviour of others, to calculate the balance of advantages and loss'. He concluded that 'here at last the intellectual faculties required are of the highest order'. Humphrey seems to assume that a complicated social system creates complicated intellectual operations ('creative intelligence', Humphrey, 1988, p. 16). This is not necessarily so. Herbert Simon (e.g. 1982) has argued that humans typically do not calculate the balance of advantages and losses in a complicated, 'optimal' way, such as prescribed by subjective expected utility theory (or its variants), but use simple 'satisficing' algorithms instead. Satisficing, a blend of sufficing and satisfying, is a word of Scottish origin that Herbert Simon introduced to characterise algorithms that successfully deal with conditions of limited time, knowledge, or computational capacities.

For instance, a person may accept the first mate who satisfies an aspiration level rather than going through the 'optimal' procedure of listing all candidates, listing all possible consequences associated with each candidate, determining the probabilities and utilities of each of these consequences, multiplying probabilities by utilities, calculating the expected utilities of all candidates and finally choosing the one with the maximum value. Even if one had the time to go through this 'optimal' procedure, the candidates may become insulted, tire of waiting, and no longer be available after all the candidates have been vetted. (There seem to be exceptions. Once I asked a rational-choice theorist from the University of Texas at Austin in which important decisions he had explicitly followed the expected utility procedure, and he answered when he chose his wife.) Nevertheless, from economics to cognitive science to optimal foraging theory, the fiction of 'optimal' computations is generally upheld. The fear is that satisficing algorithms would not be very intelligent. However, Dan Goldstein and I showed that this fear is unwarranted; simple satisficing strategies can make about as many accurate inferences about real-world environments as computationally costly rational calculations, and in less time and with less knowledge (Gigerenzer & Goldstein, 1996). If social situations can be mastered by fast and frugal satisficing algorithms, then there is little reason why more costly 'optimal' computations should have evolved instead.

Thus a system that looks complex may not demand those sophisticated (and mystical) cognitive processes that Humphrey termed 'creative intelligence'; simple processes may do the job as well. However, unless we specify these intelligent processes, complicated or simple, and actually test and simulate their performance on some adaptive task, we will not know. Therefore, a research programme on social intelligence needs to work out these satisficing algorithms that may be the building blocks of social intelligence.

To summarise, the possibility of a special social intelligence, different from technical, ecological, and other forms of intelligence, has been attributed to the alleged facts that social environments are more 'complex', 'unpredictable', or 'challenging'. Justifications such as these sound plausible but under closer inspection turn out to be either empirically empty (untestable and vague) or possibly false (they project 20th-century control over nature into the past). Last but not least, none of these supposed reasons for a special social intelligence has helped to specify the mechanisms of social intelligence, Machiavellian or otherwise.

I propose to drop this rhetoric and instead to start with a modular concept of intelligence. Modularity can justify why separate social intelligences (note the plural) are needed, and can suggest what the mechanisms actually could be. The notion of modularity is nothing new, but, as the introduction to a recent book on this topic illustrates, it means many things to many people (Hirschfeld & Gelman, 1994). There exist several important approaches to modularity (e.g. Millikan, 1984; Leslie, 1994; Pinker, 1994; Baron-Cohen, 1995). It will soon become clear which ones inspired my own speculations.

Modules for social intelligence

The modular version of the social intelligence hypothesis I propose assumes that social intelligences come in the plural, as do non-social intelligences. I will now describe the modular organisation of social intelligence. Reader be warned: from here on is speculation.

The thesis that social intelligence is modular is motivated by two reasons: the shortsightedness of natural selection and the combinatorial explosion of intelligent systems. Natural selection works without a big plan but results in specific adaptations accumulated over generations. Thus it seems unlikely that natural selection designed a general-purpose intelligence that embodies, say, the Piagetian formal operations or a Bayesian inference machine. Even if this had happened, such a general-purpose intelligence runs into the problem of combinatorial explosion, as evidenced by the frame problem in artificial intelligence: unless the infinite possibilities to combine elements and relations in a general-purpose system are drastically reduced by semantic constraints, an organism would be paralysed and unable to react in time. For instance, unless attention is constrained to specific types of interactors and interactions, and semantic structure is *a priori* built in that tells the organism what to learn, what to look for, and what to ignore, an intelligent organism would be unable to perform even the most elementary tasks: to detect predators, prey and mates, and be fast enough to survive and reproduce.

I propose the following assumptions about the nature of modular social intelligence:

1 A module for social intelligence is a faculty, not a general factor.

Intelligence is often assumed to be of one kind, one general ability that helps an organism cope with all situations – such as Francis Galton's 'natural ability,' Spearman's general intelligence factor g, and the numberless definitions that start with 'intelligence is the general ability to . . . .' The thesis that intelligence is a unified general ability has been invented only recently, in the mid-19th century, by Francis Galton, Herbert Spencer and Hippolyte Taine, among others (Daston, 1992). The idea of one general intelligence was motivated by Darwin's theory of evolution (Galton was Darwin's cousin) and seemed to provide the missing continuum between animals and humans, as well as between human races, and last but not least, between men and women.

Such a unified general ability was alien to the earlier *faculty* psychology, which dated back to Aristotle. Faculty psychology posited a collection of faculties and talents in the mind, such as imagination, memory and judgment. These faculties organised an intricate division of mental labour, and no single one nor their sum coincided with our concept of intelligence (Daston, 1992). Faculty psychology was revived, in the language of factor analysis, in the late 1930s when L. L. Thurstone claimed about seven primary mental abilities. In the second half of the 20th century, the mind has become again a crowded place. Evidence has been announced for dozens of factors of intelligence, and Guilford & Hoepfner (1971) even claimed the confirmation of some 98 factors of cognitive ability (see Carroll, 1982). Cognitive psychologists who use experiments rather than IQ tests also divide up cognition in terms of faculties (but you will not catch one using that term): deductive reasoning, inductive reasoning, problem-solving, memory, attention, judgement and decision-making, and so forth.

A modular organisation of intelligence assumes, similar to the earlier faculty psychology before Galton, several intelligences that have special designs, and not one general-purpose intelligence. The general thesis is that social intelligence is like a Swiss army knife with several special tools rather than one single general-purpose blade (Cosmides & Tooby, 1994a).

2   A module for social intelligence is domain-specific, not domain-general.

Intelligence modules, however, are not like Thurstone's primary mental abilities and faculties such as reasoning. I distinguish between two types of faculties: *domain-specific* and *domain-general*. Faculties such as deductive reasoning, memory and numerical ability (as well as such factors as 'fluid' and 'crystallised' intelligence) are assumed to treat any content identically, that is, to operate in a domain-general way. The laws of memory, for instance, in this view, are not about *what* is memorised; they are formulated without reference to content. Fodor (1983) called these domain-general faculties 'horizontal', as opposed to 'vertical' domain-specific faculties. The modularity of social intelligence, I propose, is vertical.

The doctrine of domain-general mechanisms flourished in Skinner's behaviourism, before it was generally rejected following experimental work by John Garcia and others (e.g. Garcia & Koelling, 1966). Skinner's laws of conditioning were designed to hold true for all stimuli and responses (the assumption of *equipotentiality* of stimuli). Garcia, however, showed that when the taste of flavoured water was repeatedly paired with an electric shock immediately after tasting, rats nevertheless had great difficulty learning to avoid the flavoured water. Yet in one single trial the rat can learn to avoid the flavoured water when it is followed by experimentally induced nausea, even if the nausea is 2 hours later (thus violating the law of contiguity). The rat seems to be 'prepared' by natural selection to form some associations rapidly but not others. Learning through imitation (rather than direct experience) is also reported to be domain-specific. Rhesus monkeys, for instance, reared in the laboratory, exhibit no fear toward venomous snakes. However, one will show fear if it sees another monkey emitting a fear reaction toward snakes. Yet the monkey does not become afraid of just any stimulus: if it sees another monkey emit a fear reaction toward a flower, it does not acquire a fear of flowers (Mineka & Cook, 1988; Cosmides & Tooby, 1994b). Learning by imitation of others, like learning by association, is simultaneously *enabled* and *constrained* by specific 'expectations' of what to avoid, what to fear, or more generally, what causal connections to establish. Without domain-specific mechanisms, an organism would not 'know' what to look for, nor which of the infinite possible causal connections to check. Such an organism would be paralysed by data analysis like the quantophrenic researcher who measures everything one can think of, computes correlation matrices of dinosaurian dimensions, and blindly searches for significant correlations. Despite the available evidence to the contrary, Skinner's ideal of domain generality has survived the cognitive revolution and is flourishing in present-day conceptions of the mind.

Domain generality is possibly the most influential and suspect idea in 20th-century psychology. Psychologists love to organise their field by horizontal faculties such as attention, memory, perception, problem-solving, and judgement and decision making. Terms such as these organise the chapter structure of textbooks, the specialties of scientific journals, the divisional structure in grant agencies, and the self-identity of numerous colleagues. Pick a psychologist at random at a conference and ask what she or he does. Most likely, you will get an answer such as 'I am a memory person' or 'I am in judgement and decision-making'. Psychologists tend to identify with horizontal faculties, not with domains.

I propose, in contrast, that modules for social intelligence are domain-specific. How should we think about these modules? Fodor (1983), a vehement proponent of modularity, has argued that modularity is restricted to input systems (the senses) and language, whereas central processes such as reasoning are domain-general. I term this the 'weak modularity thesis'. In his view, modules are specifically designed mechanisms for voice recognition in conspecifics, for face recognition in conspecifics, and colour perception, among others. I disagree with Fodor's opposition between modular sensory processes (and language) and general-purpose central processes. Social intelligence involves both perceptual processes and mechanisms for reasoning and inductive inference. For instance, assume there is a module for social contracts, that is, a module that enables co-operation between unrelated conspecifics for their mutual benefit. Such a module would need to incorporate both 'central' processes, such as cost–benefit computations and search algorithms for information that could reveal that one is being cheated, and sensory processes such as face recognition. Without both 'peripheral' and 'central' mechanisms, neither social contracts nor cheating detection would be possible.

What I call the 'strong modularity thesis' postulates that modules include central processes as well as sensory mechanisms (and language). The function of modules is not tied to 'peripheral' as opposed to 'central' processes. Rather, their function is to solve specific problems of adaptive significance, and to do this quickly. A problem of adaptive significance can be described as an evolutionarily recurrent problem whose solution promoted reproduction (Cosmides & Tooby, 1994b). Candidates include coalition forming and co-operation, foraging, predator avoidance, navigation and mate selection. To solve such problems, modules need to combine 'peripheral' and 'central' processes. Thus, the domains (more precisely, the 'proper' domains, see next section) of modules are important adaptive problems and not just perceptual (plus language) tasks.

3 A module for social intelligence has a proper and an actual domain.

Assume there is a social intelligence module designed for handling social contracts in a hunter–gatherer society. The *proper* domain of the module may have been the exchange of food for the mutual benefit of both parties involved in the contract (because food sharing is not too common among animals, an alternative hypothesis would be that the proper domain concerned social services such as alliance formation, see Harcourt & de Waal, 1992). Generations later, currency has been developed, and the module's representation of possible benefits and costs exchanged in a social contract needs to be expanded to tokens that can be exchanged for benefits. Soon economic systems will be invented where the exchange of hard currency is no longer the norm, and benefits and costs become more and more abstract. The *actual* domain of the module has shifted from the exchange of grain and meat to buying futures and options. The mechanisms of the module, however, perform largely the same task: a routine that leads individuals to enter into social contracts (sharing) when resources (such as meat) are highly variable and scarce; a representation of what the benefits and costs are for oneself and for one's kin; perceptual algorithms and a memory that allows identification of the partner by face, voice, or name recognition; and search processes that look for information that could reveal that one is being cheated.

Thus the *proper* domain of a module is that for which the module actually evolved; the *actual* domain is one to which the module is transferred or extended, following changes in the environment (Sperber, 1994). By being transferred to new domains, the mechanisms of the modules themselves may change; adaptations (modules) can become exaptations for new adaptations (Gould & Vrba, 1982). The distinction between proper and actual domain is a matter of degree rather than of kind, and the actual domain is most likely larger than the proper domain. Modules for social intelligence in humans seem to differ from those in primates in that they have larger actual domains, and in that the actual domains may have less overlap with the proper domain.

The actual domains of modules for human social intelligence can extend beyond the human. Anthropomorphism is social intelligence reaching out beyond *Homo sapiens*. Anthropomorphism has counted as a scientific sin since the 17th century, and earlier as a theological sin; nevertheless human intelligence cannot resist projecting human social categories, intentions and morals into non-humans (Mitchell *et al.*, 1997). Darwin himself practiced empathic anthropomorphism (but not anthropocentrism) in particular with respect to dogs; animal rights activists often invoke the same sentiment. Anthropomorphism of a less empathic nature extends to phylogenetically distant species: 'Rape' in scorpion flies and 'ant slavery' are examples. In opposition to all this, behaviourism values purifying scientific language, and a story told about the Columbia University philosopher Sidney Morgenbesser illustrates this value. After B. F. Skinner gave a talk at Columbia, Sidney stood up and said: 'Professor Skinner, I always tried to understand what the essence of behaviourism is. Now I think I know. Behaviorism is the denial of anthropomorphism for humans'.

Social intelligence can reach beyond animals and still create powerful metaphors. Dawkin's (1976) 'selfish gene' lives in a world of savage competition, exploitation and deceit. Physicists, chemists and astronomers certainly censor similar anthropomorphic descriptions in press, but in scientists' informal and private conversations, intentions are frequently attributed to particles and matter (Atran, 1990).

4   A module is activated by a triggering algorithm.

Assume there is a simple social organism with two modules for social intelligence: one deals with social contracts, the other with threats. Thus this organism knows only two ways to deal with conspecifics: to engage with them in the exchange of certain goods to their mutual benefit, and to threaten individuals to get one's way (and react when others do so). As simple as the social intelligence of this organism is, the organism needs to decide when to activate the social contract module and when the threat module. All modules cannot be activated at the same time because the very advantage of modularity is to focus attention and to prevent combinatorial explosion. For instance, the social contract module focuses attention on information that can reveal that the organism is being cheated, while this information is of no relevance for a threat module. A threat module needs to attend to information that can reveal, for instance, whether the other side is bluffing, or whether high status individuals are present who could be used for 'protected threat' (Kummer, 1988).

How is one of the two modules activated? I assume that there is a triggering algorithm that attends to a small set of cues whose presence signals either threat or social contract. These signals can include facial expressions, gestures, body movements and verbal statements. Assume the organisms do have language. A simple algorithm can quickly recognise whether a verbal statement of the type 'if you do X, then I do Y' is a threat or a social contract. If Y is a negative consequence for me, and follows X in time, then I am being threatened. If Y is a benefit for me, and the temporal sequence can be either way, then I am being offered a social contract. I call such simple rules 'triggering algorithms' because their function is to activate a module that can focus attention, emotion and behavioural responses so that fast reaction is possible.

Triggering algorithms can err, that is, not activate the appropriate module, such as mistaking a serious threat for pretend play. The likelihood of triggering the wrong module may increase when there are more than two modules, but redundancy in cues, such as verbal cues, facial cues and gestures may reduce errors.

5   Modules are hierarchically organised.

When a mind has not just two, but a large number of modules, a single triggering algorithm may be too slow to discriminate between all possibilities simultaneously. In such a socially more intelligent mind, modules can be hierarchically connected by triggering algorithms, as in a sequential decision tree. Hierarchical organisation corresponds to the idea that species started out with a few modules, to which more specialised modules were added later in phylogeny, and to Wimsatt's (1986) notion of generative entrenchment.

Assume I march through a forest at night. Visibility is poor, a storm is coming up, and I suddenly see the contours of a large dark object that seems slowly to move. A triggering algorithm needs to decide quickly whether the object is 'self-propelled' (animal or human) or not (plant or physical object) (Premack & Premack, 1994). According to the Premacks, this decision is based on the object's motion pattern. Recall the demonstrations by Fritz Heider where the motion patterns of two points in two-dimensional space make us 'see' the points as animate or inanimate, chasing, hunting, hurting, or supporting one another (e.g. Heider & Simmel, 1944). These are beautiful demonstrations, but they include no descriptions of the algorithms that make us see all these social behaviours. How could the first triggering algorithm work? A simple algorithm would analyse only external movements (such as the direction and acceleration of the object) and not internal movements (the relative movement of the body parts). For instance, if a motion pattern centres on my own position, such as an object that circles around me, or speeds up toward me, the algorithm infers a self-propelled object. Moreover, it infers a self-propelled object that takes some interest in myself. Motion patterns that centre around the object's own centre of gravity, in contrast, indicate that the object is a plant (e.g. a tree). Now, if the motion pattern indicates that the object is self-propelled, the triggering algorithm may activate a module for unrecognised self-propelled objects. This module will immediately set the organism into a state of physiological and emotional arousal, initiate behavioural routines such as stopping and preparing for running away, and activate a second, more specialised triggering algorithm whose task is to decide whether the self-propelled object is animal or human. Assume that this second triggering algorithm infers from shape and motion information that the object is human. A module for social encounters with unknown humans is subsequently activated, which initiates a search for individual recognition in memory and may initiate an appeal for voice contact in order to find out whether the other is friend or enemy, is going to threaten or help me, and so on. This is pure speculation, but one might work out the mechanisms of a hierarchical organisation along these lines.

Modules that are hierarchically organised can act quickly, as only a few branches of the combinatorial tree need to be travelled. For instance, if the first triggering algorithm had indicated that the unknown object was not self-propelled, then all subsequent information concerning whether it is human or animal, friend or enemy, or predator or prey, could have been ignored.

6 An intelligence module works with satisficing algorithms.

There are two views about the machinery of intelligent behaviour. The classical view is that the laws of probability theory or logic define intelligent processes: intelligent agents have rules such as Bayes's rule, the law of large numbers, transitive inference and consistency built in. This was the view of the Enlightenment mathematicians (Daston, 1988), to which Jean Piaget added an ontogenetic dimension, and it still is a dominant view in economics, cognitive psychology, artificial intelligence and optimal foraging theory. For instance, Bayes's rule has been proposed to model how animals infer the presence of predators and prey (Stephens & Krebs, 1986) as well as how humans reason, categorise and memorise (Anderson, 1990). The problem with this view is that in any sufficiently rich environment, Bayesian computations become mathematically so complex that one needs to assume that minds are 'Laplacean demons' that have unlimited computational power, time and knowledge. To find a way out of this problem, researchers often make unrealistic assumptions about the structure of natural environments, namely assumptions that reduce the Bayesian computations. Anderson (1990) for instance, found himself forced to make the false assumption that environmental features would be generally independent, in order to save the fiction of the Bayesian homunculus in the mind (Gigerenzer, 1991a). Despite their psychological implausibility, Laplacean demons are bustling in contemporary theories of the mind; as models of choice, categorisation, estimation and inference, among others (Gigerenzer & Murray, 1987). The rationale seems to be this: cognition is rational, Bayes's theorem defines rationality, *ergo* cognition works with Bayes's theorem. The same rationale seems to hold for other statistical tools that turned into theories of mind, such as multiple regression, Neyman–Pearson decision techniques and analysis of variance (Gigerenzer, 1991b).

The second view, the one I propose here, is that modules of social intelligence, including the triggering algorithms, work with simple 'satisficing' algorithms instead of the costly 'optimal' algorithms. There are several reasons that favour simple and specifically designed principles rather than expensive and general ones. Firstly, there is, in fact, no single method of inference — statistical or logical — that works best in all real-world contexts (Gigerenzer et al., 1989). Secondly, as mentioned before, in real-world situations, 'optimal' computations can become quickly so complex that one is forced to make highly simplifying assumptions about the environment. Thirdly, algorithms for social intelligence need to work under constraints of limited time and knowledge – for instance, one may not have the time to search for further information. Fourthly, the means and ends of social intelligence are broader than consistency (coherence) and accuracy – the accepted norms of logic and statistics. Social intelligence can involve being inconsistent (e.g. adaptive unpredictability may be optimal in competitive situations: the opponent will be unable to predict one's behaviour), taking high risks in trying to come out first (that is, options with low probabilities rather than those that maximise expected value), responding quickly rather than accurately (e.g. to make too long a pause in a conversation in order to think of the best answer can be embarrassing and seen as impolite), and making decisions that one can justify or defend afterward (Gigerenzer, 1996).

The key argument against satisficing strategies is that their simplicity raises the suspicion that they are really bad. But this need not be the case: simple principles can be quick-and-clean rather than quick-and-dirty. Consider a simple algorithm for choice called 'Take The Best,' which Dan Goldstein and I have studied in some detail (Gigerenzer & Goldstein, 1996). Take The Best infers which of two alternatives scores higher on some criterion, such as which of two food items is more dangerous, or which of two cities has a higher population. Take The Best bases decisions on one single reason, namely on the first good reason on which two alternatives differ. The first good reason can be simply that the individual does not recognise (has never heard of) one of the two alternatives. This 'recognition principle' seems to operate in domains where recognition is correlated with the variable that needs to be inferred. For instance, rats who can choose between food that they recognise and food that is new to them do not accept the new food unless they have smelled it on the breath of a fellow rat (Gallistel et al., 1991).

But how good is Take The Best? We set up a contest between Take The Best and various linear integration algorithms, including multiple regression (Gigerenzer & Goldstein, 1996). The task was to infer which of two cities has the larger population. We used as a test environment all German cities with more than 100 000 inhabitants and 10 binary predictors of population (such as whether or not a city has a soccer team in the major league). Take The Best simply goes through the predictors one by one, in the order of their validity, until it finds one in which one city has a positive value (e.g. a soccer team in the major league) and the other has not (no team or unknown). Then the inference is made that the city with the positive value is the larger, and no further predictor values are searched – it takes the best predictor that makes a difference and ignores the rest. Thus, Take The Best violates the classical standards of rationality: it does not search for all evidence (here the values of two objects on all ten predictors), and it does not integrate any evidence, and variants of Take The Best can violate transitivity. The competitors – such as multiple regression – in contrast, always used all predictors and always integrated this information. The competition was performed with millions of simulated subjects with varying degrees of limited knowledge about predictor values. Take The Best matched or outperformed all competitors in accuracy, including multiple regression, and outperformed all in speed. This surprising result demonstrates that simple psychological principles can be as accurate as costly statistical algorithms of the Laplacean demon type.

If short-sighted evolution has equipped us with simple satisficing algorithms rather than with the collected works of logic and probability theory, this result indicates that we need not necessarily worry about human rationality. The challenges are to understand what these satisficing algorithms are and to describe the structure of the environments in which they can perform well, and where they cannot. My proposal is that both the triggering algorithms and the mechanisms of the module are satisficing algorithms.

7 Satisficing algorithms combine cognitive, emotional and motivational tools to guide inference and behaviour.

In each module, various cognitive, emotional, behavioural and motivational processes are wired together. A social contract module, for instance, includes perceptual machinery to recognise different individuals; a long-term memory that stores the history of past exchanges with other individuals in order to know when to co-operate, when to defect and when to punish for defection; knowledge about what constitutes a benefit and what a cost for oneself; and emotional reactions such as anger that signal to others that one will go ruthlessly after cheaters (Cosmides & Tooby, 1992; Gigerenzer, 1995). Satisficing algorithms can use cognitive, emotional, or motivational processes vicariously as means to achieve a goal. For instance, emotional reactions (such as disgust in matters of food) can substitute for learning from experience when events are too rare or too deadly for individual learning.

The very challenge of a modular concept of social intelligence is that it crosses the established boundaries of horizontal faculties. It opens up a conception of intelligence that integrates cognition with, rather than setting it apart from, other adaptive functions such as motivations and emotions.

Experimental tests

This sketch of a modular social intelligence is speculative and there is room for improvement. Does such a theory produce testable predictions? It does, and I give one example: the thesis that there is a module for social contracts in humans. Humans are among the very few species that engage in co-operation between unrelated individuals, such as social contracts. But co-operation (reciprocal altruism) cannot evolve in the first place unless one can detect cheaters (Trivers, 1971). The thesis is that humans are equipped with a module for social contracts, which has special mechanisms, such as weighing benefits against costs, recognising individuals, and detecting when other individuals cheat. The theory was proposed first by Cosmides (1989) and has been further elaborated and experimentally tested (e.g. Cosmides & Tooby, 1989, 1992; Gigerenzer & Hug, 1992; Gigerenzer, 1995).

One testable implication of a social contract module is that if an interaction is classified as a social contract, the module will search for information that could reveal that the other party is cheating. In a social contract of the type 'If you take the benefit, then you must pay the costs', cheating is defined as 'benefit taken and costs not paid'.

Let us apply this hypothesis to a standard reasoning task that seems to have absolutely nothing to do with social intelligence. The task is known as the four card problem (or the Wason selection task). There is a conditional rule of the type 'if P then Q' such as 'if there is a "4" on one side of the card, then there is a "B" on the other'. There are four cards that have a number on one side and a letter on the other. The participant can read only one side, and the cards read '4', '5', 'A', and 'B'. The participant is asked which of these cards must be turned around in order to find out whether the rule has been violated. Peter Wason (1966), who introduced this task, and his followers believed that the correct answer is to turn around the '4' and the 'A' cards, because in propositional logic, a conditional statement 'if P then Q' is violated if and only if 'P and not-Q' is obtained. An avalanche of experimental studies showed that people sometimes reasoned according to propositional logic, sometimes not, depending on the content of the Ps and Qs. For instance, only about 10% of participants picked the 'P' and the 'not-Q' cards in rules about numbers and letters, as above, whereas this number skyrocketed to 75% when the rule was 'if an employee works on the weekend, then that person gets a day off during the week' (Gigerenzer & Hug, 1992). In the latter experiment, the four cards represented information about four previous employees who had worked (had not worked) on the weekend and did get (did not get) a day off. For more than two decades psychologists puzzled about why people sometimes reason logically and sometimes not. But no convincing answer was found. Propositional logic, which many researchers (mis)take as the yardstick of sound reasoning did not tell − it is pure syntax and mute on semantics.

A modular theory of intelligence, however, postulates that even in the cases where judgements correspond to the logical 'P and not-Q,' people are not necessarily performing logical operations. If the rule is a social contract, such as the day-off rule, then a social contract module is activated that searches for information that could reveal that the other party is cheating. The 75% who chose the 'worked on the weekend' and 'did not get a day off' cards did not perform a logical abstraction, that is, they did not infer that 'if P then Q' is violated if and only if P and not-Q was obtained. These participants chose the 'P' and 'not-Q' card for a different reason: 'P' and 'not-Q' happens to coincide with 'benefit taken' and 'costs not paid', what the module is attentive to. One way to test these competing explanations − modular social intelligence versus general-purpose logic − is to switch perspectives: to tell half of the participants that they are an employee, and the other half that they are the employer, leaving everything else as it was. If people reason by propositional logic, this should make no difference, because logic knows no perspective. If people, however, reason by a social contract module, then the perspective is the very essence. The experimental results were consistent with the postulate of a social contract module: 75% of the employees choose the cards 'worked on the weekend' and 'did not get a day off' but only 2% of the employers. The majority of employers selected the 'did not work on the weekend' and 'did get a day off' cards, which looks like the logical 'not-P and Q'. Thus, if one believes in logic as a general-purpose norm for good reasoning, then people's performance seems to be inconsistent: sometimes they reason logically and sometimes they do not. If one assumes a social contract module, however, then people are quite consistent: whether employee or employer, they search for 'benefit taken' and 'costs not paid' (Gigerenzer & Hug, 1992).

Note that these results can not be explained away by saying that the conditional in a social contract is a logical biconditional. If people treat the statement as a logical biconditional, then they would have to turn around all four cards (because both 'P and not-Q' and 'not-P and Q' violate a biconditional). Not one single employee did so, and very few of the employers. Note that participants were not looking for cheaters *per se*, but only for being cheated themselves. Our participants were not reasoning by a Kantian moral, but by a Machiavellian intelligence.

This and other experiments illustrate how social intelligence can explain apparently contradictory data in a standard laboratory task that has been assumed to reveal human irrationality. The thesis that the evolutionary theory of reciprocal altruism can enlighten us about cognitive psychology has stirred up a virulent controversy (e.g. Cheng & Holyoak, 1989; Pollard, 1990). The thought that social intelligence might exist in the syntactical world of research on reasoning has been treated by many like a virus infection. In this world where the content of reasoning is often arbitrary and irrelevant for the theory, the debate is still about which syntactical model is the right one: is it mental logic (e.g. Rips, 1994) or mental models (e.g. Johnson-Laird, 1983)? But the data, such as on the 'Machiavellian' effect of perspective on reasoning, has now been replicated several times, and some researchers have begun to adjust their theories to these data (e.g. Holyoak & Cheng, 1995a,b; Cummins, 1996).

Summing up

In 1976, Nick Humphrey wrote a stimulating essay on the social function of intellect that provided 'the single most important seed' (Byrne & Whiten, 1988a, p. 1) for *Machiavellian Intelligence*. Humphrey's paper contains stimulating ideas about social intelligence, but also the seed of a sterile research methodology. In the postscript we are told that his 'central thesis' demands 'that there should be a positive correlation across species between "social complexity" and "individual intelligence"' (Humphrey, 1988, p. 26 (originally published in 1976)). A laboratory test of social skill, Humphrey proposes, is urgently needed, which 'ought, if I am right, to double as a test of "high-level intelligence"' (p. 26). This proposal, as innocent as it looks, steers toward repeating a grave error that has swamped research on (non-social) intelligence tests. The error is to start with no theory but seductive everyday concepts such as social skill and creative intelligence, then go on to design tests to measure these vague concepts, and to pray to heaven that these tests miraculously transform loose thinking into precise mechanisms of intelligence.[1] Despite prayers that were backed up by statistics, some 90 years of factor analysing and correlating IQ tests has not noticeably increased our understanding of the mechanisms of human intelligence. I fear that Humphrey's proposal to look for correlations between some tests for social complexity, social skill and individual intelligence will be doomed to the same failure.

The alternative is to start boldly and theoretically. The challenge is to design the possible mechanisms of social intelligence, and to test these by means of experiment, observation and simulation. The mechanisms of a modular social intelligence I have outlined, as speculative as they are, can serve as a start. We will have to take up some hard questions. What are the domains (proper and actual) for a given species? What is the mechanism of a module? What is the algorithm that triggers a module? If we join forces, we can do it.

Acknowledgements

I would like to thank Arnold Davidson, Ulrich Hoffrage, Geoffrey Miller, Anita Todd, Frans de Waal, Bill Wimsatt and Andy Whiten for their helpful comments on earlier drafts of this chapter.

References

Anderson, J. R. (1990). *The Adaptive Character of Thought*. Hillsdale, NJ: Lawrence Erlbaum Associastes.
Atran, S. (1990). *Cognitive Foundations of Natural History: Towards an Anthropology of Science*. Cambridge: Cambridge University Press.
Baron-Cohen, S. (1995). *Mindblindness*. Cambridge, MA: MIT Press.
Binet, A. & Simon, T. (1914). *Mentally Defective Children*. London: Edward Arnold.

---

[1] The notion of test intelligence, left undefined in its content, has had many faces, including the moral and the social (Daston, 1992). The creators of the first intelligence tests, Binet & Simon (1914), for instance, asked questions concerning social skills, such as 'Why should one judge a person by his acts rather than by his words?' Louis Terman (1916), in the first edition of the Stanford–Binet Test, expressed the intimate link between lack of intelligence and of morally inappropriate behaviour as follows: 'Every feeble-minded woman is a prostitute'. In the 1937 revision of the text (with M. A. Merrill), this sentence was deleted. Piece by piece, IQ tests became pure and puritan.

Boesch, C. & Boesch, H. (1984). Mental map in wild chimpanzees: An analysis of hammer transports for nut cracking. *Primates*, 25, 160–70.

Byrne, R. & Whiten, A. (eds) (1988). *Machiavellian Intelligence: Social Expertise and the Evolution of Intellect in Monkeys, Apes and Humans*. Oxford: Clarendon Press.

Carroll, J. B. (1982). The measurement of intelligence. In *Handbook of Human Intelligence* ed. R. J. Sternberg, pp. 29–120. Cambridge: Cambridge University Press.

Chance, M. R. A. & Mead, A. P. (1953). Social behavior and primate evolution. *Symposia of the Society for Experimental Biology, Evolution*, 7, 395–439.

Cheng, P. W. & Holyoak, K. J. (1989). On the natural selection of reasoning theories. *Cognition*, 33, 285–313.

Cosmides, L. (1989). The logic of social exchange: Has natural selection shaped how humans reason? *Cognition*, 31, 187–276.

Cosmides, L. & Tooby, J. (1989). Evolutionary psychology and the generation of culture, Part II. Case study: A computational theory of social exchange. *Ethology and Sociobiology*, 10, 51–97.

Cosmides, L. & Tooby, J. (1992). Cognitive adaptations for social exchange. In *The Adapted Mind: Evolutionary Psychology and the Generation of Culture*, ed. J. H. Barkow, L. Cosmides & J. Tooby, pp. 163–228. Oxford: Oxford University Press.

Cosmides, L. & Tooby, J. (1994a). Beyond intuition and instinct blindness: Towards an evolutionary rigorous cognitive science. *Cognition*, 50, 41–77.

Cosmides, L. & Tooby, J. (1994b). Origins of domain specificity: The evolution of functional organization. In *Mapping the Mind: Domain Specificity in Cognition and Culture*, ed. L. A. Hirschfeld & S. A. Gelman, pp. 85–116. Cambridge: Cambridge University Press.

Cummins, D. D. (1996). Evidence for the innateness of deontic reasoning. *Mind and Language*, 11, 160–90.

Daston, L. (1987). The domestication of risk: Mathematical probability and insurance 1650–1830. In *The Probabilistic Revolution: Volume 1. Ideas in History*, ed. L. Krüger, L. J. Daston & M. Heidelberger, pp. 237–60. Cambridge, MA: MIT Press.

Daston, L. (1988). *Classical Probability in the Enlightenment*. Princeton, NJ: Princeton University Press.

Daston, L. (1992). The naturalized female intellect. *Science in Context*, 5, 209–35.

Dawkins, R. (1976). *The Selfish Gene*. Oxford: Oxford University Press.

Driver, P. M. & Humphries, D. A. (1988). *Protean Behavior: The Biology of Unpredictability*. Oxford: Oxford University Press.

Fodor, J. A. (1983). *The Modularity of Mind*. Cambridge, MA: MIT Press.

Gallistel, C. R., Brown, A. L., Carey, S., Gelman, R. & Keil, F. C. (1991). Lessons from animal learning for the study of cognitive development. In *The Epigenesis of Mind: Essays on Biology and Cognition*, ed. S. Carey & R. Gelman, pp. 3–36. Hillsdale, NJ: Lawrence Erlbaum Associates.

Garcia, J. & Koelling, R. A. (1966). Relation of cue to consequence in avoidance learning. *Psychonomic Science*, 4, 123–4.

Gigerenzer, G. (1991a). Does the environment have the same structure as Bayes' theorem? *Behavioral and Brain Sciences*, 14, 495.

Gigerenzer, G. (1991b). From tools to theories: A heuristic of discovery in cognitive psychology. *Psychological Review*, 98, 254–67.

Gigerenzer, G. (1995). The taming of content: Some thoughts about domains and modules. *Thinking and Reasoning*, 1, 324–33.

Gigerenzer, G. (1996). Rationality: Why social context matters. In *Interactive Minds: Life-span Perspectives on the Social Foundation of Cognition*, ed. P. Baltes & U. M. Staudinger, pp. 319–46. Cambridge: Cambridge University Press.

Gigerenzer, G. & Goldstein, D. (1996). Reasoning the fast and frugal way: Models for bounded rationality. *Psychological Review*, 103, 650–69.

Gigerenzer, G. & Hug, K. (1992). Domain-specific reasoning: Social contracts, cheating, and perspective change. *Cognition*, 43, 127–71.

Gigerenzer, G. & Murray, D. J. (1987). *Cognition as Intuitive Statistics*. Hillsdale, NJ: Lawrence Erlbaum Associates.

Gigerenzer, G., Swijtink, Z., Porter, T., Daston, L., Beatty, J. & Krüger, L. (1989). *The Empire of Chance: How Probability Changed Science and Everyday Life*. Cambridge: Cambridge University Press.

Gould, S. J. & Vrba, E. S. (1982). Exaptation – a missing term in the science of form. *Paleobiology*, 8, 4–15.

Guilford, J. P. & Hoepfner, R. (1971). *The Analysis of Intelligence*. New York: McGraw-Hill.

Harcourt, A. H. & de Waal, F. B. M. (eds) (1992). *Coalitions and Alliances in Humans and Other Animals*. Oxford: Oxford University Press.

Heider, F. & Simmel, M. (1944). An experimental study of apparent behavior. *American Journal of Psychology*, 57, 243–59.

Hirschfeld, L. A. & Gelman, S. A. (1994). Toward a topography of mind: An introduction to domain specificity. In *Mapping the Mind: Domain Specificity in Cognition and Culture*, ed. L. A. Hirschfeld & S. A. Gelman, pp. 3–35. Cambridge: Cambridge University Press.

Holyoak, K. J. & Cheng, P. W. (1995a). Pragmatic reasoning with a point of view. *Thinking and Reasoning*, 1, 289–313.

Holyoak, K. J. & Cheng, P. W. (1995b). Pragmatic reasoning from multiple points of view: A response. *Thinking and Reasoning*, 1, 373–88.

Humphrey, N. K. (1988). The social function of intellect. In *Machiavellian Intelligence: Social Expertise and the Evolution of Intellect in Monkeys, Apes and Humans*, ed. R. W. Byrne & A. Whiten, pp. 13–26. Oxford: Clarendon Press. (Original work published in 1976).

Johnson-Laird, P. N. (1983). *Mental Models*. Cambridge, MA: Harvard University Press.

Kummer, H. (1988). Tripartite relations in hamadryas baboons. In *Machiavellian Intelligence: Social Expertise and the Evolution of Intellect in Monkeys, Apes and Humans*, ed. R. W. Byrne & A. Whiten, pp. 113–21. Oxford: Clarendon Press.

Kummer, H., Daston, L., Gigerenzer, G. & Silk, J. (1997). The social intelligence hypothesis. In *Human by Nature: Between Biology and the Social Sciences*, ed. P. Weingart, P. Richerson, S. D. Mitchell & S. Maasen, pp. 157–79. Hillsdale, NJ: Lawrence Erlbaum Associates.

Leslie, A. (1994). ToMM, ToBY, and Agency: Core architecture and domain specificity. In *Mapping the Mind: Domain Specificity in Cognition and Culture*, ed. L. A. Hirschfeld & S. A. Gelman, pp. 119–48. Cambridge: Cambridge University Press.

Miller, G. F. (1997). A review of sexual selection and human evolution: How mate choice shaped human nature. In *Evolution and Human Behavior: Ideas, Issues, and Applications*, ed. C. Crawford & D. Krebs. Hillsdale, NJ: Lawrence Erlbaum Associates. (In press).

Millikan, R. (1984). *Language, Thought, and Other Biological Categories*. Cambridge, MA: MIT Press.

Milton, K. (1988). Foraging behaviour and the evolution of primate intelligence. In *Machiavellian Intelligence: Social Expertise and the Evolution of Intellect in Monkeys, Apes and Humans*, ed. R. W. Byrne & A. Whiten, pp. 285–305. Oxford: Clarendon Press.

Mineka, S. & Cook, M. (1988). Social learning and the acquisition of snake fear in monkeys. In *Social learning: Psychological and Biological Perspectives*, ed. T. R. Zentall & B. G. Galef, pp. 51–73. Hillsdale, NJ: Lawrence Erlbaum Associates.

Mitchell, S. D., Daston, L., Sesardic, N., Sloep, P. & Gigerenzer, G. (1997). In the service of pluralism and interdisciplinarity. In *Human by Nature: Between Biology and the Social Sciences*, ed. P. Weingart, P. Richerson, S. D. Mitchell & S. Maasen, pp. 103–50. Hillsdale, NJ: Lawrence Erlbaum Associates.

Pinker, S. (1994). *The Language Instinct*. London: Penguin Press.

Pollard, P. (1990). Natural selection for the selection task: Limits to social exchange theory. *Cognition*, 36, 195–204.

Premack, D. & Premack, A. J. (1994). Moral belief: Form versus content. In *Mapping the Mind: Domain Specificity in Cognition and Culture*, ed. L. A. Hirschfeld & S. A. Gelman, pp. 149–68. Cambridge: Cambridge University Press.

Rips, L. J. (1994). *The Psychology of Proof: Deductive Reasoning in Human Thinking*. Cambridge, MA: MIT Press.

Simon, H. A. (1982). *Models of Bounded Rationality*. Cambridge, MA: MIT Press.

Smith, P. K. (1988). The cognitive demands of children's social interactions with peers. In *Machiavellian Intelligence: Social Expertise and the Evolution of Intellect in Monkeys, Apes and Humans*, ed. R. W. Byrne & A. Whiten, pp. 94–109). Oxford: Clarendon Press.

Sperber, D. (1994). The modularity of thought and the epidemiology of representations. In *Mapping the Mind: Domain Specificity in Cognition and Culture*, ed. L. A. Hirschfeld & S. A. Gelman, pp. 39–67. Cambridge: Cambridge University Press.

Stephens, D. W. & Krebs, J. R. (1986). *Foraging Theory*. Princeton, NJ: Princeton University Press.

Terman, L. M. (1916). *The Measurement of Intelligence*. Boston, MA: Houghton Mifflin Co.

Terman, L. M. & Merrilll, M. A. (1937). *Measuring Intelligence*. Boston, MA: Houghton Mifflin Co.

Todd, P. M. & Miller, G. F. (1995). The role of mate choice in biocomputation: Sexual selection as a process of search, optimization, and diversification. In *Evolution and Biocomputation: Computational Models of Evolution. Lecture Notes in Computer Science no. 899*, ed. W. Banzof & F. H. Eeckman, pp. 169–204. New York: Springer-Verlag.

Trivers, R. L. (1971). The evolution of reciprocal altruism. *Quarterly Review of Biology*, 46, 35–57.

Wason, P. C. (1966). Reasoning. In *New Horizons in Psychology*, ed. B. M. Foss, pp. 135–51. Harmondsworth: Penguin.

Whiten, A. & Byrne, R. W. (1988a). The Machiavellian intelligence hypotheses. In *Machiavellian Intelligence: Social Expertise and the Evolution of Intellect in Monkeys, Apes and Humans*, ed. R. W. Byrne & A. Whiten, pp. 1–9. Oxford: Clarendon Press.

Whiten, A. & Byrne, R. W. (1988b). Taking (Machiavellian) intelligence apart. In *Machiavellian Intelligence: Social Expertise and the Evolution of Intellect in Monkeys, Apes and Humans*, ed. R. W. Byrne & A. Whiten, pp. 50–65. Oxford: Clarendon Press.

Wimsatt, W. C. (1986). Developmental constraints, generative entrenchment, and the innate-acquired distinction. In *Integrating Scientific Disciplines*, ed. P. W. Bechtel, pp. 185–208. Dordrecht: Martinus-Nijhoff.

Wynn, T. (1988). *The Evolution of Spatial Competence*. Urbana, IL: University of Illinois Press.

11 The Technical Intelligence hypothesis: An additional evolutionary stimulus to intelligence?

RICHARD W. BYRNE

Suppose the Machiavellian intelligence hypothesis *is* right, and the problems created by social complexity were indeed an important spur to increasing intelligence during primate and human evolution. Do we then need to assume that this effect was operating constantly and universally? Not necessarily. It is perfectly possible that intellectual capacity was increased at *several* different points in the ancestral line leading to humans, and that these events were caused by evolutionary responses to quite different circumstances. And what of non-primates? Are all signs of specialisation in extra brain capacity to be explained in the same way? Clearly this is rather unlikely.

The question is, which *particular* observed facts does the Machiavellian intelligence hypothesis explain, if any? On a rather grand interpretation, as perhaps suggested by '*Social Expertise and the Evolution of Intellect in Monkeys, Apes and Humans*' (the subtitle of *Machiavellian Intelligence*, Byrne & Whiten, 1988), the need to handle social complexity would be the stimulus to *all* intellectual advances throughout the evolutionary ancestry of humans and primates. On the most narrow interpretation, the hypothesis would assert only that social complexity lies behind certain specific differences in ability between the haplorhine and strepsirhine primate groups. This more modest claim is already strongly supported by current evidence. What we must do, is first locate the evolutionary events that contributed to the eventual pre-eminence of human intellect. Only then can we tentatively assign causes, in the form of selective pressures that promoted change.

To judge from brain size, a rather easier variable to measure than intelligence, there are two immediately obvious branch points in primate evolution (i.e. origin points for new clades, monophyletic groups) at which we should look for a selective pressure causing intellectual change:

- the haplorhine (monkey and ape) clade, which differs from the strepsirhine (lemur and loris) clade in that haplorhines typically have relatively larger brains, and in particular, a greater investment in neocortex;
- the *Homo* clade, which shows another increase in relative (and absolute) brain size, preceding the great range expansion ('Out of Africa') and subsequent development of sophisticated stone tools.

Both events have been already subject to much discussion, and − in this volume and elsewhere − the case has been made that a need to deal with increased social complexity promoted the changes. In this chapter, I will argue that there is yet a third important evolutionary event in the ancestry of human mental evolution:

- the Great Ape clade, descendants of a common ancestor at about 16 million years ago, including the modern orangutan, gorilla, the two chimpanzees and ourselves, shows a cognitive advance in comparison to the Old World monkeys and other haplorhines.

I will argue that an explanation *complementary* to Machiavellian intelligence is needed to understand the changes involved in this development. And whereas in the past there has been a tendency to view social and ecological pressures as *alternative* theories for the origins of enhanced intelligence in primates, I argue that both may be necessary to understand human intellectual origins.

Why the Machiavellian intelligence idea is right

Taking 'intelligence' as a convenient inclusive label for a range of cognitive skills, without any necessary implication of a *single* underlying processing system in the brain, monkeys and apes are found to be more intelligent than strepsirhine primates, and most other mammalian groups.

This is shown in the evidence that forms much of the substance of this book (and see also de Waal, 1989; Cheney & Seyfarth, 1990; Harcourt & de Waal, 1992; Byrne, 1995). Abundant evidence documents that for monkeys and apes:

- long-term social relationships are formed,
- gains and losses in competitive encounters are often decided by triadic interactions,
- individuals can rely on third-party support, and often depend on a network of allies,
- in the case of Old World species at least, it appears that grooming is used to build up this network and active reconciliation is used to make repairs to strained relationships,
- considerable social manoeuvring is shown, in the widespread use of tactical deception and in the use of co-operation in agonism,
- individuals (at least of some species) distinguish and classify others of their species, for instance by their dominance rank, affiliation and group membership.

In addition to this well-documented social sophistication, monkeys and apes possess brains substantially larger for their body sizes than most other mammals (Jerison, 1973), despite the high metabolic cost of brain tissue (Armstrong, 1983). Given the allometric scaling rules that apply to primate brains, this means they invest heavily in neocortex; and neocortex is a brain region known to be involved in flexible, cross-modal integration and other 'intelligent' functions.

This haplorhine investment in neocortex, indexing a strong selection pressure for cognition, has been used to test between alternative theories of the origin of haplorhine intelligence. Dunbar (1992, 1995; and see Chapter 9) compared neocortical ratio, the ratio of the volume of the neocortex to that of the rest of brain, against a simple correlate of social complexity and several possible measures of environmental complexity. He took average group size to index social complexity, and residuals of range area and day journey length — when effects of body size had been removed by regression — and the extent of use of extracted foods, to index environmental complexity. (Note that none of these indices is an ideal one, but they are probably the best that can be used at present: see Byrne, 1996b.)

Only social complexity predicted neocortical investment, and Barton

(1996) was able to confirm this result with a method that identifies corre-lations across *independent* evolutionary events, avoiding problems of phylogenetic bias. Further, Byrne (1993, 1996b) showed that a *direct* measure of manipulative social skill, the frequency of using tactical decep-tion, was well predicted in primates by neocortical ratio. Thus, those haplorhine primates with relatively large brains (and this variation is itself largely a function of the neocortex size) use social manoeuvring more than others, and tend to live in larger groups.

The Machiavellian intelligence hypothesis does a good job of explaining these facts, as follows. Having to live in a large group (for some unspeci-fied reason, perhaps a function of predation pressure) led, over an evol-utionary timescale, to increased social complexity, creating an environ-ment in which individuals with greater social skills were advantaged. Thus brain (neocortex) increases were positively selected. This explains not only the quantitative variation at the individual species level within haplorhines, but the grade-shift between strepsirhine and haplorhine pri-mates (Passingham, 1982; Barton, 1996). The socially simple strep-sirhines – not needing large brains – can subsist on a reliable but low energy diet, a largely folivorous one; in contrast, the socially more com-plex haplorhines typically require high energy fruit (or meat) diets to sup-port their higher investment in metabolically costly brain tissue. Indeed, Barton's (1996) analysis found that frugivory correlated with larger brains among haplorhine primates, an effect independent of – but much smaller than – that of group size.

This tidy picture is completed by noting that what the social skills of haplorhines depend on, cognitively, is ultimately a matter of simple *learn-ing efficiency*. Remembering a large number of individuals and their varied traits, remembering histories of past relationships with many individuals, learning who can be relied upon in co-operative manoeuvres, learning a repertoire of tactics of deception – all these things need efficient learning and large memory capacity. True, some of these skills could be made even more sophisticated with a 'theory of mind' understanding of other individuals as complex, intentional agents. But there is no evidence for such ability generally in haplorhines (e.g. Byrne & Whiten, 1992; Toma-sello & Call, 1994), and possession of theory of mind is not necessary for the case. If monkeys' social skill is indeed based on efficient learning and memory, we can make an immediate link with the many studies (reviewed by Passingham, 1982) showing faster learning by monkeys, especially large-brained Old World species such as the rhesus macaque, in the less-simple laboratory tasks such as the discrimination learning set. Rapid learning and efficient memory, having evolved because of social profits, evidently also allow benefits in quite different, non-social tasks (see Byrne, 1995, for a fuller discussion).

Convergent evolution of relatively large brains in animals other than primates provides supportive evidence for the Machiavellian intelligence hypothesis, since large brains are found chiefly in groups noted for social complexity and quick learning – carnivores and pinnipeds are obvious examples (Jerison, 1973). Furthermore, within some taxa not closely related to primates, such as insectivorous bats, the same relationship has been found between relative brain enlargement and social group size (see Chapter 9).

Why then is not subtle social manipulation, such as tactical deception, more widespread? Repeated requests to the research community have produced almost no reliable evidence of tactical deception in non-primate mammals, even among highly social species such as wolves, wild dogs, hyaenas, lions, etc (see Chapter 5, for a summary). However, as pets under the artificial conditions of captivity, cats and dogs readily learn tactics of deception that they employ against owners and other pets (this evidence comes from personal communications from owners, often backed by carefully observed descriptive data; see Byrne, 1997). This should not surprise us, if learning underlies acquisition of most tactical deception. The circumstances that allow learning of deceptive tactics are frequent ones for pets, but occur rarely in the wild. For instance, to learn the 'fake predator' tactic (e.g. Byrne & Whiten, 1985; Cheney & Seyfarth, 1990) of signalling a predator as a distraction in a problematic social circumstance, without any insight as to its mental means of operation, requires that the conjunction of a real predator and similar problem circumstances has occurred in the past. Domestic dogs who bark at non-existent postmen (to distract other dogs or their owners), may have had experience of hundreds of 'trials', given the daily arrival of a real postman. In contrast, with the rarity of predator sightings in the wild a primate would be lucky to get one or two trials in its lifetime to learn such a tactic by trial-and-error. Any deceptive strategy or tactic will be frequency-dependent (Wiley, 1983), and tactical deception in primates is evidently rather uncommon. Nevertheless, all groups of haplorhine primate do *occasionally* acquire tactics of deception (Byrne & Whiten, 1992). In animals like social carnivores – relatively large-brained mammals, but nevertheless less quick to learn than primates – it would perhaps not be surprising if the rate of occurrence of hard-to-learn tactics were too low to detect. Alternative explanations are also possible. Carnivores are most often social in order to facilitate co-operation, not to reduce predation as is normal in primates (van Hooff & van Schaik, 1992); their interests may therefore less often be served by tactical deception within the group. Also, far fewer groups of social carnivores than primates have yet been studied in the intensive and detailed way needed to reveal such subtle tactics.

Perhaps we can explain all *neocortical* expansions as a consequence of selection for social skill? Most obviously relevant to human evolution is the grade-shift towards greater investment in brain tissue seen with the advent of African *Homo erectus*, a species showing massive brain enlargement well before any evidence of human culture. Aiello & Dunbar (1993) indeed argue that this shift had a similar origin to the haplorhine one, caused by the social complexity of even-larger groups. Thus human technical and social skills, even language, are proposed to have originated as responses to social complexity. (As in the case of most theories about early hominid evolution, we must realise that it may never be possible to go beyond plausible speculations of this kind.)

What Machiavellian intelligence fails to explain

There is, however, a problem. Haplorhine primates are a varied group, and one branch of them, the great apes, appears cognitively rather different to the rest. Since great apes includes *Homo*, this could mean that *another* jump in mental sophistication occurred, between the two noted above.

There would still be no difficulty for the Machiavellian intelligence hypothesis if these differences were shadowed by systematic correlations with group size and with neocortical enlargement — but they are not. Great apes do *not* live in bigger or socially more complex groups than monkeys. The group sizes and social structures of great ape species are highly varied, from the solitary living orangutans to the multi-male, multi-female communities of chimpanzees; but these differences are matched or exceeded by variation within monkey societies. Only the belief that great apes are 'cleverer' leads researchers sometimes to suggest that ape social lives are more complex than those of monkeys; to then use this difference in social complexity to explain apes' greater intelligence would be circular logic. Furthermore, great ape brains do *not* show evidence of particularly strong selection for brain size increase, compared with monkeys. True, their brains are large in absolute terms since great apes are large animals, but when allometric scaling is used to examine brain size relative to body size, or neocortex size relative to the rest of the brain, the ratios are unexceptional, and typical of haplorhines (Deacon, 1990; Dunbar, 1992). Several monkey species in fact have larger relative brain sizes, and larger neocortical ratios, than some great apes. For instance, baboons 'should' be more intelligent than gorillas, to judge from their relative investment in neocortex.

Yet, in conflict with this 'neocortical IQ' approach, it seems that *all* great apes are cognitively more sophisticated than *any* monkey species. The evidence for this assertion is a mixed bag, but cumulatively it is fairly impressive (see Byrne, 1995, for details). Differences emerge, not in what great apes do — which is in practice often much the same as what monkeys do — but in how they do it. For instance, as noted above, all haplorhine primate groups show occasional use of tactical deception, and most cases of this can plausibly be explained as a result of very rapid learning, capitalising on the reinforcement of fortuitously beneficial — but accidental — actions. However, a minority cannot, without gross distortion of the meaning of 'plausible' (Byrne & Whiten, 1991). These unusual cases, each of which strongly suggests insightful planning rather than blind conditioning, are found only among the records of deception from great apes, and come from all four non-human species. Deception data thus point to great apes, but not monkeys, having some sort of 'theory of mind' about the deceptive intentions and malleable beliefs of other individuals.

Though usually restricted to chimpanzee/macaque comparisons, subsequent direct laboratory tests of theory of mind have generally borne out this difference (e.g. Povinelli *et al.*, 1992a,b and see Chapter 6). Similarly, occasional but striking hints of mental sophistication are reported in chimpanzees, but not in any of the equally well-studied monkey species. These include deliberate instructional teaching (Boesch, 1991; and see Chapter 7), and indulgence in very risky and apparently unnecessary actions that seem unlikely to have evolved by genetical selection, but whose potential future benefits are clear to those with foresight, such as the deliberate killing of a baby leopard in the presence of its mother (Hiraiwa-Hasegawa *et al.*, 1986; see Byrne, 1995 for other examples). Also, individuals of all four great ape species have been taught gestural or ideographic 'languages' with some success (see especially, Savage-Rumbaugh *et al.*, 1993). This has yet to be attempted with any monkey, but great apes show a flexibility in gestural communication that appears lacking in monkeys; development of the use of novel communicative gestures has been seen in both chimpanzees (Tomasello *et al.*, 1989, 1994) and gorillas (Tanner & Byrne, 1993, 1996).

The ape/monkey difference in cognitive approach is apparent not just in the social world. The common chimpanzee and the orangutan are the only primate species to manufacture and use tools for subsistence in the wild, and many tool types have now been described (McGrew, 1992b; van Schaik *et al.*, 1996). In captivity, all great apes commonly use and make tools, and the manufacture of stone tools has been induced in orangutans and pygmy chimpanzees (Wright, 1972; Toth *et al.*, 1993). Monkeys, especially capuchins, also sometimes develop tool use in captivity; but when tested carefully it appears that they do not understand the task in a representational, cause–effect fashion (Visalbergi & Trinca, 1989; Visalberghi & Limongelli, 1994; Westergaard & Suomi, 1993); they sometimes make highly revealing errors that suggest they have simply acquired a habit by associative conditioning. After apparently mastering the technique of probing for food in a transparent tube, a capuchin monkey will enthusiastically try to probe with a rod that is much thicker than the opening, one that is much too short to reach, or even with a flexible chain. Capuchins that have learnt to break nuts with stones and use twigs to extract the kernel, still repeatedly try to break the nut with blows of the thin twig or use stones to extract kernels! These are not the sort of errors that are seen in natural chimpanzee behaviour (Goodall, 1986); and indeed when tested on a similar task to that used with capuchin monkeys, chimpanzees often succeeded, and without ever making this sort of error (Limongelli *et al.*, 1995). Although other explanations are possible, it seems that, while monkeys may learn to use objects as tools, they lack an understanding of what *specifications* a good tool needs to meet. In the wild, chimpanzees demonstrate that they possess just this mental specification of a tool when they select suitable objects well in advance of the anticipated use as a tool (Boesch & Boesch, 1984), or deliberately prepare a tool before carrying it to the site of use (Goodall, 1986).

A related skill, not meeting the strict definition of tool-use, but shown by all non-human great apes and no species of monkey, is the activity often called 'nest-building'. Each night, and often during day-time rests as well, every adult or independent juvenile great ape constructs a sleeping place, using leaves and branches; the term 'bed', used by Japanese primatologists, is a more helpful descriptor than 'nest'. The sophistication of the construction varies, from a (largely terrestrial) mountain gorilla's day-bed, just a few large leaves plucked and positioned to make a comfortable place to sit, to the elaborate bed high in the canopy constructed by a chimpanzee or orangutan for its night rest (orangutans also construct platforms to give them shelter from heavy rain). Starting often at a fork in a slender tree, branches are bent back (often breaking, but remaining attached by flexible bark) and held with the prehensile feet or other hand, one on top of the other, eventually resulting in a slightly cupped platform several feet across; researchers who have tried sleeping in these nests report the beds firm and comfortably springy! Of course, many species other than apes construct nests, including some strepsirhine primates; but no other haplorhine primates do, and it is tempting to relate the skill displayed in constructing these beds to the same species' facility with tools.

Another sphere in which great apes differ qualitatively from monkeys is in their imitative capacity – though whether this is best seen as a social or a technical achievement is equivocal. The ability to imitate is often taken to imply 'theory of mind' understanding of the goals of others (e.g. Tomasello, 1990; Whiten & Byrne, 1991); however, an alternative view is that it requires understanding of behaviour, not mind – or even neither, relying only on cross-modal transfer (Heyes, 1993; Mitchell, 1993). Regardless of the implications, it does seem that monkeys have great difficulty in imitating (see Visalberghi & Fragaszy, 1990; Whiten & Ham, 1992), whereas there is increasing evidence for imitation in great apes (Byrne & Burne, 1993; Russon & Galdikas, 1993, 1995; Tomasello *et al.*, 1993; Byrne & Russon, 1998). Largely, this evidence supports the idea that great apes imitate at 'program-level' (Byrne, 1994), copying the relational structure of actions and the overall co-ordinated organisation of behaviour, but not the details and idiosyncrasy of execution that happen to be observed. This is evidently more than is normally implied by the term cross-modal transfer, but points mainly to a sophisticated representation of *behaviour*, including cause–effect relations, in great apes (see also Gómez, 1991).

Monkeys do stand out quantitatively from most other animals, in that they give evidence of extensive social knowledge, and show the rapid learning of tactics that depend on this large data-base. However, unlike great apes, they are *qualitatively* no different from species in many other mammalian groups. Great apes' various accomplishments, both in social and technical problem-solving, suggest that they — like humans, but unlike monkeys and most other animals — have a *representational* understanding of the world, one that can support simple computation. In everyday terms, they can *think*. Since the ape/monkey difference does not correlate with relative investment in brain size and neocortical extension, we must presume that mental representation of the world and its problems is either an emergent property of very large brains, a side-effect of greater overall size (as suggested by Gibson, 1990, for instance); or a software difference in the way information is handled in the cortex (as suggested by Byrne, 1995).

Notice that, while the skills of monkeys are empirically closely linked to social problems, this does not apply to the further sophistication seen in apes, which has shown up in a wide range of spheres. If my speculations are correct, and all the skills peculiar to great apes depend on a memory format capable of *abstract problem representation*, the original evolutionary selection pressure that led to this might have been in any one of the spheres in which we now see it demonstrated. Once able mentally to represent problems, the ability thus to 'simulate' possible actions and compute the possible outcomes that would result can be applied to any sort of problem: what a rival or an offspring might do if its knowledge is limited or wrong, what a predator might do in the future if not treated firmly now, what type of twig or stone will be useful for a particular task, and how to modify inadequate physical material to meet task specifications.

What possible selection pressure might have been the stimulus to this fundamental change in memory organisation? That is, what natural problems confront great apes that monkeys do not meet, or if they do, are somehow less challenging for monkeys?

Explaining great apes' representational minds

An obvious starting point is to revisit those theories proposed to explain general intellectual specialisation: while they may have been inferior to the Machiavellian intelligence hypothesis for explaining the neocortical expansion of haplorhines, they might help us understand the ape/monkey difference.

Cognitive maps

In recent debates the major alternative theory has been the idea that complexity of the feeding environment selected for what in psychology is called a 'cognitive map'; that is to say, a mental representation (and corresponding neural substrate) that allows efficient navigation in a rich and complicated world, changing over time as well as space. Milton (1981, 1988) championed this as the explanation for the large brains of the spider monkey, a species with large ranges that enable it to obtain year-round access to patchily distributed fleshy fruit. She compared this to the smaller-brained howler monkey, a species able to eat coarser foods and so able to fall back on relatively common and easy-to-find items when fruit becomes locally scarce.

There are three difficulties with the cognitive maps hypothesis:

- the general failure, noted above, to explain primate brain size as a function of range size or day journey length (Dunbar, 1992; but remember the unsatisfactory nature of these measures);

- the distinct possibility that in recent primate evolution diet has changed bodies more rapidly than brains, so the small *relative* brain size of folivores is artefactual (see Byrne, 1994, 1996b);

- the very remarkable memory abilities of small birds such as jays, nutcrackers and marsh tits, which hint that no great amount of cortical tissue would be needed for the cognitive map tasks presented by primates' environments.

Cache-storing birds' level of ability is associated with selective hippocampal enlargement (Krebs *et al.*, 1989), which admittedly shows that bigger cognitive maps require more brain tissue; however, in primates, range size and complexity are not linked to hippocampal size (Barton & Purvis, 1994). Specifically with respect to the ape/monkey difference, many monkeys have ranges as large and diets as varied and patchy as those of great apes.

But great apes *do* differ in one obvious way from all monkeys, and this may salvage the cognitive map hypothesis. As noted by one of the idea's originators, Mackinnon (1978), great apes are all much *heavier* than any monkey or lesser ape, and thus have higher travel costs; the inefficiency for long-distance travel of the brachiating mode of locomotion used by apes exacerbates their problems. Furthermore, the Old World monkeys (i.e. the direct feeding competitors of the great apes) have digestions specialised for dealing with unripe fruit, whereas their ape competitors must get to fruits just when they are ripe. Thus it can at least be argued that the selective advantages of having a good spatio-temporal memory for food sources would be greater for great apes than for monkeys, even those with an apparently equivalent fleshy-fruit diet. The plausibility of this modified version of the hypothesis could be strengthened by calculating the energetic cost per unit distance travelled, for individuals of a number of ape and monkey species, and comparing this to their absolute brain sizes. (Since relative brain and neocortex sizes do not separate apes and monkeys, this hypothesis can only be tested if it predicts absolute increases in brain size.)

Simulation of movement

Alternatively, great apes' problems of locomotion might have *directly* selected for a different sort of intelligence, as suggested by Povinelli & Cant (1995). They argue that, for an arboreal brachiator that is physically large and thus vulnerable to severe injury from falling, moving through forest presents a technically demanding engineering problem. Small-bodied lesser apes and quadrupedal monkeys do not face this challenge. The great ape has to manoeuvre its heavy body by swinging itself and by setting small trees in motion to aid its progress; Cant and Povinelli argue that the ability to 'externalise' the view of one's own body as an independent entity would give a distinct selective advantage in delicate clambering problems – and indirectly lead to the ability to recognise this entity as oneself when seen in a mirror. Although devised to explain the ability of great apes, but not monkeys, to recognise themselves in mirrors (see Parker *et al.*, 1994), the hypothesis has more far-reaching implications. It implies the formation of a representational model of a problem in the ape's mind, in order to 'simulate' the task before attempting it: and as we have already noted, this is just the capacity that could lead to the suite of ape/monkey differences that have been observed. However, it is unclear how this interesting hypothesis might be tested.

Constructional skills

Bed-construction techniques are shown in all non-human great apes, as described above, and they involve a sophisticated use of attached objects not shown by monkeys. One might propose that they reflect an ability needed by the great apes' common ancestor, one that led to it developing the representational understanding we observe today in other spheres. The need for arboreal beds presumably derives, once more, from the large size of great apes compared with monkeys (though large monkeys such as baboons regularly sleep at night high in trees, sitting on bare branches or against the main trunk). Bed construction is regularly observed in zoos, and the techniques used are surely deserving of more detailed study[1], both observational and experimental, which might potentially lead to a test of this idea.

Skilled feeding techniques

Great apes differ from monkeys in yet another way than their size and mode of locomotion, and this points to a fourth hypothesis for the selective pressure that could have favoured representational comprehension. In a variety of ways great apes show *technical skill* in gathering food from sources that are nutritious but present difficulties.

All populations of chimpanzees use tools to feed on insects that are hidden and protected by their nests, 'fishing' into narrow holes with flexible probes; soldier-caste insects attack the probes, and if removed carefully can thus be extracted from the holes (see McGrew, 1992b, for details of chimpanzee subsistence feeding techniques). Some chimpanzee populations additionally use longer, rigid wands to 'dip' into bivouacs of the aggressive African safari ant *Dorylus*; ants of the soldier caste swarm in abundance up the wand, and the chimpanzee loosely grasps the wand with its other hand, then with a stripping motion sweeps the mass of insects into the hand – and eats rapidly to minimise its bites. An understanding of the relation between tool form and function is particularly clearly shown by the successive use of more than one type of tool in the pursuit of a single goal: a tool-set. Chimpanzees at Ndoki (Congo) regularly do just this, employing strong, pointed twigs to force entry to termite nests, then using thin, flexible herb stems to extract the termites (Suzuki *et al.*, 1995). Occasional 'one-off' records in other populations show that all chimpanzees have this potential; for instance, Brewer & McGrew (1990) describe a chimpanzee successively employing four sticks of differing thickness and length, to get the honey in a nest of wild bees: a strong tool to break a hole in the casing, a slender probe to investigate inside, and so on. It was long thought that this sort of tool-based subsistence activity was unique to the common chimpanzee, but one population

---

[1] Since those words were written, Frith & Hohmann (1996) have published a careful comparative analysis of great ape nest building, arguing that the evolution of construction skills enabled ancestral apes to sleep near food sources, so competing effectively with monkeys.

of orangutans has now been recorded using tools in a similar way (van Schaik *et al.*, 1996). These skills not only show an understanding of objects-as-tools, but they also require delicate co-ordination of the two hands, and in some cases more than one stage of processing must be sequenced correctly.

One possibility, then, is that an increasing need for sophisticated tool use selected for great ape intelligence. It is a puzzle that all great apes in captivity show tool-making skill, yet only the common chimpanzee and one population of orangutans do so with regularity under natural conditions. This has led several researchers to speculate that tool-making may have been found in the great ape clade's common ancestor, but has since been 'given up' by modern gorillas, pygmy chimpanzees and most populations of orangutans (see McGrew, 1992a). If so, then whatever needs for tool-making were felt by that ancestral species might have led to the cognitive advance shown in all its descendants. However, since we cannot determine what these needs were, and since any explanation is suspect that proposes that a character was derived in the common ancestor of a clade, yet is now shown by only two species out of five in it, these speculations are rather unsatisfying.

An alternative but related hypothesis highlights the concealed and hard-to-extract nature of the food itself. Parker & Gibson (1977, 1979; see also Parker *et al.*, 1994; Gibson, 1986) pointed out that species that obtain hidden food resources, yet lack specialised anatomy to do so (such as an aye-aye's middle finger, or a woodpecker's long tongue) have a problem. Where the need to forage extractively is year-round and restricted to plant foods, they argued that specialised foraging mechanisms would be expected; this applies to the gorilla, which 'pulls tubers from the ground with his massive strength' (Gibson, 1986). However, where the need arises seasonally and over a wide range of foods, as they proposed was the case for the ancestral great ape (which they suggested to resemble the modern common chimpanzee in its ecology), and independently in the capuchin monkey, 'sensorimotor' intelligence would be favoured and intelligent tool use would result (Parker & Gibson, 1977, p. 634; Gibson, 1986, p. 99).

On the face of it, this theory is beset with difficulties. In addition to the unsatisfying nature, noted above, of proposing that the common ancestor of all great apes was a tool user, a second difficulty for the theory is that the tool use of capuchins appears to be of a non-representational, trial-and-error sort, as reviewed above. When the hypothesis was first formulated, capuchins were treated as 'ape-like' in their intelligence and tool-use, but there is now no good reason to suggest capuchins have representational intelligence. This is difficult to reconcile with the extractive foraging hypothesis, without the assumption that capuchins just happened not to possess the genetic variation necessary to develop in the way that ancestral great apes did. While evolution is of course always limited by the genetic variation available, it is again rather unsatisfying to propose this as an explanation with species as closely related as ape and monkey, especially when the structure concerned – the neocortex of the brain – is present in both. Indeed, the generality of extractive foraging among other mammals and birds has been used to question the whole idea that it was a significant influence in the development of primate intelligence (King, 1986). Part of the problem seems to be the link with tool use, in particular, and the absence of tool use in wild capuchins, gorillas, pygmy chimpanzees and most populations of orangutans. Were this link to be broken, the emphasis on the problem posed by certain hard-to-extract foods would bring it closer to the next theory to be considered, below.

Understanding the significance of great apes' tool use has been slowed, I believe, because the *fact* of a primate using a tool has dominated researchers' attention, rather than the *manner* in which the tool is employed. Certainly, the way common chimpanzees employ tools, in a complex *organisational structure*, does suggest considerable representational understanding. Using a tool may be of no significance in itself; capuchin's tool use in captivity, and the extractive foraging of the various other animals that show it, are embedded in no such elaborate organisations of action. However, complex organisation of action might, in principle, be shown in other ways of foraging than by tool using. With this new perspective, I suggest that we should re-examine the feeding behaviour of apes other than the common chimpanzee, for complex skills that perhaps happen not to benefit from tool use. This will bring us to the final theory that may potentially explain the origin of representational understanding in great apes.

Ironically, in view of what was formerly believed to be the gorilla style of feeding (as in the quotation, above), on current evidence the laurels for complex organisation of feeding sequences go to the mountain gorillas of the Virunga Volcanoes in Rwanda (Byrne & Byrne, 1991, 1993; Byrne, 1996a). All the major diet items available to this population are physically defended in some way – spines, stings, hard casing, tiny clinging hooks.

Each problem requires a very different technique to deal with it, and each technique involves several sequential stages. Throughout, the two hands are used together in different but synchronised roles. Subsequences (of various numbers of steps) can be repeated iteratively until some criterion (a subgoal) is reached, when the main sequence continues; they thus function as subroutines. These characteristics show that the gorillas' mental programs are organised *hierarchically*, not in the linear chains of actions that associative learning generates. Nevertheless, juveniles attain adult levels of efficiency by the time they are weaned at 3–4 years old. Unlike the skilled tool-use of chimpanzees and orangutans, which is employed only occasionally and even then only by a subset of the population (chiefly females), the hierarchical programs of gorilla food preparation are employed every day by every individual. Speed and efficiency in obtaining this potentially nutritious but time-consuming vegetarian diet must be at a premium, for such a large mammal with a simple gut living in a cold environment. Orangutans, particularly in the dipterocarp forests on the impoverished soils of Borneo, forests known for erratic mast-fruiting, may face similarly severe tests of skill in dealing with hard, physically defended fruit (Galdikas & Vasey, 1992; A. E. Russon, personal communication, reports orangutan feeding techniques strongly reminiscent of those of gorillas in their complexity). Only the pygmy chimpanzee, vaunted for the intelligence it shows in captive situations, cannot at present be added to this constellation of apes showing manual skill in feeding; however, this is probably a reflection of the small amount of fieldwork yet carried out on the natural feeding behaviour of the species.

The skills that great apes must have, to build complex programs of actions for plant or insect gathering, differ qualitatively from anything seen in monkeys. Indeed, primatologists have been so little impressed with manual feeding techniques in monkeys that precise comparisons are difficult: monkey techniques are largely undocumented. Where comparison has been made, monkey techniques seem 'unprincipled', varying their choice of actions from food item to food item in a way that strongly suggests a string of simple actions, each triggered in reaction to the immediate stimuli presented by the food, rather than an organised and systematic plan of approach (Harrison, 1996). The need of all great apes to obtain food of considerably higher quality than their competitors among Old World monkeys, noted above, and the cheek pouches of these monkeys that make rapid collection and removal of items feasible, give a clear ecological reason for the existence of a stronger selection pressure for skilled feeding techniques in the ancestral great ape than in monkeys.

The systematic approach of great apes to manual problems suggests an underlying common factor of *flexible plan-building*. Once again, we have come up against signs of a representational understanding in apes — this time, of the organisation of behaviour itself.

As a hypothesis to explain the qualitative ape/monkey difference in intelligence, the logic here would be that:-

- ancestral great apes, perhaps rather similar in their behavioural ecology to orangutans of today, were subject to selective pressure for more efficient feeding;

- large body size, slow and inefficient locomotion, unspecialised guts and the lack of cheek pouches, all exacerbated this problem;

- its solution was an ape-specific ability to organise behaviour into hierarchical programs of mutually co-ordinated actions to achieve goals: in other words, to *plan*;

- planning requires a *mental representation* of actions, and this representational ability then applied to physical objects, allowing them to be specified in an abstract way as potential tools;

- in turn, representational ability could be applied to other individuals, allowing them to be treated as active agents with *intentions*.

In support of this hypothesis, all great apes show food extraction or processing techniques that are technically demanding in some way, whereas monkeys do not. Parallelling this difference in technical challenge is a matching difference in comprehension, both social and mechanical: to over-simplify, monkeys show fast learning, apes show insight. Further, as noted by King (1994) specifically for the chimpanzee, complexity of foraging skill may result in an ensuing need for a long period of apprenticeship and 'social information donation', meshing well with the evidence of imitation and (occasional) teaching in great apes but not monkeys.

Gibson (1990) goes further in arguing that complex manipulative behaviours, in particular skills of hierarchical organisation and construction, have selected for larger (absolute) brain sizes in the great apes. (She relates this to the extractive foraging and tool use hypothesis, discussed above, but there seems no need to do so.) If so, then it might be argued that the large bodies of great apes are a secondary consequence of a need to possess a large brain, an intriguing reversal of the usual chain of logic.

Conclusions

The Technical intelligence hypothesis is as much of a *Just So* story as the Machiavellian intelligence hypothesis was, when first proposed. Similarly, it is not a unitary theory, but a banner for a collection of several (at least four), partly-linked hypotheses, all of which point to some technical, mechanical selective pressure as the origin of the ape/monkey grade-shift in intelligence. However, very large body size, locomotion by brachiation, the representational use of tools, construction of sleeping beds, and the ability to build hierarchical programs of actions, are all unique to great apes: separately or in some combination they are then *in principle* suitable candidate hypotheses to explain a special adaptation of the great apes. This does not seem to be the case for the other explanations yet proposed, those that point to omnivorous extractive foraging *per se* or social complexity as the evolutionary selective pressure of greatest moment. It needs to be emphasised that this hypothesis is intended to *complement* the Machiavellian intelligence explanation, which is certainly a better explanation of the earlier haplorhine rise in intelligence, and might (or might not) explain the later hominid one that led to *Homo erectus*.

Testing *between* the four versions of Technical intelligence hypothesis will not be easy, since in several ways they are similar in their starting point. All point to aspects of *efficiency in foraging behaviour* (where this is interpreted broadly, to include the ability to sleep safely in unrestricted locations, and to brachiate safely in tropical forests during ranging). This premium on efficiency is seen as *more necessary for great apes* than monkeys, because of their large size, the difficulties of brachiation for distance travel, and their reliance on high quality diet. Equally, all treat the undoubted sophistication of apes in social areas (including theory of mind, and mirror self-recognition) as a secondary effect, derived from possession of a representational format for knowledge that evolved in the technical sphere, and which still has a primary function in dealing with the technical problems met by wild great apes.

The chief differences between the different versions are likely to arise in the format of the representations, that would best do the job that they purport to be the evolutionary origin of modern ape mental capacity.

Would these representations be *maps*, isometric to the two-dimensional or three-dimensional world and containing memory information about locations within it; or *structural representations*, suitable for problems in the dynamics of brachiation, or statics of building beds; or *hierarchical control structures* for organising behaviour? Teasing these apart is a task beyond the scope of this chapter, or – probably – current empirical evidence. However, acceptance that some sort of Technical intelligence hypothesis is needed is dependent only on accepting that there *is* an ape/monkey difference in intelligence, whereas there is no comparable difference in the social challenges faced by members of the two taxa.

Acknowledgements

My thanks go to Kathleen Gibson, Barbara King, Andrew Whiten and especially to Louise Barrett for reading and commenting helpfully on earlier drafts of this chapter, and to Anne Russon for many stimulating discussions of issues related to it.

References

Aiello, L. C. & Dunbar, R. I. M. (1993). Neocortex size, group size and the evolution of language. *Current Anthropology*, 34, 184–93.

Armstrong, E. (1983). Metabolism and relative brain size. *Science*, 220, 1302–4.

Barton, R. A. (1996). Neocortex size and behavioural ecology in primates. *Proceedings of the Royal Society of London, Series B*, 263, 173–7.

Barton, R. A. & Purvis, A. (1994). Primate brains and ecology: Looking beneath the surface. In *Current Primatology: Proceedings of the XIVth Congress of the International Primatological Society*, ed. J. R. Anderson, J. J. Roeder, B. Thierry & N. Herrenschmidt, pp. 1–9. Strasbourg: Université Louis Pasteur.

Brewer, S. & McGrew, W. C. (1990). Chimpanzee use of a tool-set to get honey. *Folia Primatologica*, 54, 100–4.

Boesch, C. (1991). Teaching in wild chimpanzees. *Animal Behaviour*, 41, 530–2.

Boesch, C. & Boesch, H. (1984). Mental map in wild chimpanzees: An analysis of hammer transports for nut cracking. *Primates*, 25, 160–70.

Byrne, R. W. (1993). Do larger brains mean greater intelligence? *Behavioral and Brain Sciences*, 16, 696–7.

Byrne, R. W. (1994). The evolution of intelligence. In *Behaviour and Evolution* ed. P. J. B. Slater & T. R. Halliday, pp. 223–6. Cambridge: Cambridge University Press.

Byrne, R. W. (1995). *The Thinking Ape: Evolutionary Origins of Intelligence*. Oxford: Oxford University Press.

Byrne, R. W. (1996a). The misunderstood ape: Cognitive skills of the gorilla. In

Reaching into Thought: The Minds of the Great Apes, eds. A. E. Russon, K. A. Bard & S. T. Parker, pp. 111–30. Cambridge: Cambridge University Press.

Byrne, R. W. (1996b). Relating brain size to intelligence in primates. In *Modelling the Early Human Mind*, ed. P. A. Mellars & K. R. Gibson, pp. 49–56. Cambridge: Macdonald Institute for Archaeological Research.

Byrne, R. W. (1997). What's the use of anecdotes? Attempts to distinguish psychological mechanisms in primate tactical deception. In *Anthropomorphism, Anecdotes, and Animals: The Emperor's New Clothes? Biology and Philosophy*, ed. R. W. Mitchell, N. S. Thompson & L. Miles, pp. 134–50. New York: SUNY Press.

Byrne, R. W. & Byrne, J. M. E. (1991). Hand preferences in the skilled gathering tasks of mountain gorillas (*Gorilla g. beringei*). *Cortex*, 27, 521–46.

Byrne, R. W. & Byrne, J. M. E. (1993) The complex leaf-gathering skills of mountain gorillas (*Gorilla g. beringei*): Variability and standardization. *American Journal of Primatology*, 31, 241–61.

Byrne, R. W. & Russon, A. E. (1998). Learning by imitation: A hierarchical approach. *Behavioral and Brain Sciences*. (In press).

Byrne, R. W. & Whiten, A. (1985). Tactical deception of familiar individuals in baboons. *Animal Behaviour*, 33, 669–73.

Byrne, R. W. & Whiten, A. (eds) (1988). *Machiavellian Intelligence: Social Expertise and the Evolution of Intellect in Monkeys, Apes and Humans*. Oxford: Clarendon Press.

Byrne, R. W. & Whiten, A. (1991). Computation and mindreading in primate tactical deception. In *Natural Theories of Mind: Evolution, Development and Simulation of Everyday Mindreading*, ed. A. Whiten, pp. 127–41. Oxford: Basil Blackwell.

Byrne, R. W. & Whiten, A. (1992). Cognitive evolution in primates: Evidence from tactical deception. *Man*, 27, 609–27.

Cheney, D. L. & Seyfarth, R. M. (1990). *How Monkeys see the World: Inside the Mind of Another Species*. Chicago: University of Chicago Press.

Deacon, T. W. (1990). Fallacies of progression in theories of brain-size evolution. *International Journal of Primatology*, 11, 193–236.

de Waal, F. (1989). *Peacemaking Among Primates*. Cambridge, MA: Harvard University Press.

Dunbar, R. I. M. (1992). Neocortex size as a constraint on group size in primates. *Journal of Human Evolution*, 20, 469–93.

Dunbar, R. I. M. (1995). Neocortex size and group size in primates: A test of the hypothesis. *Journal of Human Evolution*, 28, 287–96.

Fruth, B. & Hohmann, G. (1996). Nest building behavior in the great apes: The great leap forward? In *Great Ape Societies*, ed. W. C. McGrew, L. F. Marchant & T. Nishida, pp. 225–40. Cambridge; Cambridge University Press.

Galdikas, B. M. F. & Vasey, P. (1992). Why are orangutans so smart? In *Social Processes and Mental Abilities in Non-human Primates*, ed. F. D. Burton, pp. 183–224. Lewiston, NY: Edward Mellon Press.

Gibson, K. R. (1986). Cognition, brain size and the extraction of embedded food resources. In *Primate Ontogeny, Cognitive and Social Behaviour*, ed. J. G. Else & P. C. Lee, pp. 93–105. Cambridge: Cambridge University Press.

Gibson, K. R. (1990). New perspectives on instincts and intelligence: Brain size and the emergence of hierarchical mental constructional skills. In *'Language' and Intelligence in Monkeys and Apes: Comparative Developmental Perspectives*, ed. S. T. Parker & K. R. Gibson. Cambridge: Cambridge University Press.

Gómez, J. C. (1991). Visual behaviour as a window for reading the mind of others in primates. In *Natural Theories of Mind: Evolution, Development and Simulation of Everyday Mindreading*, ed. A. Whiten, pp. 195–207. Oxford: Basil Blackwell.

Goodall, J. (1986). *The Chimpanzees of Gombe: Patterns of Behavior*. Cambridge, MA: The Belknap Press.

Harcourt, A. H. & de Waal, F. B. (eds) (1992). *Coalitions and Alliances in Humans and Other Animals*. Oxford: Oxford University Press.

Harrison, K. (1996). Skills used in food processing by vervet monkeys, *Cercopithecus aethiops*. PhD thesis, University of St. Andrews.

Heyes, C. M. (1993). Imitation, culture and cognition. *Animal Behaviour*, 46, 999–1010.

Hiraiwa-Hasegawa, M., Byrne, R. W., Takasaki, H. & Byrne, J. M. (1986). Aggression towards large carnivores by wild chimpanzees of Mahale Mountains National Park, Tanzania. *Folia Primatologica*, 47, 8–13.

Jerison, H. J. (1973). *Evolution of the Brain and Intelligence*. New York: Academic Press.

King, B. J. (1986). Extractive foraging and the evolution of primate intelligence. *Human Evolution*, 1, 361–72.

King, B. J. (1994). Primate infants as skilled information gatherers. *Pre-and Perinatal Psychology Journal*, 8, 287–307.

Krebs, J. R., Sherry, D. F., Healy, S. D., Perry, V. H. & Vaccarino, A. L. (1989). Hippocampal specialization in food storing birds. *Proceedings of the National Academy of Sciences of the U.S.A.*, 86, 1388–90.

Limongelli, L., Boysen, S. T. & Visalberghi, E. (1995). Comprehension of cause-effect relations in a tool-using task by chimpanzees (*Pan troglodytes*). *Journal of Comparative Psychology*, 109, 18–26.

Mackinnon, J. (1978). *The Ape Within Us*. London: Collins.

McGrew, W. C. (1992a). Why is ape tool use so confusing? In *Comparative Socioecology: The Behavioural Ecology of Humans and Other Mammals*, ed. V. Standen & R. A. Foley, pp. 457–72. Oxford: Blackwell Scientific Publications.

McGrew, W. C. (1992b). *Chimpanzee Material Culture: Implications for Human Evolution*. Cambridge: Cambridge University Press.

Milton, K. (1981). Distribution patterns of tropical plant foods as a stimulus to primate mental development. *American Anthropologist*, 83, 534–48.

Milton, K. (1988). Foraging behaviour and the evolution of intellect in monkeys, apes and humans. In *Machiavellian Intelligence: Social Expertise and the Evolution of Intellect in Monkeys, Apes and Humans*, ed. R. W. Byrne & A. Whiten, pp. 285–305. Oxford: Clarendon Press.

Mitchell, R. W. (1993). Mental models of mirror-self-recognition: Two theories. *New Ideas in Psychology*, 3, 295–325.

Parker, S. T. & Gibson, K. R. (1977). Object manipulation, tool use, and sensorimotor intelligence as feeding adaptations in early hominids. *Journal of Human Evolution*, 6, 623–41.

Parker, S. T. & Gibson, K. R. (1979). A developmental model for the evolution of language and intelligence in early hominids. *Behavioral and Brain Sciences*, 2, 367–408.

Parker, S. T., Mitchell, R. W. & Boccia, M. L. (eds) (1994). *Self-awareness in Animals and Humans: Developmental Perspectives*. Cambridge: Cambridge University Press.

Passingham, R. E. (1982). *The Human Primate*. Oxford: W. H. Freeman.

Povinelli, D. J. & Cant, J. G. H. (1995). Arboreal clambering and the evolution of self-conception. *Quarterly Journal of Biology*, 70, 393–421.

Povinelli, D. J., Nelson, K. E. & Boysen, S. T. (1992a). Comprehension of role reversal in chimpanzees: Evidence of empathy? *Animal Behaviour*, 43, 633–40.

Povinelli, D. J., Parks, K. A. & Novak, M. A. (1992b). Role reversal by rhesus monkeys but no evidence of empathy. *Animal Behaviour*, 44, 269–81.

Russon, A. E. & Galdikas, B. M. F. (1993). Imitation in free-ranging rehabilitant orangutans. *Journal of Comparative Psychology*, 107, 147–61.

Russon, A. E. & Galdikas, B. M. F. (1995). Constraints on great apes' imitation: Model and action selectivity in rehabilitant orangutan (*Pongo pygmaeus*) imitation. *Journal of Comparative Psychology*, 109, 5–17.

Savage-Rumbaugh, E. S., Murphy, J., Sevcic, R. A., Brakke, K. E., Williams, S. L. & Rumbaugh, D. (1993). Language comprehension in ape and child. *Monographs of the Society for Research in Child Development*, 58, 1–256

Suzuki, S. Kuroda, S. & Nishihara, T. (1995). Tool-set for termite-fishing by chimpanzees in the Ndoki Forest, Congo. *Behaviour*, 132, 219–35.

Tanner, J. E. & Byrne, R. W. (1993). Concealing facial evidence of mood: Evidence for perspective-taking in a captive gorilla? *Primates*, 34, 451–6.

Tanner, J. E. & Byrne R. W. (1996). Representation of action through iconic gesture in a captive lowland gorilla. *Current Anthropology*, 37, 162–73.

Tomasello, M. (1990) Cultural transmission in the tool use and communicatory signaling of chimpanzees? In *'Language' and Intelligence in Monkeys and Apes: Comparative Developmental Perspectives*, ed. S. T. Parker & K. R. Gibson, pp. 274–311. Cambridge: Cambridge University Press.

Tomasello, M. & Call, J. (1994). Social cognition of monkeys and apes. *Yearbook of Physical Anthropology*, 37, 273–305.

Tomasello, M., Gust, D. & Frost, G. T. (1989). A longitudinal investigation of gestural communication in young chimpanzees. *Primates*, 30, 35–50.

Tomasello, M., Savage-Rumbaugh, E. S. & Kruger, A. C. (1993) Imitative learning of actions on objects by children, chimpanzees, and enculturated chimpanzees. *Child Development*, 64, 1688–705:

Tomasello, M., Call, J., Nagell, C., Olguin, R. & Carpenter, M. (1994). The learning and use of gestural signals by young chimpanzees: A trans-generational study. *Primates*, 35, 137–54.

Toth, N., Schick, K. D., Savage-Rumbaugh, E. S., Sevcik, R. A. & Rumbaugh, D. M. (1993). *Pan* the tool-maker: Investigations into the stone-tool-making and tool-using capabilities of a bonobo (*Pan paniscus*). *Journal of Archaeological Science*, 20, 81–91.

van Hooff, J. A. R. A. M. & van Schaik, C. P. (1992). Cooperation in competition: The ecology of primate bonds. In *Coalitions and Alliances in Humans and Other*

Animals, ed. A. H. Harcourt & F. B. M. de Waal, pp. 357–89. Oxford: Oxford University Press.

van Schaik, C. P., Fox, E. A. & Sitampol, A. F. (1996). Manufacture and use of fats in wild Sumatran orangutans: Implications for human evolution. *Naturwissen Schaften*, 83, 186–8.

Visalberghi, E. & Fragaszy, D. (1990). Do monkeys ape? In *'Language' and Intelligence in Monkeys and Apes*, ed. S. T. Parker & K. R. Gibson, pp. 247–73. Cambridge: Cambridge University Press.

Visalberghi, E. & Limongelli, L. (1994). Lack of comprehension of cause–effect relations in tool-using capuchin monkeys (*Cebus apella*). *Journal of Comparative Psychology*, 108, 15–22.

Visalberghi, E. & Trinca, L. (1989). Tool use in capuchin monkeys: Distinguishing between performing and understanding. *Primates*, 30, 511–521.

Westergaard, G. C. & Suomi, S. J. (1993). Use of a tool-set by capuchin monkeys (*Cebus apella*). *Primates*, 34, 459–62.

Whiten, A. & Byrne, R. W. (1991). The emergence of meta-representation in human ontogeny and primate phylogeny. In *Natural Theories of Mind: Evolution, Development and Simulation in Everyday Mindreading*, ed. A. Whiten, pp. 267–81. Oxford: Basil Blackwell.

Whiten, A., & Ham, R. (1992). On the nature and evolution of imitation in the animal kingdom: Reappraisal of a century of research. In *Advances in the Study of Behaviour*, vol. 21, ed, P. J. B. Slater, J. S. Rosenblatt, C. Beer & M. Milinski, p. 239–83. New York: Academic Press.

Wiley, R. H. (1983). The evolution of communication: Information and manipulation. In *Animal Behaviour*, vol. 2. *Communication*, ed. T. R. Halliday & P. J. B. Slater, pp. 156–89. Oxford: Blackwell Scientific Publications.

Wright, R. V. S. (1972). Imitative learning of a flaked-tool technology: The case of an orangutan. *Mankind*, 8, 296–306.

12 Protean primates: The evolution of adaptive unpredictability in competition and courtship

GEOFFREY F. MILLER

Introduction: Unpredictability, animacy and psychology

Nature cloaks herself in many modes of unpredictability. Science advances in part by recognising and distinguishing these modes (see Kruger *et al.*, 1987). Statistical mechanics modelled the complexity of fluids using stochastic principles. Quantum theory accepted the noisiness of elementary particles. Chaos theory revealed that many dynamical systems show extreme sensitivity to initial conditions. Evolutionary theory showed how random variation plus cumulative selection could yield organic complexity. Such progress in physics and biology has not been matched by psychology. Although unpredictability is a hallmark of animal behaviour, it has been the bane of the behavioural sciences. Variation in behaviour, whether across species, situation, space, or time, has usually been attributed either to adaptation or to error, with adaptation narrowly defined as systematic (if complex) correspondence between environmental conditions and behavioural tactics, and error narrowly defined as raw behavioural noise. Psychology's favourite statistical shibboleth, analysis of variance, assumes that behaviour can be explained by the interaction of environmental determinants and random, non-adaptive noise.

This chapter examines a type of behaviour that is both adaptive and noisy, both functional and unpredictable, and that has therefore been overlooked by most behavioural scientists. The difficulty of predicting animal behaviour may be much more than a side-effect of the complexity of animal brains. Rather, the unpredictability may result from those brains having been selected over evolutionary history to baffle and surprise all of the would-be psychologists who preceded us. To appreciate why psychology is hard, we have to stop thinking of brains as physical systems full of quantum noise and chaos, or as computational systems full of informational noise and software bugs. We have to start thinking of brains as biological systems that evolved to generate certain kinds of adaptive unpredictability under certain conditions of competition and courtship.

Genuine unpredictability is the best defence against predictive mindreading

The Machiavellian intelligence hypothesis suggests that apes and humans have evolved special cognitive adaptations for predicting and manipulating the behaviour of other individuals (Humphrey, 1976; Byrne & Whiten, 1988; Whiten & Byrne, 1988; and see Chapter 1). These adaptations are postulated to include a 'theory of mind' module for attributing beliefs and desires to others, to better predict their behaviour (see Dennett, 1988; Leslie, 1994; Baron-Cohen, 1995; Chapter 6). Suppose these hypotheses are right. Would evolution stop there, with everyone able to predict and manipulate each other's behaviour, or would counter-strategies also be expected to evolve? In a society of Machiavellian psychoanalysts, individuals that are harder to predict and manipulate must have selective advantages.

In their classic paper on mindreading and manipulation, Krebs & Dawkins (1984) identified only two defences an animal might use against having its actions predicted by a hostile 'mindreader': concealment (of telltale intention cues), and active deception (by generating false cues). They overlook the classic third option, familiar to all military strategists, sports coaches and game theorists, who routinely confront the problem of stopping an enemy from predicting and preparing for their next move: randomness. Genuine unpredictability. The kind that submarine commanders used in World War II when they threw dice to determine their zig-zagging paths during dangerous patrols against surface ships. Thus, resistance to mindreading may take several major forms: (a) hiding intentions (the Poker Face strategy), (b) tactical deception and disinformation (the KGB strategy), and (c) adaptive unpredictability (the Protean strategy). Because these strategies are useful under different circumstances at different times, we might expect that they will tend to evolve together in a repertoire of social defences against mindreading. However, the Protean strategy has been much neglected compared to the Poker Face and

KGB strategies. Also, while the Poker Face and KGB strategies remain vulnerable to the co-evolution of smarter intention-sensing and deception-foiling capacities (see Chapters 5, 6 and 7), there is no real defence against genuine unpredictability. Thus, the Protean strategy may be the only evolutionarily stable strategy in the arms race against Machiavellian intelligence.

The Protean strategy's usefulness has been overlooked because evolution was widely assumed to produce deterministic mechanisms of animal behaviour. Descartes wrote of animals as automata; ethologists wrote of sign stimuli and simple releasing mechanisms; sociobiologists wrote of genes for specific behaviours. Such determinism makes sense for behaviours that deal with inanimate objects, but was extended too easily to behaviours subject to mindreading. For example, Krebs & Dawkins (1984, p. 384) suggested that 'Natural selection itself will favour male sea otters whose behaviour happens to take advantage of the lawfulness of female behaviour. The effect is that the male manipulates the female in much the same way as he manipulates a stone . . . animals respond in mechanical, robot-like fashion to key stimuli'. Further, their notion of mindreading was based on using statistical laws to exploit the supposed predictability of animal behaviour: 'For an animal, the equivalent of the data-collection and statistical analysis is performed either by natural selection acting on the mind-reader's ancestors over a long period, or by some process of learning during its own lifetime' (Krebs & Dawkins, 1984, p. 386).

This view of animals as intuitive statisticians suggests some obvious counter-measures. Anything that psychologists try to eliminate from their laboratory experiments can be useful against intuitive psychologists in the wild. Skew their distributions. Dehomogenise their variances. Bias their samples. Add confounds. Regress to the mean. Introduce order effects, practice effects, fatigue effects, maturation effects, expectancy effects, prestige biases, interviewer biases and social desirability biases. Confound their reliability and validity. But these are just ways to delay enemies from discovering the real determinants of your behaviour. The best protection is to undermine the determinants themselves to some degree: increase 'residual variance' in one's behaviour to erode the validity of an opponent's correlations, ANOVAs, MANOVAs and path analyses. Squirt some noise into your behaviour and their intuitive statistics will suffer.

This argument may seem silly. The notion of cognition as intuitive statistics, though once popular (e.g. Peterson & Beach, 1967), is problematic (Gigerenzer & Murray, 1987). But the accuracy of perception and cognition should be undermined by noise in the input, whether one models cognition as intuitive statistics, cognitive psychology flowcharts, neural networks, knowledge-based systems, or dynamical systems theory. Genuine unpredictability is an objective, information-theoretic feature of behaviour, so would affect any information-processing system that tries to perceive and predict the behaviour, no matter what cognitive metaphor one prefers. Thus, the Protean strategy should often prove useful, especially in primate social behaviour. But to build a foundation for understanding social proteanism in primates, we must review three things: the notion of psychological selection from evolutionary theory, the notion of mixed strategies from game theory, and the notion of protean behaviour from ethology.

Psychological selection: How minds guide evolution

One of Darwin's greatest achievements was to naturalise the role that mind plays in guiding evolution. He discarded grandiose religious ideas about God as Cosmic Designer and philosophical ideas about Reason willing itself into existence (e.g. as in works by Hegel, Schopenhauer, Spencer and Lamarck), and explained simply how animal perceptual systems can act as selective forces to shape the fantastic forms and varieties of flowers (Darwin, 1862), domesticated animals (Darwin, 1868), and courtship traits (Darwin, 1871). Particularly in his analysis of female choice, Darwin (1871) started to develop a general theory of ornaments based on regularities of animal perception such as sensitivity to colour, symmetry, repetition and novelty (see Miller, 1993). However, his incipient theory of what I have called 'psychological selection' (Miller, 1993) was not taken forward by anyone at first, largely because Wallace (1889) and others proved so skeptical about the possibility of 'aesthetic choice' by female animals (see Cronin, 1991). Perception was viewed mainly as a selective force that operates between species to shape morphological adaptations, such as the appearance of fruit, flowers, camouflage, warning coloration and mimicry (see Wallace, 1870, 1889; Morgan, 1888; Cott, 1940). This hostility towards Darwin's ideas about the role of minds as selective forces within species, affecting behaviour and not just morphology, probably delayed the development of the Machiavellian intelligence hypothesis by about a century, from Darwin (1871) to Humphrey (1976).

Recently though, there has been an explosion of interest in psychological selection – going under a variety of terms such as 'sensory drive' (Endler, 1992), 'sensory exploitation' (Ryan, 1990), 'signal selection' (Zahavi, 1991), and 'the influence of receiver psychology on the evolution of animal signals' (Guilford & Dawkins, 1991). However, most such theory continues to emphasise how minds shape bodies, not how minds shape other minds. A few exceptions are some analyses of communication (Dawkins & Krebs, 1978), deception (Krebs & Dawkins, 1984; Byrne & Whiten, 1988), self-deception (Trivers, 1985), and animate motion perception (Miller & Freyd, 1993).

We lack a general theory of how minds can select other minds within a species. This is a major gap in evolutionary theory, because cognition can guide evolution in such powerful and surprising ways. For example, the evolutionary dynamics that arise when mate choice interacts with natural selection may lead to much faster evolutionary innovation, optimisation and diversification (Miller, 1994a; Miller & Todd, 1993, 1995; Todd & Miller, 1993). Developing a useful theory of psychological selection will require identifying fundamental regularities in perception and cognition that emerge repeatedly through convergent evolution, and that could shape the evolution of behaviour within or across species. The Machiavellian intelligence hypothesis offers one such regularity: animals living in complex social groups should regularly evolve mental adaptations for social perception, prediction, manipulation and exploitation. This regularity in turn sets up reliable selective pressures favouring countermeasures such as intention-hiding, tactical deception and social proteanism. But to understand just how these pressures operate, we must turn to game theory.

Differential game theory: Mixed strategies in pursuit and evasion

The idea of a mixed strategy from game theory is best introduced with an example. In the game of *Matching Pennies*, two players each have a coin. Every turn, each player secretly turns her coin heads-up or tails-up. Then the coins are revealed. If the first player, in the role of 'matcher', has turned up the same side as her opponent (e.g. both coins are heads), then she wins a dollar from her opponent. If the coins mismatch (e.g. one is heads, the other tails), then she must pay a dollar to her opponent. Players can repeat this game turn after turn, producing long sequences of heads and tails, until one player goes broke, or, as more often happens, becomes lividly frustrated.

The roles of 'matcher' and 'non-matcher' seem different, but their goals are fundamentally the same: predict what the opponent will do, and then do whatever is appropriate (matching or not matching) to win the turn. All that matters is to find out the opponent's intentions. The ideal offensive strategy then is to be the perfect predictor: figure out what the opponent is doing based on her past behaviour, extrapolate her strategy to the next move, make the prediction, and win the turn. But there is a remarkably easy way to defeat this prediction strategy, by playing unpredictably:

> 'In playing Matching Pennies against an at least moderately intelligent opponent, the player will not attempt to find out the opponent's intentions but will concentrate on avoiding having his own intentions found out, by playing irregularly "heads" and "tails" in successive games'
>
> (Von Neumann & Morgenstern, 1944, p. 144).

If a player picks heads with probability $\frac{1}{2}$ and tails with probability $\frac{1}{2}$, then no opponent, no matter how good a predictor they are, can do better than break even in this game. This half-heads, half-tails strategy is an example of a 'mixed strategy', because it mixes moves unpredictably. Perhaps the most important and interesting result from Von Neumann & Morgenstern (1944) was that every two-player, zero-sum game of incomplete information with multiple saddle points (which, in technical terms, covers most of the interesting games you could play against someone) has an optimal strategy that is mixed rather than pure. The utility of mixed strategies has also been shown for many situations of pursuit and evasion studied by 'differential game theory' (Isaacs, 1965; Yavin & Pachter, 1987; for a review see Miller & Cliff, 1994a). For example, game theorists have designed 'electronic jinking' systems to generate unpredictable flight paths for military aircraft so they can evade guided missiles, by analogy to gazelles jinking erratically to avoid cheetahs (Forte & Shinar, 1989).

Evolutionary game theory (Maynard Smith, 1982) has also recognised the optimality of mixed strategies in many contests between animals. But mixed strategies are usually assumed to evolve as behavioural polymorphisms across a population rather than as unpredictable behaviour within an individual. Also, evolutionary game theory has focused mostly on single-step games (such as sex-ratio determination or the Hawk–Dove game: see Maynard Smith, 1982) and discrete-step games (such as the iterated prisoner's dilemma: see Axelrod, 1984). The literature on differential pursuit–evasion games has been strangely overlooked despite its obvious relevance to predator–prey interactions, dominance contests, sexual harassment and play behaviour. Dave Cliff and I have tried to fill this gap by developing simulations of co-evolution between pursuit and evasion strategies, implemented by genetically specified neural networks with noise parameters that evolve to implement proteanism (Miller & Cliff, 1994a,b; Cliff & Miller, 1996).

Protean behaviour theory: Unpredictable evasion by animals

A striking historical coincidence: four years after Michael R. A. Chance co-authored one of the foundational papers in Machiavellian intelligence (Chance & Mead, 1953), he became one of the first biologists to recognise the adaptive significance of unpredictable behaviour in animals, with a paper titled 'The role of convulsions in behaviour' (Chance, 1957; see also Chance & Russell, 1959). Researchers had long been puzzled by 'audiogenic seizures' in laboratory rats: when laboratory technicians accidentally jangle their keys, some laboratory rats go into bizarre convulsions. But Chance (1957) found that if the rats are provided with hiding places (little rat-huts) in their cages, they simply run and hide when keys are jangled; thus, the convulsions may be facultative defensive behaviours rather than pathological oddities. Convulsions would make it much more difficult for a predator to catch and hold the convulsing animal. Shortly after, Roeder (1962) found that moths tumble and loop unpredictably when hit by bat ultrasound (signalling a predator's approach); Roeder & Treat (1961) found such tumbling much more effective at bat-evasion than passive tumbling or predictable fleeing (see May, 1991, for recent review).

Humphries & Driver (1970) termed this sort of adaptively unpredictable behaviour 'protean behaviour', after the mythical Greek river-god Proteus, who eluded capture by continually, unpredictably changing form. Their book *Protean Behaviour: The Biology of Unpredictability* (Driver & Humphries, 1988) presents a detailed theory and many ethological observations. Though they did not cite game theory, they made analogies between protean behaviour in animals, unpredictable feints in human sports and randomising methods in military strategy.

The adaptive logic of proteanism is simple. Animals generally evolve perceptual and cognitive capacities to entrain, track and predict the movements of other biologically-relevant animals such as prey, predators and potential mates (Camhi, 1984; Premack, 1990; Freyd, 1992; Miller & Freyd, 1993). Such predictive abilities mean that unpredictable behaviour will often be favoured in many natural pursuit–evasion situations. For example, if a rabbit fleeing from a fox always chose the single apparently shortest escape route, the very consistency of its behaviour would make its escape route more predictable to the fox, its body more likely to be eaten, and its genes less likely to replicate. Predictability is punished by hostile animals capable of prediction. Thus, the effectiveness of almost any behavioural tactic can be enhanced by endowing it with characteristics that cannot be predicted by an evolutionary opponent (Driver & Humphries, 1988). Evolutionarily recurring pursuit–evasion contests will usually result in arms races between perceptual capacities for predicting animate motion, and motor capacities for generating protean behaviour (Miller & Freyd, 1993).

Along with directional fleeing, protean escape behaviours are probably the most widespread and successful of all behavioural anti-predator tactics, being used by virtually all mobile animals on land, under water and in the air. Driver & Humphries (1988) review ethological observations from hundreds of species, including insects, fish, birds and mammals. Human proteanism is obvious in any competitive sport: good boxers use unpredictable feints and attacks, and good rugby players use unpredictable jinks. Predators can also exploit unpredictability to confuse prey, as when weasels do 'crazy dances' to baffle the voles that they stalk, or when Australian aborigine hunters do wild dances to mesmerise the kangaroos that they hunt (Driver & Humphries, 1988). Of course, proteanism is typically used at one level of behavioural description (e.g. the trajectory through the environment), and is consistent with maintenance of orderly behaviour at other levels (e.g. posture, locomotor gait, obstacle avoidance, perceptual scanning). A possible exception is convulsive 'death throes', when injured prey use wild, desperate, unpredictable movements to escape from the clutches of predators.

Patterns of animal play behaviour reveal the importance of proteanism. Most animal play is play-chasing and play-fighting (Fagen, 1981), and includes intense practice in pursuit and evasion, prediction and proteanism, anticipation and violation of expectations. Judging by the relative play time devoted to learning different skills, foraging for plant foods and navigating through space is much easier than catching prey, escaping from predators, or fighting conspecifics. These latter skills are harder because they demand the robust, continuous, dynamic control of one's own body in competition with the continuous, dynamic movements of a motivated, well-adapted opponent (Miller & Cliff, 1994a,b). Insofar as primates rehearse proteanism in juvenile play, they probably use it as adults to avoid predators, attack prey and compete for dominance.

Unpredictability can be useful at many levels of biological organisation. When threatened, octopi, cuttlefish and sea pansies use 'colour convulsions' across the fast-response chromataphores on their skin, quickly going through different colour patterns to defeat the search images (perceptual expectations) used by their predators (Driver & Humphries, 1988). Animals in groups use unpredictable movements, complex motion patterns, and confusing colouration (e.g. zebra stripes or shiny fish scales) to confuse predators. Selection for unpredictability can favour the evolution of large differences between individuals, as when animals within a species evolve 'aspect diversity' (polymorphic colouration or behaviour) through 'apostatic selection' (Clarke, 1962) that favours low-frequency traits (e.g. because predators' use of search images penalises common appearances).

Co-evolution itself can be viewed as a pursuit–evasion contest between lineages rather than between individuals. From this perspective, sexual recombination makes sense as a protean strategy that unpredictably mixes up genes so as to 'confuse' pathogens (Hamilton *et al.*, 1990). Indeed, this proteanism argument is one of the leading explanations for the evolution of sex itself (Ridley, 1993). Despite proteanism's importance, it has been long overlooked in biology, because complex order rather than useful chaos was assumed to be the defining feature of Darwinian adaptations (see Miller, 1993).

Can animals really randomise?

For decades, experimental psychologists have investigated whether humans can generate sequences of numbers, letters, or motions that obey various tests of mathematical randomness. Dozens of papers suggested that Reichenbach (1934/1949) was correct in suggesting that humans tend to alternate too much (heads–tails–heads–tails) and don't produce enough long runs (heads–heads–heads–heads). Tune's (1964) review concluded that 'humans are incapable of generating a random series of selections from a finite number of alternatives', and Wagenaar's (1972) review concluded 'Producing a random series of responses is a difficult, if not impossible task for humans, even when they are explicitly instructed'. Complex models were advanced to explain the 'heuristics', 'biases', or 'cognitive constraints' underlying these failures of randomisation (e.g. G. A. Miller & Frick, 1949; Kahneman & Tversky, 1972; Treisman & Faulkner, 1987).

However, most such studies were artificial in the extreme, typically requiring isolated subjects to write down a series of numbers on paper with instructions such as 'be as random as possible'. Rapoport & Budescu (1992) found that sequences come much closer to genuine mathematical randomness when they are generated by subjects playing a real, face-to-face, strictly competitive game (e.g. Matching Pennies), than when they are generated by isolated subjects trying to write down 'random sequences'. Even without explicit competition, other researchers have shown that animal and human subjects can learn to generate almost perfectly random sequences when given good feedback (Neuringer, 1986; Lopes & Oden, 1987; Neuringer & Voss, 1993). The randomisation abilities of monkeys and apes could be tested by having them play a variant of the penny-hiding game, used by Baron-Cohen (1992) to show that autistics lacking a theory of mind are poor at randomisation in two-person zero-sum games.

The recent skepticism about animals' capacities for varied, unpredictable, novel behaviour is ironic because such capacities were fundamental to Behaviorist theories of operant conditioning, which drew explicit parallels between learning and evolution. For example, Skinner (1974) and Campbell (1960) saw random exploratory behaviour as analogous to genetic mutations, and reinforcement as analogous to natural selection. Without a reasonably unpredictable, varied set of initial behaviours for reinforcement to 'shape', the development of complex behavioural repertoires would be impossible. A classic volume titled *Functions of Varied Experience* (Fiske & Maddi, 1961) demonstrates the sophistication of Behaviorist reasoning about the importance of behavioural variation, before the computer metaphor and cognitive psychology conflated behavioural variation with noisy information and malfunctioning programmes.

From unpredictable evasion to social proteanism

The strongest arguments about proteanism have come from studies of pursuit–evasion contests, whether in game theory, evolutionary simulation, or behavioural biology. Would unpredictability still prove adaptive if we shift attention from trajectories through physical space to more abstract trajectories through the space of possible social behaviours? When would 'social proteanism' be selected?

There are two levels at which social proteanism makes sense: strategic choices and tactical details. Roughly, social strategies include things such as coalition-forming, peace-making, short-term mating, long-term consorting and dominance-challenging; tactics include specific implementations of strategies to exploit local, temporary conditions. Many social strategies are subject to frequency-dependent selection. Examples include the balance between aggressiveness and bluffing in the Hawk–Dove game (Maynard Smith, 1982), between deceptive and honest signals in animal signal theory (Zahavi, 1975; Dawkins & Krebs, 1978), and between extroversion and introversion in evolutionary personality psychology (Buss, 1991; Wilson, 1994). As Maynard Smith (1982) pointed out, any frequency-dependent balance can be implemented either between individuals, as a genetic polymorphism, or within an individual, as unpredictable strategic variation over time. Thus, social proteanism can function to make one's strategic choices unpredictable. But every strategy, every social action or reaction, can also vary in its tactical details, including time, space, style, rhythm, movements, signals, targets and allies. Introducing uncertainty into each of these tactical variables can render the action more unpredictable, more impervious to counter-measures, and hence more effective.

In general, social proteanism can be viewed as the ultimate extension of Trivers' (1985) theory of adaptive self-deception, which postulates that hiding one's intentions from oneself allows one to better hide them from others. Genuine proteanism means that no part of one's nervous system knows what you will do next, because your actions will be generated stochastically. Thus, it would be impossible to leak 'intention cues' to others, because there are no specific intentions. Anywhere that adaptive self-deception might be useful, social proteanism might be even more useful. Indeed, the evolution of social proteanism might act as a brake on Machiavellian intelligence arms races, by undermining the possibility of further improvements in social prediction and manipulation: proteanism casts an oily fog over the dark world of mindreading (cf. Chapter 6).

The following sections outline six examples of social proteanism that we might expect to find in primates with high levels of Machiavellian intelligence. These examples are largely speculative, but I have two defences. Firstly, for methodological and statistical reasons, it would be extremely hard to notice social proteanism if you weren't looking for it, so the absence of relevant primate data – so far – is not surprising (Miller, 1993). Few primatologists seemed to notice tactical deception until Byrne & Whiten (1988) suggested there were good reasons to expect it. Secondly, it would be strange if the mixed-strategy game theory that applies to rabbits zig-zagging to escape foxes (Driver & Humphries, 1988), simulated robots evolving noisy neural networks for evasion (Miller & Cliff, 1994b), and military aircraft jinking erratically to avoid guided missiles (Forte & Shinar, 1988), did not apply to those craftiest of animals, the primates.

Example 1: Protean anger thresholds

Suppose alpha males could adopt one of two strategies for setting their 'anger threshold' that determines when they will punish insults to their dominance (e.g. encroachments on their resources or females). With the Old Faithful strategy, the anger threshold is set so that aggressive punishment is generated only if an insult exceeds a fixed magnitude, T. With the Mad Dog strategy though, the anger threshold is probabilistic, so punishment occurs if an insult exceeds a variable magnitude chosen from a normal distribution with mean T and high variance. Which strategy will work better? Subordinates can quickly learn Old Faithful's anger threshold, and can do anything below magnitude T with impunity. If T is set so anger is only incurred by actual copulation with a female, the subordinates could still groom and provision females at will, establishing useful alliances that increase their claim to alpha status. But subordinates face terrible uncertainty with Mad Dog: can they get away with even a minute of grooming a female this time? Maybe they did last time, but maybe not this time. Against the Mad Dog strategy, any insult, however slight, risks retaliation – but Mad Dog doesn't incur the time, energy and injury costs of having a fixed low threshold either. The uncertainty does most of the work of intimidating subordinates. As Betzig (1986) emphasised, the definition of despotism is the power of *arbitrary* life and death over subordinates, and many despots have used the Mad Dog strategy to great effect. This argument about protean anger thresholds would also apply to thresholds for sexual jealousy, sexual coercion, aggressive weaning conflict, aggressive sibling rivalry, juvenile temper tantrums, group warfare, etc. However, indiscriminate use of Mad Dog may worry one's allies in addition to unnerving one's opponents, so it should be used selectively and sparingly.

Example 2: Protean promiscuity and concealed ovulation

The outcome of sperm competition is fairly unpredictable in mammals (see Baker & Bellis, 1995). Females can exploit this fact by mating promiscuously with several males during ovulation, so that there is profound uncertainty about paternity: a male will seldom risk infanticide for fear that the infant he's killing may be his own (Hrdy, 1981; Small, 1993). Promiscuity uses proteanism to confuse paternity. Likewise, concealed ovulation introduces uncertainty about the timing of fertility and hence the paternity of offspring. Most female primates in multi-male groups seem to use either protean promiscuity or concealed ovulation to protect against infanticide.

Obviously, proteanism would also help a female in the choice of when and where to arrange a covert copulation with a subordinate male. The more predictable such sneaky acts, the more risk they incur from dominant males who are trying to mate-guard their females and predict sneaky copulations. Protean lust may be a good strategy: if a female does not know herself when she will be overcome with desire for a subordinate, she cannot leak cues of intended deception to other males. The impulsiveness of some human sexual encounters may reflect such a strategy. Of course, protean timing need not imply indiscriminate mate choice, or indiscreet choice of mating place.

Example 3: Protean grudges, forgiveness and reciprocity

Nowak (1990) and Nowak & Sigmund (1992) showed that generous tit-for-tat (GTFT), a stochastic strategy, could evolve and thrive in evolutionary simulations of the noisy, iterated prisoner's dilemma. GTFT co-operates even after an opponent's defection at some non-zero probability (e.g. one third of the time), and its unpredictability is the key to its success. In Nowak's noisy prisoner's dilemma, accidental defections can occur even if both players try to co-operate. This means that the traditional tit-for-tat (TFT) strategy can get locked into infinite cycles of defection as a result of a single mistake. GTFT is more forgiving, but it is impossible to predict exactly when it will co-operate after a defection, so its generosity is hard to exploit. Indeed, allowing GTFT to evolve is one of the most powerful ways to catalyse the evolution of reliable co-operation in the iterated prisoner's dilemma. By allowing probabilities of co-operation after defection to evolve slowly and continuously, Nowak & Sigmund (1992) got full co-operation to evolve where it never could have evolved in one big jump.

This simple simulation has profound implications for reciprocity, exchange and social relationships (for background, see Chapter 2). Individuals who forgive defectors after a predictable interval can be exploited repeatedly. Those who forgive after an unpredictable interval are much tougher to exploit. One might even speculate that grudges should decay according to a Poisson distribution over time. Unpredictable grudges also make it harder for potential defectors to estimate the costs of losing a co-operative partner, such that risk-averse would-be defectors may continue co-operating in the face of this uncertainty. Thus, proteanism can even promote the evolution of reciprocity.

Example 4: Group co-operation through protean cost–benefit lotteries

Group co-operation may be facilitated by randomising processes that make it hard to predict the distribution of costs and benefits from co-operation (Miller, 1994b). An analogy to meiosis shows why: just as the gene-randomising process of meiosis is necessary to promote peaceful cell division during gamete production, and this peace is disrupted by 'meiotic drive' that biases gene allocation among gametes (Hurst, 1992), a cost–benefit lottery may help promote group harmony during high-risk, co-operative activity.

Such lotteries work best when co-operation produces individual fitness pay-offs with a positive mean value and a high variance, and with positive and negative outcomes that are fast, final, unpredictable and unshareable (such as successful fertilisation or death). These conditions make it stupid to defect before the lottery and impossible to defect after the lottery. The main resource lotteries in human evolution were probably co-operative hunting, co-operative warfare and co-operative sexual coercion. For example, Tooby & Cosmides (1993) suggested that the development of projectile weapons may have facilitated the evolution of human co-operative warfare, by making the outcome of warfare more unpredictable to the individual but more beneficial to the winning group. A fast hail of projectiles imposes a more unpredictable survival lottery than an afternoon of hand-to-hand combat, so individual defection is less likely. Moreover, warriors or hunters may draw lots at random to decide who will lead a dangerous raid. Co-operative sexual coercion by males can also function as a reproductive lottery, because the outcome of sperm competition among multiple males is not predictable (see Baker & Bellis, 1995).

Randomisation has happier uses. When a Hutterite (type of American fundamentalist) community grows too large, it splits into two groups, and ownership of the original home site is assigned by lottery (Wilson & Sober, 1994). Some of the apparently idiotic, essentially random divination methods used by hunters to predict where prey will be found (e.g. throwing stones on maps of the local environment) may function not only to distribute search effort efficiently (under an optimal foraging model), but to allow collective decision-making without individual guilt or recrimination should the day's efforts prove futile (Campbell, 1974). More recently, Britain's adoption of a national lottery could be construed as a convenient way of promoting national unity and an illusion of fairness in the face of apparently indestructible class divisions and economic collapse. Also, Gigerenzer (1996) has emphasised how in-group variation can implement a form of 'adaptive coin-flipping' that benefits the group, though it can be maintained by individual-level selection. In sum, if competition between groups has been important in human evolution (Wilson & Sober, 1994), then we would expect to find evidence of cognitive adaptations that facilitate in-group lotteries. This lottery strategy for group co-operation could complement more deterministic egalitarian models (see Chapters 13 and 14).

Example 5: Proteanism, polymorphism and personality

Unpredictable variation can prove adaptive between individuals as well as within individuals. Clark (1962) postulated that 'apostatic selection' in favour of low-frequency body types and behaviours could maintain substantial morphological and behavioural polymorphism in a species. For example, birds have more trouble finding and eating snails in species with high levels of polymorphism in shell colour and pattern, because the birds' perceptual expectations don't work as well (Driver & Humphries, 1988). The same argument could apply to polymorphism at other levels: the predictive power of Machiavellian intelligence may favour greater diversity in 'personality' (i.e. social-strategic specialisation across the lifespan). Evolutionary personality psychologists such as Buss (1991) and

Wilson (1994) recognise that frequency-dependent selection can maintain genetic variation in personality traits, but they neglect this possible apostatic effect. Consider how much easier social interactions would be if every individual one encountered had exactly the same personality – i.e. the same social-strategic repertoire, the same goals, the same tastes in mates and friends, the same thresholds for anger or gratitude, etc. Social complexity is not just a function of the number and quality of social relationships in a group (cf. Dunbar, 1993; see also Chapter 9), but also of the interindividual variations in personality that must be perceived, remembered, and strategised about. Given Machiavellian intelligence, apostatic selection may favour a rapid diversification of personality types, and may maintain behavioural polymorphisms at higher levels than they would otherwise attain. Sexual selection through mate choice may exert additional apostatic pressures, insofar as variety-seeking mechanisms such as the Coolidge Effect (Dewsbury, 1981) favour individuals with unusual appearances and behaviours. Just as predictive social intelligence can favour social proteanism within individuals, it can favour a greater diversity of personality across individuals.

Example 6: Proteanism as a learning-inhibitor, cognition-blocker and stress-inducer

Unpredictability, aside from making short-term prediction hard, also makes learning hard. It has been suggested earlier in this chapter that behavioural noise interferes with intuitive statistics. Behavioral noise will also interfere with almost any type of inductive learning about behaviour. It's more difficult to puzzle out the determinants of another agent's behaviour if their behaviour is indeterministic.

Proteanism has a host of other nasty psychological effects on opponents; these can be characterised using the language of cognitive psychology. Proteanism makes top-down perceptual expectations less useful, so makes perception slower and less accurate. It demands attention by violating expectations, interfering with other 'controlled processing' tasks. It interferes with category learning by decreasing the utility of prototypes and blurring boundaries. It undermines schema-based reasoning by reducing the validity of social schemata. It overloads memory, by requiring the storage of heterogenous ensembles of episodic memories, rather than simple, representative exemplars. It introduces uncertainty, confusion and conflict at almost every stage of cognition. Research on human judgement and decision-making shows that we are not only risk-averse, but uncertainty-averse (Ellsberg, 1961; Hogarth & Kunreuther, 1989), and proteanism capitalises on these aversions.

Proteanism could also induce debilitating levels of physiological stress in opponents. Many studies have shown that lack of control over an unpredictable environment causes stress, depression, disease and feelings of helplessness (see Seligman, 1975). Sapolsky (1994) notes that 'Unpredictability makes stressors much more stressful'. Low-quality predictive information does not help: especially stressful are vague warnings of an upcoming menace that will occur at an unpredictable time, and against which few precautions can be taken. For example, a male primate rising in rank could benefit by 'warning' an alpha male that a takeover attempt is imminent, without providing any tactical details; the alpha's resulting worries and stress could make the takeover more likely to succeed. Conversely, the alpha could use the Mad Dog strategy to impose continuous, debilitating stress on potential challengers. Dominants may have evolved a tacit understanding that by using proteanism to induce sufficient long-term learned helplessness in rivals, their immune systems and energy reserves will be sufficiently compromised that pathogens and predators will finish them off, with little risk to the dominant.

From social proteanism to creative intelligence?

One rarely-examined assumption of the Machiavellian intelligence hypothesis is that domain-specific social cognition (e.g. a theory of mind module) is uniquely likely to facilitate the evolution of full-blown, human-level intelligence and creativity. The assumption seems plausible at first, but I cannot see its real logical force. It *seems* a short step from the capacity to attribute beliefs and desires to other agents, to the capacities for language, metacognition, episodic memory, creativity and long-term planning. But the same reasoning could predict that it is only a short evolutionary step from beaver dams to Greek architecture, from depth perception to representational painting, from social insect colonies to Marxism, and from echolocation to radar. The formal similarities can hide huge evolutionary gaps. Evolution tends to produce domain-specific cognitive modules tightly adapted to specific, evolutionarily recurring tasks (Cosmides & Tooby, 1994; Chapter 10). We do not yet have any theory about which such domain-specific capacities are likely to have more domain-general spin-offs. Furthermore, there are good functional arguments for relative domain-generality being a primitive rather than an advanced state for most cognitive capacities: the longer a capacity is under selection, the more automatic, unconscious, domain-specific, encapsulated and specialised it is expected to become (Cosmides & Tooby, 1994). Thus, the apparent flexibility of social cognition in great apes may reflect it evolutionary recency (i.e. its primitiveness, inconvenience, inefficiency, unreliability and general looseness). In another 20 million years, perhaps mindreading in the great apes would become as encapsulated, specialised and unconscious as web-spinning in the spider. The sloppy boundaries of social cognition in apes may have little direct relation to the evolution of more domain-general human intelligence.

Proteanism is different, because its evolution provides one critical substrate for creative thought: the capacity for rapid, unpredictable generation of highly variable alternatives. Almost every modern theory of learning and cognition relies upon some mechanism of random variation and selective retention (Campbell, 1960). Studies of human creativity have long stressed the interplay between random generation (e.g. brainstorming, divergent thinking, remote associations) and selective evaluation (see Boden, 1991). The most baffling and poorly explained feature of creative thought is the mechanism of random generation, whether mythologised as the creative muse, deified as divine inspiration, or rationalised as 'divergent thinking'. The theory of protean behaviour (Driver & Humphries, 1988; Miller, 1993) seems to offer the first evolutionary explanation for this crucial randomisation mechanism, and thus leads to the first naturalistic account of the evolution of human creativity.

A problem arises: why don't all animals with capacities for protean evasion of predators develop human-level creative thought? One might expect that randomisation capacities, plus basic capacities for mentally representing one's environment, plus generic natural selection for intelligence, would produce creative thought in almost all species capable of proteanism. But it hasn't. Evolution seems to abhor intelligence, and avoids it whenever possible. Even worse, most semi-smart species that have evolved social proteanism (e.g. apes, and maybe some dolphins, whales and elephants) do not go on to evolve human-style creative intelligence.

The easy way out of this quandary is to 'pull a Steven Jay': invoke historical contingency, genetic drift, epistasis, heterochrony, local optima, or some other dark refuge of anti-adaptationism (Gould, 1989), and suggest that one lineage with social proteanism, social intelligence, social creativity, large brains and good luck just happened to evolve human cognition. But we must face the hard facts: full-blown creative cognition is so rare, expensive and complex that it must have evolved under *direct* selection (Foley, 1992; Miller, 1993) – not through the happy overlap of cognitive capacities selected for other functions. Social proteanism just provides one important mechanism (randomisation) that could have been 'exapted' for creative intelligence; it doesn't lead straight to humans up some evolutionary ladder. The next section outlines one possible model of direct selection for creative intelligence. It takes social proteanism as a starting point, but requires sexual selection to do most of the work.

From proteanism to creativity: Runaway sexual selection for unpredictability-indicators?

Suppose that capacities for proteanism became an important component of primate social intelligence, especially in apes and early hominids. Insofar as proteanism contributed to competitive success, along with size, strength, health and social skills, we might expect that mate choice mechanisms would evolve to favour exaggerated displays of proteanism, along with displays of size, strength, health and social skills (see Andersson, 1994). The more important proteanism becomes in social competition and survival, the more likely it is to be advertised and elaborated in courtship. Once proteanism came under the influence of mate choice, three new processes could come into play.

Firstly, Zahavi's (1975) handicap principle might predict that only proteanism-displays that are costly (e.g. energetically expensive) would be reliable, so proteanism-displays would probably become elaborated and specialised, leading to special 'protean courtship displays' that might bear little resemblance to the original social protean tactics. However, skill at proteanism is almost as hard to fake as other features relevant to mate choice (e.g. size, strength, health, status), because proteanism can be directly assessed by capacities for social prediction. So proteanism-displays in courtship may evolve to be quite distinct from social proteanism in competition, and their informational features may become elaborated (e.g. into unpredictability at higher and higher levels of cognitive or strategic performance), but they need not become elaborated in physical magnitude, e.g. through exaggerated movements. Thus, human lovers sometimes whisper creative jokes, metaphors and stories to each other, using proteanism elaborated at the level of cognitive content, but not at the level of physical size or intensity – unlike most other products of sexual selection, such as 5 foot long peacock tails, or 120 decibel humpback whale songs.

Secondly, under Ryan's (1990) sensory exploitation model, any intrinsic sensory biases that favoured unpredictability could exert an influence on mate choice, so could select for proteanism. We know of such a sensory bias already: neophilia (selective attention to the novel and the unexpected). Nervous systems rely heavily on expectations, and usually evolve mechanisms to detect violations of expectations. These novelty-detectors direct attention to environmental features that require deeper, more focused cognitive processing. Thus, neophilia tends to favour proteanism because unpredictability attracts attention. Darwin (1871) attached great importance to neophilia in explaining the diversity and rapid evolutionary turnover of bird plumage: 'It would appear that mere novelty, or slight changes for the sake of change, have sometimes acted on female birds as a charm, like changes of fashion with us'. Some female birds have been shown to prefer male birds who have larger song repertoires, allowing greater diversity and novelty of performance (Catchpole, 1987; Podos et al., 1992). Such neophilia probably accounts for the astounding complexity and variety of songs by blackbird, nightingales, mockingbirds, parrots and mynahs. Moving from birds to primates, Small (1993) emphasised neophilia in primate mate choice: 'The only consistent interest seen among the general primate population is an interest in novelty and variety. Although the possibility of choosing for good genes, good fathers, or good friends remains an option open to female primates, they seem to prefer the unexpected'. Neophilia in humans has been studied most extensively as 'sensation-seeking' (Zuckerman, 1984), and 'openness': one of the 'Big Five' personality traits (see Buss, 1991). Both sensation-seeking and openness are moderately heritable, as illustrated by the recent discovery of the 'novelty-seeking' polymorphism of the D4DR dopamine receptor gene (see Cloninger et al., 1996). Human neophilia is also the foundation of the art, music, television, film, publishing, drug, travel, pornography and fashion industries, which account for a substantial proportion of the global economy. Martindale (1990) has documented the importance of neophilia in the development of diverse artistic, literary and musical styles over history. If birds, primates and humans show heritable neophilia, early hominids probably did too, and this neophilia in mate choice could have exerted strong, directional selection in favour of human-level creativity.

Thirdly, under Fisher's (1930) runaway sexual selection model, any initial, heritable preference for proteanism, whether due to indicator mechanisms or neophilic biases, can lead to positive-feedback dynamics that elaborate both the mate preference and the preferred trait. The runaway process works because preferences become genetically correlated ('linked') with the traits they prefer, and this genetic linkage drives the process even in the face of substantial natural selection and biased mutation (Pomiankowski et al., 1991). Runaway is especially likely given a 'directional preference' of the more-is-better variety (Kirkpatrick, 1987; Miller & Todd, 1993).

What sort of behaviours could possibly advertise capacities for behavioural unpredictability, variability and novelty? Any behaviour that humans consider 'creative' would work: art, music, humour, language, metaphors, stories, concepts, ideologies – in short, almost all of human culture can function to advertise proteanism. Protean sexuality may be manifest in the incredible variety of sexual foreplay and intercourse positions observed in bonobos or 'pygmy chimpanzees' (see de Waal, 1989). But full-blown, creative, protean courtship displays seem unique to humans. Creativity strips proteanism down to its bare essentials: the innovative, unpredictable recombination of recognisable perceptual, conceptual, or performative elements. The more abstracted away from real social tactics such creativity becomes, the more accurate and specialised a proteanism-indicator it is. Thus, most of the human mind's capacities that have baffled evolutionary theorists from Wallace (1889) onwards might be illuminated by considering their functions as protean courtship displays.

Of course, in all such displays we see an interplay between proteanism and ritualisation, both of which increase the effectiveness of the display signal (see Krebs & Davies, 1987, chapter 14). Ritualisation increases impact through the use of repetition, high intensity, strong contrasts, alerting signals and stereotypy in basic units (Huxley, 1966; Krebs & Davies, 1987), whereas proteanism attracts attention, creates memorable juxtapositions, and produces humour by violating expectations. Ritualised themes and protean variations, and ritualised units and protean combinations, are common in human culture. Language combines ritualised grammar, phonology, semantics and conversational norms with protean sentence structure, intonation, word choice, story plot and expressive content. Music combines ritualised rules of tonality, rhythmicity, melody and harmony, and protean inventions and variations in particular songs. Art combines ritualised representational and stylistic conventions with protean composition, content and individual style. Displays without any orderly elements are incomprehensible; those without protean elements are boring. The optimal cultural courtship display is the virtuosic combination of recognisable semantic elements in novel combinations with new emergent meanings.

This hypothesis adds a new stage to the Machiavellian intelligence model: here, the transition from monkeys to apes and early hominids may reflect the evolution of new social-competitive skills, but the transition from early hominids to modern humans represents the evolution of new courtship skills. Selection for ecological and technological intelligence has probably been over-emphasised in human evolution theories (cf. Chapters 8 and 11). Adaptations for gathering, hunting, navigating and tool-making merely allowed our ancestors to bear the energetic burden of growing such large courtship ornaments, i.e. brains (see Foley, 1992; Aiello & Wheeler, 1995). Still, we need to develop empirical tests that distinguish not only between ecological and social models of encephalisation (as in Byrne, 1995), but also, within the social realm, between social-competitive and sexual-selective models.

The Machiavellian intelligence hypothesis has lumped together all possible selection pressures that can emerge from behavioural interactions between conspecifics. Since the vast majority of runaway processes that result in fast elaborations of behavioural capacities probably occur within species, the Machiavellian hypothesis scored an easy win over other, much weaker theories of human mental evolution (e.g. intelligence through tool-making, hunting, gathering, neoteny, drift, or gene-culture co-evolution). But it is time to ask about the relative contributions of each distinctive relationship type to hominid and human evolution: though inter-related, we should try to avoid conflating parent–offspring interactions, reciprocity, competition for social status, between-group competition, mate choice, etc. My bets are on mate choice as the mainspring of human mental evolution, because the runaway processes of sexual selection are the best-established and most thoroughly modelled (see Miller, 1993; Andersson, 1994; Miller & Todd, 1995), and result in adaptations such as bird song, whale song and courtship dances that are most similar to the products of human creative intelligence. All social competition is ultimately reproductive competition, and sexual selection through mate choice is at the heart of reproduction competition. My view therefore differs somewhat from that of Whiten & Byrne (1988, p. 3), who downplayed sexual selection in suggesting that 'In the earlier paper [Chance & Mead, 1953] an important *misconception* was that sexual relationships represent the essence of primate life, and the key "problem" requiring cleverness' (my italics). Agreed, primatologists used to overplay the centrality of male–male aggressive sexual conflict, but sexual competition more broadly construed is the very heart of primate and human social life.

Conclusions

Social behaviour in primates and humans shows many regularities, but we must not assume that predictable regularity is always adaptive. Given the predictive capacities postulated by the Machiavellian intelligence hypothesis, we would expect a co-evolutionary arms race to ensue in competitive domains such as competition and courtship, between social prediction and social proteanism. Of course, in more co-operative relationships between kin, friends and lovers, we might expect social intelligence to favour social predictability rather than unpredictability. A general theory of how social intelligence can select for unpredictability under some conditions and predictability under other conditions might account for the evolution not only of social proteanism in competition and creativity in courtship, but also of empathy, reliability and intimacy. Further research with primates and humans could investigate not only our capacities for mindreading others, but our capacities for making our own minds harder or easier to read, by switching from unpredictability in some contexts to predictability in others.

This chapter has reviewed the psychological selection theory, differential game theory, and protean behaviour theory relevant to understanding the adaptive value of unpredictability, and has developed six examples where such unpredictability could prove adaptive in primate social behaviour. We also saw how runaway sexual selection may tend to elaborate social proteanism into various protean courtship displays such as art, music, humour and language. The bridge from primate social intelligence to human cultural intelligence was crossed not through social-competitive pressures for Machiavellian intelligence, but through mate-choice pressures for Protean intelligence. We humans, and most of what we do – including chapters for books such as this – are the happy result.

Acknowledgements

This research was supported by: an NSF-NATO Post-Doctoral Fellowship, RCD-9255323, NSF Research Grant INT-9203229, an NSF Graduate Fellowship, NSF grant BNS90–21684 to Roger Shepard, the University of Sussex, the University of Nottingham, and the Max Planck Society. For helpful discussions, comments and/or collaboration, thanks to Rosalind Arden, Simon Baron-Cohen, Richard Byrne, Dave Cliff, Donald Campbell, Leda Cosmides, Helena Cronin, Franz de Waal, Dan Dennett, Peter Driver, Robin Dunbar, Robert Foley, Jennifer Freyd, Gerd Gigerenzer, John Maynard Smith, Roger Shepard, Elliot Sober, Peter Todd, John Tooby and Andy Whiten.

References

Aiello, L. C. & Wheeler, P. (1995). The expensive tissue hypothesis: The brain and the digestive system in human and primate evolution. *Current Anthropology*, 36, 199–221.

Andersson, M. B. (1994). *Sexual Selection*. Princeton, NJ: Princeton University Press.

Axelrod, R. (1984). *The Evolution of Cooperation*. New York: Basic Books.

Baker, M. & Bellis, M. (1995). *Human Sperm Competition*. London: Chapman & Hall.

Baron-Cohen, S. (1992). Out of sight or out of mind? Another look at deception in autism. *Journal of Child Psychology and Psychiatry*, 33, 1141–55.

Baron-Cohen, S. (1995). *Mindblindness*. Cambridge, MA: MIT Press.

Betzig, L. (1986). *Despotism and Differential Reproduction: A Darwinian View of History*. Hawthorne, NY: Aldine.

Boden, M. (1991). *The Creative Mind*. New York: Basic Books.

Buss, D. M. (1991). Evolutionary personality psychology. *Annual Review of Psychology*, 42, 459–91.

Byrne, R. (1995). *The Thinking Ape: Evolutionary Origins of Intelligence*. Oxford: Oxford University Press.

Byrne, R. & Whiten, A. (eds) (1988). *Machiavellian Intelligence: Social Expertise and the Evolution of Intellect in Monkeys, Apes, and Humans*. Oxford: Clarendon Press.

Camhi, J. M. (1984). *Neuroethology: Nerve Cells and the Natural Behavior of Animals*. Sunderland, MA: Sinauer.

Campbell, D. (1960). Blind variation and selective retention in creative thought as in other knowledge processes. *Psychological Review*, 67, 380–400.

Catchpole, C. K. (1987). Bird song, sexual selection and female choice. *Trends in Evolution and Ecology*, 2, 94–7.

Chance, M. R. A. (1957). The role of convulsions in behavior. *Behavioral Science*, 2, 30–45.

Chance, M. R. A. & Mead, A. (1953). Social behavior and primate evolution. *Symposia of the Society for Experimental Biology: Evolution*, 7, 395–439.

Chance, M. R. A. & Russell, W. M. S. (1959). Protean displays: A form of allaesthetic behavior. *Proceedings of the Zoological Society of London*, 132, 65–70.

Clarke, B. C. (1962). The evidence for apostatic selection. *Heredity*, 24, 347–52.

Cliff, D. & Miller, G. F. (1996). Co-evolution of pursuit and evasion. II: Simulation methods and results. In *From Animals to Animals 4: Proceedings of the Fourth International Conference on Simulation of Adaptive Behaviour* (SAB96), ed. P. Maes, M. Mataric, J.-A. Meyer, J. Pollack & S. W. Wilson, pp. 506–15. Cambridge, MA: MIT Press.

Cloninger, C. R., Adolfsson, R. & Svrakic, N. M. (1996). Mapping genes for human personality. *Nature Genetics*, 12, 3–4.

Cosmides, L. & Tooby, J. (1994). Origins of domain specificity: The evolution of functional organization. In *Mapping the Mind: Domain Specificity in Cognition and Culture*, ed. L. A. Hirschfeld & S. A. Gelman, pp. 85–116. Cambridge: Cambridge University Press.

Cott, H. B. (1940). *Adaptive Coloration in Animals*. London: Methuen.

Cronin, H. (1991). *The Ant and the Peacock: Altruism and Sexual Selection from Darwin to Today*. Cambridge: Cambridge University Press.

Darwin, C. (1862). *On the Various Contrivances by Which Orchids are Fertilized by Insects*. London: John Murray.

Darwin, C. (1868). *On the Variation of Animals and Plants under Domestication*. London: John Murray.

Darwin, C. (1871). *The Descent of Man, and Selection in Relation to Sex*, 2 vols. London: John Murray.

Dawkins, R. & Krebs, J. R. (1978). Animal signals: Information or manipulation? In *Behavioral Ecology: An Evolutionary Approach*, 2nd edn, ed. J. R. Krebs & N. B. Davies, pp. 282–309. Oxford: Blackwell Scientific Publications.

de Waal, F. (1989). *Peacemaking among Primates*. Cambridge, MA: Harvard University Press

Dennett, D. (1988). The intentional stance in theory and practice. In *Machiavellian Intelligence: Social Expertise and the Evolution of Intellect in Monkeys, Apes and Humans*, ed. R. W. Byrne & A. Whiten, pp. 180–202. Oxford: Clarendon Press.

Dewsbury, D. A. (1981). Effects of novelty on copulatory behavior: The Coolidge effect and related phenomena. *Psychological Bulletin*, 89, 464–82.

Driver, P. M. & Humphries, N. (1988). *Protean Behavior: The Biology of Unpredictability*. Oxford: Oxford University Press.

Dunbar, R. (1993). Coevolution of neocortical size, group size, and language. *Behavioral and Brain Sciences*, 16, 681–735.

Ellsberg, D. (1961). Risk, ambiguity, and the Savage axioms. *Quarterly Journal of Economics*, 75, 643–99.

Endler, J. A. (1992). Signals, signal conditions, and the direction of evolution. *American Naturalist*, 139, S125-S53.

Fagen, R. (1981). *Animal Play Behavior*. Oxford: Oxford University Press.

Fisher, R. A. (1930). *The Genetical Theory of Natural Selection*. Oxford: Clarendon Press.

Fiske, D. W. & Maddi, S. R. (1961). *Functions of Varied Experience*. Homewood, IL: Dorsey Press.

Foley, R. (1992). Ecology and energetics of encephalization in hominid evolution. In *Foraging Strategies and Natural Diet of Monkeys, Apes and Humans*, ed. A. Whiten & E. M. Widdowson, pp. 63–72. Oxford: Oxford University Press.

Forte, I. & Shinar, J. (1989). Improved guidance law design based on the mixed-strategy concept. *Journal of Guidance, Control, and Dynamics*, 12, 739–45.

Freyd, J. J. (1992). Dynamic representations guiding adaptive behavior. In *Time, Action and Cognition: Towards Bridging the Gap*, ed. F. Macar, V. Pouthas & W. J. Friedman, pp. 309–23. Dordrecht: Kluwer Academic Publishers.

Gigerenzer, G. (1996). Rationality: Why social context matters. In *Interactive Minds: Life-span Perspectives on the Social Foundations of Cognition*, ed. P. B. Baltes & U. Staudinger, pp. 319–46. Cambridge: Cambridge University Press.

Gigerenzer, G. & Murray, J. L. (1987). *Cognition as Intuitive Statistics*. Hillsdale, NJ: Lawrence Erlbaum Associates.

Gould, S. J. (1989). *Wonderful Life*. New York: Norton.

Guilford, T. & Dawkins, M. S. (1991). Receiver psychology and the evolution of animal signals. *Animal Behavior*, 42, 1–14.

Hamilton, W. D., Axelrod, R. & Tanese, R. (1990). Sexual reproduction as an adaptation to resist parasites: A review. *Proceedings of the National Academy of Sciences of the U.S.A.*, 87, 3566–73.

Hogarth, R. M. & Kunreuther, H. C. (1989). Risk, ambiguity, and insurance. *Journal of Risk and Uncertainty*, 2, 5–35.

Hrdy, S. B. (1981). *The Woman That Never Evolved*. Cambridge, MA: Harvard University Press.

Humphrey, N. (1976). The social function of intellect. In *Growing Points in Ethology*, ed. P. P. G. Bateson & R. A. Hinde, pp. 303–17. Cambridge: Cambridge University Press.

Humphries, D. A. & Driver, P. M. (1970). Protean defense by prey animals. *Oecologia*, 5, 285–302.

Hurst, L. D. (1992). Intragenomic conflict as an evolutionary force. *Proceedings of the Royal Society of London, Series B*, 248, 135–40.

Huxley, J. (1966). A discussion of ritualisation of behaviour in animals and man: Introduction. *Philosophical Transactions of the Royal Society of London, Series B*, 251, 247–71.

Isaacs, R. (1965). *Differential Games*. New York: John Wiley.

Kahneman, D. & Tversky, A. (1972). Subjective probability: A judgment of representativeness. *Cognitive Psychology*, 3, 430–54.

Kirkpatrick, M. (1987). The evolutionary forces acting on female preferences in polygynous animals. In *Sexual Selection: Testing the Alternatives*, ed. J. W. Bradbury & M. B. Andersson, pp. 67–82. New York: John Wiley.

Krebs, J. R. & Dawkins, R. (1984). Animal signals: Mindreading and manipulation. In *Behavioral Ecology: An Evolutionary Approach*, 2nd edn, ed. J. R. Krebs & N. B. Davies, pp. 380–402. Oxford: Blackwell Scientific.

Krebs, J. R. & Davies, N. B. (1987). *An Introduction to Behavioral Ecology*, 2nd edn. Oxford: Blackwell Scientific Publications.

Kruger, L., Gigerenzer, G. & Morgan, M. S. (eds) (1987). *The Probabilistic Revolution*. Vol. 2. *Ideas in the Sciences*. Cambridge, MA: MIT Press.

Leslie, A. (1994). ToMM, ToBY, and Agency: Core architecture and domain specificity. In *Mapping the Mind: Domain Specificity in Cognition and Culture*, ed. L. A. Hirschfeld & S. A. Gelman, pp. 119–48. Cambridge: Cambridge University Press.

Lopes, L. L. & Oden, G. C. (1987). Distinguishing between random and nonrandom events. *Journal of Experimental Psychology: Learning, Memory, and Cognition*, 13, 392–400.

Martindale, C. (1990). *The Clockwork Muse*. New York: Harper Collins.

May, M. (1991). Aerial defense tactics of flying insects. *American Scientist*, 79, 316–28.

Maynard Smith, J. (1982). *Evolution and the Theory of Games*. Cambridge, Cambridge University Press.

Miller, G. A. & Frick, F. C. (1949). Statistical behavioristics and sequences of responses. *Psychological Review*, 56, 311–24.

Miller, G. F. (1993). Evolution of the Human Brain Through Runaway Sexual Selection: The Mind as a Protean Courtship Device. Ph.D. thesis, Stanford University Psychology Department. (Available through UMI microfilms.)

Miller, G. F. (1994a). Exploiting mate choice in evolutionary computation: Sexual selection as a process of search, optimization, and diversification. In *Evolutionary Computing: Proceedings of the 1994 Artificial Intelligence and Simulation of Behavior (AISB) Society Workshop*, ed. T. C. Fogarty, pp. 65–79. Berlin: Springer-Verlag.

Miller, G. F. (1994b). Beyond shared fate: Group-selected mechanisms for cooperation and competition in fuzzy, fluid vehicles. *Behavioral and Brain Sciences*, 17, 630–1.

Miller, G. F. & Cliff, D. (1994a). Co-evolution of Pursuit and Evasion: Biological and Game-theoretic Foundations. Cognitive Science Research Paper CSRP-311, University of Sussex.

Miller, G. F. & Cliff, D. (1994b). Protean behavior in dynamic games: Arguments for the co-evolution of pursuit-evasion tactics in simulated robots. In *From Animals to Animats 3: Proceedings of the Third International Conference on Simulation of Adaptive Behavior*, ed. D. Cliff, P. Husbands, J. A. Meyer, & S. Wilson, pp. 411–20. Cambridge, MA: MIT Press/Bradford Books.

Miller, G. F. & Freyd, J. J. (1993). Dynamic Mental Representations of Animate Motion: The Interplay Among Evolutionary, Cognitive, and Behavioral Dynamics. Cognitive Science Research Paper CSRP-290, University of Sussex.

Miller, G. F. & Todd, P. M. (1993). Evolutionary wanderlust: Sexual selection with directional mate preferences. In *From Animals to Animats 2: Proceedings of the Second International Conference on Simulation of Adaptive Behavior*, ed. J.-A. Meyer, H. L. Roitblat & S. W. Wilson, pp. 21–30. Cambridge, MA: MIT Press.

Miller, G. F. & Todd, P. M. (1995). The role of mate choice in biocomputation: Sexual selection as a process of search, optimization, and diversification. In *Evolution and Biocomputation: Computational Models of Evolution*, ed. W. Banzaf & F. H. Eeckman, pp. 169–204. Berlin: Springer-Verlag.

Morgan, C. L. (1888). Natural selection and elimination. *Nature*, **August 16**, 370.

Neuringer, A. (1986). Can people behave 'randomly'? The role of feedback. *Journal of Experimental Psychology: General*, 115, 62–75.

Neuringer, A. & Voss, C. (1993). Approximating chaotic behavior. *Psychological Science*, 4, 113–9.

Nowak, M. A. (1990). Stochastic strategies in the prisoner's dilemma. *Theoretical Population Biology*, 47, 93–112.

Nowak, M. A. & Sigmund, K. (1992). Tit for tat in heterogenous populations. *Nature*, 355, 250–2.

Peterson, C. R. & Beach, L. R. (1967). Man as an intuitive statistician. *Psychological Bulletin*, 68, 29–46.

Podos, J., Peters, S., Rudnicky, T., Marler, P. & Nowicki, S. (1992). The organization of song repertoires in song sparrows: Themes and variations. *Ethology*, 90, 89–106.

Pomiankowski, A., Iwasa, Y. & Nee, S. (1991). The evolution of costly mate preferences. I. Fisher and biased mutation. *Evolution*, 45, 1422–30.

Premack, D. (1990). The infant's theory of self-propelled objects. *Cognition*, 36, 1–16.

Rapoport, A. & Budescu, D. V. (1992). Generation of random series in two-person strictly competitive games. *Journal of Experimental Psychology: General*, 121, 352–63.

Reichenbach, H. (1934/1949). *The Theory of Probability*. Translated by E. Hutten & M. Reichenbach. Berkeley, CA: University of California Press. (First published in German in 1934).

Ridley, M. (1993). *The Red Queen: Sex and the Evolution of Human Nature*. London: Viking.

Roeder, K. D. (1962). The behavior of free-flying moths in the presence of artificial ultrasonic pulses. *Animal Behavior*, 10, 300–4.

Roeder, K. D. & Treat, A. E. (1961). The detection and evasion of bats by moths. *American Scientist*, 49, 135–48.

Ryan, M. J. (1990). Sexual selection, sensory systems, and sensory exploitation. *Oxford Surveys of Evolutionary Biology*, 7, 156–95.

Sapolsky, R. (1994). *Why Zebras Don't Get Ulcers: A Guide to Stress, Stress-Related Diseases, and Coping*. San Francisco, CA: W. H. Freeman.

Seligman, M. (1975). *Helplessness: On Depression, Development, and Death*. San Francisco, CA: W. H. Freeman.

Skinner, B. F. (1974). *About Behaviorism*. New York: Alfred A. Knopf.

Small, M. (1993). *Female Choices: Sexual Behavior of Female Primates*. Ithaca, NY: Cornell University Press.

Tooby, J. & Cosmides, L. (1993). The evolutionary psychology of coalitional aggression. Paper presented at the Fifth Annual Meeting of the Human Behavior and Evolutionary Society, Binghampton University, NY, August 4–8, 1993.

Todd, P. M. & Miller, G. F. (1993). Parental guidance suggested: How parental imprinting evolves through sexual selection as an adaptive learning mechanism. *Adaptive Behavior*, 2 , 5–47.

Treisman, M. & Faulkner, A. (1987). Generation of random sequences by human subjects: Cognitive operations or psychological process? *Journal of Experimental Psychology: General*, 116, 337–55.

Trivers, R. (1985). *Social Evolution*. Menlo Park, CA: Benjamin/Cummings.

Tune, G. S. (1964). Response tendencies: A review of some relevant literature. *Psychological Bulletin*, 61, 286–302.

Von Neumann, J. & Morgenstern, O. (1944). *Theory of Games and Economic Behavior*. Princeton, NJ: Princeton University Press.

Wagenaar, W. A. (1972). Generation of random sequences by human subjects: A critical survey of literature. *Psychological Bulletin*, 77, 65–72.

Wallace, A. R. (1870). *Contributions to the Theory of Natural Selection*. London: Macmillan.

Wallace, A. R. (1889) *Darwinism: An Exposition of the Theory of Natural Selection, with Some of its Applications*. London: Macmillan.

Whiten, A. & Byrne, R. (1988). Tactical deception in primates. *Behavioral and Brain Sciences*, 11, 233–73.

Wilson, D. S. (1994). Adaptive genetic variation and human evolutionary psychology. *Ethology and Sociobiology*, 15, 219–35.

Wilson, D. S. & Sober, E. (1994). Re-introducing group selection to the human behavioral sciences. *Behavioral and Brain Sciences*, 17, 585–654.

Yavin, Y. & Pachter, M. (eds) (1987). *Pursuit-evasion Differential Games*. Amsterdam: Pergamon Press.

Zahavi, A. (1975). Mate selection – a selection of handicap. *Journal of Theoretical Biology*, 53, 205–14.

Zahavi, A. (1991). On the definition of sexual selection, Fisher's model, and the evolution of waste and of signals in general. *Animal Behavior*, 42, 501–3.

Zuckerman, M. (1984). Sensation seeking: A comparative approach to a human trait. *Behavioral and Brain Sciences*, 7, 413–71.

13 Egalitarian behaviour and the evolution of political intelligence

CHRISTOPHER BOEHM

The puzzle of egalitarian society

The common ancestor of humans and the African great apes was a non-monogamous ape, one that lived in a closed social network and exhibited hostile relations between groups with stalking and killing of conspecifics by males. Wrangham (1987) deduced these ancient traits conservatively by tallying behaviours that humans share with all three African apes. However, the presence or absence of social dominance hierarchy was left in abeyance – even though hierarchies are all too apparent in chimpanzees, gorillas, bonobos, and Neolithic and modern humans. The problem, presumably, was that human foragers, being egalitarian, have been taken to exist without any significant hierarchy; this erroneous assumption has seriously confused the assessment of our own political nature.

More recently, Knauft (1991) has likened our political evolution to a 'U-shaped curve'. He does assume our common ancestor lived hierarchically, but points out that this approach to social life disappeared for a long span of evolutionary time until it returned with chiefdoms, civilisation and modern nations. Focusing on the 'simple-foragers' in whose bands evolved the genes we now carry, Knauft characterises them as largely lacking hierarchy in the form of dominance relations or stratification among the males, and as exhibiting little or no leadership and very low levels of inter-group violence.

Recent work of my own (Boehm, 1993) has questioned the first of these assumptions. I have suggested that among foragers hierarchical behaviour did not actually disappear but rather it assumed a radically different form. The hypothesis, tested successfully against a large number of world societies, was that the direction of domination was redirected so that the group as a whole kept its alpha-male types firmly under its thumb, instead of *vice versa*. Thus, humans did not lose the great ape dispositions to dominance behaviour (see Boehm 1982, 1984), but rather as nomadic prehistoric foragers they put them to a very different use, a pattern continued by the sedentary, tribal egalitarians who emerged with agriculture. By examining a large sample of extant foragers and tribesmen, I have documented that moral sanctioning is the specific vehicle for keeping dominance tendencies neutralised (Boehm, 1993), and this ability of subordinates to influence the degree of hierarchy in their groups has been aptly characterised as 'counter-domination' (Erdal & Whiten, 1994; see also Erdal & Whiten, 1996). I emphasise that foragers' suppression of individualistic, hierarchy-forming tendencies is essentially conscious and deliberate; it is just one of many possible expressions of human political intelligence.

Political intelligence can be defined as the decision-making capacity that enables social animals to further their self-interest in situations that involve rivalry and questions of power and leadership. Many species act mainly as individuals (e.g. Schelderup-Ebbe, 1922); bluffing, backed up by fighting, is the tool of the confidently ambitious, while flight, deference and gestures of appeasement are the tools of the fearful subordinate. In various species the result can be either a non-linear dominance order or a linear one, with an alpha male or female on top (see Bernstein & Gordon, 1974). For humans, I shall explore the poorly understood evolutionary transition from hierarchy to equality by comparing the political intelligence and behavioural dispositions of egalitarian humans with those of *Pan troglodytes*. In this instance chimpanzees serve as a particularly useful (if referential) proxy for our common ancestor because of their exceptionally well-studied coalition behaviour.

Chimpanzee politics

Chimpanzees learn about power by watching adults, and through play that is largely social and agonistic (Goodall, 1986): young chimpanzees sharpen their fighting and bluffing skills as they learn to inhibit their aggressive behaviour within the group. Such 'training' stimulates the growth of 'political IQ', and it is heavily involved with innate dispositions for dominance and submission. Years of practice prepare adults to be politically fluent in behaviours such as bluff, threat, attack, defence, avoidance and appeasement. The result is a territorial community in which the females have rough dominance rankings but males have a predictably linear hierarchy that regulates access to mating opportunities, desirable food sources, and position during travel, and provides leadership roles on patrol and in resolving conflicts (Nishida, 1979; Goodall 1986).

Wild chimpanzees live in male hierarchies that can be determined by studying the emission of pant-grunts by subordinates (Goodall, 1986). These submissive signals are uni-directional for any stable adult male dyad, and are used by all adult females greeting adult males. If neither male uses this greeting, the two are engaged in a dominance instability. Such a contest can be protracted, and it ends only when one party decides to enter into a subordinate role by pant-grunting, or dies. As with humans who live in stratified societies with strong leaders, chimpanzees work politically as individuals but also in small groups: they form political coalitions that compete for privileged access to resources or power. De Waal's (1982, 1992) pioneering work on captive chimpanzees at Arnhem Zoo provides a psychologically convincing description of their political machinations as they vie for higher rank and more breeding partners.

Acoustically the pant-grunt is a bi-directional rough-sounding vocalisation that can escalate, along a continuum, from a quiet, barely-voiced grunting sound to a much louder rasping pant-bark, or to a high-pitched pant-scream. A pant-scream carries with it a high fear component, but even so the subordinate is desisting from flight and trying to greet his superior. The latter's level of arousal can be read by an observer attentive to hair erection, direction of attention, facial expression and postural components of display or impending attack. On the subordinate's part, there is an array of submissive gestures, postures and facial expressions that combine with sleeking of the hair to communicate submission and appeasement. An alternative tactic is avoidance, and at Gombe I have seen subordinates making risky leaps from the top of one tree to the lower branches of another to save themselves from active attacks. Subordinates tend to scream continuously when under attack.

Individuals engaged in dominating seldom vocalise, but they erect their hair, assume postures that can be read as being aggressive, often display and sometimes attack. At close range they also may use a soft-cough as a mild warning that seems to be equivalent to the arm-threat, and occasionally they use the waa-bark as a long-range warning from their position of dominance. Many dominance interactions are determined by 'shorthand', as it were. The dominant individual merely erects hair or stands up bristling, and an adequate message has been sent. Chimpanzee political intelligence includes the sending and reading of highly nuanced signals.

The usual result of these behaviours is a stable linear male hierarchy with an alpha individual having clear-cut pre-eminence over the others. However, there are always young males trying to move up through the hierarchy, and they create instabilities as they advance. Some males are very good at playing the political game; others seem less able, or less motivated (Goodall, 1990). De Waal's (1982) captive data correlate with what is observed in the wild, with one major exception. Wild females forage alone or often with just one or two companions, fail to develop coalition partners, and are not major players in the male quest for power. Confined to a small piece of real estate, de Waal's captive females exhibit far more involvement. However, an alpha female ran the group at first, when there were no adult males, and subsequently the Arnhem Zoo females banded together to keep the alpha male they preferred in place. Such long-term control by a coalition of individually subordinate females has not been reported in the wild.

A solo male chimpanzee cannot compete for rank very effectively, for his competitors work through expedient power-coalitions. They do so on a basis that de Waal (1982) has called 'Machiavellian' because of similarities to cleverly expedient power-seeking in our own species. However, chimpanzee applications of power are not entirely competitive. One fascinating use of power is the quelling of disputes and active fights (see Boehm, 1992), and there is also reconciliation and reassurance behaviour (de Waal, 1989).

In a typical power-intervention the alpha male displays toward the protagonists, scatters them, then sits ready to intervene again. However, a variety of substrategies and tactics may be used, and some minor conflicts are controlled just by vocalisations. In serious conflicts as many as three males have been reported to collaborate in breaking up a fight, and a Gombe intervenor may successively threaten each protagonist individually, directing his threats so as to move them away from each other (Boehm, 1994a). Other tactics are also used. I personally observed the number two male prying apart two adolescent combatants who were grappling and fighting with biting, and once a female was observed to remove an object, to be used in an impending display, from the hand of a male (J. Goodall, personal communication). After decades of research at Gombe there are just these two incidents, but the same behaviours are observed frequently at Arnhem (de Waal, 1982). We are obviously dealing with a complicated, flexible and potentially innovative political intelligence here.

Large-group coalitions in the wild

Chimpanzee power-coalitions are not limited just to groups of two or three males seeking better positions. Elsewhere (Boehm, 1992) I have described how wild chimpanzees also form coalitions of all the males. They do this regularly to go on patrols to exploit the resources of strangers, protect their own resources, attack and kill neighbouring males or females with infants, acquire females ready to breed, and bluff against enemy patrols. Chimpanzees also go hunting as groups that collaborate in capturing and sharing prey (Goodall, 1986), and this can be taken as 'political' behaviour insofar as bush pigs, male colobus and male baboons actively defend their groups. Likewise, chimpanzees occasionally mob or even attack predators such as leopards, as observed by Byrne & Byrne (1988; see also Boesch, 1991). At Gombe, we have 8 mm video footage of a large python being 'mobbed' by watchful chimpanzees. To drive it away, they issued alarm calls whenever it moved and engaged in branching displays. All of these behaviours involve calculations of power.

To a field observer, an established alpha male seems a despot of sorts. However, this is far from being true in human terms. Our despots not only take a lion's share of resources, but execute their own policies by mobilising the entire group for action whether people like it or not. Those who disobey may be fined, killed, tortured, or otherwise punished because the despot has abundant coercive force at hand. A chimpanzee alpha male does gain special access to resources by means of threat or application of force, and he enjoys a similarly intimidating role. However, he lacks soldiers and policemen and he cannot impose his own decisions on the group coercively when it comes to collective activities such as going on patrol, hunting, or mobbing predators.

If the entire group wants to be led, the alpha male definitely can influence its behaviour. In a 'group decision' videotaped at Gombe by field assistant Yahaya Almasi, an enemy group spotted the study-group's patrol first and began to vocalise hostilely, at a distance (Boehm, 1994a; see also Boehm, 1991). The study-group males were not all present and they were indecisive, showing both fear and some tendency to respond aggressively. As the alpha male moved forward and tensely scanned the valley other males directed their attention toward him and *vice versa*. Finally, alpha male Goblin took the lead in displaying across the hillside and vocalising, and the rest instantly followed suit. As will be seen, the ability of an entire group to reach unanimous political decisions will figure heavily in the evolutionary explanation of egalitarian society.

The power of subordinates

In many primate species subordinates have substantial power. At first blush a well-established chimpanzee alpha male dominates his group decisively. His routine intimidation displays are directed at all, and a chorus of screams is emitted as subordinates rapidly climb trees. However, having gained a safe distance they are prone to issue hostile waa-barks of protest. Fear gears them to submit or to avoid, but defiance leads them to protest vocally as individuals and in certain contexts they become actively defiant.

Coalitions of subordinate males regularly try to unseat the alpha male, and there is also an important unique observation from Gombe. When Wilkie displaced Goblin as alpha male, Goblin, largely recovered from serious wounds, returned to make his political comeback. A very large coalition of adolescent/young adult males ganged up on the former alpha and drove him away (J. Goodall, personal communication). This one-time behaviour in the wild also has a parallel at Arnhem, where the large coalition of captive *females* regularly manipulates the male hierarchy (de Waal, 1982).

Individual subordinates also appear to 'control' dominants in certain limited contexts, as when reproductively available females gain a favoured position in meat-sharing groups (see Stanford *et al.*, 1994) or a low-ranking adult male makes a solo kill and this is not expropriated (Goodall, 1986). However, the main route to political power for a subordinate is to enter into a small coalition directed at unseating the alpha male.

It appears, then, that subordinates may sometimes control those who would otherwise dominate them if their immediate motivation is exceptional or if they can find safety in numbers. I shall suggest that such aggressive types of subordinate behaviour, some of which are assumed to be present also in the common ancestor of chimpanzees and humans, constituted a pre-adaptation for the emergence of human foragers with their egalitarian approach to political life. In explaining the human potential for egalitarian behaviour, tendencies to form subordinate coalitions will receive special attention.

Human societies of 'equals'

Human foragers living in nomadic bands are always egalitarian, and so are the non-foraging people that anthropologists refer to as 'tribesmen' (Sahlins, 1968; see also Evans-Pritchard, 1940; Bohannan, 1954). Egalitarian societies have been formally defined along dimensions of ranking (Fried, 1967) and leadership (Middleton & Tait, 1958; Service, 1962, 1975). There are no social classes, nor even any very pronounced differences of rank, and very weak leadership is joined with a consensual mode of making group decisions. Relations between males seem to be far more co-operative and cordial than competitive and agonistic. Earlier descriptions probably over-emphasised absence of strong leadership or ranking, and the degree of co-operativeness, and tended to downplay aggressiveness in general. This stereotype has been revised (e.g. Lee, 1979; Knauft, 1991), and it is recognised that homicide rates among foragers are quite high by human standards.

If all humans were egalitarian, we could hypothesise that chimpanzee nature and human nature were very different, indeed. However, Kummer (1971) and Knauft (1991) have pointed out the similarity between modern human social and political forms and those of primates that live in pronounced social dominance hierarchies. By contrast, human egalitarian societies seem totally different. This inconsistency has intrigued anthropologists. Most investigations of forager egalitarianism have noted that there exists an egalitarian ethos, a distinctive set of values that extols equality of adults or adult males. However, they then proceed to attribute egalitarian behaviour to 'levelling mechanisms,' conceived as social or ecological forces that automatically reduce hierarchy (see Fried, 1967). Social factors include sharing of large-game meat or an unstable group composition that works against hierarchy; natural factors include dispersed resources that promote nomadic movement (see Boehm, 1993).

There are two problems with such explanations. One is that anthropologists, hesitant to tackle the issue of human nature, seldom ask why levelling mechanisms are necessary in the first place. The second problem is that human intentions are left out of the picture.

Intentional levelling

In the interest of finding a single causal explanation for all egalitarian societies, I surveyed hundreds of reports of egalitarian societies to look for any mechanism they might all share. My working hypothesis was that egalitarian behaviour could be the result of intentional and vigilant policing of alpha types by the entire group, and that moral sanctioning was instrumental in keeping pronounced male hierarchies from forming (Boehm, 1993).

This hypothesis had two important implications. Firstly, if confirmed, it would demonstrate that the main causal forces that held egalitarian societies in place were not mainly ecological, demographic, or social-structural, but *intentional*. Secondly, and more fundamentally, it would demonstrate that powerful forces were still working to promote the growth of hierarchy in modern *Homo sapiens*. Otherwise, such vigilant policing by subordinates would not be necessary.

The specific findings were that a range of deliberate sanctions were being applied to individuals (including leaders) who became too competitive or dominating or tried to gain some real authority. At the core of this explanation was social control: political upstarts, if they were not kept in line simply by fear of gossip, were criticised, ridiculed, ostracised, exiled, or even executed if they managed to achieve substantial domination through intimidating others one at a time (Boehm 1993). If they were leaders, they could also be deposed or deserted.

Thus, while an egalitarian society in equilibrium may give the *impression* that the males are equal because human nature, itself, is egalitarian, my hypothesis goes in quite another direction. Human nature, similarly to chimpanzee nature, is heavily disposed to status rivalry and domination as well as co-operation (Boehm, 1984), and without some very *decisive* 'counter-domination' (defined below) by the entire group, ranking and dominant leadership are likely to assert themselves to produce an orthodox dominance hierarchy with substantial power at the top.

My research demonstrated that hierarchical forces were far from absent, but that significant power was being exerted from the bottom up in a way that kept hierarchical tendencies neutralised in many areas. Rather than an alpha male dominating his group as subordinates, the subordinates were keeping their would-be alpha males under their thumbs. Because dominant force or the threat thereof is used very consistently by small human groups when they act collectively as moral communities, one might view the resulting societal arrangement to be a 'reverse dominance hierarchy'. I say this because dominance is being routinely but decisively neutralised through counter-domination behaviour; this is possible because the subordinates are able to definitively hold down the potential dominators in their midst (see Boehm 1993, 1994b).

I emphasise this point because Erdal & Whiten (1994, 1996), in spite of many convergences in our thinking, have taken issue with my use of the term 'reverse dominance hierarchy'. They hold that counter-domination merely keeps orthodox dominance tendencies at an incipient level insofar as leaders are still recognised and used by bands.

I find Erdal & Whiten's (1994, 1996) notion of 'counter-domination' quite useful; indeed, it applies to forces that are also found in virtually every non-egalitarian human society from chiefdoms to nations: an abusive leader will always stir resentment, and often those beneath him can exert some control or depose him. However, at the same time these societies expect and tolerate – or welcome – substantial authority on the parts of leaders, allow leaders to make decisions independently of group consensus meetings, and fail to define their leaders as 'firsts-among-equals'. These are orthodox dominance hierarchies. By contrast, egalitarian bands and tribes see to it that the authority of leaders does not develop beyond a critical bare minimum, insist on making their decisions as entire groups with leaders as mere facilitators, and make a point of not granting leaders or other over-achievers a formal political status that is other than 'equal'. For me, this is a difference of kind that deserves typological recognition.

Erdal and Whiten seem to view egalitarian society more as a mere end-point on a political continuum, and an empirical continuum of sorts does, indeed, exist as one looks from bands to tribes to chiefdoms to primitive kingdoms. However, I see 'egalitarian society' as meriting a political type unto itself because the group's moral authority so dominantly manipulates its ablest and most aggressive individuals, and particularly because it is distinguished by an egalitarian ethos. Perhaps 'neutralised dominance hierarchy' would incorporate both of our interpretations (see Boehm, 1995) so long as it is agreed that the subordinates are firmly in charge and are guided by an egalitarian ideology.

Leaving typologies aside, with respect to the facts, Erdal & Whiten's (1996) extensive survey of 24 band-level societies goes far beyond the modest but representative coverage of band-level societies in Boehm (1993), and corroboratively shows informal leadership, absence of authority and counter-dominance to be as widely reported among foragers as it is among tribesmen.

The critical role of social scale

It is a puzzle that apparently human groups began to form 'orthodox', ape-like hierarchies only after the invention of agriculture. Changes in the gene pool were unlikely to have triggered this very rapid transition, and anthropologists (e.g. Service, 1975) are not certain exactly how it took place. However, I can at least suggest why egalitarian society seems to have stayed in place as long as human nomads continued their foraging way of life, and why egalitarianism continued in much the same form after sedentary tribal groups arose with the domestication of plants and animals.

The key lies in social scale and its effect on political dynamics. It is characteristic of egalitarian societies that leadership is kept weak deliberately, and an unintended effect is that decisive, authoritative conflict intervention (such as that found among chimpanzees or in human chiefdoms) is absent. As a result, when there is a really serious conflict within an egalitarian band or tribe the unit quickly splits (see von Furer-Haimendorf, 1968). One cause of conflict is male jealousy over women, and another is factional tendencies.

As small human communities grow to a certain size they stop behaving like a single 'family' and develop factions (e.g. Chagnon, 1983). Decisive factionalisation interferes with finding a moral consensus, for members of factions tend to back their own people. Furthermore, the stronger faction tends to take over group leadership. This interferes, obviously, with the vigilant maintenance of an egalitarian order because the group is no longer in a position to unite and moralistically block the moves of a political upstart. What enables an egalitarian system to stay in place, mechanically, is the fact that when group size reaches the critical mass for factions to develop, the group quickly splits because of interfactional quarrels. Otherwise, the more powerful faction can dominate and the egalitarian order becomes compromised.

It was probably a combination of factors that finally led egalitarians to compromise their ideals and countenance strong, hereditary chiefs. One may have been sedentarisation with the greater population density it brought. Another was a practical attachment to land being cultivated, which made fissioning more costly. Another may have been the resulting intensive territorial warfare, for allowing a group to fission weakens its ability to resist enemies. All of these factors could have led to the strengthening of the hands of leaders who were trying to resolve conflicts in order to keep the group together. Another factor could have been special personal characteristics of leaders who were able to assume some real authority – without taking the bit into their teeth and stirring counter-domination tendencies.

Chiefdoms

In egalitarian societies even though a weak leader helps to facilitate group consensus, such a process can fail. If it does, the band simply reconstitutes itself or melts into other groups. With chiefdoms leadership becomes significantly authoritative, and hereditary within certain higher-ranking clans (see Service, 1975). This is not to say that the power of leaders becomes absolute. Potentially, counter-domination by subordinates plays a part in all human societies (Boehm, 1993). A legitimately very strong chief who (as locally defined) severely abuses his power can be overthrown, or executed. Kings (in non-literate kingdoms) are more difficult to sanction with professional soldiers to back them, but revolts are still possible. Modern democracies keep in place institutionalised methods of impeachment, and even in totalitarian societies there is some possibility of rebellion or assassination.

Egalitarians not only define virtually any use of authority outside the family as morally illegitimate, but philosophically they define political relations among adults, or at least among the adult (often, male) household heads, as being 'equal'. This refers to exerting authority or control, and more generally to trying to place yourself above another. However, such groups do recognise individuals of merit, and they actually encourage individual competition in certain areas such as hunting (Balikci, 1970), or tribal warfare (Chagnon, 1983). They often have a recognised 'group leader', and accord him (or her) a special status so long as there is no arrogation of power.

In spite of such vigilance, egalitarian followers do occasionally lose control of their would-be alpha types, as when powerful shamans manage to intimidate and control their groups (see Boehm, 1993). There are examples of dominant upstarts being executed on various continents, so this seems to be a general if rare phenomenon. It may well be that one way to develop a chiefdom is to experience a domination episode in which a newly powerful leader turns his power to the common good, or somehow avoids being sanctioned, and manages to found a dynasty by inspiring a judicious mixture of respect and fear (see also Service, 1975).

Could chimpanzees create an egalitarian society?

Under present environmental conditions, it seems unlikely that wild chimpanzees could decisively neutralise their own hierarchical tendencies on a long term and orderly basis as human egalitarians do. However, one can consider wild chimpanzees' coalition behaviour as a model for pre-adaptations likely to have been present in the mutual ancestor. This potential has been used consistently in captivity by females to control the alpha male in important respects, and in the wild, ephemerally, to keep the former alpha male from reasserting his dominance. However, to institutionalise a definitive ascendancy of subordinates over dominants, a moral community may be necessary. This provides a verbal definition of undesirable behaviours, a communication network that constantly tracks people's behaviour, a tradition of sanctioning deviants, including political deviants, and a group able to make its decisions collectively.

Certain monkeys appear to make collective decisions (e.g. Kummer, 1971; Boehm, 1978) as do chimpanzees (see Boehm, 1991). However, there is no evidence for a consensus process similar to that of humans, by which the majority pressures dissenters to go along with the group. To achieve such unity requires vigorous persuasion and sometimes political arm-twisting (Boehm, 1993). The result is a group that makes a habit of arriving at and executing a common policy, and such a group is in a position to regularly keep the politically ambitious in line.

The subordinate adults of a chimpanzee community appear to resent the intimidation displays of the alpha male, and purely in terms of *motive* this is surely an important pre-adaptation (see also Boehm 1982, 1984). Other behaviours that feed into what Erdal & Whiten (1994, pp. 177) have referred to as 'counter-domination', what Knauft (1994, pp. 182) refers to as an 'aversion to subordination', and I refer to as 'ambivalence over submission because dominance tends to be more satisfying' (Boehm, 1994b, pp. 179), have been detailed by Erdal & Whiten (1996). However, when it comes to coupling such negative affects with deeds, the compelling chimpanzee political tendency is for males in the wild to compete *individualistically*, either as individuals or in small coalitions, for higher personal rank. Another practical problem is that their fission–fusion communities usually remain quite dispersed, and chimpanzee victims of domination cannot communicate specifically enough to tell other group members about what has transpired in a temporarily isolated subgroup. The group has no way to pool its information, and the same can be said of our prelinguistic common ancestor. Neither developed a moral community.

The moral community and its political functions

It would be easy just to say that language made possible the development of egalitarian society, for a human type of communication made feasible both the definition of a preferred political order, and the tracking of political deviants so that they could not freely intimidate group members when they were alone. However, there is a profound difference between humans with their collectively arrived at moral codes and chimpanzees with their far more individualised reactions to group life.

A human moral community amounts to a strongly latent coalition of the entire group, which actively unites to deal with deviants. The sanctions it exerts are powerful enough to call such behaviour 'political' whether the deviance itself consists of incest, thievery, being too aggressive, or being politically ambitious. A group of wild chimpanzees may form a very large coalition to episodically banish a former alpha male, or captives may continuously deny some of the alpha's power. By contrast, with humans morality unifies the group on a long-term basis so that alpha domination is terminated definitively.

Members of this moralistic coalition are ever-watchful; they gossip constantly, and they stand ready to sanction a whole range of behaviours ranging from transgressions against the gods to political upstartism. In effect, such coalitions tend to remain activated because deviance-prone individuals are often pushing the moral envelope. As a result of this recurrent tension all humans have moral values (see Kluckhohn, 1952), and they develop distinctive local themes that amount to an 'ethos' (see Kroeber, 1948). It is the egalitarian ethos that defines all of the household heads in a small group to be equal as political actors, and in effect provides a political charter for the social architecture of the group.

Elsewhere (Boehm, 1982), I have constructed a scenario for prehistoric political evolution that suggests that the moral community was a necessary prerequisite for the emergence of egalitarian bands. It was needed because otherwise tendencies to form either small, individualistic coalitions or large, mutually hostile factions would have precluded the kind of concerted group action that is needed to definitively neutralise male hierarchy. The conclusion was that the moral community had to appear first, before the egalitarian political order, and that it arose as a response to social problems such as incest, murder, lying, cheating, stealing, or whatever.

Here I suggest an alternative scenario. It is possible that the very first social problem that led a human group to coalesce as a moral community was actually that of alpha-male domination, and that when the rank-and-file unanimously branded their too-dominating top male as a social undesirable, group-morality (as I have defined it, largely following Durkheim, 1933) was invented. The question remains, as to the degree of communication skill that was needed for such political dynamics to come into play. The accomplishments of the female chimpanzees at Arnhem Zoo suggest that we should not set the threshold too high.

Political intelligence

A more direct comparison of chimpanzee and human capacities for making political calculations will be useful at this point. Decisions are an important interface between genotype and phenotype (Pulliam & Dunford, 1980) and this applies to social behaviour. Political intelligence evolves through decisions about whether to try to dominate or submit, and both relate directly to reproductive success. Dominators tend to control reproductive resources, while those who inexpediently fail to submit may physically endanger themselves – or invest their energies to little point. At the individual level, chickens have the intellectual wherewithal to make such decisions. However, making decisions as coalitions is associated with unusually large brains and a high degree of sociality, such as that found in primates, dolphins and other highly social mammals (see Harcourt & de Waal, 1992).

The chimpanzee version of large-brained sociality involves a number of well described dominance-and-submission behaviours that involve triads or more. I have discussed competition for rank through small coalitions, conflict interventions, whole-group aggressive behaviours in the anti-predator and territorial fields, and a few rare instances of large-group coalitions directed by subordinates against dominant members of the same group. All of these behaviours involve making decisions as groups, and some of these decisions are quite complex. There is little doubt that chimpanzees, given different environments, would be capable of other variants of coalition behaviour, as well.

In terms of political intelligence, a chimpanzee must be particularly good at sizing up situations involving competition or agonism. This involves reading signals given by both superiors who may attack and others who may be useful as coalition partners. The political 'computations' become quite intricate. A wild group may have several coalitions competing simultaneously, and with fission–fusion social life they meet, compete and form small coalitions under a variety of circumstances. The concomitant calculations push chimpanzee political intelligence to its limits in natural situations, and they are likely to affect reproductive success.

The result is an animal that is capable of inventing unusual coalition behaviours. For example, while interventions in conflicts normally involve triads, sometimes two or three individuals join in the control role (Boehm, 1994a). At a still higher level, patrols of up to a dozen males make decisions about how to deal with other large patrols, and with smaller stranger-groups of varying sizes (Goodall, 1986; see also Boehm, 1991). Earlier, I raised the question of whether chimpanzees are capable of neutralising their own political hierarchies as humans do, by putting coalition behaviour to a novel and complicated long-term use. While this may be questionable, I believe that these political skills of apes provide a critically-needed pre-adaptive wherewithal for the decisive neutralisation of orthodox dominance hierarchy.

To explain the transition from alpha-male hierarchy in the common ancestor to decisive suppression of hierarchy by subordinates among human foragers, one needs among other things a political theory of mind, a theory of genotypic dispositions, and an understanding of how individual behavioural strategies ramify to create group social and political life. The political intelligence of humans living in egalitarian societies with their very effective collectivised counter-domination behaviour may be not too different from that of chimpanzees in certain basic ways. The dispositions to domination and subordination appear to be similar, as are tendencies for strong male leaders to emerge in groups and tendencies for subordinates to form coalitions. What humans do that chimpanzees do not do, is to create stable, permanent, whole-group anti-hierarchical coalitions that are actively held in place by a vigilantly defiant rank-and-file, people guided by a well-developed ideology. These *potential* subordinates act dominantly whenever necessary to suppress the power of politically ambitious males, and thereby decisively reverse the direction of domination. The result is an egalitarian society with its predictable and devastating use of ridicule, ostracism and execution as tools of counter-domination.

In comparing humans with chimpanzees as a referential model (see Tooby & DeVore, 1987) I have suggested that differences in group spatial distribution and composition, along with substantial differences in communication potential, play a part in making such counter-domination possible. I also have fixed on moral consensus as the cultural binder that makes a human coalition-of-the-whole-group so effective at heading off individual or subgroup dominance. The question arises, as to whether this last factor involves a vastly different kind of political intelligence than that possessed by wild chimpanzees.

Egalitarian foragers are guided by conscious and verbally articulated political strategies, for their ethos lays out the do's and the don'ts of exercising power. There is explicit praise of co-operativeness, modesty, and generosity, and sharp condemnation of over-aggressive behaviours that serve greed or intimidate or control others (Boehm, 1993). This amounts to a political compact that reflects the ambivalence in human nature that will be discussed presently, and participation involves a personal strategy. As a forager male, my chances of becoming alpha in my small band are 1 in 15, while my chances of being dominated by another male are 15 to 1. However, if I am willing to give up on the alpha possibility, then I can at least be certain that I will never be dominated. As long as the other political actors in the group agree with me, we can neutralise the social dominance hierarchy that would emerge otherwise. In effect, we move the locus of power to the whole group, and make our decisions by consensus because we have precluded strong leadership.

There exists a large literature on the sharing of meat among foragers, and early treatments tend to depict such sharing as though it were basically spontaneous and devoid of ambivalence. Erdal & Whiten (1994) have taken a more realistic position in their discussion of 'vigilant sharing' of large-game meat. In effect, group members make certain that the powerful, the greedy, and those prone to cheat do not make a mockery of a co-operative, uncentralised redistribution system that is well-supported by the egalitarian ethos.

In the political lifestyle that I have been discussing, in effect it is political power, not meat, that is being shared out equally. Among foragers, and among tribesmen as well, whenever necessary the rank-and-file neutralise their own personal political mobility in order to avoid domination, and they do so deliberately. Their political intelligence helps them to understand this system they have created, and to keep it going through the application of social pressure and sanctions. The fact that virtually every band-level society ever described by an ethnographer remains undominated by alpha types is a testimonial to their uncanny skills at social engineering.

Evolution of specific political dispositions

Many millennia of dealing with a new, hyper-co-operative type of political organisation changed not only the nature of political intelligence, but some of the specific behavioural dispositions that underlie that intelligence. We know for certain that humans have lost not only the long erectible hair of chimpanzees, but also genetically well set up dominance displays and specialised submissive vocalisations like those seen in chimpanzees and the other two African great apes.

Egalitarian political life changed the behavioural context of domination and submission behaviour within the foraging band so radically that we may assume the behavioural genotype was modified. I say so because surely egalitarian bands go back at least to the appearance of Cro-Magnons, and this would have allowed well over a thousand generations (see Wilson, 1975) for selection forces to act on whatever genes were involved. With subordinates in control, domination was exerted collectively, while individual submission was no longer directed at dominant individuals but, in effect, at the entire group. While dominance, submission and resentment of being dominated continued as general traits present in the common ancestor, this radical alteration in the structure of hierarchy surely had an impact on selection pressures that shaped these three basic dispositions. For one thing, it became less dangerous for subordinate types to express defiant hostility to those capable of dominating them, because they now had the security of numbers. For another, the rewards for being individualistically competitive and dominating one's fellows were reduced significantly because meat sharing was equalised, and because in many other contexts selfishly aggressive behaviour was punished by social sanctioning. Whereas criticism and ridicule produce stress and modify a deviant's behaviour, in a highly social species ostracism, exile and execution affect reproductive success far more directly.

In effect, if surely not in intention, people acting in groups were altering gene pools by singling out *individualistic* dominance behaviours that had been genetically rewarded in the past, and suppressing them quite decisively. However, they were still using dominance behaviour *collectively* in order to suppress it at the individual level. Tendencies to dominate, although surely modified, remained robust. This may help to explain why, after at least many dozens of millennia of egalitarian behaviour, the species was not constrained to remain egalitarian as group size and complexity increased.

When humans operate politically in smallish social groups larger than families, counter-dominant tendencies are very likely to result in an egalitarian political order. When social scale of local groups increases beyond the level of bands or small tribal segments, counter-domination does continue as a political force, but the local definition of legitimate authority becomes far more 'permissive' of authority. Eventually, this allows orthodox, ape-like hierarchies to form. This cultural transition was possible not because human nature is a blank slate, but because a flexible set of political dispositions combined with a formidable political intelligence. This allowed radically different political forms to emerge, depending on environmental circumstances as these affected the cultural definition of legitimate political authority. Modern democracy, with a strong and continuous exertion of counter-dominant behaviour that is rather similar to what takes place in bands and tribes, provides us with an interesting compromise between the two extremes of egalitarian control-from-below *versus* despotic domination-from-above.

Broader natural selection issues

Prehistoric egalitarian society evolved in a species that achieved high degrees of co-operation in policing deviants, in acquiring and sharing food, and in caring for one another (Boehm, 1982). Such co-operativeness has posed major explanatory problems for scientists who rely upon a 'Darwinian' individual-selectionist paradigm. 'Altruism' has become a kind of bogey-man, one that has stimulated explanations through inclusive fitness (see Wilson, 1975) or 'reciprocal altruism' (Trivers, 1971), but very seldom through 'group-selection'. Indeed, ever since Williams (1966) demonstrated the fallacy of assuming that obviously useful group functions were a product of group selection, individual selection theory (Lewontin, 1970) has reigned very aggressively (see Wilson & Sober, 1994).

The crux of Williams' attack was that individual selection effects are very robust, whereas group effects are, where they exist, very weak by comparison; subsequently, the consensus has been that all but impossibly high rates of group extinction are needed for such weak group effects to make a serious difference in supporting altruistic traits (Wilson, 1975). Alexander (1974) has suggested that human warfare might fulfill such extinction criteria, but it is difficult to estimate how long humans have been practicing intensive warfare. Recently, however, Wilson & Sober (1994) have more seriously challenged exclusive reliance on individual selectionist arguments. Here, I shall briefly suggest how the human egalitarian career could figure in group selection arguments (see also Boehm, 1996, for a more complete account).

It is individual variation within the group that helps to make individual effects so much more powerful than group effects, and of course it is individual variation at the *phenotypic* level that natural selection acts upon. What egalitarian behaviour does is to drastically lessen phenotypic differences among individuals who normally would be competing on a highly uneven basis. In particular, dietary protein and breeding partners are no longer 'monopolised' by alpha male types. The result is a drastic reduction of adaptively significant phenotypic variation among males and their households, and this gives a greater *relative* edge to group effects that support so-called 'altruistic' behaviours such as co-operation, sharing, or patriotic self-sacrifice.

The 'balance of power' between group and individual effects needs to be extensively 're-modelled' in the light of egalitarian political arrangements. Not only is there a drastic suppression of individual differences at the level of phenotype due to egalitarian sanctioning of upstarts, but consensual decisions of bands also serve to obliterate individual differences in foraging behaviour. The consensual approach to emergency decision-making also has the effect of amplifying the power of group-effects when different groups come to different coping decisions (Boehm, 1978; see also Boehm, 1996). In tandem, suppression of *individual* phenotypic variation and amplification of *group* phenotypic variation make for a significant shift in the division of labour between group and individual effects, a shift that makes it less difficult to explain co-operation and altruism.

Our ambivalent political nature

I do not think it is profitable to try to characterise human nature as being 'egalitarian' or 'despotic', or 'peaceful' or 'warlike', even though such labels make for lively debate. It is far more likely that our nature is many-faceted and internally contradictory, and that political behaviour often involves a trade-off between dispositions that work in opposition in certain contexts. The result is psychological ambivalence and flexible behavioural compromise in specifiable directions (e.g. Boehm, 1989, 1994b; see also Campbell, 1965). In exemplifying this general theory my examples have been ambivalence over killing neighbours in blood feuds

(Boehm, 1989) and ambivalences of chimpanzees and humans in following a subordinate role (Boehm, 1995). Erdal & Whiten (1994, 1996) have arrived at similar conclusions with respect to human dispositions that affected political evolution.

Like other primates, humans in a subordinate position have to set aside their dominant tendencies and submit (or avoid) because of fear, but such a response is not regulated by the neurological equivalent of an 'on–off' switch. With chimpanzees, we saw that individuals who readily submit to intimidation displays also exhibit and *communicate* feelings of defiance, while if an instability exists between two males you often see both of them screaming with fear even as they mutually try to intimidate each other (de Waal 1982). These are instances of psychological ambivalence – and behavioural compromise – that derive directly from conflict between genetic dispositions.

For people, one can describe finer nuances of such political ambivalence. The attraction of occupying a position of control that involves domination can be considerable, but the countervailing attractions of submission include freeing oneself from the stress of competition, being protected, and getting to identify with a powerful or charismatic leader. Thus, submission brings with it the positive rewards of followership but also, as with chimpanzees, resentment and a tendency toward defiance because being in control tends to bring greater rewards. When humans in small societies work to remain egalitarian, they are choosing to emphasise the defiant side of this ambivalence, the side that favours avoidance of domination. However, the outcome is rather complicated. In effect, they are setting aside individualistic domination, and submission as well, to opt for independence of action (e.g. Gardner, 1991) as a brilliant compromise. They stabilise this political compromise by collectively outlawing serious competition leading to domination among the local group's main political actors.

Conclusion

This analysis links egalitarian rule by subordinates among humans with coalition behaviour of chimpanzees, whose political intelligence involves a noteworthy potential when it comes to countering domination. Chimpanzees form power-coalitions of the entire community in a number of contexts, and they definitely possess the *potential* to do so in a way that controls the occupancy of the alpha role or manipulates its functions. Our formidable human political intelligence works with similar dispositions to dominance, submission and defiance, but it can more definitively reshape our social hierarchies to create novel socio-political forms that remain stable.

There are two profound differences between chimpanzees and humans in this area. One is the moral community, with its high degree of dependency upon cultural tradition and language. Moral communities make decisions about how they should live, and the effects on human life are pervasive because moral communities gossip and track everyone's behaviour. By contrast, for the most part the social order of chimpanzees is automatically organised by a social dominance hierarchy (see Goodall 1982). Morality makes a radically egalitarian outcome possible for humans because morality involves a permanent coalition of an entire watchful community. Morality and social control are inexorably inter-twined with politics, for the all-powerful moral community defines what is politically legitimate and applies its sanctions accordingly.

The second difference is that humans are able to conceive of and execute rather complicated political blueprints. Modern 'intentional communities' have received considerable attention (e.g. Wilson & Sober, 1994), and I have suggested that non-literate egalitarian societies are similarly intentional (Boehm 1993): on an informal basis, the egalitarian ethos of a band or tribal community makes it quite clear what kind of social life is desired ideally, and deliberate social sanctioning makes political reality approach the local ideal of individual autonomy and equality rather closely.

Chimpanzee political intelligence is keen, and particularly in the case of males it is oriented to achieving upward mobility. The underlying 'drive' is basically individualistic, but chimpanzees very readily form small coalitions to advance their personal interests co-operatively. The political intelligence of humans is still better adapted to co-operation, and because of our distinctive blend of cultural capacity and morality, foragers can actually think about and discuss the kind of social and political order they wish to live in. In this context, they form a coalition of the entire group to deliberately sanction deviants. For political behaviour this introduces the need for a substantial element of 'lower level teleology' in our explanations, be the subjects monkeys (Jolly, 1988), apes (Boehm, 1991), or humans (Boehm, 1978, 1996); I have focused heavily on intentions in this discussion precisely because humans manage to keep their bands and tribes egalitarian on a conscious basis, guided by the egalitarian ethos.

Egalitarian human foragers, with their impressive political intelligence and very small sovereign groups, were the first great political architects. So far, we have been unable to replicate their amazing achievements when we try to execute radically egalitarian blueprints as nations. However, in democracies we settle for a compromise in which effective counter-domination rather than 'total equality' is the realistic focus, and we do rather well at keeping that particular political compromise in place.

Acknowledgements

The author thanks Paul J. Bohannan, Donald T. Campbell, Andrei Simic and Andy Whiten for commenting on this chapter, and is grateful to the H. F. Guggenheim Foundation and the National Endowment for Humanities for grants that supported investigation of political egalitarianism.

References

Alexander, R. D. (1974). The evolution of social behavior. *Annual Review of Ecology and Systematics*, 5, 325–84.

Balikci, A. (1970). *The Netsilik Eskimo*. New York: Doubleday.

Bernstein, I. S. & Gordon, T. P. (1974). The function of aggression in primate societies. *American Scientist*, 62, 304–11.

Boehm, C. (1978). Rational preselection from Hamadryas to *Homo sapiens*: The place of decisions in adaptive process. *American Anthropologist*, 80, 265–96.

Boehm, C. (1982). The evolutionary development of morality as an effect of dominance behavior and conflict interference. *Journal of Social and Biological Sciences*, 5, 413–22.

Boehm, C. (1984). Can social hierarchy and egalitarianism both be ascribed to the same causal forces? *Politics and the Life Sciences*, 1, 12–14.

Boehm, C. (1989). Ambivalence and compromise in human nature. *American Anthropologist*, 91, 921–39.

Boehm, C. (1991). Lower-level teleology in biological evolution: Decision behavior and reproductive success in two species. *Cultural Dynamics*, 4, 115–34.

Boehm, C. (1992). Segmentary 'warfare' and the management of conflict: Comparison of East African chimpanzees and patrilineal–patrilocal humans. In *Coalitions and Alliances in Humans and Other Animals*, ed. A. H. Harcourt & F. B. M. de Waal, pp. 137–73. Oxford: Oxford University Press.

Boehm, C. (1993). Egalitarian behavior and reverse dominance hierarchy. *Current Anthropology*, 34, 227–54.

Boehm, C. (1994a). Pacifying interventions at Arnhem zoo and Gombe. In *Chimpanzee Cultures*, ed. R. W. Wrangham, W. C. McGrew, F. B. M. de Waal & P. G. Heltne, ed. pp. 211–26. Cambridge, MA: Harvard University Press.

Boehm, C. (1994b). Reply to Erdal and Whiten: 'On human egalitarianism: An evolutionary product of Machiavellian status escalation?' *Current Anthropology*,

35, 178–80. [This article by Erdal and Whiten was a critique of my 1993 article on egalitarian behaviour].

Boehm, C. (1995). Neutralizing the human social dominance hierarchy: Egalitarian society and Machiavellian Intelligence. Paper presented at Mellon Symposium on the Evolution of Egalitarian Relationships, organised by A. Whiten at Emory University, Department of Anthropology, April 21–22, 1995.

Boehm, C. (1996). Emergency decisions, cultural-selection mechanics, and group selection. *Current Anthropology*, 37, 763–93.

Boesch, C. (1991). The effects of leopard predation on grouping patterns in forest chimpanzees. *Behaviour*, 117, 220–41.

Bohannan, P. J. (1954). The migration and expansion of the Tiv. *Africa*, 24, 2–16.

Byrne, R. W. & Byrne, J. M. (1988). Leopard killers of Mahale. *Natural History*, 97, 22–6.

Campbell, D. T. (1965). Ethnocentric and other altruistic motives. In *Nebraska Symposium on Motivation*, ed. D. Levine, pp. 283–311. Lincoln, NA: University of Nebraska Press.

Chagnon, N. (1983). *Yanomamo: The Fierce People*. New York: Holt, Rinehart and Winston.

Durkheim, E. (1933). *The Division of Labor in Society*. New York: Free Press.

Erdal, D. & Whiten, A. (1994). On human egalitarianism: An evolutionary product of Machiavellian status escalation? *Current Anthropology*, 35, 175–84.

Erdal, D. & Whiten, A. (1996). Egalitarianism and Machiavellian intelligence in human evolution. In *Modelling the Early Human Mind*, ed. P. A. Mellars & K. R. Gibson. pp. 139–50. Cambridge: McDonald Institute for Archaeological Research.

Evans-Pritchard, E. E. (1940). *The Nuer: A Description of the Modes of Livelihood and Political Institutions of a Nilotic People*. Oxford: Clarendon Press.

Fried, M. H. (1967). *The Evolution of Political Society: An Essay in Political Anthropology*. New York: Random House.

Furer-Haimendorf, C. von (1967). *Morals and Merit: A Study of Values and Social Controls in South Asian Societies*. Chicago: University of Chicago Press.

Gardner, P. (1991). Foragers' pursuit of individual autonomy. *Current Anthropology*, 32, 543–58.

Goodall, J. (1982). Order without law. *Journal of Social and Biological Structures*, 5, 345–52.

Goodall, J. (1986). *The Chimpanzees of Gombe: Patterns of Behavior*. Cambridge, MA: The Belknap Press.

Goodall, J. (1990). *Through a Window*. New York: Houghton-Mifflin.

Harcourt, A. H. & de Waal, F. B. M. (eds) (1992). *Coalitions and Alliances in Humans and Other Animals*. Oxford: Oxford University Press.

Jolly, A. (1988). The evolution of purpose. In *Machiavellian Intelligence: Social Expertise and the Evolution of Intellect in Monkeys, Apes, and Humans*, ed. R. W. Byrne & A. Whiten, pp. 363–78. Oxford: Clarendon Press.

Kluckhohn, C. (1952). Values and value-orientations in the theory of action: An exploration in definition and classification. In *Toward a General Theory of Action*, ed. T. Parsons & E. Shils, pp. 395–418. Cambridge, MA: Harvard University Press.

Knauft, B. B. (1991). Violence and sociality in human evolution. *Current Anthropology*, 32, 391–428.

Knauft, B. B. (1994). Reply to Erdal and Whiten. *Current Anthropology*, 35, 181–2.

Kroeber, A. L. (1948). *Anthropology*. New York: Harcourt-Brace.

Kummer, H. (1971). *Primate Societies: Group Techniques of Ecological Adaptation.* Chicago: Aldine.

Lee, R. B. (1979). *The !Kung San, Men, Women, and Work in a Foraging Society.* Cambridge: Cambridge University Press.

Lewontin, R. C. (1970). The units of selection. *Annual Review of Ecology and Systematics*, 1, 1–18.

Middleton, J. & Tait, D. (eds) (1958). *Tribes Without Rulers: Studies in African Segmentary Systems.* London: Routledge and Kegan Paul.

Nishida, T. (1979). The social structure of chimpanzees of the Mahale mountains. In *The Great Apes*, ed. D. A. Hamburg & E. R. McCown, pp. 73–122. Menlo Park, CA: Benjamin/Cummings.

Pulliam, H. & Dunford, C. (1980). *Programmed to Learn: An Essay on the Evolution of Culture.* New York: Columbia University Press.

Sahlins, M. (1968). *Tribesmen*. New York: Prentice-Hall.

Schelderup-Ebbe, T. (1922). Beitrage zur Sozial psychologie des Haushuhns. *Zeitschrift Psychologie*, 88, 225–52.

Service, E. R. (1962). *Primitive Social Organization: An Evolutionary Perspective.* New York: Random House.

Service, E. R. (1975). *Origin of the State and Civilization: The Process of Cultural Evolution.* New York: Norton.

Stanford, C. B., Wallis, J., Mpongo, E. & Goodall, J. (1994). Hunting decisions in wild chimpanzees. *Behaviour*, 131, 1–18.

Tooby, J. & DeVore, I. (1987). The reconstruction of hominid behavioral evolution through strategic modeling. In *The Evolution of Human Behavior: Primate Models*, ed. W. G. Kinzey, pp. 183–238. Albany, NY: SUNY Press.

Trivers, R. L. (1971). The evolution of reciprocal altruism. *Quarterly Review of Biology*, 46, 35–57.

Waal, F. B. M. de (1982). *Chimpanzee Politics: Power and Sex among Apes.* New York; Harper and Row.

Waal, F. B. M. de (1989). *Peacemaking Among Primates.* Cambridge, MA: Harvard University Press.

Waal, F. B. M. de (1992). Coalitions as part of reciprocal relations in the Arnhem chimpanzee colony. In *Coalitions and Alliances in Humans and Other Animals*, ed. A. Harcourt & F. B. M. de Waal, pp. 233–58. Oxford: Oxford University Press.

Williams, G. C. (1966). *Adaptation and Natural Selection: A Critique of Some Current Evolutionary Thought.* Princeton, NJ: Princeton University Press.

Wilson, D. S. & Sober, E. (1994). Reintroducing group selection to the human behavioral sciences. *Behavioral and Brain Sciences*, 17, 585–654.

Wilson, E. O. (1975). *Sociobiology: The New Synthesis.* Cambridge, MA: Harvard University Press.

Wrangham, R. (1987). African apes: The significance of african apes for reconstructing social evolution. In *The Evolution of Human Behavior: Primate Models*, ed. W. G. Kinzey, pp. 51–71. Albany, NY: SUNY Press.

14 Social intelligence and language: Another Rubicon?

ESTHER N. GOODY

Like the first volume of *Machiavellian Intelligence* this successor is concerned with the role of social intelligence in primate evolution. The editors note 'three principal branch points' in primate evolution at which selective pressures for intellectual change need to be identified, of which the *Homo* line is the last (Chapter 1). The *Homo* line is characterised by 'massive brain enlargement, and extensive stone tool use, (see p. 14). My own chapter begins by looking briefly at questions raised by this astonishing trajectory from apes to *Homo sapiens sapiens*. If Machiavellian social intelligence can be traced from the strepsirhine line to its greater elaboration in apes, was it further refinement of this form of social intelligence by which the apes bootstrapped themselves to fully human intelligence? If so, were there no new characteristics linked to the hominid transition? The editors suggest that this may have occurred as a legacy from ape intelligence, or as a consequence of 'social bias' in solving problems of survival in the changing conditions of hominid ecology. Another possibility they note is the 'specific development of a social *module* or *modules*, independent from other modules used for non-social tasks' (see p. 14).

What form might a 'social bias' have taken? How would a 'social module' operate? Both would seem to involve some sort of linking of cognitive processes and social *inter*action. Indeed primate social intelligence can be seen as the progressively effective cognitive mapping of the interdependency of own and others' actions. Here primate cognitive mapping of feeding territories (Milton, 1988) may have been a precursor of the cognitive modelling of contingent interaction. This is a shift from mapping of static territory 'out there' to mapping of others' *actions* 'out there' in relation to an animal's own intentions. Clearly the latter is far more cognitivly demanding: it requires imputing intentions to others on the basis of their actions, it requires that own intentions be modelled as actions, and it involves constant amendment of the cognitive model in response to own and the other's strategic choices. In the first volume, Byrne & Whiten (1988) presented evidence that this led to monkey and ape social intelligence, which is particularly characterised by skill in deceiving other monkeys and apes. They suggested that this Machiavellian intelligence introduced a competitive dynamic, with those most skilled at deception having a reproductive advantage, their deception-skilled descendents being harder to deceive and thus needing even greater social intelligence to deceive others, and so on. This Machiavellian ratchet is seen as likely to have contributed significantly to the emergence of hominid social intelligence, the last of the three branch points of primate evolution.

But given the huge evolutionary gap between apes and *Homo sapiens* — in brain size, culture and language — might we not expect some new element in the Machiavellian equation? This chapter suggests that a gradually emerging proto-language among early hominids would have progressively augmented ape social intelligence in several ways: language itself would have to be incorporated in cognitive representations of own and others' intentions; language permits more effective classification and storage of information, and thus more effective use of memory; language-in-use is a powerful tool for the co-operative construction of meaning; language-in-use is a new sort of tool for co-operation between individuals; and language is a tool for constructing socio-cultural devices for co-operation among members of a community.

It is suggested that early proto-language, and subsequent increasingly complex forms of spoken language, should be thought of as a new sort of tool for thinking with and for acting with. The emergence of spoken language would have provided a new tool for co-operation at the same time that it can only be used through co-operation. Where ape Machiavellian intelligence seeks to outwit others, social intelligence built on language must achieve a framework for co-operation if conversational meanings are to be understood.

Background

When I was writing the Introduction to *Questions and Politeness: Strategies in Social Interaction* (Goody, 1978a) Nicholas Humphrey sent me a copy of his paper 'The social function of intellect' (Humphrey, 1976). The suggestion that chimps were actively engaged in solving the problem of the likely responses to them of other chimps was very exciting. It led me to a view of interaction as based on the reciprocal cognitive modelling of contingent responses. Such a view was consistent with findings that a great deal of human behaviour can be understood in terms of the attribution of intention to others (Humphrey, 1976, p. 12–13). In pursuing this theme in a series of working papers (E. N. Goody, unpublished results) it proved useful to designate this form of cognitive modelling as *anticipatory interactive planning* (AIP). But if apes were able to cognitively model reciprocal contingencies of action, how did this skill become transformed as humans acquired the new tool of spoken language? Language is used to manage social relationships in complex ways in greetings used to create 'debts' of respect (Goody, 1972), and in the ways in which relative status constrains the meaning of questions (Goody, 1978b). Indeed these uses of language *construct* the social relationships that make up society, while at the same time being themselves products of that society. If in addition to the immense possibilities language provides for sharing information, it is also central to the construction and management of *social* relationships, then language-using primates had a new tool of immense potential for social intelligence. But what would evidence for such cognitive modelling of contingencies look like? And what kind of evidence might there be for the role of language in this modelling?

This chapter draws mainly on contributions to *Social Intelligence and Interaction* (Goody, 1995c) in order to pursue the question of how the emergence of language might effect the cognitive modelling of reciprocally contingent action.[1] It also considers the related question of how a modelling of contingent action augmented by language would be reflected in socio-cultural forms. One of the most helpful clarifications arising from discussion of these chapters was that several contributors understood *anticipatory interactive planning* to be necessarily conscious and intentional. This is not so. Cognitive modelling of the contingent responses of others is not seen as necessarily taking place within awareness, indeed this cannot always be the case (see discussion of Drew's work below, and Drew (1995), Streeck (1995) and Levinson (1995). AIP is to be taken as

---

[1] The chapters in *Social Intelligence and Interaction* resulted from papers presented and discussed at a workshop on *Some implications of a social origin of human intelligence* held at the Wissenschaftskolleg zu Berlin in May, 1990. Stephen Levinson and Penny Brown helped to organise the seminar, for which the Wissenschaftskolleg provided funding and hospitality.

cognitive modelling that is often below awareness, but may of course also be consciously worked out.

Implications of a gradual emergence of language for hominid social intelligence

In their Introduction, the editors of this volume raise the question of the selective pressures for the transition from ape to hominid intelligence. They suggest some combination of ape machiavellian intelligence with a social bias in solving problems encountered by early hominids. Yet of the features that clearly distinguish humans from their ape relatives – massive increase in brain size, complex material and social cultures, and spoken language – the role of language has scarcely been considered. If we take seriously the social nature of ape intelligence, surely a tool for *communication between individuals* like language must have played a key role.

There are interesting reasons for this omission arising from the way language itself has been studied. Following considerable scholarly and speculative discussion of the origins of language during the 18th and 19th centuries, Darwin's theory of evolution precipitated a deluge of crackpot papers on language origins. This led to despair at the difficulty of grounding such work scientifically. When the Société de Linguistique de Paris was founded in 1866 the bye-laws included a prohibition on publication of papers discussing the origins of language. While individual scholars continued to address this question, it came to be generally considered as outside the domain of scientific study.

This self-imposed embargo on exploring the origins of language has been reinforced in the 20th century by the work of linguists such as N. Chomsky (e.g. Chomsky, 1972) who see the cognitive capacity for grammar and syntax as genetically coded in humans. There seemed little point in devoting attention to language origins, since the genetic changes involved were taken as an occurrence that set the form for subsequent grammatical structures. Although very different in character, these two scholarly positions have until very recently effectively inhibited linguists from asking questions about how human language might have emerged.[2]

---

[2] There is a striking parallel here with the embargo in behavioural psychology on the study of mental processes. Nothing was to be studied that could not be studied experimentally and measured. What went on in the mind was to be considered as a 'black box' whose contents and processes were unknowable. Paradoxically, this meant that most mental processes were excluded from research. The recent resurgence of interest in the nature and dynamics of the origin of spoken language led in 1983 to the foundation of the *Language Origins Society*, and to its journal, *LOS Forum*.

Archaeological and anthropological work has followed a similar path, placing the emergence of complex language at the end of the trajectory of hominid evolution. In a recent collection of papers, *Modelling the Early Human Mind*, Paul Mellars discussion of language links its first significant influence to 'the Human Revolution' of 40 000 bp (Mellars, 1996). His argument is based on the first clearly identified evidence of human use of culturally shaped representations in burials and cave art; language involves symbolic thought, and these are the first evidence of symbols. Archaeological evidence is based on what has been preserved from the past, almost entirely 'bones and stones'. The problem is that speech does not fossilise.

Since linguists and archaeologists concurred that spoken language was only recently acquired by early *Homo sapiens*, it is not surprising that there should be little discussion of the role of language in the hominid adaptation of social intelligence. However, given the level of Machiavellian intelligence achieved by apes, if we are to look for some sort of specialised hominid social intelligence of increasing power, it seems very unlikely that it would not incorporate some sort of language. And as the editors remind us, the major evolutionary advances are best seen as gradual adaptations of a number of related features.

Scholars stress the gradual nature of increase in brain size (from around 400 cc for apes to 1200–1300 cc for *Homo sapiens sapiens*), but they have tended to interpret this as meaning that brain size itself played no significant role in hominid emergence. Gibson (1993) has recently challenged this view, arguing that brains are enormously expensive for human metabolism and that such a three- to fourfold increase would only have occurred if brains were of central importance to the improving cognitive skills of successive hominid species. She stresses the role that larger brains would play in increasing information-processing capacities, linking this to emergent skills in tool use, language and social intelligence. ' . . . since human social intelligence, tool use and language all depend on quantitative increases in brain size and its associated information processing capacities, none could have suddenly emerged full-blown like Minerva from the head of Zeus. Rather, like brain size, each of these intellectual capacities must have evolved gradually' (Gibson, 1993, p. 251). Gibson regards these capacities as interdependent so that none could have reached the fully human level of complexity in isolation from the others.

In the last few years a few scholars have also begun to suggest that some form of early language might have preceded complex language as we know it today. Lyons (1988) and Donald (1991) propose that a gestural language might have preceded spoken language. Bickerton (1990) suggests a spoken proto-language consisting essentially of a simple lexicon. Dunbar argues that when early hominids came to live in larger groups the primate mode of sustaining social relations through reciprocal grooming would have become ineffective; at this point he suggests that vocalisations came to play an increasing role in social intercourse (Aiello & Dunbar, 1993; Dunbar, 1993).

However, apparently still influenced by the Chomskian paradigm of a genetic mutation as the origin of modern syntax and grammar, these scholars insist that complex language appeared late, and then as a structure separate from early forms of proto-language. This allows them to explore possible dynamics of early language without relating these to the nature of complex language. Yet despite their various arguments against the construction of complex language from the building blocks provided by proto-language, such a progression appears in fact far more likely. William Foley now provides a framework for this articulation in *Anthropological Linguistics*.

Unlike those who have previously addressed the problem of the emergence of language, Foley takes seriously the essential nature of language as a mode of communication *between* individuals. Also unlike formal linguists who study the products of language (syntactically correct sentences, as sentences), he is concerned with language-in-use. This is the 'action tradition' of linguistics that has recently come into prominence, based on the analysis of *conversation* (Gumperz, 1982; Levinson, 1983; Brown & Levinson, 1987; Clark, 1992; Drew, 1995; Streeck, 1995). For Foley the dynamic of evolutionary change is the co-adaptation through 'structural coupling' of organism and environment. Co-adaptations that are stable over time come to be genetically coded, leading to what Maturana & Varela (1987) term evolutionary drift. In higher animals new adaptations are increasingly transmitted by learning (as with a language), or by a combination of genes and learning. When communication takes the form of spoken language, speakers engage in structural coupling through exchanging speech.

Foley proposes that spoken language first emerged as early hominids came to exchange an increasing number of distinctive calls, the earliest words. Even a tripling of the three dozen distinctive calls recorded for chimpanzees would, he suggests, have overloaded the auditory perceptive space leading to processing problems, and presumably new cognitive structures emerged to handle this. Further extension of processing capacity would be gained by combining words.[3] Simple combinations of words in this early lexicon would have been early proto-language. Citing the work of Aiello & Dunbar (1993) on the relationship between group size and the emergence of language to replace grooming for servicing of social relationships, Foley suggests that proto-language would have been already well established with *Homo habilis*.[4]

The lexical resources of proto-language would have gradually increased, up to several hundred words. The significantly larger brain of *Homo erectus* would have been more adept at framing and comprehending longer sequences of signs, and thus sequences of words would have become longer. Longer sequences of words would have placed new demands on short-term memory, leading to its extension. However, as size of lexicon and length of sequences of words increased, new processing problems would arise, and this may have led to the first complex symbolic units, perhaps containing proto-phonemes, though these were probably not utilised systematically. Foley considers it unlikely however that *Homo erectus* had 'crossed the bridge to fully modern language'.[5] This, he suggests, occurred with archaic *Homo sapiens* with the serialisation of component units, composed internally of hierarchical structures (for instance, noun phrases and verb phrases, hierarchically embedded). Evidence that archaic *Homo sapiens* had cognitive control over hierarchically construed composite units comes from their tool technology in which hafted tools first appear. These are composite tools, made from functionally different components combined into a new tool that has a use different from its components. Composite tools can be seen as the manual analogue of linguistic hierarchical structure and, following the homology between manual action

---

[3] Foley notes that this skill would have been well within the capacities of early hominids, as apes have been shown able to combine signs of American Sign Language in meaningful ways. Because Foley's book was in draft and then in press while this chapter was being written, it has been necessary to paraphrase rather than quote directly from the published book, as page numbers were not available. I am most grateful to Professor Foley for making this critically relevant material available to me while he was preparing the manuscript. Apologies to the reader for the absence of page references; readers are urged to consult *Anthropological Linguistics*, published in March 1997.

[4] This dating is consistent with other features of *Homo habilis*: preferential right handedness, associated with strong lateralisation of the brain; and hemispheric asymmetry with enlargement of left hemisphere areas associated with language in modern humans.

[5] Foley cites as evidence for this the fact that the *Homo erectus* tool kit remained unchanged for nearly 1 million years, and from endocasts it appears that neurological components of the brain had not fully developed.

and language[6], are, he suggests, the first evidence in the hominid line for true syntax: the hierarchical organisation of grammatical constituents in lower units. Such a hierarchical organisation of language is termed by linguists the paradigmatic side of grammar; the syntagmatic (i.e. serialising of units) is much older, going back in the hominid line to *Homo habilis* (Foley, 1997).

The burst of cultural activities reflected in the Hominid Revolution some 150 000 years later may have reflected, Foley suggests, the emergence of the propositional bearing function of speech. This would have facilitated the linguistic function of reference, and with this the possibility of providing a semantic description of things. This 'metalinguistic awareness' is the *awareness* that meaning is conveyed by signs. While early hominids in fact conveyed meaning by signs, with metalinguistic awareness, the construction of meaning can become the object of speech, as well as its vehicle. Perhaps a remote analogy would be with a fish becoming aware that it swims in water. It is at this point in the archaeological record that we have evidence of *Homo sapiens* intentionally constructing representations in cave art that have been seen as having a magical role in hunting.

We can now raise again the question of how the gradual emergence of spoken language might have augmented the social intelligence of apes. If ape social intelligence involves the cognitive modelling of others' contingent responses, early language itself must now have been a component of such models. In addition to modelling the actions others might make in response to their own, successive species of hominids would have had to model the meanings of calls/words, sequences of words, hierarchically organised sequences of words, and complex reference.

Structural coupling and the construction of meaning through language

Foley suggests that the first stage in the emergence of proto-language would have been an increase in the number of distinctive calls, and that many such calls would lead to cognitive processing difficulties. But surely something new is happening here. How is the meaning of new calls estab-

---

[6] There is a growing literature on the probability of a close relationship between cognitive foundations of tool use and manufacture and those of language. There is no space to discuss this here, but see Greenfield (1991) and chapters in Gibson & Ingold (1993).

lished among the members of the group? How does it come about that all members agree on what each new distinctive call means? This is the problem of establishing shared meanings for a lexicon, and Hutchins & Hazlehurst (1995) have proposed a very interesting model of what this would have to involve.

Using the operation of an autoprocessor as a template, they show that for one individual to establish a cognitive representation of something seen, visual input must be matched to representation, and this checked against what is seen (visual output). Many individuals can thus each create their own representations. But linking words to such representations requires an entirely new level of representations and matching output. As before, visual input needs to be matched to representation, but now this is matched to a word — which they term an *artefact* in order to stress that it is a 'ready-made thing in the world'; and the artefact must be spoken, as verbal output. But what is spoken (verbal output) by one individual is heard by another (verbal input). Here the heard artefact is matched to a cognitive representation of the artefact, *and* to a cognitive representation of the thing the artefact/word represents. Both for speaker and for hearer there is a two-stage matching process between verbal input and verbal output. Verbal input must be matched against a cognitive representation of the thing it represents, and this representation matched against the artefact.

How might such artefacts/words come to be agreed upon among members of a community? How might all come to 'mean' the same thing by the same artefact? Using computer simulation, the linking of two autoprocessor circuits by verbal input/output, this model was run for sets of five 'individuals' given the task of assigning distinctive 'words' to images of the 12 phases of the moon. After some 50 000 trials matching each individual with each of the others (as speaker and as hearer), all members of a set came to assign the same 'word' to each of the phases of the moon. Hutchins & Hazlehurst (1995) make no claims that this model literally expresses the process of establishing shared meanings for words representing 'things in the world'. But they do suggest that to achieve this would require some 'artefact' that can both be cognitively modelled, and spoken by some and heard by others.

This model has two critical implications for the impact of spoken language on the social intelligence of apes. First, it requires many repeated exchanges of tentative word/object associations between pairs of members of a community. This is 'structural coupling' in action. Maturana & Varela

(1987) say that it is as structural couplings extend over time that each shapes the other. And the effective 'unit' is not the individual but the 'network of relations' between individuals. Here this network links cognitive representations of overlapping pairs of individuals with their vocal expression as this is spoken and heard. The second implication is that the sharing of word/artefact meanings creates and requires a lexicon of words that exist 'in the world', independently of individual members of a community. These are what Bickerton (1990) terms 'secondary representations'. They are artefacts/tools for thinking with. It is in this sense that spoken language must have been the earliest form of what Hutchins (1991) elsewhere terms 'distributed cognition': a cognitive property of the group that exists independently of its individual members.[7]

When hominids used language for the co-operative construction of meaning, Machiavellian deceit encountered reciprocity.

Co-operative construction of meaning in conversation

Several of the chapters in *Social Intelligence and Interaction* (Goody, 1995c) focus on the study of 'language in use', or, what Maturana and Varela call 'languaging'. The primary data for such research is drawn from conversation in natural settings. The relatively unobtrusive records that can be made using tape recordings and video recordings permit close analysis of what is said, how it is said, and how the contributions of participants are inter-related. Such material has dramatically shifted the perspective from the structure of isolated sentences (grammar and syntax) and their 'truth value', to a view of conversation as a jointly constructed process during which meanings emerge. The unit of analysis can be said to have shifted from one sentence to people engaging in dialogue, conversation. This requires us to see language as inherently and of necessity a social product. Indeed these analyses are windows on the procedures through which two people are able to co-ordinate their joint production of meaning.

One of these collaborative procedures is discussed in Streeck's (1995) chapter 'On projection'. His research data are video films of conversation that permit the close analysis of the relationship of gesture and speech in

---

[7] I have slightly rephrased Hutchins' definition in the 1991 paper, as this was framed in the context of 'the division of cognitive labour' (p. 284ff). Given the treatment by Hutchins and Hazlehurst of words as 'artefacts' which are made by the exchange of form-meaning mappings between individuals, this wording seems reasonable.

sequences of interaction. He has worked with people in several different societies, Phillipine, Thai, German, American, Japanese, and can thus consider both similarities across societies and cultural specificity. These records show minute patterns of co-ordination of gesture and of speech on parallel levels, and across levels, and that these patterns take a form that signals ahead the meanings about to be conveyed. Streeck terms these tentative trajectories 'projections', 'prefatory components of things to come', or 'pre's'.

Pre's foreshadow or project something that comes after them, to prepare the scene. They allow other participants a certain premonition as to what this actor might be up to next. In his data, pre's take a number of regular patterned forms across the samples from different cultures: the minimal units are preliminary noises – 'er', 'uh' . . . and micro-moments of silence. At the other extreme are fully developed pre-sequential utterances such as 'Can I ask you a question?' – a preliminary question to gain permission for asking a question. Intermediate pre's may be in the form of gestures in 'prefatory slots', or minor routines that manage 'repairs' where the intended trajectory is briefly deflected, such as managing the search for a better word. By looking at these sequences as they alternate between speakers Streeck finds that one speaker's trajectory is continuously adapted to the other's responses. This mutual adaptation occurs both at the level of gesture and at the level of speech.

An example will make this mutuality clearer. Here is a Thai conversation about inappropriateness of the weather for wearing summer clothes (only the English is given here).

> The first speaker [A] initiates the topic saying "You can rarely use it",
> accompanied by a wiggle, then scratching her face.
> [A]   "What it is, uh . . . it is not, not, [clapping her hands] not, not, not suit—"
> Then both women speak together
> [B]   "Not suitable in this weather"
> [A]   "Not suitable in this climate"
> [folding her hands].
>
> (Streeck 1995, p. 90)

In discussing this and other data on gesture in conversational pre's Streeck shows that gestures of each influence the way the other participates. As in this example, touching the face has the effect of making the other divert gaze from the speaker's face, and serves to 'leave her space' to find the words she needs to express her idea. When she is ready to proceed, another gesture [here clapping] and/or continued repetition of a linking word invite the other to help her search. The folding of hands marks the speaker's completion of the successful introduction of this topic. He has found that gestures used in this way tend to start before the words, and to decay before the verbal element is completed. 'Action gestures precede their speech affiliates. They unfold and often decay before the word arrives.' (Streeck, 1995, p. 100). Here gesture acts as a prefatory component of the verbal utterance to come. Another mode in which gesture serves to synchronise conversation is in the mirroring of one speaker's posture or hand movements by the other, seemingly without conscious attention.

Pre's may involve speech alone, as in this example in which three American children argue about an assignment. Leola is about to present Wallace with the evidence for her view by reading aloud the instructions. While Leola leads in this exchange, very soon she and her friend Carolyn are reading the instructions in unison.

> LEOLA: "You see. Here it say. How man. How
> CAROLYN: How
> LEOLA: many words can you make out of these five letters.
> CAROLYN: many words can you make out of these five letters.
> (Streeck, 1995, p. 93).

Speaking in unison is a special case of the successful accomplishment of a pre trajectory in which the joint, interdependent, nature of conversation is unusually transparent.

Sociolinguists have devoted considerable attention to another domain of the organisation of conversations that deals with solving 'problems' arising as talk proceeds. These 'repairs' are often initiated by pre's, as in the 'sound stretch: 'Welllll . . ' or 'Nooooo . . . ,' The repair may then range in explicitness from self-correction . . . 'I mean . . ' and requests for clarification . . . . 'What did you say?' to collaborative repair involving both speakers. Self-initiation of repair often follows an indication of 'trouble ahead' (perhaps a frown or puzzled look on the other's face). Typically there is a shift from individual to collaborative repair. Searching for a word is a common form of repair in which this shift occurs, as illustrated in the first example above.

Most of Streeck's data are too complex to reproduce here since they show multiple mutualities between channels and between actors: mutualities of gesture, of linkages across words and phrases, of contingent adaptation between gestural and verbal components of a trajectory, and of 'socially intelligent action formats'. This interdependent construction of meaning is perhaps most evident in the fact that pre's are initially tentative, projections of *possible* trajectories. They may be abandoned, and may only be identifiable as pre's when a sequence has developed through sustaining responses. Each of the examples in Streeck's analysis reveals 'language and behaviour as phenomena *in progression, unfolding towards (possible) completion*' (Streeck, 1995, p. 106). This unfolding he characterises as the 'collaborative organisation of talk'.

But how is this collaboration achieved? This is a deceptively simple question, yet one that is fundamental for understanding the role of spoken language in being human. Streeck's material on posture and gesture argues strongly for a level of co-ordination that occurs without awareness. This is clearest in one person's adjustment of posture to match the other's, or the picking up of a cup shortly after the other has done so. We might see this as 'motor modelling' of the other's actions.[8] Because it is expressed in action we know it happens. But may this not provide an insight also into the necessarily invisible cognitive modelling of the other's talk-and-action? For this same 'deep patterning' appears in some of the verbal forms. As Streeck suggests, despite the diversity of particular instances, '... pre's seem to point to an underlying organization, a design feature of the human interaction order itself' (Streeck, 1995, p. 87–8). 'It appears that this design is an imprint of a rather generic social intelligence' (p. 106).

Yet just as any particular conversation is carried on in a particular language (Thai, German . . .) so the realisation of the collaborative construction of meaning in a conversation is carried on through culturally given formats that permit foresight, and are learned by individual speakers. The detailed data show differences between cultures as well as consistent patterns across them.

Culturally given formats presumably emerge in the millions of conversations of a particular socio-cultural world over a long period. They emerge as speakers sharing the same culture and language collaborate to

---

[8] My video records of children's role play in Baale (northern Ghana) show minute modelling of adult posture and gesture when playing at adult tasks they have not yet carried out in the household or farm (Goody, 1993).

solve similar problems of meaning and understanding. Critically, they come to exist in this socio-cultural world independently of individual speakers. This process can be seen as expressing the model proposed by Hutchins & Hazlehurst (1995) for establishing shared lexical meaning, but here artefacts are cultural formats and not words. Without being aware of them young speakers learn these through their own participation in myriad conversations. Such cultural formats are 'tools for collaboration' of a special kind. They are tools that are inherently dyadic; scripts for two actors. And because both actors are 'reading from the same cultural script' collaboration can be achieved.

If synchrony of gaze and gaze aversion are examples of cerebral hardware for collaborative interaction, cultural formats that permit foresight can be seen as software — written to solve culturally framed problems and installed anew in each of us through participation in conversations. But, to paraphrase Hutchins and Hazlehurst, both are a special kind of programme for linking two actors into a *shared* circuit.

Drew (1995) is concerned with the sequential patterns or organisations in talk-in-interaction, with conversations. Describing several sets of patterns, he asks how this regularity relates to the speaker's planning of what s/he wants to say. Starting from the position that social intelligence consists at least in part of cognitive models of action that can underlie meaningful communicative behaviour, he notes that incorporating models of the other's responses highlights the role of reciprocity. 'The predictability of some contingent subsequent action(s) is part of "mentally modelling" the likely behaviour/responses of their co-interactants, which hence underpins the strategic nature of selecting a current action' (Drew, 1995, p. 111). In conversation, 'The ability to anticipate subsequent verbal actions, performed in turns at talk, and to select or design a current action (turn) accordingly, would seem to rest on the cognitive representation of *sequences* of actions' — 'the discernable shapes, patterns, organizations or regularities which may be associated with, or which may be the products of, the progressivity of participants' decisions about "what to say next" in response to what has just been said. . . . Thus underlying AIP is some mental representation of interaction sequences' (Drew, 1995, p. 111).

Therefore, Drew asks whether a current turn-at-talk might be produced with an eye to an anticipated future slot or move in a sequence. He first considers the possibility that such cognitive modelling may involve the conscious use by speakers of knowledge of sequential patterns, as is often the case in formal greeting exchanges.[9] Certain sequences are so conventionalised as to be, in effect, part of the vernacular language. This is particularly clear for sets of paired forms where if one speaker produces the first part, the other is virtually required to respond in a particular way. Questions–answers (see Goody, 1978b), like greetings (Goody, 1972), invitations, accusations and requests may take this form. The constraint here is both normative and embedded in linguistic form. As such it is both a way of securing a predictable response (a strategic *action*) and provides the interlocutor with a clear model of what the speaker intends. However, as with the trajectories initiated by pre's, how the conversation will in fact develop further remains open to subsequent contingencies.

While many sequential patterns of three or more turns can be identified in conversation, Drew finds these to be organised rather differently and to have less predictive power for subsequent responses. These extended patterns include 'teases', patterns that serve to avoid disagreement, and pre-sequences (see above). While these several kinds of sequential patterning are also conversational routines, they clearly involve a weaker form of predictability. They are perhaps better characterised as 'cautious' procedures for reaching conversational goals in ways that enlist the co-operation of the other and avoid upsetting or antagonizing her.[10] It is doubtful that speakers consciously decide to employ such routines, and certainly not in the form of a worked-out sequence of moves. Of 'teases' Drew writes that the shape of these sequences is not being orientated to by co-participants. It is discernable by the analyst because of the regularity of the patterning. This in turn is due to the fact that participants are trying to solve common interactional problems using 'typical ways/moves'. It is a product of the resulting turn-by-turn progression through a series of 'typical' interactional contingencies. It is not the product of participants' mental representation of a projected sequence, and the exploitation of a move within such a sequence. In avoidance of disagreement the participants' orientation to projectable next slots is implicit. In pre-sequences it may be explicit, but need not

[9] The fact that greeting exchanges are often taught to children to ensure their mastery of polite behaviour marks greetings as objects of conscious planning. It is significant that to omit the appropriate formal greeting may be taken as intended insult; it is assumed to be under conscious control, and speakers are held accountable for producing it.

[10] This is an underlying design feature shared with the wide class of 'politeness phenoma' so well analysed by Brown & Levinson (1987).

be so. They are manifestly initiated with an interactional goal in view.

In sum, many patterns or organisations of conversational sequence are not evidence of conscious interactional planning by participants. The regularity of patterning is due to common response to interactional contingencies. Nevertheless, it may be the case that the sequential organisation remains part of community members' conscious linguistic/interactive repertoire and permits the 'projection' or anticipation of future moves of the sequence. Such anticipation of the unfolding of a sequence can be incorporated in pursuing the goal of an interaction (Drew, 1995, p. 120).

Drew suggests that most cases of exploitation of anticipated or projected sequential routines will probably fluctuate around the borderline between cognitive strategies and conscious strategies (citing Heritage 1990/91, p. 121–2). He gives several examples where it is clear that a move is made in an interactional sequence that exploits the way it is expected to develop. A cognitive strategy, cognitive modelling of the anticipated sequence, is clearly involved; whether this is also a conscious strategy is usually opaque, and need not be the case for the action to follow the cognitive model.

> There can be little doubt that, whilst structures of sequences of turns/actions are part of the cognitive processes through which the coherence of these sequences was produced in the first place in the course of interaction, the mental models of such structures may not be conscious, articulated resources. Sequential structures are some of the *procedures* whereby co-participants discover the meaning in, and goals behind, one another's utterances: that is, they are procedures which lie behind participants' analysis of meaning/ action . . . . Participants' understandings of what the other means, or is up to, are indeed the conscious rational products of routines which themselves may not generally be subject to conscious modelling or deliberation. The social intelligibility and perceived rationality of talk-in-interaction is the product of procedures – including sequential structures – which are part of learned programs which underlie social intelligence. (Drew, 1995, p. 132–3)

He concludes that the evidence 'causes us to vacillate between regarding [communicative strategies] as empirical instances of procedural, programmable cognitive strategies, to the possibility that they are instances of speakers' conscious strategies in anticipating how to achieve certain outcomes in projected sequences' (Ibid, p. 136).

Just as communicative strategies need not be located at the conscious level of intentionality of speakers, this need not be the case with other elements associated with the cognitive modelling of contingent responses such as 'planning', 'anticipation', 'predictability' and 'control'. He sees it as consistent to regard the 'mental imaging' of interactive sequences as cognitive procedures for action and interpretation, and not as part of overt social knowledge. 'Social intelligence may consist of social procedures for action and interpretation, without these procedures becoming the objects of conscious articulation (in the mind at least) on the occasion of their use.' (Ibid, p. 112)

Formal properties of Machiavellian intelligence and the co-operative construction of meaning

In discussing the 'social bias' in human intelligence, Levinson (1995) points out that Machiavellian reasoning has the formal properties of agonistic interaction. It is a zero sum game in which it is possible to calculate relative utilities of each move in advance of play. He contrasts this with the inherent 'impossibility' of being able to know what another means in 'the cooperative game of pure coordination' where each option of each player will yield zero pay-off *unless it is matched by the co-ordinating option of the other player.* Zero sum games *merely* require decision trees for different contingencies; co-ordination games require deep reflexive thinking about other minds. 'Both win if, and only if, each does what the other expects each to do; otherwise both lose. In a zero sum game one's own preferences are clear in advance; in a co-ordination game it doesn't much matter which action is taken so long as it matches the other's expectations. Zero sum games can be reduced to relatively simple mathematics but nobody knows if a mathematics for co-ordination games could even be formulated.... Strictly speaking *Machiavellian Intelligence* is child's play, a lower-order computational ability: *Humeian intelligence* (coordination through implicit contract) is the adult stuff' (italics in original: Levinson, 1995, pp. 226–7).

One sees here the basis of the fascination with whether apes have a 'theory of mind' and how this relates to human capacities for 'mind-reading' (Premack & Woodruff, 1978; Dennett, 1988; Premack, 1988; Whiten 1991, 1993). However, attempts to model an ape–human continuum of theories of mind have failed to take account of the role of language in modelling the implications that one's actions might have for the expectations, emotions, self-esteem and intentions of other actors. The tool of language permits modelling of others' expectations and intentions with words that have *shared* meaning. Whiten (1993) discusses the ape capacity for metarepresentation of intentions. With spoken language, hominids are capable of *public*, shared, representation. While apes may indeed have a theory of mind, they lack the words with which to make internal representations the topic of co-operative construction of meaning. To reduce the distinction between implicit and explicit to 'just meaning intentions can be talked about' fails to account for what happens to cognitive representations when they are shared by means of artefacts/words. In the model proposed by Hutchins & Hazlehurst (1995) this involved representing both the intention and the artefact, and the artefact is used by others to map the same intention. Thus human mindreading in fact incorporates both the artefacts/ meanings shared with others (words, cognitive procedures) and reflects the ongoing process of the collaborative making of meaning. In the absence of the tool of spoken language, apes lack these tools for thinking with and for exchanging information about intentions. Human mindreading goes on in the structural coupling through language between self and other, as well as in individual heads.

Yet we are left with the question of how this co-ordination of meanings is possible, given the extreme computational complexity involved in arriving at correct inferences of others' intentions where the goal is mutual understanding. Here Grice's theory (1957) of communication based on intention attribution makes a critical contribution. Grice sees communication as achieved when a recipient recognises the specific intention behind the production of a communicative act. The importance of this view lies in the fact that both speaker and addressee are necessary for the communicative act. The speaker's act is only completed by its recognition by the addressee. This is an elegant model for structural coupling through language. The working out of Grice's theory involves conditions that must hold for the speaker to ascertain that the addressee has understood his intention correctly. All of these are based on the Principle of Co-operation: that both speaker and addressee are using language in a way to make the mutual understanding of intentions possible. Grice proposes a number of axioms that permit the realisation of the Co-operative Principle. Here it is sufficient to note that all successful spoken communication refers back to the premise of co-operation between speakers. The contrast with Machiavellian deception is striking and fundamental.

Pragmatic meaning

If cognitive procedures and culturally framed routines co-ordinate the conscious collaborative production of conversational meanings in talk-in-interaction, each speaker nevertheless retains her individuality in this process. Good's (1995) insightful discussion of the fluidity of pragmatic meaning brings together the account of meaning as constructed in conversation and Byrne & Whiten's (1988) view of intelligence as being typified by the problem of how to deceive, and how to take account of the possibility of others' deception. With them he sees that possibilities for deception imply both strategies for deceiving and for countering deception. The implications are an ever-expanding series of nested contingencies. How have these been responded to by language-using primates? Good (1995) argues that given the possibility of deception, the most effective use of language will be one that permits maximum flexibility in managing the way meanings are projected and negotiated. He suggests that in practice, in use, language has elaborated possibilities for ambiguity and for retrospective reinterpretation − 'hindsight'. This permits speakers to disavow an initial implication if this later proves uncomfortable, or inconsistent with meanings that emerge as the conversation proceeds. Indeed it opens the way for later recasting of meanings long after a conversation has ended.

From this perspective the whole domain of pragmatics can be seen as a way of managing levels of meaning that become relevant, or recede, as the conversation continues. Pragmatics has developed in modern linguistics from Austin's (1975) insight that much of the meaning in conversation cannot be accounted for by the lexical, dictionary, meaning of the words used. 'Why haven't you come to see me?' can be either an invitation or a complaint. Which is intended must be ascertained by the addressee on the basis of his knowledge of past encounters with the speaker. But even then, the addressee can recast the meaning by the way he responds, turning a potential complaint into an invitation: 'I'd love to, what about Sunday?'; or vice versa, turning an invitation into a complaint 'Sorry, I have been terribly busy with the new house.' This level of meaning is termed 'illocutionary force' in contrast to the 'locutionary' meaning of the words by themselves. Good (1995) suggests that its great importance in human conversation arises from the fact that language permits the introduction of *time* as a factor in managing meaning. Even in the short time span of a single conversation, emerging meanings may alter earlier understandings. Where language-in-use deals with past and future events, possibilities for deception and for re-interpretation are multiplied. The initial vagueness of pragmatic meaning resides in the way it was determined by personal memories and current context, rather than in lexical and grammatical forms. What can later be recalled of the conversation will again be subject to memories and context. Since the initial meaning was pragmatically conveyed neither speaker can be held accountable by reference to the actual words, leaving recollection vulnerable to subsequent interests and experiences.

Spoken language, then, introduces the tools for making past and future events the subject of present negotiations of meaning. But since meanings are largely pragmatic, they are subject to recasting while this takes place, as they will be again tomorrow, and forever. There is a nice irony in the fact that language permits both a greatly increased precision in collaborative construction of meanings, and, through pragmatic meanings and a new ability to represent time, ensures fluidity and ambiguity. It is a further paradox that the possibilities of the subtle ambiguity and fluidity of pragmatic meanings and the representation of time must have increased as language became more complex and more powerful.

Our repertoire of language tools must thus be extended to include conventions for establishing pragmatic meanings. That these are both linguistic and socio-cultural can be seen in the analysis of how questions have meaning in Gonja conversations (Goody, 1978b). There are linguistic forms that specify that a question is being asked; but how a question is understood depends in part on the relative social positions of speaker and addressee. Position in the social structure heavily constrains the meaning of questions. This is a pragmatic variation in the meaning of a sign that is dependent on a property of its user. There are also a number of cultural idioms for questions: for example, questions involving a joking challenge require a joking response that takes its force from role expectations and has no 'truth value' at all; rhetorical questions in a court setting elicit norms relevant to the case being tried, and so on. Tools for constructing pragmatic meaning are 'made of language' but shaped by social structure and by cultural forms.

Spoken language provides tools for thinking and acting with
socially constructed artefacts: Predictability and accountability

There is clear evidence then that today ordinary human conversations are
still carried out in ways that depend on the constant close reciprocal monitoring of signals ranging from words, to gestures, to facial expressions,
to grammar and syntax, to 'passive' markers of social status such as cloth-
ing and accent.

On the level of interaction, work by ethnomethodologists has shown
that we are continuously engaged in establishing and monitoring common
meanings in order to be able to interact effectively (Garfinkel, 1967;
Heritage, 1984). Those who regularly interact together establish implicitly
shared routines for accomplishing even simple joint activities such as
eating a meal or watching television. Each participant comes to expect
the others to continue to act as they have previously acted in the same
situation. When such a participant fails to behave as expected this leads
to attempts by the others to secure explanations for the deviation and to
restore the expected behaviour. Participants hold each other to be
'accountable' when they deviate from established joint routines.[11] It is
this sort of process that underlies what has come to be acknowledged as
the 'social construction of reality' (Berger & Luckmann, 1967). Accountability is central to structural coupling between individuals in close relationships. The mechanism of accountability is nicely consistent with the argument that the modelling of the contingent responses of others is enhanced
by the predictability of those responses (Goody 1995a).

How might the emergence of spoken language have effected the predictability of others' behaviour?

It follows from the discussion of the sharing of lexical meanings and
language-in-use, that once spoken language exists, it modifies the social
intelligence of apes in two ways at least. Firstly, spoken language provides
a shared lexicon in terms of which both participants think about, cognitively model, their experience and goals. Thus participants tend to use the
same categories, assume similar premises, share values and understand
each other's goals. This must enhance the accuracy of modelling contingent interdependence.

---

[11] Garfinkel's (1967) brillliant experiments, usually carried out by students in natural situations,
sometimes resulted in high levels of hostility from participants whose expectations were unexpec-
tedly violated.

—*Spoken language is a tool for thinking with – a cognitive tool.*
—*But language embodies* shared *meanings – spoken language means* thinking with socially constructed schemata.

Secondly, spoken language is used as a way of influencing others to act in accordance with the strategy suggested by modelling contingent interdependence.

—*Spoken language is a tool for acting with.*
—*Spoken language is a tool that permits acting on others using shared schemata;* as such *it is a tool with which we 'get inside each others' heads.*

Both as a tool for thinking with, and as a tool for acting with, language-in-use produces cultural artefacts that become part of the ecological reality of our socio-cultural worlds. Three of these most fundamental cultural constructs are *roles, rules* and *communicative genres.*

Spoken language, classification and the labelling of roles

It is clear that primates use categories in relating to the world, and may even make different signals in response to different categories, as with vervet monkeys' differentiation of responses to different kinds of predator. However, only a language appears to permit the intentional use of a symbol/word in the absence of the object it represents. With the use of reference in speech it becomes possible to label categories, and to use category labels in speaking to others (as well as for thinking with). Indeed Levinson (1995) argues that language works in part through the cognitive process of decoding meanings by reference to a known stereotype. By linking what was said to known attributes of the speaker and the situation, the number of possible meanings is sharply reduced for the addressee.[12]

One of the most robust universal characteristics of human societies is some form of terminology that categorises kinds of relative; anthropologists refer to these as *kinship terms.* There is a considerable anthropological literature on the nature of the relationship between kin terms and behaviour. Kin terms tend to indicate rights and duties that shape expectations of how people in these roles will act; obviously this does not

---

[12] This is the process of 'grounding' conversational meaning discussed by Clark (1992) in *Arenas of Language Use.*

guarantee that people will necessarily act accordingly. The most important terms refer to core social roles (Goody, 1984).

Kin terms then act as labels for a kind of relative, and also imply socio-culturally shaped expectations of rights and obligations *vis-à-vis* other kinds of relatives. In her sensitive discussion of kinship among the Nayaka hunter–gatherers of central India, Bird-David (1995) notes that at first children and youths have only nicknames, but in adulthood they come to be addressed almost exclusively by kin terms that are used and learned as reciprocals of the complementary roles. Thus 'He calls me *tamma(n)* [younger brother] so I call him *anna(n)* [older brother].' And she notes that such kin terms are often called across the hamlet to engage a person in this role. Here we see both one aspect of Nayaka social structure – that relative age of those in a sibling relationship is important, and how individuals come to be inducted into active participation in these key role relationships (Bird-David, 1995)

The fascinating discussion of the nature of the role of 'father' in human societies provides a particularly vivid instance of how labels for kin roles may influence social forms. This turns on the fact that, in the absence of any manifest physiological continuity between a man and his offspring, for people outside the influence of western scientific discourse there is no evident physiological basis for the role of 'father'.[13] Nevertheless there is always some term for this role (variously defined depending on other aspects of the social structure.) Fortes (1983) holds that the emergence of the role of father marked the beginning of human society since it is necessarily *socially* defined; further, he points out that the role of father is linked to the internalisation of rules without which people cannot live together in society. Although Fortes does not mention it, the social creation of a role must have depended on spoken language to separate particular individual fathers from the generic 'father role' (as with other kin terms). Wilson (1980), taking a very different view of the origin of human society, also sees the emergence of the role of 'father' as pivotal, and for him it is linked to the human capacity for making promises, i.e. commitments for the future. Again the vehicle for role emergence must have been a spoken language.

While it is likely that kin roles were the earliest social roles, there is

---

[13] See the extended debate about whether Trobriand Islanders knew of the physiological relationship between fathers and their offspring in Barnes (1961), Leach (1967) and Sprio (1968). Also see Fortes (1983) and Wilson (1980).

probably no society in which additional social roles have not emerged. Even in very simple societies there are usually political roles (warrior–warrior, elder–subordinate), economic roles (hunter–hunter, weapon/tool maker–warrior/farmer) and ritual roles (diviner–supplicant, ritual expert–congregation). One index of increasing social complexity is the number of roles and the networks of links between them.

Spoken language, roles and the emergence of 'rules'

The naming of regularities of behaviour associated with positions in a social structure as roles linked to recognised rights and obligations is a feature of all human societies. Such roles are 'cultural things' in that they exist as part of the socio-cultural world independently of particular individuals who may 'be' fathers or warriors at any given time. Social roles make the cognitive modelling of social contingency significantly more efficient in several ways related to increasing the predictability of the responses of others. Most obvious is the making explicit of what a role occupant – say a father – *is* in this society. Anthropologists recogonise that Trobriand fathers are very different from Nuer fathers; but how do the members of a particular society know 'how to be a father'? Once a role is labelled comments and criticism of the behaviour of individual holders make explicit the expectations on which it is based, and comments and criticisms can only be made explicit through language.

There is another characteristic feature of social roles that has great power in making social interactions more predictable. This is their dyadic nature. Fatherhood implies sonhood and daughterhood; to be a wife you must have a husband, an older sibling requires a younger sibling, and so on. With family roles we have a labelling of key reciprocal *interdependencies* arising from kinship. Given the human capacity for the co-operative construction of meaning in interaction, what is actually expected of occupants of family roles emerges in the first instance in the kinship practice of a given society. Fathers make claims on their sons, and sons in turn make claims on their fathers. But in a world of spoken language such reciprocal expectations become explicit. It is in this way that explicit role expectations become models for individuals for their own behaviour. It is clear what is involved in being a 'good English/middle class/Nuer father', and boys and men internalise this model as a standard relevant to their own behaviour.[14]

---

[14] Of course girls and women also internalise cultural models of male roles, but models for the opposite gender have a different relation to the construction of the self.

The second new dynamic, based on the dyadic nature of social roles, is the reciprocal sanctioning of deviations from expected behaviour. Garfinkel's (1967) experiments have revealed the universal character of the discomfort that we feel when expectations based on customary, routinised interaction are not met. When social roles come to be labelled these expectations become explicit, and widely shared. Now deviations are matters of public comment and may be sanctioned, perhaps by a delegation of elders, or by legal means depending on the social system. Levi-Strauss (1963) has suggested that it was the invention of the incest taboo that marked the beginning of human society. It has become clear that humans are not the only species that avoids mating between close kin. But as the only species with spoken language we have indeed invented *rules* – about incest among other things. Both early roles and early rules appear to have centred around the dynamics of close kinship.

The dyadic nature of social roles and the accountability of role occupants for their behaviour are socio-cultural procedures for the replication of structural couplings of individuals in the same roles within a society.

Like roles, rules are also 'cultural things' that exist in the socio-cultural world apart from individual actors (Bourdieu, 1977). Both roles and rules have a dual existence – they shape the cognitive modelling of contingent action, they are tools for thinking with;[15] and they frame and shape interaction, they are tools for acting with. If we return to the question of how language would have altered the challenges of early hominid existence one answer is that language creates two new sorts of *socio-cultural* tool – new socio-cultural tools for thinking with, and new socio-cultural tools for acting with.[16]

Language-in-use generates cultural tools for managing social interaction on many levels.

In fact language is a tool for *making tools* for thinking and acting with. Roles and rules could well have appeared with early proto-language since they are based on the labelling of classification that simple reference makes

---

[15] Levi-Strauss (1963) and Fortes (1987) both discuss totemism in these terms, though in very different ways.

[16] Language would of course markedly increase memory, both through 'chunking' of items under category labels, and because of the effects of conversation on recall. However, it is argued that these tools for thinking with raise cognitive capacities to a new 'power'. New tools for thinking with, language in the first instance, then roles and rules, and finally grammatical language could have led to *disjunctive* changes, where the increment in memory capacity is an incremental change.

possible. As language becomes more complex it is also a more powerful tool-making tool. This is best seen in studies that reveal the power of conversational genres such as politeness forms (Brown & Levinson, 1987), questions (Goody, 1978a,b; Keenan *et al.*, 1978), and irony (Brown, 1995) to shape both form and meaning. Such conversational genres are tools for doing particular important tasks with spoken language (being polite while pursuing a goal; getting information in ways appropriate to status difference; making comments by using language in a non-literal, safe, way). They work because as socio-culturally defined genres they are also 'cultural things', to which individuals have shared access. Since they are learned, they form a quasi-standardized mode of interacting for unacquainted individuals in similar settings.

Indeed Luckmann (1995) has argued that conversational genres also perform a critical task in the articulation of individuals by managing the key problem in communication of *reciprocal adjustment of perspectives*. Where a conversational genre is shared by members of a community, ethnic group or social class, it acts as a mode of synchronising the joint construction of meaning within this group. In fact it seems likely that this is one of the main ways in which group identities are both expressed and created (see also Bakhtin, 1986; Wertsch, 1991).

Co-operation and the dialogue template

From the replicated exchange of verbal input and output necessary for establishing lexical meanings, to the close synchrony of gesture and utterance between people in making conversational meanings, to the conversion of recurrent modes of solving conversational problems into culturally shaped genres, language-in-use creates and facilitates collaboration between speakers. Dialogue, literally 'speaking alternately', is our specially human mode of structural coupling, perhaps the fundamental form of human sociality. It is as though humans were designed for dialogue; we seem to think with a dialogue template.[17]

One expression of this is the internal dialogue we hold with ourselves. Indeed Vygotsky (1986) argues on the basis of experimental studies that conscious thought is internalised speech. Our dialogue bias appears when

---

[17] It has recently been argued that human thnking follows a narrative mode in which events and their participants are linked in chains of meaning (Bruner, 1986, 1990; Carrithers, 1995). There is no space to develop this here, but narrative can be seen as based on the reciprocal entailment of successive elements of dialogue.

we try to hold conversations with new-born infants (Ryan, 1974; Goody, 1978b), and with pets. Dialogue can be seen as the basis for such socio-cultural practices as divination (Zeitlyn, 1995) and prayer (Goody, 1995b).

Social intelligence and language: Another Rubicon?

The social intelligence of apes models the contingent responses of other apes. Ethological evidence suggests that whether it is used for deception or co-operation this modelling relies on inference about the responses of others based on knowledge of past interactions. With the gradual emergence of spoken language hominid modelling of the responses of others is augmented by shared cognitive artefacts. Cognitive models in individual heads now use the *same representations* – words, phrases, hierarchically ordered phrases. The establishing of shared meanings for words must have required cognitive procedures for exchanging mappings of form on meaning between speakers and hearers. These procedures would have been used, or extended, to manage the collaborative construction of meaning in conversation. For it is recognised that for language-in-use, meaning is an emergent property of collaboration between speakers. Conversational meaning requires both the grand artefact of language, and the *co-operative* use of this tool. The tool/artefact is shared by members of the community – both in individual heads and 'in the world'. Spoken language is *realized only in use between them.*

Such close reciprocal monitoring of each others' speech would be predicted by the Hutchins & Hazlehurst (1995) model for the initial establishing of a lexicon through repeated exchanges of sign/form mappings as spoken/heard utterances. Early spoken language may have resulted from, and progressively refined, new patterns of joint attention to and cognitive processing of utterances.

The fact that once a lexicon has been established a speaker hears the same 'word' as does his listener may have been the crucial factor in escaping from the private worlds of thought into the shared social world of spoken language. Lexicons and spoken languages exist 'in the world', apart from the minds of individual speakers. As proto-languages became more complex, elements of structure – negation, question forms, tense, embedding of clauses, etc – presumably came, like vocabulary, to be part of the learned language. Today fluent speakers are not aware of using grammatical structures, and indeed are often unable to describe them. What must have begun as shared conventional usage have become routinised cognitive strategies, and on some level, genetically expressed. Yet even with these refined tools for language use, evidence from recent research (e.g. Drew, 1995 and Streeck, 1995, discussed above) shows that the construction of shared meanings in conversation continues to require the sort of close reciprocal monitoring through which proto-languages presumably emerged.

Grice (1957) has argued that even with such close attention, conversational meaning is only possible because speakers abide by the Principle of Co-operation. In essence this means that speakers use vocabulary, grammar and conventions of conversation in ways that will lead hearers to correctly understand the meanings they intend to convey. Of course individuals can and do use language to deceive. But spoken language would never have emerged unless most people, most of the time, followed conventional usage. Otherwise meaningful conversations would have been impossible; indeed there would have been neither lexicons nor conventions of grammar to transmit to later generations. For spoken language to effectively convey meanings speakers must follow the conventions, and hearers must be able to count on their doing so. Co-operation was necessary not only in constructing each meaningful conversation; it was increasingly necessary in using learned and shared conventions that made it possible to talk about complex matters such as the past and the future, beliefs and intentions, social roles and social rules. Perhaps the very necessity of co-operation in order to use emergent spoken language created the conditions for the slow but progressive elaboration of language itself.

The Principle of Co-operation is clearly a very different matter from the Machiavellian skill at deception that has been held to characterise monkey and ape behaviour. It would seem that the emergence of spoken language cannot then have been the product of simply an increasing skill in deception. If W. Foley's analysis is roughly correct, the gradual emergence of spoken language may well have been integral to the progressive increase in cranial capacities and tool use of the hominids. When finally the shared meanings shaped by spoken language came to be represented in the ritual use of colour, in cave paintings and in carving this does indeed seem to mark a revolutionary change. The objectifying of shared meanings in these lasting forms not only expresses complex cultural patterns, but would simultaneously have been a medium for co-ordinating culturally powerful activities. With such activities, spanning the domains of politics, economics, religion and kinship we have the basic repertoire of modern human cultures. It is striking indeed that from this point it was but a short time, perhaps 35 000 years, until the earliest forms of writing appeared. This great revolution seems to have occurred with the objectification of shared meanings for purposes beyond simple subsistence. It appears to have created the new socio-cultural resources for the elaborate co-ordination of roles and rules that underlie fully modern human societies.

Acknowledgement

Particular thanks are due to friends who took time to comment on various drafts of this chapter; to the editors, Richard Byrne and Andrew Whiten, and to Phyllis Lee, John Gumperz, David Good, Verena Stolke, Jack Goody, Paul Mellars and Robert Hinde.

References

Aiello, A. C. & Dunbar, R. I. M. (1993). Neo-cortex size, group size and the evolution of language. *Current Anthropology*, 34, 184–93.

Austin, J. L. (1975). *How To Do Things with Words*, 2nd edn, ed. J. O. Urmson & M. Sbisà. Cambridge, MA: Harvard University Press (1st published in 1962).

Bakhtin, M. M. (1981). *The Dialogic Imagination: Four Essays*, ed. M. Holquist. Austin, TX: University of Texas Press.

Bakhtin, M. M. (1986). *Speech Genres and Other Late Essays*, eds. C. Emerson & M. Holquist. Austin, TX: University of Texas Press.

Barnes, J. A. (1961). Physical and social kinship. *Philosophy of Science*, 28, 296–9.

Berger, P. & Luckmann, T. (1967). *The Social Construction of Reality*. London: Allen Lane.

Bickerton, D. (1990). *Language and Species*. Chicago: University of Chicago Press.

Bird-David, N. (1995). Hunter-gatherers' kinship organization: Implicit roles and rules. In *Social Intelligence and Interaction*, ed. E. N. Goody, pp. 68–84. Cambridge: Cambridge University Press.

Bourdieu, P. (1977). *Outline of a Theory of Practice*. Cambridge: Cambridge University Press.

Brown, P. (1995). Politeness strategies and the attribution of intentions: The case of Tzeltal irony. In *Social Intelligence and Interaction*, ed. E. N. Goody, pp. 153–74. Cambridge: Cambridge University Press.

Brown, P. & Levinson, S. (1987). *Politeness: Some Universals in Language Usage*. Cambridge: Cambridge University Press.

Bruner, J. S. (1986). *Actual Minds, Possible Worlds*. Cambridge, MA: Harvard University Press.

Bruner, J. S. (1990). *Acts of Meaning*. Cambridge, MA: Harvard University Press.

Byrne, R. W. (1995). The ape legacy: The evolution of Machiavellian intelligence and anticipatory interactive planning. In *Social Intelligence and Interaction*, ed. E. N. Goody, pp. 37–52. Cambridge: Cambridge University Press.

Byrne, R. W. & Whiten, A. (eds) (1988). *Machiavellian Intelligence: Social Expertise and The Evolution of Intellect in Monkeys, Apes and Humans.* Oxford: Clarendon Press.

Carrithers, M. (1995). Stories in the social and mental life of people. In *Social Intelligence and Interaction*, ed. E. N. Goody, pp. 261–76. Cambridge: Cambridge University Press.

Chomsky, N. (1972). *Language and Mind.* New York: Harcourt Brace Jovanovich.

Clark, H. H. (1992). *Arenas of Language Use.* Chicago and Stanford: University of Chicago Press.

Dennett, D. C. (1988). The intentional stance in theory and practice. In *Machiavellian Intelligence: Social Expertise and the Evolution of Intellect in Monkeys, Apes and Humans*, ed. R. W. Byrne & A. Whiten, pp. 180–222. Oxford: Clarendon Press.

Donald, M. (1991). *Origins of the Modern Mind.* Cambridge, MA: Harvard University Press.

Drew, P. (1995). Interaction sequences and anticipatory interactive planning. In *Social Intelligence and Interaction*, ed. E. N. Goody, pp. 111–38. Cambridge: Cambridge University Press.

Dunbar, R. (1993). Coevolution of neocortical size, group size and language in humans. *Behavioral and Brain Sciences*, 16, 681–735.

Foley, W. A. (1997). *Anthropological Linguistics: An Introduction.* Oxford: Blackwell Scientific Publications.

Fortes, M. (1983). *Rules and the Emergence of Society.* Royal Anthropological Institute Occasional Papers, No. 39. London: Royal Anthropological Institute.

Fortes, M. (1987). Totem and taboo. In *Religion, Common Morality and the Person.* ed. J. Goody, pp. 110–45. Cambridge: Cambridge University Press.

Garfinkel, H. (1967). *Studies in Ethnomethodology.* Englewood Cliffs, NJ: Prentice Hall.

Gibson, K. R. (1993). Tool use, language and social behavior in relation to information processing capacities. In *Tools, Language and Cognition in Human Evolution*, ed. K. R. Gibson & T. Ingold, pp. 251–70. Cambridge: Cambridge University Press.

Gibson, K. R. & Ingold, T. (eds) (1993). *Tools, Language and Cognition in Human Evolution.* Cambridge: Cambridge University Press.

Gómez, J. C. (1991). Visual behaviour as a window for reading the mind of others in primates. In *Natural Theories of Mind: Evolution, Development and Simulation in Everyday Mindreading*, ed. A. Whiten, pp. 195–207. Oxford: Basil Blackwell.

Good, D. (1995). Where does foresight end and hindsight begin? In *Social intelligence and Interaction*, ed. E. N. Goody, pp. 139–49. Cambridge: Cambridge University Press.

Goody, E. N. (1972). 'Greeting', 'begging' and the presentation of respect. In *The Interpretation of Ritual*, ed. J. S. LaFontaine, pp. 39–71. London: Tavistock Press.

Goody, E. N. (1978a). Introduction. In *Questions and Politeness: Strategies in Social Interaction*, ed. E. N. Goody, pp. 1–16. Cambridge: Cambridge University Press.

Goody, E. N. (1978b). Towards a theory of questions. In *Questions and Politeness:*

Strategies in Social Interaction, ed. E. N. Goody, pp. 17–43, Cambridge: Cambridge University Press.

Goody, E. N. (1984). The persistence of core roles across space and time. In *Female Migrants and the Work Force: Domestic Repercussions*. Special Issue. *Anthropologica NS*, 26, 123–34.

Goody, E. N. (1993). Informal learning of adult roles in Baale. In *Images d'Afrique et Sciences Sociales: Les pays lobi, birifor et dagara*, ed. M. Fieloux & J. Lombard, with J.-M. Kambou-Ferrand, pp. 483–91. Paris: Karthala-ORSTOM

Goody, E. N. (1995a) Introduction: Some implications of a social origin of intelligence. In *Social Intelligence and Interaction*, ed. E. N. Goody, pp. 1–33. Cambridge: Cambridge University Press.

Goody, E. N. (1995b). Social intelligence and prayer as dialogue. In *Questions and Politeness: Strategies in Social Interaction* ed. E. N. Goody, pp. 206–20. Cambridge: Cambridge University Press.

Goody, E. N. (ed.) (1995c). *Social Intelligence and Interaction*. Cambridge: Cambridge University Press.

Greenfield, P. (1991). Language, tools and brain: The ontogeny and phylogeny of hierarchically organized sequential behaviour. *Behavioral and Brain Sciences*, 14, 531–95.

Grice, H. P. (1957). Meaning. *Philosophical Review*, 66, 337–88.

Gumperz, J. J. (1982). *Discourse Strategies*. Cambridge: Cambridge University Press.

Harcourt, A. H. & de Waal, F. B. M. (eds) (1992). *Coalitions and Alliances in Humans and Other Animals*. Oxford: Oxford University Press.

Heritage, J. (1984). *Garfinkel and Ethnomethodology*. Cambridge: Cambridge University Press.

Heritage, J. (1990/91). Intention, meaning and strategy: Observations on constraints in interactional analysis. *Research in Language and Social Interaction*, 24, 311–22.

Humphrey, N. (1976). The social function of intellect. In *Growing Points in Ethology*, ed. P. P. G. Bateson & R. A. Hinde, pp. 303–17. Cambridge: Cambridge University Press.

Hutchins, E. (1991). The social organization of distributed cognition. In *Perspectives on Socially Shared Cognition*, ed. L. B. Resnick, J. M. Levine & S. D. Teasley, pp. 283–307. Washington, DC: American Psychological Association.

Hutchins, E. & B. Hazlehurst (1995). How to invent a shared lexicon: The emergence of shared form-meaning mappings in interaction. In *Social intelligence and interaction*, ed. E. N. Goody, pp. 53–67. Cambridge: Cambridge University Press.

Keenan, E. Ochs, B. B. Schieffelin & Platt, M. (1978). Questions of immediate concern. In *Questions and Politeness: Strategies in Social Interaction*, ed. E. N. Goody, pp. 44–55. Cambridge: Cambridge University Press.

Leach, E. R. (1967). Virgin birth. *Proceedings of the Royal Anthropological Society for 1966*, pp. 39–49. London: Royal Anthropological Institute.

Levinson, S. (1983). *Pragmatics*. Cambridge: Cambridge University Press.

Levinson, S. (1995). Interactional bias in human thinking. In *Social Intelligence and Interaction*, ed. E. N. Goody, pp. 221–60. Cambridge: Cambridge University Press.

Levi-Strauss, C. (1963). *Totemism*. Boston, MA: Beacon Press.

Lieberman, P. (1991). *Uniquely Human: The Evolution of Speech, Thought and Selfless Behaviour*. Cambridge, MA: Harvard University Press.

Lyons, J. (1988). Origins of language. In *Origins: The Darwin Lectures*, ed. A. C. Fabian, pp. 141–66. Cambridge: Cambridge University Press.

Luckmann, T. (1995). Interaction planning and intersubjective adjustment of perspectives by communicative genres. In *Social Intelligence and Interaction*, ed. E. N. Goody, pp. 175–86. Cambridge: Cambridge University Press.

Maturana, H. R. & Varela, F. J. (1987). *The Tree of Knowledge: The Biological Roots of Understanding*. Boston, MA: New Science Library

Mellars, P. (1996). Symbolism, language and the Neanderthal mind. In *Modelling the Early Human Mind*, ed. P. Mellars & K. Gibson, pp. 15–32. Cambridge: McDonald Institute Monographs.

Milton, K. (1988). Foraging behaviour and the evolution of primate intelligence. In *Machiavellian Intelligence: Social Expertise and the Evolution of Intellect in Monkeys, Apes and Humans*, ed. R. W. Byrne & A. Whiten pp. 285–305. Oxford: Clarendon Press.

Premack, D. (1988). 'Does the chimpanzee have a theory of mind?' revisited. In *Machiavellian Intelligence: Social Expertise and the Evolution of Intellect in Monkeys, Apes and Humans*, ed. R. W. Byrne & A. Whiten, pp. 160–79. Oxford: Clarendon Press.

Premack, D. & Woodruff, G. (1978). Does the chimpanzee have a theory of mind? *Behavioral and Brain Sciences*, 1, 515–26

Ryan, J. (1974). Early language development: Towards a communicational analysis. In *The Integration of the Child in a Social World*, ed. M. Richards, pp. 185–213. Cambridge: Cambridge University Press.

Spiro, M. E. (1968). Virgin birth, parthenogenesis and physiological paternity. *Man*, 2, 242–61.

Streeck, J. (1995). On projection. In *Social Intelligence and Interaction*, ed. E. N. Goody, pp. 87–110. Cambridge: Cambridge University Press.

Vygotsky, L. (1986). *Thought and Language*. Cambridge, MA: Massachusetts Institute of Technology Press.

Wertsch, J. V. (1991). *Voices of the Mind: A Sociocultural Approach to Mediated Action*. London: Harvester Wheatsheaf.

Whiten, A. (1993). Evolving a theory of mind. In *Understanding Other Minds: Perspectives from Autism*, ed. S. Baron-Cohen, H. Tager Flusberg & D. J. Cohen, pp. 367–96. Oxford: Oxford University Press.

Whiten, A. (ed.) (1991). *Natural Theories of Mind: Evolution, Development and Simulation of Everyday Mindreading*. Oxford: Basil Blackwell.

Wilson, P. J. (1980). *Man, the Promising Primate: The Conditions of Human Evolution*. New Haven, CT: Yale University Press.

Zeitlyn, D. (1995). Divination as dialogue: Negotiation of meaning with random responses. In *Social Intelligence and Interaction*, ed. E. N. Goody, pp. 189–205. Cambridge: Cambridge University Press.

Index

aboutness 165
accidental actions 165–6
accountability in relationships 386
Adapted Mind theory 106
affiliative tendency 26
aggression
  anger thresholds 323–4
  baboon consort studies 53–9
  managing aggression 38–43
  retaliatory behaviour 128–31, 146
  see also coalitions
alarm calls
  in vervet monkeys 11
  misusing 195
alliances 30–8
  see also coalitions
altruism 91–2, 358
  altruistic socialisers 92
  see also co-operation
amygdala 250–3
anger thresholds 323–4
anthropomorphism 275
anticipatory interactive planning 368
ants 92
apostatic selection 320, 326–7
arboreal clambering (as engineering
  problem) 300
art 332–3, 370
asocial learning *see* individual learning
attachment studies 94
attention 161–5
audiogenic seizures 318
autism 154–5, 162, 321

babies
  eye-contact 87
  false beliefs 137
  infant crying 98
  mother–child bonding 94
baboons
  consort studies 53–65, 69–73
  deception 7
  food discrimination 216

friendships 26
gelada 29
grooming behaviour 29
intelligence 295
object manipulation 186
reciprocity 33
sleeping habits 301
social relationships 51
spatial memory 220, 229
tripartite relations 264
see also hamadrya baboons
bats 245–6, 250
  bat-evasion 318
Bayes's theorem 278
bed construction 296–7, 300–1
behavioural after-effects 191
behaviourism 272, 275, 321
birds
  brain size 241, 242, 257, 299
  cognitive mapping 257, 299
  neophilia in 331
  perceptual expectations 326
blue monkeys 28
bluffing 342
bond *see* friendship
brachiation (arboreal clambering) 300
brain size 7, 16, 241–58, 290, 291–2,
  370
  birds 241, 242
  body size and 15–16, 242, 243–4
  ecological correlates 241–3
  mammals 242
  metabolic rate and 244
  primates 241, 246–50

calls *see* vocalisations
capuchin monkeys
  grooming behaviour 36
  imitation 6, 182
  object manipulation 186, 296, 302
cause–effect understanding 9
  see also mindreading
Chance, M.R.A. 318

cheaters *see* deception
chickens 123–5
chiefdoms 351
children 86–106
  conflict resolution 97–106
  mindreading 145–6, 151–6
  visual attention 163
  see also babies; infants
chimpanzees 50–1
  coalitions 31, 343, 344, 346, 352–3
  consolation 42
  deception 156–61
  donating expertise 194–6
  ecological knowledge 186–8
  equivalent to 3 year old child 146
  food discrimination 218, 231
  food scrounging 192–3
  gesturing 296
  grooming behaviour 29, 36, 184–5
  imitation 182, 184
  intentional/accidental contrast 165–6
  object manipulations 187, 195, 196, 264
  political intelligence 342–6, 352, 354–7
  raised in isolation 231
  reciprocity 33, 34
  self-medication 187–8
  self-recognition 10
  sorting abilities 210
  spatial memory 219, 229
  tactical deception 193–4
  theory of mind 51, 144–5
  third party conflict resolution 41–2
  visual attention 162–5
Chomsky, N. 369
Churchill, Winston 106
classification/sorting 209–20
co-action 191
co-evolution 320
co-operation 358
  coalitions 30–8
  genuine tit-for-tat 324–5
  group co-operation 325–6
  human studies 103, 281–3
  language and 383, 391–3
  monkeys *versus* chimps 9
  theory of mind and 9
  versus manipulation 4
co-ordination, zone of 67
coalitions 30–8, 241
  chimpanzee 31, 343, 344, 346, 352–3

human 353–4
cognition 61–3, 65, 68–73
  cognitive ethology 66
  as conversation 70
cognitive evolution 244–6, 249, 254–9
cognitive mapping 15, 257, 298–300, 366–7
  see also language
communication 92
  non-human primates 175
  communicative repertoire 184
comparative method 95–6
comparative psychology 258–9
competition mechanisms 4
complexity 3, 59–63, 105
  versus complication 61
  see also social complexity
conciliation (in children) 98, 105
conflict resolution 41–3
  in children 97–106
consolation 42
consort studies 53–65, 69–73
  case studies 79–85
  protean lust and 324
  protean sexuality 332
contagion 177
conventionalisation 180, 184
convulsions 318
Coolidge effect 327
counter-deception 150
  retaliation 128–31, 146
counter-domination 342, 348–60
courtship skills 330, 332, 333
creativity 328–34
cultural/social learning 5–6, 176–90

Darwin, Charles 106, 275, 315, 331
death throes 319
deception 7, 60, 87–8, 112–43
  deceptive box test 154
  definition of 115
  functional (definition of) 113, 115, 116
  in baboons 7
  in children 153–6
  in chimps/orangutans 156–61
  in domestic chickens 123–5
  in honeybees 131–3
  in rhesus monkeys 125–31
  in stomatopods 118–21
  in vervet monkeys 133–5
  intentional (definition of) 113, 122

deception (*cont.*)
  language and 383–4
  lying/untruths 91
  prerequisites for 94
  social contract module and 281–3
  see also tactical deception
desire 324
despotism 323
  child studies 104
  chimpanzee studies 345
differential game theory 316–18
domain specificity 3–4, 11–12
  social intelligence and 272–4
domestic chickens 123–5
dominance 185
  chimpanzees 342–6
  human societies 341–2, 347–51
  monkeys 4

ecological cognition 185–9
  versus social cognition 256–8
ecological learning *see* individual learning
egalitarian behaviour 341–65
Einstein, Albert 106
emulation 177, 182
encephalisation 241–3, 333
  see also brain size
enculturation 182
ethnocentrism 102
evolution of cognition 244–6, 249, 254–9, 290
evolutionary drift 371
evolutionary game theory 317–18
evolutionary psychology 258–9
expectations, violation of 385–6
experience projection 150–1
exploiting others 174–206
  in chimpanzees 6–7
extractive foraging 16, 90, 302–3
  brain size and 16, 258

face recognition 5
false belief 153–7
  see also deception
feeding skill 301–6
  greater need in apes than monkeys 304
feeding/food calls 123–31
flexible plan building 305
folivory 15, 242–3, 244, 292
folk taxonomies 213–14
food calls 123–31

food discrimination 215–18, 231, 304
food sharing/scrounging 190–4, 356
foraging 207–39
  foraging niche hypothesis 240, 241
  see also extractive foraging
Freud, Anna 94
Freud, Sigmund 93, 94
friendship 26–30
  benefits of 29–30
  child studies 93, 101
  cultivation of 35–8
  definition of 54
  repair of 27, 38–41
frugivory 241, 242, 244, 245–6, 292

Galton, Francis 271
game theory 316–18
gaze following 162
gelada baboons 29
gestures/gesturing 296
  language and 371, 375–8
gorillas 184
  feeding techniques 186–7, 302, 303–6
  gesturing 296
  imitative learning 6
  intelligence 295
  scrounging 190, 191
  self-recognition 10
grooming 4, 26–7, 229
  alliances and 35–8
  friendship and 28–9
  in chimpanzees 29, 36, 184–5
  neocortex size and 250
  tamarin monkeys 231
group living 3
  chimpanzee 343, 345
  group-morality 353–4
grudges 325
guenons 27

hamadryas baboons
  grooming behaviour 29
  inter-baboon proximity 230
  social complexity 4
handicap principle 330
hippocampal enlargement 244, 299
honeybees 131–3
howler monkeys 218–19, 299

imitation 177, 178–83, 190
  definition of 178
  evidence 181

imitation (*cont.*)
  in great apes 181, 182, 183, 184, 297
  in monkeys 5–6, 182, 272–3, 297
  methods 181
  program-level 6, 297
imitative learning *see* imitation; social
  learning
implicit mindreading 150
incest taboo 389
individual learning 176, 180
  associative learning 176, 177
  instrumental learning 176, 177
  relation to social learning 176
infants
  false beliefs 137
  infant crying 98
  mindreading 145–6
  see also babies
information
  active falsification 122, 135–6
  withholding/suppressing 122, 135–6
  see also deception
insects 257
intelligence 2–3
  haplorhine/strepsirhine 14, 290, 291–2
  monkey/ape 14, 294–307
  species differences 3, 258–9
  see also Machiavellian intelligence
    hypothesis; social intelligence
intelligence tests 284
intent 147
intentionality 368
  intentional deception 121–2
  intentionality detector 165
  theory of mind and 10
intervening variables 150

joint attention 162

kinship 387–90

language 332, 353, 366–97
  ape-language studies 7, 51, 295–6
  language aquisition 162
  origins/evolution 369–75
  role in egalitarianism 353
learning 207–32
  how unpredictability interferes with
    327–8
  instrumental conditioning 89
  life-long 175
  neural mechanisms 259

speed of 292–3
lemurs 3, 185
lying/untruths 91

macaque monkeys
  consolation 42
  dominance ranks 185
  food discrimination 215, 217–18
  food handling/expertise 175, 186, 188
  food scrounging 191
  foraging studies 220–3, 229–32
  grooming behaviour 28, 36, 38
  imitative learning 272
  memory studies 223–8
  mindreading 161
  reciprocity 33, 34
  reconciliation 39–40
  sorting abilities 212
  surrogate mothers 231
  third party conflict resolution 41–2
  visual system 255
Machiavelli, Niccolò 94, 178–9
Machiavellian intelligence hypothesis
    1–23, 52, 207, 264
  scope of 1, 13–14, 290–4, 333
  shortcomings 294–8, 328
  see also social intelligence
Machiavellianism 12–13, 73–4
manipulation 12, 92, 146
  object manipulation 186–7, 305
  see also tool-use
matching pennies game 316–17
mate choice 333–4
  neophilia in 331
  protean promiscuity 324
maternal coaching 195
maternal tolerance 192
mediation 41–3
memory studies 207–32
mindblindness 154
mindreading 105, 144–73, 382–3
  defences against *see* deception; protean
    behaviour
mirror self-recognition 10, 300
misrepresentation 154, 155
mixed strategies 316–18
monkeys
  blue monkeys 28
  deception in 125–31, 133–5
  howler monkeys 218–19, 299
  imitation in 5–6, 182, 272–3, 297
  monkey *versus* chimp co-operation 9

monkeys (*cont.*)
  monkey/ape intelligence 294–306
  muriquis 27
  night monkeys 27
  spider monkeys 188–9, 299
  squirrel monkeys 27–28
  titi monkeys 229, 232
  tool-use 296
  see also capuchin monkeys; macaque
    monkeys; rhesus monkeys; tamarin
    monkeys; vervet monkeys
mother–child bonding 94
muriquis monkeys 27
music 332

natural psychology *see* mindreading
navigational intelligence 74–5
neocortex 245, 256, 291
neocortical enlargement 3, 245–50, 256,
  291–2, 295
neophilia 331
nest/bed construction 296–7, 300–1
neural nets 255–6
newborn *see* babies
night monkeys 27
noisy behaviour 312
novelty-seeking 331

omnivore's paradox 218
ontogenetic ritualisation 180
orangutans
  demonstration teaching 195–6
  ecological expertise 189
  false belief studies 160–1
  food discrimination/skills 215, 216,
    304
  imitative learning 6
  self-recognition 10
  tool-use 301, 302
  visual attention 164
ostracism 357
  child studies 103

pacifying 41–3
parallel processing 255–6
paranoia 94
paternity uncertainty 324
peer groups (child studies) 99–104
personality 326–7
Piaget, J. 90, 278
pigeons 212
play behaviour 95–6, 101

proteanism and 319–20
political intelligence 341–65
polymorphism, behavioural 326–7
Popper, K. 93, 94
prelief 156
pretence 156
priming 177–8, 180, 190
The Prince (Machiavelli) 178
program-level imitation 6, 297
promiscuity 324
protean behaviour/intelligence 95, 267,
  313–15, 318–40
proximal development 67
psycho-analysis 93
psychological selection 315–16
punishment 128–31
pursuit-evasion games 316–18
  protean behaviour and 319

randomisation 320–1
  group co-operation and 326
rats 272, 279
reciprocal altruism *see* co-operation
reciprocity 25, 33–4
  generous tit-for-tat 324–5
  tit-for-tat tactic 86, 103
reconciliation 5, 38–41
  child studies 98–9
  chimpanzee studies 344
  definition of 39
repair (of relationship) 27, 38–41
representation 300, 382–3
response facilitation 177
retaliatory behaviour 128–31, 146
rhesus monkeys
  food calling 125–31
  theory of mind 9
  see also macaque monkeys
ringtailed lemurs 185
ritualisation 180, 332
rodents 257
runaway sexual selection 104–5, 332

'satisficing' algorithms 269–70, 278–81
scrounging 190–4
  tolerated scrounging 192–4
seeing–knowing 8
self-deception, adaptive 322
self-medication (zoopharmacognosy)
  187–8
self-recognition 10, 300
sensory drive 316

sensory exploitation 316, 331
sex, evolution of 320
sexual consort studies 53–65, 69–73
  case studies 79–85
  protean lust and 324
  protean sexuality 332
sexual selection theory 104–5, 332
shared attention 162
sharing of food 190–4, 356
sheep 25
signal selection 316
situated action 66–7, 69–73
skeptical receivers 131–5
Skinner, B.F. 272, 275
sleeping near the enemy (SNE) 63–5,
  69–73
  case studies 79–85
social cognition 254–9
social complexity 2, 4–7, 59–63
  carnivores 14
  cetaceans 14
  as conceptual cul-de-sac 266–7
  primates 68–73
social contract module 281–3
social intelligence 50, 52, 91–4, 264
  hypothesis 264–84
  innateness of 87
  modular concept 270–84
  see also Machiavellian intelligence
  hypothesis
social learning 5–6, 176–90
social manipulation 2
social meta-learning 87
social referencing 162
social relationships
  definition of 25–6
  repair of 27, 38–41
social status acquisition 102–4
sociobiological theory 51
sorting/categorisation 209–20
spatial memory/cognition 244–5
spatial relations (proximity) 27
Spencer, Herbert 271
spider monkeys 188–9, 299
squirrel monkeys 27–8
statistical methods 278
stimulus enhancement 177
stomatopods 118–21
stories/story-telling 89–90
stress, how unpredictability increases
  328
superorganisms 24

symbolic cognition 180
symbolic representation 370

tactical deception 113, 147–8
  definition of 115
  in non-primates 293–4
  in primates 162, 193–4
Taine, Hippolyte 271
tamarin monkeys
  grooming behaviour 231
  spatial memory 219–20, 229
teaching 194–6
  coaching 195
  demonstration 195–6
  opportunity 195
technical intelligence 16, 289–311
telepathy 150, 151
termite-fishing 187, 188
theory of mind 7–11, 51, 52, 137, 313
  in children 151–3
  in chimps 8–9, 51, 144–5, 295
  in great apes 295
  role of language 382–3
  see also mindreading
Tinbergen, Niko 148
tit-for-tat tactic 86, 103
  generous tit-for-tat 324–5
titi monkeys 229, 232
tool-making 16, 90
  see also technical intelligence
tool-use 16–17, 303
  by capuchin monkeys 6, 296, 302
  by chimpanzees 187, 195, 196, 264,
    296, 301–4
  composite 372
  non-representational 296, 302
tree rats 191
trust 94

unpredictability 267–8
untruths/lying 91

vervet monkeys
  food discrimination 216
  grooming behaviour 36, 37–8
  imitative learning 5–6
  reciprocity 33
  skepticism 133–5
  social complexity 5
Vian, Boris 106
vision system of primates 255–6
visual attention 162–5

visual occlusion 9
vocalisations 27–8
  alarm calls 11
  alarm calls (misusing) 195
  deceptive signalling 114–18, 123–31
  food calls 123–31
  in chimpanzees 343–4
  in vervet monkeys 11
  skepticism and 133–5

social intercourse and 371
  see also language
volition (reading) 165–6
Vygotsky, L. 66, 72

xenophobia 102

zoopharmacognosy (self-medication)
  187–8

9 780521 550871